# GREGG SHORTHAND DICTIONARY

**A Compilation of Shorthand Outlines for 34,055 Words;**
**1,314 Names and Geographical Expressions;**
**1,368 Frequently Used Phrases;**
**and 120 Abbreviations**

# GREGG SHORTHAND DICTIONARY

## Diamond Jubilee Series

### Second Edition

**John Robert Gregg**

**Louis A. Leslie**

**Charles E. Zoubek**

Shorthand Written by Charles Rader

**Gregg Division | McGraw-Hill Book Company**

New York St. Louis Dallas San Francisco
Düsseldorf Johannesburg Kuala Lumpur London
Mexico Montreal New Delhi Panama
Rio de Janeiro Singapore Sydney Toronto

Cover and Title Design / Gail Young

**Library of Congress Cataloging in Publication Data**

Gregg, John Robert, 1867-1948.

Gregg shorthand dictionary.

(Diamond jubilee series)

1. Shorthand—Gregg—Dictionaries. I. Leslie, Louis A., date. joint author. II. Zoubek, Charles E., date. joint author. III. Title.

Z55.5.G7 1974 653'.427'03 73-12581

ISBN 0-07-024632-7

ISBN 0-07-024633-5 (mini. ed.)

**Gregg Shorthand Dictionary, Diamond Jubilee Series**
**Second Edition**



34567890DODO098765

ISBN 07-024632-7

# FOREWORD

*Gregg Shorthand Dictionary, Diamond Jubilee Series, Second Edition,* is divided into four parts:

Part One contains, in alphabetic order, the shorthand outlines for 34,055 words. However, these 34,055 words represent a considerably larger vocabulary, as many simple derivatives of these words have been omitted—those ending in *-ing* and *-s,* for example.

Part Two contains, in alphabetic order, the shorthand outlines for 1,314 entries for personal and geographical names.

Part Three contains, in alphabetic order, the shorthand outlines for 1,368 phrases frequently used in business dictation.

Part Four contains shorthand outlines for 120 abbreviations.

It is easily possible to construct briefer outlines for many of the scientific and literary words for which full outlines are given in this dictionary. It is not advisable to do so, however, unless the writer is certain that he will use those briefer outlines with sufficient frequency to justify the effort of learning them. Otherwise, the brief, but half-remembered, outlines will cause mental hesitation that will result in slower, rather than faster, writing.

Research techniques using high-speed motion pictures have proved that most shorthand writers actually write each outline at about the same speed, regardless of the speed of the dictation. That is why the writer who can take dictation at only 100 words a minute writes each outline as rapidly as it is written by another writer taking the same material at 200 words a minute. What, then, is the difference between the two writers?

The difference is that the writer who can write 100 words a minute is consuming time thinking, pausing, hesitating. The writer who can write 200 words a minute does not need to stop to think. He writes the outlines little, if any, faster than the 100-word writer, but the 200-word writer writes *continuously.*

The problem of increasing shorthand speed, therefore, is actually a problem of decreasing hesitations in writing. What causes hesitations in writing? They are caused by the struggle of the mind to remember and use the abbreviating material provided in the shorthand system.

The fewer shortcuts and exceptions the mind must remember and use, the easier it is for the writer to decrease or eliminate the hesitations that reduce speed. Therefore, any attempt by the writer to manufacture additional shortcuts is more likely to reduce his speed than to increase it, unless the new shortcuts are used in his daily work with such frequency that they readily become automatized.

The experience of expert shorthand writers of every system is conclusive in establishing the inadvisability of attempting to gain speed by devising and learning lists of brief outlines. Longer outlines that are quickly constructed by the mind under pressure of dictation give the writer more speed; the attempt to remember and use large numbers of abbreviated outlines tends to reduce the writer's speed.

There is often room for some difference of opinion as to the most appropriate outline for a word. This dictionary offers outlines that have been discussed and considered by experts. Sometimes an apparently obvious improvement in an outline will actually create the danger of a conflict in reading. More often an outline different from that provided in this dictionary would be individually satisfactory but would not be consistent with the outlines for other members of the same word family.

Of one thing the reader may be sure—every outline in this dictionary is the result of serious thought and consideration. Where possible alternate outlines exist, each alternate has been discussed and considered. This dictionary as a whole represents the accumulated experience of all those who have worked with Gregg Shorthand since its first publication in 1888.

The compilers of this dictionary are confident that this volume will render a valuable service to the shorthand writer by placing at his disposal a facile and fluent outline for any word or phrase in which he may be interested.

*The Publishers*

# PART ONE

Part One of the Second Edition of *Gregg Shorthand Dictionary, Diamond Jubilee Series,* contains shorthand outlines for 34,055 words, arranged in alphabetical order.

Of these 34,055 words, more than 100 did not appear in the First Edition. Some are words that have been added to the language in the last decade—*skyjacker, disadvantaged, miniskirt, Amtrak.* Some are words that have been added to the language as a result of advances in technology—*astroturf, circuitry, recycling, blast-off, splashdown.* Some are words that were rarely used in the past but because of changes in the times, are today frequently used—*racist, multiethnic, ecology.*

Experience has proved that those using a shorthand dictionary often consult it for the simple words formerly omitted from shorthand dictionaries or for rare and unusual words likewise formerly omitted.

The present list, therefore, includes many of the apparently simple words formerly omitted. Most readily apparent will be the addition of the many rare and unusual words that experience has proved are wanted by users of a list such as this.

Many words are included because the shorthand learner, while still in school, has occasion to use them in his schoolwork. For this reason many mathematical, mineralogical, chemical, botanical, and physiological terms are included. For the same reason many literary words are included, words that are usually of no business value but that the high school or college learner uses in his schoolwork. The bulk of the vocabulary, however, consists of words generally used in business-office dictation.

It must be remembered, too, that in many types of office work the stenographer may have occasion to use these scientific or literary words. The editor's stenographer will need the literary words. The professor's secretary will need many of the mathematical or chemical or physiological words—according to the professor's field of interest.

Consistency, rather than brevity of outline, has been the guiding principle in the construction of the shorthand outlines in this dictionary. The fastest shorthand outline (within reasonable limits) is the outline that requires the least mental effort, the outline that is written consistently and analogically. The speed of a shorthand outline is not to be judged by its brevity to the eye, nor even by its facility for the hand; it is to be judged by the speed with which it may be constructed by the mind and supplied by the mind to the hand.

Many shorthand writers experience difficulty in understanding the principle that guides the shorthand author in devising shortcuts. If the preceding paragraph is true, why are there *any* shortcuts? Why not write out everything in full? The secret of the good shortcut is the frequency of use of the word or phrase. If a dictator says *bacteriological* day after day, the shorthand writer should, of course, use a very brief shortcut for that word. Because of this extreme frequency of use, the shortcut will come as quickly to the mind as though the word has been written in full.

There is no value, however, in having every shorthand writer learn a shortcut for a word like *bacteriological,* for some dictators may never use the word, and if it should occur infrequently in the dictation, the mental effort needed to recall the word would require far more time than would have been necessary to write it in full.

It is strongly urged, therefore, that the outline in this dictionary be accepted as the normal outline for any expression unless that expression occurs so frequently in the writer's dictation that learning a shortcut for it is thoroughly justified. A long list of seldom-used shortcuts can be a very heavy burden on the mind and will almost invariably result in decreasing the writer's shorthand speed rather than increasing it. As a famous shorthand reporter of an earlier generation once said, "The longer I write shorthand, the *longer* I write shorthand."

ab′a·cus
a·baft′
ab′a·lo′ne
a·ban′don
a·ban′doned
a·ban′don·ment
a·base′
a·based′
a·base′ment
a·bash′
a·bat′a·ble
a·bate′
a·bat′ed
a·bate′ment
ab′bess
ab′bey
ab′bot
ab·bre′vi·ate
ab·bre′vi·at′ed
ab·bre′vi·a′tion
ab′di·cate
ab′di·cat′ed
ab′di·ca′tion
ab·do′men
ab·dom′i·nal
ab·duct′
ab·duc′tion
a·bed′
ab′er·ra′tion
ab′er·ra′tion·al
a·bet′
a·bet′ted
a·bet′tor
a·bey′ance
ab·hor′
ab·horred′
ab·hor′rence
ab·hor′rent
a·bide′
a·bil′i·ty
ab′ject
ab′ju·ra′tion
ab·jure′
ab·jured′
ab·jure′ment
ab′la·tive
ab′laut
a·blaze′
a′ble
a′ble-bod′ied
ab·lu′tion
a′bly
ab′ne·ga′tion
ab·nor′mal
ab′nor·mal′i·ty
ab·nor′mi·ty
a·board′
a·bode′
a·bol′ish
a·bol′ished
ab′o·li′tion
ab′o·li′tion·ism
ab′o·li′tion·ist
a·bom′i·na·ble
a·bom′i·na·bly
a·bom′i·nate

a·bom′i·na′tion
ab′o·rig′i·nal
ab′o·rig′i·ne
a·bor′tive
a·bound′
a·bound′ing·ly
a·bout′
a·bove′
ab·rade′
ab·rad′ed
ab·ra′sion
ab·ra′sive
ab′re·ac′tion
a·breast′
a·bridge′
a·bridged′
a·bridg′ment
a·broad′
ab′ro·gate
ab′ro·gat′ed
ab′ro·ga′tion
ab′ro·ga′tive
ab·rupt′
ab·rupt′ly
ab·rupt′ness
ab′scess
ab′scessed
ab·scis′sa
ab·scis′sion
ab·scond′
ab·scond′ed
ab·scond′er

ab′sence
ab′sent
ab′sen·tee′
ab′sen·tee′ism
ab′sent·ly
ab′sinthe
ab′so·lute
ab′so·lute·ly
ab′so·lute·ness
ab′so·lu′tion
ab′so·lut·ism
ab′so·lut·ist
ab·solve′
ab·solved′
ab·sorb′
ab·sorbed′
ab·sorb′en·cy
ab·sorb′ent
ab·sorb′ing·ly
ab·sorp′tion
ab·sorp′tive
ab·stain′
ab·stained′
ab·stain′er
ab·ste′mi·ous
ab·ste′mi·ous·ly
ab·ste′mi·ous·ness
ab·sten′tion
ab′sti·nence
ab′sti·nent
ab′sti·nent·ly
ab′stract

ab·stract′ed
ab·stract′ed·ly
ab·strac′tion
ab·strac′tion·ist
ab′stract·ly
ab·struse′
ab·struse′ness
ab·surd′
ab·surd′i·ty
ab·surd′ly
a·bun′dance
a·bun′dant
a·bun′dant·ly
a·buse′
a·bused′
a·bu′sive
a·bu′sive·ly
a·bu′sive·ness
a·but′
a·but′ment
a·but′tal
a·but′ted
a·but′ter
a·bysm′
a·bys′mal
a·byss′
a·ca′cia
ac′a·dem′ic
a·cad′e·mi′cian
a·cad′e·mies
a·cad′e·my
A·ca′di·an

a·can′thus
ac·cede′
ac·ced′ed
ac·cel′er·an′do
ac·cel′er·ant
ac·cel′er·ate
ac·cel′er·at′ed
ac·cel′er·a′tion
ac·cel′er·a′tive
ac·cel′er·a′tor
ac·cel′er·a·to′ry
ac′cent
ac·cent′ed
ac·cen′tu·ate
ac·cen′tu·at′ed
ac·cen′tu·a′tion
ac·cept′
ac·cept′a·bil′i·ty
ac·cept′a·ble
ac·cept′ance
ac′cep·ta′tion
ac·cept′ed
ac′cess
ac·ces′si·bil′i·ty
ac·ces′si·ble
ac·ces′sion
ac·ces′so·ry
ac′ci·dence
ac′ci·dent
ac′ci·den′tal
ac′ci·den′tal·ly
ac·cip′i·trine

ac·claim′
ac·claimed′
ac′cla·ma′tion
ac·clam′a·to′ry
ac·cli′mate
ac·cli′mat·ed
ac′cli·ma′tion
ac·cli′ma·ti·za′tion
ac·cli′ma·tize
ac·cli′ma·tized
ac·cliv′i·ty
ac′co·lade′
ac·com′mo·date
ac·com′mo·dat′ed
ac·com′mo·dat′ing·ly
ac·com′mo·da′tion
ac·com′mo·da′tive
ac·com′pa·nied
ac·com′pa·ni·ment
ac·com′pa·nist
ac·com′pa·ny
ac·com′plice
ac·com′plish
ac·com′plished
ac·com′plish·ment
ac·cord′
ac·cord′ance
ac·cord′ed
ac·cord′ing·ly
ac·cor′di·on
ac·cost′
ac·cost′ed

ac·count′
ac·count′a·bil′i·ty
ac·count′a·ble
ac·count′an·cy
ac·count′ant
ac·count′ed
ac·cou′tered
ac·cou′ter·ment
ac·cred′it
ac·cred′it·ed
ac·cre′tion
ac·cru′al
ac·crue′
ac·crued′
ac·cu′mu·late
ac·cu′mu·lat′ed
ac·cu′mu·lates
ac·cu′mu·la′tion
ac·cu′mu·la′tive
ac·cu′mu·la′tor
ac′cu·ra·cy
ac′cu·rate
ac′cu·rate·ly
ac′cu·sa′tion
ac·cu′sa·tive
ac·cu′sa·to′ry
ac·cuse′
ac·cused′
ac·cus′er
ac·cus′ing·ly
ac·cus′tom
ac·cus′tomed

ace
a·cerb′
a·cer′bic
a·cer′bi·ty
ac′e·tate
a·ce′tic
ac′e·tone
a·cet′y·lene
ache
ached
a·chiev′a·ble
a·chieve′
a·chieved′
a·chieve′ment
ach′ro·mat′ic
ach′ro·mat′i·cal·ly
a·chro′ma·to′sis
ac′id
a·cid′i·fi·ca′tion
a·cid′i·fi′er
a·cid′i·fy
a·cid′i·ty
ac′i·do′sis
ac′id·proof′
a·cid′u·late
a·cid′u·lat′ed
a·cid′u·lous
ac·knowl′edge
ac·knowl′edged
ac·knowl′edg·ment
ac′me
ac′ne
ac′o·lyte
ac′o·nite
a′corn
a·cous′tic
a·cous′ti·cal
a·cous′ti·cal·ly
a·cous′tics
ac·quaint′
ac·quaint′ance
ac·quaint′ance·ship
ac·quaint′ed
ac′qui·esce′
ac′qui·esced′
ac′qui·es′cence
ac′qui·es′cent
ac·quire′
ac·quired′
ac·quire′ment
ac·quires′
ac′qui·si′tion
ac·quis′i·tive
ac·quis′i·tive·ness
ac·quit′
ac·quit′tal
ac·quit′ted
a′cre
a′cre·age
ac′rid
a·crid′i·ty
ac′rid·ly
ac′ri·mo′ni·ous
ac′ri·mo′ni·ous·ly
ac′ri·mo′ni·ous·ness
ac′ri·mo′ny
ac′ro·bat
ac′ro·bat′ic
ac′ro·bat′i·cal·ly
ac′ro·bat′ics
a·crop′o·lis
a·cross′
a·cryl′ic
act
act′ed
ac·tin′ic
ac·tin′i·um
ac′tion
ac′tion·a·ble
ac′ti·vate
ac′ti·vat′ed
ac′ti·va′tion
ac′ti·va′tor
ac′tive
ac′tive·ly
ac′tiv·ist
ac·tiv′i·ty
ac′tiv·ize
ac′tor
ac′tress
ac′tu·al
ac′tu·al′i·ties
ac′tu·al′i·ty
ac′tu·al·ly
ac′tu·ar′i·al
ac′tu·ar′y

ac′tu·ate
ac′tu·at′ed
a·cu′i·ty
a·cu′men
ac′u·punc′ture
a·cute′
a·cute′ness
ad′age
a·da′gio
ad′a·mant
ad′a·man′tine
a·dapt′
a·dapt′a·bil′i·ty
a·dapt′a·ble
ad′ap·ta′tion
a·dapt′ed
a·dapt′er
a·dap′tive
add
add′ed
ad·den′da
ad·den′dum
ad′der
ad′dict
ad·dict′ed
ad·dic′tion
ad·di′tion
ad·di′tion·al
ad·di′tion·al·ly
ad′di·tive
ad′dle
ad′dled

ad·dress
ad·dressed′
ad′dress·ee′
Ad·dres′so·graph
ad·duce′
ad·duced′
ad·duct′
ad·duc′tion
ad·duc′tive
ad·duc′tor
ad′e·noid
ad′e·nol′o·gy
ad′e·no′ma
a·dept′
ad′e·qua·cy
ad′e·quate
ad′e·quate·ly
ad′e·quate·ness
ad·here′
ad·hered′
ad·her′ence
ad·her′ent
ad·he′sion
ad·he′sive
ad·he′sive·ness
a·dieu′
ad′i·pose
ad′i·pos′i·ty
ad·ja′cen·cy
ad·ja′cent
ad′jec·ti′val
ad′jec·tive

ad·join′
ad·joined′
ad·journ′
ad·journed′
ad·journ′ment
ad·judge′
ad·judged′
ad·ju′di·cate
ad·ju′di·cat′ed
ad·ju′di·ca′tion
ad·ju′di·ca′tive
ad·ju′di·ca′tor
ad′junct
ad′ju·ra′tion
ad·jur′a·to′ry
ad·jure′
ad·jured′
ad·just′
ad·just′a·ble
ad·just′ed
ad·just′er
ad·just′ment
ad′ju·tan·cy
ad′ju·tant
ad·min′is·ter
ad·min′is·tered
ad·min′is·tra′tion
ad·min′is·tra′tive
ad·min′is·tra′tive·ly
ad·min′is·tra′tor
ad·min′is·tra′trix
ad′mi·ra·ble

ad′mi·ra·bly
ad′mi·ral
ad′mi·ral·ty
ad′mi·ra′tion
ad·mire′
ad·mired′
ad·mis′si·bil′i·ty
ad·mis′si·ble
ad·mis′sion
ad·mit′
ad·mit′tance
ad·mit′ted
ad·mit′ted·ly
ad·mix′ture
ad·mon′ish
ad′mo·ni′tion
ad·mon′i·to′ry
a·do′be
ad′o·les′cence
ad′o·les′cent
a·dopt′
a·dopt′ed
a·dop′tion
a·dop′tive
a·dor′a·ble
ad′o·ra′tion
a·dore′
a·dored′
a·dor′ing·ly
a·dorn′
a·dorned′
a·dorn′ment
ad·re′nal
ad·ren′al·ine
a·drift′
a·droit′
a·droit′ly
a·droit′ness
ad·sorb′
ad·sorp′tion
ad′u·la′tion
ad′u·la·to′ry
a·dult′
a·dul′ter·ant
a·dul′ter·ate
a·dul′ter·at′ed
a·dul′ter·a′tion
a·dul′ter·er
a·dul′ter·ous
a·dul′ter·y
a·dult′hood
ad·um′brate
ad·um′brat·ed
ad′um·bra′tion
ad·vance′
ad·vanced′
ad·vance′ment
ad·van′tage
ad′van·ta′geous
ad′vent
Ad′vent·ist
ad′ven·ti′tious
ad·ven′ture
ad·ven′tur·er
ad·ven′ture·some
ad·ven′tur·ess
ad·ven′tur·ous
ad′verb
ad·ver′bi·al
ad·ver′bi·al·ly
ad′ver·sar′y
ad·ver′sa·tive
ad·verse′
ad·verse′ly
ad·ver′si·ty
ad·vert′
ad′ver·tise
ad·ver′tise·ment
ad′ver·tis′er
ad·vice′
ad·vis′a·bil′i·ty
ad·vis′a·ble
ad·vise′
ad·vised′
ad·vis′ed·ly
ad′vi·see′
ad·vise′ment
ad·vi′so·ry
ad′vo·ca·cy
ad′vo·cate
ad′vo·cat′ed
ad·vow′son
adz
ae′gis
ae·o′li·an
ae′on

a'er·ate
a'er·at'ed
a'er·a'tion
a'er·a'tor
a·e'ri·al
a'er·o·nau'ti·cal
a'er·o·sol
a'er·o·space
aes·thet'ic
af'fa·bil'i·ty
af'fa·ble
af'fa·bly
af·fect'
af'fec·ta'tion
af·fect'ed
af·fect'ed·ly
af·fect'ing·ly
af·fec'tion
af·fec'tion·ate
af·fec'tion·ate·ly
af'fec·tiv'i·ty
af·fi'ance
af·fi'anced
af·fi'ant
af'fi·da'vit
af·fil'i·ate
af·fil'i·at'ed
af·fil'i·a'tion
af·fin'i·ty
af·firm'
af·firm'a·ble
af'fir·ma'tion
af·firm'a·tive
af·firm'a·to'ry
af·firmed'
af·fix'
af·fixed'
af·fla'tus
af·flict'
af·flict'ed
af·flic'tion
af·flic'tive
af'flu·ence
af'flu·ent
af·ford'
af·ford'ed
af·for'est
af·for'est·a'tion
af·fray'
af·fright'
af·fright'ed
af·front'
af·front'ed
af'ghan
a·field'
a·fire'
a·flame'
a·float'
a·foot'
a·fore'said'
a·fore'thought'
a·fore'time'
a·foul'
a·fraid'
Af'ro-A·mer'i·can
aft'er
aft'er·beat'
aft'er·care'
aft'er·clap'
aft'er·deck'
aft'er-din'ner
aft'er·ef·fect'
aft'er·glow'
aft'er·growth'
aft'er·guard'
aft'er·hatch'
aft'er·hold'
aft'er·im'age
aft'er·life'
aft'er·math
aft'er·most
aft'er·noon'
aft'er·part'
aft'er·taste'
aft'er·thought'
aft'er·time'
aft'er·ward
a·gain'
a·gainst'
a·gape'
ag'ate
ag'ate·ware'
a·ga've
age
aged
age'less

a'gen·cy
a·gen'da
a·gen'dum
a'gent
a·ger'a·tum
ag·glom'er·ate
ag·glom'er·at'ed
ag·glom'er·a'tion
ag·glom'er·a'tive
ag·glu'ti·nate
ag·glu'ti·na'tion
ag·glu'ti·na'tive
ag'gran·dize
ag·gran'dize·ment
ag'gra·vate
ag'gra·vat'ed
ag'gra·vat'ing·ly
ag'gra·va'tion
ag'gre·gate
ag'gre·ga'tion
ag·gres'sion
ag·gres'sive
ag·gres'sor
ag·grieve'
ag·grieved'
a·ghast'
ag'ile
a·gil'i·ty
ag'i·o
ag'i·tate
ag'i·tat'ed
ag'i·ta'tion
ag'i·ta'tor
a·gleam'
ag'nate
ag·nos'tic
ag·nos'ti·cism
a·gog'
ag'o·nize
ag'o·nized
ag'o·niz'ing·ly
ag'o·ny
a·grar'i·an
a·gree'
a·gree'a·bil'i·ty
a·gree'a·ble
a·gree'a·ble·ness
a·greed'
a·gree'ment
ag'ri·cul'tur·al
ag'ri·cul'ture
a·gron'o·my
a·ground'
a'gue
a·head'
a·hoy'
a·hun'gered
aid
aid'ed
ai·grette'
ai'guil·lette'
ail
ai·lan'thus
ailed
ai'ler·on
ail'ment
aim
aim'less
air
air'brush'
air'-dry'
aired
air'field'
air'freight
air'i·ly
air'lin'er
air'mail'
air'man
air'plane'
air'port'
air'ship'
air'sick'
air'space'
air'tight'
air'way'
air'wor'thy
air'y
aisle
a·jar'
a·kim'bo
a·kin'
al'a·bas'ter
a·lac'ri·ty
al'a·mo
a·larm'
a·larmed'

a·larm'ing·ly
a·larm'ist
a·las'
al'ba·core
al'ba·tross
al·bi'no
al'bum
al·bu'min
al·bu'mi·nous
al'che·mist
al'che·my
al'co·hol
al'co·hol'ic
al'co·hol·ism
al'co·hol·ize
al'cove
al'der
al'der·man
al'der·man'ic
Al'der·ney
a'le·a·to'ry
a·lem'bic
a·lem'bi·cate
Al'e·mite
a·lert'
a·lert'ly
a·lert'ness
ale'wife'
al'ex·an'drite
al·fal'fa
al'ge·bra
al'ge·bra'ic
Al·ge'ri·an
a'li·as
al'i·bi
al'i·dade
al'ien
al'ien·a·bil'i·ty
al'ien·a·ble
al'ien·ate
al'ien·at'ed
al'ien·a'tion
al'ien·ist
a·light'
a·lign'
a·lign'ment
a·like'
al'i·men'ta·ry
al'i·men·ta'tion
al'i·mo'ny
al'i·quant
al'i·quot
a·live'
a·live'ness
a·liz'a·rin
al'ka·li
al'ka·lin'i·ty
all
al·lay'
al·layed'
al'le·ga'tion
al·lege'
al·leged'
al·leg'ed·ly
al·le'giance
al'le·gor'i·cal
al'le·go·rize
al'le·go'ry
al'le·gret'to
al·le'gro
al'ler·gen
al·ler'gic
al'ler·gy
al·le'vi·ate
al·le'vi·at'ed
al·le'vi·a'tion
al'ley
al'ley·way'
al·li'ance
al·lied'
al'li·ga'tor
al·lit'er·ate
al·lit'er·a'tion
al·lit'er·a'tive
al·lit'er·a'tive·ly
al'lo·ca·ble
al'lo·cate
al'lo·cat'ed
al'lo·ca'tion
al'lo·cu'tion
al'lo·path
al'lo·path'ic
al·lop'a·thy
al·lot'
al·lot'ment
al·lot'ted

al·low′
al·low′a·ble
al·low′ance
al·lowed′
al·low′ed·ly
al·loy′
al·loy′age
al·loyed′
all′spice′
al·lude′
al·lud′ed
al·lure′
al·lured′
al·lure′ment
al·lur′ing·ly
al·lu′sion
al·lu′sive
al·lu′sive·ly
al·lu′sive·ness
al·lu′vi·al
al·lu′vi·um
al·ly′
al′ma·nac
al·might′y
al′mond
al′mon·er
al′most
alms
alms′house′
a·lo′di·um
al′oe
a·loft′
a·lo′ha
a·lone′
a·long′
a·long′side′
a·loof′
a·loof′ly
al′o·pe′ci·a
a·loud′
al·pac′a
al′pha·bet
al′pha·bet′ic
al′pha·bet′i·cal
al′pha·bet·ize
al·read′y
al′so
al′tar
al′tar·piece′
al′ter
al′ter·a·ble
al′ter·a′tion
al′ter·a′tive
al′ter·cate
al′ter·ca′tion
al′tered
al′ter·nate
al′ter·nat′ed
al′ter·na′tion
al·ter′na·tive
al′ter·na′tor
al·though′
al′ti·graph
al·tim′e·ter
al′ti·pla′no
al·tis′si·mo
al′ti·tude
al′to
al′to·geth′er
al′tru·ism
al′tru·ist
al′tru·is′tic
al′tru·is′ti·cal·ly
al′um
a·lu′mi·na
a·lu′mi·nate
a·lu′mi·nif′er·ous
a·lu′mi·no′sis
a·lu′mi·num
a·lum′na
a·lum′nae
a·lum′ni
a·lum′nus
al·ve′o·lar
al·ve′o·lus
al′ways
a·lys′sum
a·mal′gam
a·mal′gam·ate
a·mal′gam·at′ed
a·mal′gam·a′tion
a·man′u·en′sis
am′a·ranth
am′a·ran′thine
a·mass′
a·massed′

am′a·teur′
am′a·teur′ish
am′a·teur′ism
am′a·tive
am′a·tive·ness
am′a·to′ry
a·maze′
a·mazed′
a·maze′ment
a·maz′ing·ly
Am′a·zon
Am′a·zo′ni·an
am·bas′sa·dor
am·bas′sa·do′ri·al
am·bas′sa·do′ri·al·ly
am·bas′sa·dress
am′ber
am′ber·gris
am′bi·dex·ter′i·ty
am′bi·dex′trous
am′bi·dex′trous·ly
am′bi·dex′trous·ness
am′bi·ent
am′bi·gu′i·ty
am·big′u·ous
am·big′u·ous·ly
am·big′u·ous·ness
am·bi′tion
am·bi′tious
am·bi′tious·ly
am·biv′a·lence
am·biv′a·lent

am′ble
am·bro′si·a
am·bro′si·al
am·bro′si·al·ly
am′bro·type
am′bu·lance
am′bu·lant
am′bu·la·to′ry
am′bus·cade′
am′bush
a·mel′io·rate
a·mel′io·rat′ed
a·mel′io·ra′tion
a·mel′io·ra′tive
a′men′
a·me′na·bil′i·ty
a·me′na·ble
a·mend′
a·mend′ed
a·mend′ment
a·men′i·ty
A·mer′i·can
A·mer′i·can·i·za′tion
A·mer′i·can·ize
am′e·thyst
a′mi·a·bil′i·ty
a′mi·a·ble
am′i·ca·bil′i·ty
am′i·ca·ble
a·mid′ships
a·midst′
a·miss′

am′i·ty
am′me′ter
am·mo′ni·a
am·mo′ni·um
am′mu·ni′tion
am·ne′si·a
am′nes·ty
a·moe′ba
a·mong′
a·mongst′
a·mor′al
am′o·rous
am′o·rous·ly
am′o·rous·ness
a·mor′phous
a·mor′ti·za′tion
a·mor′tize
a·mor′tized
a·mount′
a·mount′ed
a·mour′
am·per′age
am′pere
am·phet′a·mine
am·phib′i·an
am·phib′i·ous
am·phib′i·ous·ly
am′phi·the′a·ter
am′pho·ra
am′ple
am′pli·fi·ca′tion
am′pli·fied

am′pli·fi′er
am′pli·fy
am′pli·tude
am′ply
am·pul′la
am′pu·tate
am′pu·tat′ed
am′pu·ta′tion
am′pu·ta′tive
am′pu·tee′
Am′trak
am′u·let
a·muse′
a·mused′
a·muse′ment
a·mus′ing·ly
a·nab′o·lism
a·nach′ro·nism
a·nach′ro·nis′tic
a·nach′ro·nous
an′a·con′da
an′a·gram
an′a·lects
an′al·ge′si·a
an′al·ge′sic
an′a·log′i·cal
a·nal′o·gies
a·nal′o·gous
a·nal′o·gous·ly
an′a·logue
a·nal′o·gy
a·nal′y·ses
a·nal′y·sis
an′a·lyst
an′a·lyt′ic
an′a·lyt′i·cal
an′a·lyt′i·cal·ly
an′a·lyze
an′a·lyzed
an′a·lyz′er
an′am·ne′sis
an·ar′chic
an·ar′chi·cal
an′arch·ism
an′arch·ist
an′arch·y
an·as′tig·mat′ic
a·nath′e·ma·tize
an′a·tom′ic
an′a·tom′i·cal
a·nat′o·mist
a·nat′o·mize
a·nat′o·mized
a·nat′o·my
an′ces′tor
an′ces′tors
an·ces′tral
an′ces′try
an′chor
an′chor·age
an′chored
an′cho·rite
an·cho′vy
an′cient
an′cil·lar′y
and
an·dan′te
and′i′ron
an′ec·dot′age
an′ec·dote
a·ne′mi·a
an′e·mom′e·ter
an′e·mom′e·try
a·nem′o·ne
a·nent′
an′er·oid
an′es·the′si·a
an′es·the′si·ol′o·gy
an′es·the′sis
an′es·thet′ic
an′es·thet′i·za′tion
an·es′the·tize
an·es′the·tized
an′eu·rysm
a·new′
an′gel
an·gel′ic
An′ge·lus
an′ger
an′gered
an′gle
an′gled
an′gler
An′gli·can
An′glo-Sax′on
An·go′ra

an'gri·er
an'gri·est
an'gri·ly
an'gry
an'guish
an'guished
an'gu·lar
an'gu·lar'i·ty
an'gu·la'tion
an·hy'drous
an'i·line
an'i·mad·ver'sion
an'i·mal
an'i·mate
an'i·mat'ed
an'i·mat'ed·ly
an'i·ma'tion
an'i·ma'tor
an'i·mism
an'i·mist
an'i·mis'tic
an'i·mos'i·ty
an'i·mus
an'ise
an'ise·root'
an'kle
an'kle·bone'
an'klet
an'ky·lo'sis
an'nal·ist
an'nals
an·neal'
an·nealed'
an·nex'
an'nex·a'tion
an'nex·a'tion·ist
an·nexed'
an·ni'hi·late
an·ni'hi·lat'ed
an·ni'hi·la'tion
an'ni·ver'sa·ry
an'no·tate
an'no·tat'ed
an'no·ta'tion
an·nounce'
an·nounced'
an·nounce'ment
an·nounc'er
an·noy'
an·noy'ance
an·noyed'
an·noy'ing·ly
an'nu·al
an'nu·al·ly
an·nu'i·tant
an·nu'i·ty
an·nul'
an'nu·lar
an·nulled'
an·nul'ment
an·nun'ci·a'tion
an·nun'ci·a'tor
an'ode
an'o·dyne
a·noint'
a·noint'ed
a·nom'a·lies
a·nom'a·lous
a·nom'a·lous·ly
a·nom'a·ly
a·non'
an'o·nym'i·ty
a·non'y·mous
a·non'y·mous·ly
a·noph'e·les
an·oth'er
an'swer
an'swer·a·ble
an'swered
ant
ant·ac'id
an·tag'o·nism
an·tag'o·nist
an·tag'o·nis'tic
an·tag'o·nis'ti·cal·ly
an·tag'o·nize
an·tag'o·nized
ant·arc'tic
an'te
ant'eat'er
an'te·ced'ent
an'te·cham'ber
an'te·date'
an'te·dat'ed
an'te·lope
an'te·na'tal

an·ten′na
an·te′ri·or
an′te·room′
an′them
an·thol′o·gies
an·thol′o·gist
an·thol′o·gize
an·thol′o·gy
an′thra·cite
an′thrax
an′thro·poid
an′thro·po·log′i·cal
an′thro·pol′o·gy
an′ti·bod′y
an′tic
an′ti·christ′
an·tic′i·pate
an·tic′i·pat′ed
an·tic′i·pa′tion
an·tic′i·pa·to′ry
an′ti·cli′max
an′ti·cline
an′ti·dote
an′ti·gen
an′ti·knock′
an′ti·mo′ny
an·tin′o·my
an·tip′a·thies
an·tip′a·thy
an·tiph′o·nal
an·tip′o·des
an′ti·quar′i·an

an′ti·quar′y
an′ti·quat′ed
an·tique′
an·tiqued′
an·tiq′ui·ty
an′ti·sep′sis
an′ti·sep′tic
an′ti·sep′ti·cal·ly
an′ti·so′cial
an′ti·tank′
an·tith′e·ses
an·tith′e·sis
an′ti·thet′i·cal
an′ti·tox′in
an′ti·trust′
ant′ler
ant′lered
an′to·nym
an′trum
an′vil
anx·i′e·ty
anx′ious
anx′ious·ly
an′y
an′y·bod′y
an′y·one
an′y·thing
an′y·way
an′y·where
a·or′ta
a·or′tic
a·pace′

a·part′
a·part′ment
ap′a·thet′ic
ap′a·thet′i·cal·ly
ap′a·thy
a·pe′ri·ent
a·per′i·tive
ap′er·ture
a′pex
a′pex·es
a·pha′si·a
a′phid
aph′o·rism
aph′o·ris′tic
a′pi·a·rist
a′pi·ar′y
ap′i·cal
ap′i·ces
a·piece′
a·poc′a·lypse
ap′o·gee
A·pol′lo
a·pol′o·get′ic
a·pol′o·get′i·cal
a·pol′o·gies
a·pol′o·gist
a·pol′o·gize
a·pol′o·gized
a·pol′o·gy
ap′o·plec′tic
ap′o·plex′y
a·pos′ta·sy

a·pos′tate
a·pos′tle
apʹos·tol′ic
apʹos·tol′i·cal
a·pos′tro·phe
a·pos′tro·phize
a·poth′e·carʹy
ap′o·thegm
a·pothʹe·o′sis
ap·pall′
ap·palled′
ap·pall′ing·ly
ap′pa·nage
apʹpa·ra′tus
apʹpa·ra′tus·es
ap·par′el
ap·par′eled
ap·par′ent
apʹpa·ri′tion
ap·peal′
ap·pealed′
ap·peal′ing·ly
ap·pear′
ap·pear′ance
ap·peared′
ap·peas′a·ble
ap·pease′
ap·peased′
ap·pease′ment
ap·peas′ing·ly
ap·pel′lant
ap·pel′late
apʹpel·la′tion
apʹpel·lee′
ap·pend′
ap·pend′age
apʹpen·dec′to·my
ap·pend′ed
ap·penʹdi·ci′tis
ap·pen′dix
ap·pen′dix·es
apʹper·ceive′
apʹper·ceived′
apʹper·cep′tion
apʹper·cep′tive
apʹper·tain′
apʹper·tained′
ap′pe·tite
ap′pe·tizʹer
ap′pe·tizʹing·ly
ap·plaud′
ap·plaud′ed
ap·plause′
ap′ple
ap′ple·jackʹ
ap′ple·nutʹ
ap′ple·sauceʹ
ap·pli′ance
apʹpli·ca·bil′i·ty
ap′pli·ca·ble
ap′pli·cant
apʹpli·ca′tion
ap′pli·caʹtor
ap·plied′
apʹpli·qué′
ap·ply′
ap·point′
ap·point′ed
ap·pointʹee′
ap·poin′tive
ap·point′ment
ap·por′tion
ap·por′tioned
ap·por′tion·ment
ap′po·site
apʹpo·si′tion
ap·praisʹal
ap·praiseʹ
ap·praised′
ap·praisʹer
ap·prais′ing·ly
ap·pre′ci·a·ble
ap·pre′ci·a·bly
ap·pre′ci·ate
ap·pre′ci·atʹed
ap·preʹci·a′tion
ap·pre′ci·aʹtive
ap·pre′ci·aʹtive·ly
apʹpre·hend′
apʹpre·hend′ed
apʹpre·hend′ing·ly
apʹpre·hen′sion
apʹpre·hen′sive
apʹpre·hen′sive·ly
apʹpre·hen′sive·ness
ap·pren′tice

ap·pren'ticed
ap·pren'tice·ship
ap·prise'
ap·prised'
ap·proach'
ap·proach'a·ble
ap·proached'
ap'pro·ba'tion
ap'pro·ba'tive
ap'pro·ba'tive·ness
ap·pro'pri·ate
ap·pro'pri·at'ed
ap·pro'pri·ate·ly
ap·pro'pri·ate·ness
ap·pro'pri·a'tion
ap·prov'al
ap·prove'
ap·proved'
ap·prov'ing·ly
ap·prox'i·mate
ap·prox'i·mat'ed
ap·prox'i·mate·ly
ap·prox'i·ma'tion
ap·pur'te·nance
ap·pur'te·nant
a'pri·cot
A'pril
a'pron
ap'ro·pos'
apse
ap'sis
apt

ap'ti·tude
apt'ly
apt'ness
aq'ua·ma·rine'
aq'ua·relle'
a·quar'i·um
aq'ua·scu'tum
a·quat'ic
aq'ua·tint'
aq'ue·duct
a'que·ous
aq'ui·line
Ar'ab
ar'a·besque'
A·ra'bi·an
Ar'a·bic
ar'a·bil'i·ty
Ar'ab·ist
ar'a·ble
a·rach'nid
a·rach'noid
a·rag'o·nite
Ar'a·ma'ic
ar'ba·lest
ar'bi·ter
ar'bi·tra·ble
ar'bi·trage
ar·bit'ra·ment
ar'bi·trar'i·ly
ar'bi·trar'i·ness
ar'bi·trar'y
ar'bi·trate

ar'bi·trat'ed
ar'bi·tra'tion
ar'bi·tra'tive
ar'bi·tra'tor
ar'bor
ar·bo're·al
ar·bo're·ous
ar'bo·re'tum
ar·bu'tus
arc
ar·cade'
ar·cad'ed
Ar·ca'di·a
ar·ca'num
arch
ar'chae·ol'o·gist
ar'chae·ol'o·gy
ar·cha'ic
arch'an'gel
arch'an·gel'ic
arch'bish'op
arch'dea'con
arch'di'o·cese
arch'du'cal
arch'duch'ess
arch'duch'y
arch'duke'
arch'er
arch'er·fish'
arch'er·y
ar'che·typ'al
ar'che·type

arch′fiend′
ar′chi·pel′a·go
ar′chi·tect
ar′chi·tec·ton′ic
ar′chi·tec′tur·al
ar′chi·tec′tur·al·ly
ar′chi·tec′ture
ar′chi·trave
ar′chives
ar′chi·vist
arch′ly
arch′ness
arch′way
arc′tic
ar′dent
ar′dent·ly
ar′dor
ar′du·ous
ar′du·ous·ly
are
a′re·a
a·re′na
ar′gent
ar′gen·tif′er·ous
ar′gon
Ar′go·naut
ar′got
ar′gu·a·ble
ar′gue
ar′gued
ar′gu·ment
ar′gu·men·ta′tion
ar′gu·men′ta·tive
Ar′gy·rol
a′ri·a
ar′id
a·rid′i·ty
a·right′
a·rise′
a·ris′en
ar′is·toc′ra·cy
a·ris′to·crat
a·ris′to·crat′ic
a·rith′me·tic
ar′ith·met′i·cal
ark
arm
ar·ma′da
ar′ma·dil′lo
ar′ma·ment
ar′ma·ture
arm′chair
armed
Ar·me′ni·an
arm′ful
arm′hole′
ar′mi·stice
arm′let
ar′mor
ar′mored
ar·mo′ri·al
ar′mor·y
arm′pit′
arm′rest′
arm′scye′
ar′my
ar′ni·ca
a·ro′ma
ar′o·mat′ic
a·round′
a·rouse′
ar·peg′gio
ar·raign′
ar·raigned′
ar·raign′ment
ar·range′
ar·ranged′
ar·range′ment
ar·rang′er
ar′ras
ar·ray′
ar·rayed′
ar·rear′age
ar·rears′
ar·rest′
ar·rest′er
ar·rhyth′mic
ar·riv′al
ar·rive′
ar·rived′
ar′ro·gance
ar′ro·gant
ar′ro·gant·ly
ar′ro·gate
ar′ro·gat′ed
ar′ro·ga′tion

ar′row
ar′row·head′
ar′row·head′ed
ar′row·wood′
ar′row·y
ar~~roy′o~~
ar′se·nal
ar′se·nate
ar·sen′ic
ar·sen′i·cal
ar′se·nide
ar′se·nite
ar′son
ar′son·ist
art
ar·te′ri·al
ar′ter·y
art′ful
art′ful·ly
ar·thrit′ic
ar·thrit′i·cal
ar·thri′tis
ar′thro·plas′ty
ar′ti·choke
ar′ti·cle
ar′ti·cled
ar·tic′u·late
ar·tic′u·lat′ed
ar·tic′u·la′tion
ar·tic′u·la′tive
ar′ti·fact
ar′ti·fice
ar·tif′i·cer
ar′ti·fi′cial
ar′ti·fi′ci·al′i·ty
ar′ti·fi′cial·ly
ar·til′ler·ist
ar·til′ler·y
ar′ti·san
art′ist
ar·tis′tic
art′ist·ry
art′less
Ar′y·an
as
as′a·fet′i·da
as·bes′tos
as·cend′
as·cend′an·cy
as·cend′ant
as·cend′er
as·cen′sion
as·cent′
as′cer·tain′
as′cer·tain′ment
as·cet′ic
as·cet′i·cism
as·ci′tes
a·scor′bic
as′cot
as·cribe′
as·cribed′
as·crip′tion
a·sep′sis
a·sep′tic
ash
a·shamed′
ash′en
ash′es
ash′lar
a·shore′
ash′pit′
ash′wort′
ash′y
A′sian
A′si·at′ic
a·side′
as′i·nine
as′i·nin′i·ty
ask
a·skance′
a·skew′
a·slant′
a·sleep′
asp
as·par′a·gus
as′pect
as′pen
as·per′i·ty
as·perse′
as·persed′
as·per′sion
as′phalt
as·phal′tic
as′pho·del
as·phyx′i·a

as·phyx′i·ate
as·phyx′i·a′tion
as′pic
as·pir′ant
as′pi·rate
as′pi·rat′ed
as′pi·ra′tion
as′pi·ra′tor
as·pire′
as·pired′
as′pi·rin
as′sa·gai
as·sail′
as·sail′ant
as·sailed′
as·sas′sin
as·sas′si·nate
as·sas′si·nat′ed
as·sas′si·na′tion
as·sault′
as·sault′ed
as·say′
as·sayed′
as·say′er
as·sem′blage
as·sem′ble
as·sem′bled
as·sem′bler
as·sem′bly
as·sent′
as·sent′ed
as·sent′ing·ly

as·sert′
as·sert′ed
as·ser′tion
as·ser′tive
as·ser′tive·ly
as·sess′
as·sess′a·ble
as·sessed′
as·sess′ment
as·ses′sor
as·ses′sor·ship
as′set
as·sev′er·ate
as·sev′er·a′tion
as′si·du′i·ty
as·sid′u·ous
as·sid′u·ous·ly
as·sign′
as·sign′a·ble
as′sig·na′tion
as·signed′
as′sign·ee′
as·sign′ment
as′sign·or′
as·sim′i·la·ble
as·sim′i·late
as·sim′i·lat′ed
as·sim′i·la′tion
as·sim′i·la′tive
as·sim′i·la·to′ry
as·sist′
as·sist′ance

as·sist′ant
as·sist′ed
as·sists′
as·size′
as·so′ci·ate
as·so′ci·at′ed
as·so′ci·a′tion
as·so′ci·a′tive
as′so·nance
as′so·nant
as·sort′
as·sort′ed
as·sort′ment
as·suage′
as·suaged′
as·sum′a·ble
as·sum′a·bly
as·sume′
as·sumed′
as·sum′ed·ly
as·sump′sit
as·sump′tion
as·sur′ance
as·sure′
as·sured′
as·sur′ed·ly
as·sur′ed·ness
as·sur′er
As·syr′i·an
as′ter
as′ter·isk
a·stern′

as′ter·oid
as·the′ni·a
as·then′ic
asth′ma
asth·mat′ic
as′tig·mat′ic
a·stig′ma·tism
as·ton′ish
as·ton′ish·ing·ly
as·ton′ish·ment
as·tound′
as·tound′ed
as·tound′ing·ly
a·strad′dle
as·trag′a·lus
as′tra·khan
as′tral
a·stray′
a·stride′
as·trin′gen·cy
as·trin′gent
as′tro·dome
as·trol′o·ger
as·trol′o·gy
as′tro·nau′tics
as·tron′o·mer
as′tro·nom′i·cal
as·tron′o·my
as′tro·phys′i·cal
as′tro·phys′i·cist
as′tro·phys′ics
as′tro·turf
as·tute′ly
as·tute′ness
a·sun′der
a·sy′lum
a′sym·met′ric
a′sym·met′ri·cal
a·sym′me·try
at
at′a·rax′i·a
at′a·vism
at′a·vis′tic
a′the·ism
a′the·ist
a′the·is′tic
ath′e·nae′um
A·the′ni·an
ath′lete
ath·let′ic
ath·let′ics
a·thwart′
at′mos·phere
at′mos·pher′ic
at′oll
at′om
at′om·at′ic
a·tom′ic
at′om·is′tic
at′om·ize
at′om·ized
at′om·iz′er
a·ton′al
a′to·nal′i·ty
a·tone′
a·toned′
a·tone′ment
a′tri·um
a·tro′cious
a·tro′cious·ly
a·troc′i·ty
at′ro·phied
at′ro·phy
at′ro·pine
at·tach′
at·tached′
at·tach′ment
at·tack′
at·tack′er
at·tain′
at·tain′a·ble
at·tain′der
at·tained′
at·tain′ment
at′tar
at·tempt′
at·tempt′ed
at·tend′
at·tend′ance
at·tend′ant
at·ten′tion
at·ten′tive
at·ten′tive·ly
at·ten′tive·ness
at·ten′u·ate
at·ten′u·at′ed

at·ten′u·a′tion
at·test′
at′tes·ta′tion
at·tests′
at′tic
at·tire′
at·tired′
at′ti·tude
at′ti·tu′di·nize
at·tor′ney
at·tor′neys
at·tract′
at·tract′ed
at·trac′tion
at·trac′tive
at·trac′tive·ly
at·trib′ute
at·trib′ut·ed
at′tri·bu′tion
at·trib′u·tive
at·tri′tion
at·tune′
at·tuned′
a·twit′ter
a·typ′i·cal
au′burn
auc′tion
auc′tioned
auc′tion·eer′
au·da′cious
au·da′cious·ly
au·dac′i·ty

au′di·bil′i·ty
au′di·ble
au′di·bly
au′di·ence
au′di·o
au′di·om′e·ter
au′dio·vis′u·al
au′dit·ed
au·di′tion
au′di·tor
au′di·to′ri·um
au′di·to′ry
au′ger
aught
aug·ment′
aug′men·ta′tion
aug·ment′a·tive
aug·ment′ed
au′gur
au′gured
au′gu·ry
au·gust′
Au′gust
aunt
au′ra
au′ral
au′re·ole
au′ri·cle
au·ric′u·lar
au·rif′er·ous
au·ro′ra
au·ro′ral

aus′cul·tate
aus′cul·ta′tion
aus′pice
aus′pic·es
aus·pi′cious
aus·tere′
aus·tere′ly
aus·ter′i·ty
Aus·tral′ian
Aus′tri·an
au·then′tic
au·then′ti·cate
au·then′ti·cat′ed
au·then′ti·ca′tion
au′then·tic′i·ty
au′thor
au·thor′i·tar′i·an
au·thor′i·ta′tive
au·thor′i·ta′tive·ly
au·thor′i·ty
au′thor·i·za′tion
au′thor·ize
au′thor·ized
au′thor·ship
au′to·bi′o·graph′i·cal
au′to·bi·og′ra·phy
au·toch′tho·nous
au′to·clave
au·toc′ra·cy
au′to·crat
au′to·crat′ic
au′to·crat′i·cal·ly

au′to·graph
au′to·in·tox′i·ca′tion
au′to·mat′ic
au′to·ma′tion
au·tom′a·tize
au·tom′a·ton
au′to·mo·bile′
au·ton′o·mize
au·ton′o·mous
au·ton′o·my
au′top·sies
au′top·sy
au′to·sug·ges′tion
au′tumn
au·tum′nal
aux·il′ia·ry
a·vail′
a·vail′a·bil′i·ty
a·vail′a·ble
a·vailed′
av′a·lanche
av′a·rice
av′a·ri′cious
av′a·ri′cious·ly
av′a·tar′
a·venge′
a·venged′
av′e·nue

a·ver′
av′er·age
av′er·aged
a·ver′ment
a·verred′
a·verse′
a·ver′sion
a·vert′
a·vert′ed
a′vi·ar′y
a′vi·a′tion
a′vi·a′tor
av′id
a·vid′i·ty
av′id·ly
av′i·ga′tion
av′o·ca′do
av′o·ca′tion
a·void′
a·void′a·ble
a·void′ed
a·vow′al
a·vow′ed·ly
a·vun′cu·lar
a·wait′
a·wait′ed
a·wake′
a·wak′en

a·wak′ened
a·ward′
a·ward′ed
a·ware′
a·ware′ness
a·wash′
a·way′
awe
awe′some
aw′ful
aw′ful·ly
awk′ward
awk′ward·ly
awk′ward·ness
awl
awn′ing
a·woke′
a·wry′
ax
ax′i·om
ax′i·o·mat′ic
ax′is
ax′le
a·za′le·a
az′i·muth
Az′tec
az′ure
az′u·rite

# B

bab′bitt
bab′ble
ba·boon′
ba′by
Bab′y·lo′ni·an
bac′ca·lau′re·ate
bac′cha·nal
bac′cha·na′li·an
bach′e·lor
bach′e·lor·hood′
ba·cil′lus
back
back′ache′
back′board′
back′bone′
back′break′er
back′drop′
back′er
back′fire′
back′gam′mon
back′ground′
back′hand′

back′hand′ed
back′lash′
back′log′
back′saw′
back′slide′
back′slid′er
back′spin′
back′stage′
back′stamp′
back′stitch′
back′stop′
back′stroke′
back′track′
back′ward
back′ward·ness
back′wash′
back′wa′ter
back′woods′
ba′con
bac·te′ri·a
bac·te′ri·al
bac·te′ri·cid′al

bac·te′ri·cide
bac·te′ri·o·log′i·cal
bac·te′ri·ol′o·gy
bac·te′ri·um
bad
badge
badg′er
bad′i·nage′
bad′lands′
bad′ly
bad′min·ton
bad′ness
baf′fle
baf′fled
bag
ba·gasse′
bag′a·telle′
bag′gage
bagged
bag′pipe′
bail
bailed

bail′ee'
bail'iff
bail'i·wick
bail'ment
bait
baize
bake
Ba'ke·lite
bak'er
bak'er·y
bal'ance
bal'anced
bal·bo'a
bal·brig'gan
bal'co·ny
bald
bal'da·chin
bal'der·dash
bald'ness
bal'dric
bale
baled
bale'ful
balk
ball
bal'lad
bal'last
balled
bal′le·ri'na
bal'let
bal·let'o·mane
bal·lis'tics
bal·loon'
bal·loon'ist
bal'lot
ball'play′er
ball'room′
balm
bal'sa
bal'sam
bal′sam·if'er·ous
bal'us·ter
bal′us·trade'
bam·boo'
bam·boo'zle
bam·boo'zled
ban
ba'nal
ba·nal'i·ty
ba·nan'a
band
band'age
ban·dan'na
band'box′
ban·deau'
band'ed
ban'de·role
ban'di·coot
ban'dit
band'mas′ter
ban′do·leer'
band'stand′
ban'dy
bane'ful
bang
bang'board′
banged
bang'le
ban'ish
ban'ish·ment
ban'is·ter
ban'jo
bank
bank'book′
banked
bank'er
bank'rupt
bank'rupt cy
banned
ban'ner
banns
ban'quet
ban'quet·ed
ban'shee
ban'tam
ban'ter
ban'tered
ban'ter·ing·ly
ban'yan
ban'zai'
bap'tism
bap·tis'mal
Bap'tist
bap·tize'
bap·tized'
bap·tize'ment

bar
barb
bar·bar′i·an
bar·bar′ic
bar′ba·rism
bar·bar′i·ty
bar′ba·rous
bar′be·cue
barbed
bar′ber
bar′ber′ry
bar·bette′
bar′bi·tu′rate
bard
bare
bare′back′
bared
bare′faced′
bare′foot′
bare′head′ed
bare′ly
bare′ness
bar′gain
bar′gained
barge
barge′man
bar′i·tone
bar′i·um
bark
bar′ley
bar′maid′
barn
bar′na·cle
barn′yard′
bar′o·gram
bar′o·graph
ba·rom′e·ter
bar′o·met′ric
bar′on
bar′on·age
bar′on·ess
bar′on·et
bar′on·et·cy
ba·ro′ni·al
bar′o·ny
ba·roque′
bar′rack
bar′ra·cu′da
bar·rage′
bar′ra·try
bar′rel
bar′ren
bar′ren·ness
bar′ri·cade′
bar′ri·cad′ed
bar′ri·er
bar′ris·ter
bar′row
bar′ter
bar′tered
bas′al
ba·salt′
bas′cule
base
base′board′
based
base′less
base′ly
base′ment
base′ness
bas′er
bas′est
bash′ful
bas′ic
bas′i·cal·ly
ba·sil′i·ca
bas′i·lisk
ba′sin
ba′sis
bask
bas′ket
bas′ket·ball′
bas′ket·work′
bas′-re·lief′
bass
bas′si·net′
bas′so
bas·soon′
bass′wood′
bast′ed
bas′ti·na′do
bas′tion
bat
batch
bath
bathe

bathed
bath'er
bath'house′
ba'thos
bath'robe′
bath'room′
ba·tiste'
ba′ton'
bat·tal'ion
bat'ten
bat'tened
bat'ter
bat'tered
bat'ter·y
bat'tle
bat'tled
bat'tle·ment
bat'tle·ship′
bawl
bawled
bay'ber′ry
bay'o·net
bay'o·net′ed
bay'ou
ba·zaar'
be
beach
beached
beach'comb′er
bea'con
bead
bead'ed

bea'dle
bead'work′
bea'gle
beak
beak'er
beam
beamed
bean
bear
bear'a·ble
beard
beard'ed
bear'er
bear'ish
bear'skin′
beast
beast'li·ness
beast'ly
beat
beat'en
beat'er
be′a·tif'ic
be·at′i·fi·ca'tion
be·at'i·fy
beat'ings
beat'nik
beau'te·ous
beau'ti·ful
beau'ti·ful·ly
beau'ti·fy
beau'ty
bea'ver

be·calm'
be·calmed'
be·came'
be·cause'
beck'on
beck'oned
be·cloud'
be·come'
be·com'ing·ly
be·com'ing·ness
bed
be·daub'
bed'bug′
bed'cham′ber
bed'clothes′
bed'ded
be·deck'
be·dev'il
be·dev'iled
bed'fel′low
be·diz'en
bed'lam
bed'post′
bed'rid′den
bed'rock′
bed'roll′
bed'room′
bed'side′
bed'spread′
bed'spring′
bed'stead
bed'time′

bee
beech
beef
beef'steak'
bee'line'
beer
bees'wax'
bee'tle
be·fall'
be·fell'
be·fit'
be·fog'
be·fore'
be·fore'hand'
be·friend'
be·fud'dle
be·fud'dled
beg
be·get'
beg'gar
begged
be·gin'
be·gone'
be·go'ni·a
be·got'
be·grime'
be·guile'
be·guiled'
be'gum
be·gun'
be·half'
be·have'

be·hav'ior
be·hav'ior·al
be·hav'ior·ism
be·head'
be·head'ings
be·held'
be·he'moth
be·hest'
be·hind'
be·hold'
be·hold'en
be·hold'er
be·hoove'
beige
be·jew'el
be·jew'eled
be·la'bor
be·lat'ed
be·lat'ed·ly
belch
be·lea'guer
be·lea'guered
bel'fry
Bel'gi·an
be·lie'
be·lief'
be·liev'a·ble
be·lieve'
be·lit'tle
be·lit'tled
bell
bel'la·don'na

bell'bird'
bell'boy'
bel'li·cose
bel'li·cos'i·ty
bel·lig'er·ence
bel·lig'er·en·cy
bel·lig'er·ent
bel·lig'er·ent·ly
bel'lowed
bel'lows
be·long'
be·longed'
be·long'ings
be·lov'ed
be·low'
belt
belt'ed
bel've·dere'
be·moan'
be·moaned'
be·mused'
bench
bend
bend'ed
be·neath'
ben'e·dic'tion
ben'e·fac'tion
ben'e·fac'tor
ben'e·fac'tress
be·nef'i·cent
ben'e·fi'cial
ben'e·fi'ci·ar'y

ben'e·fit
ben'e·fit'ed
be·nev'o·lence
be·nev'o·lent
be·night'ed
be·nign'
be·nig'nan·cy
be·nig'nant
be·nig'ni·ty
bent
ben'zene
be·queath'
be·quest'
be·rate'
be·rat'ed
be·reave'
be·reaved'
be·reave'ment
ber'ry
berth
ber'yl
be·seech'
be·seeched'
be·seech'ing·ly
be·set'
be·side'
be·sides'
be·siege'
be·sieged'
be·smirch'
be·sot'ted
be·span'gle
be·speak'
Bes'se·mer
best
bes'tial
bes'ti·al'i·ty
be·stow'
be·stowed'
be·stride'
bet
be·take'
be·tide'
be·times'
be·to'ken
be·tray'
be·tray'al
be·tray'er
be·troth'
be·troth'al
bet'ter
bet'tered
bet'ter·ment
be·tween'
be·twixt'
bev'el
bev'eled
bev'er·age
bev'y
be·wail'
be·wailed'
be·ware'
be·wil'der
be·wil'dered
be·wil'der·ing·ly
be·wil'der·ment
be·witch'
be·witch'ing·ly
be·yond'
bez'el
bi·an'nu·al
bi·an'nu·al·ly
bi'as
bi'ased
bi'be·lot'
Bi'ble
Bib'li·cal
bib'li·o·graph'i·cal
bib'li·og'ra·phy
bib'u·lous
bi·cam'er·al
bi·car'bon·ate
bi·cen'te·nar'y
bi'ceps
bi·chlo'ride
bi·chro'mate
bi·cus'pid
bi'cy·cle
bid
bid'der
bide
bi·en'ni·al
bi·en'ni·um
bier
bi·fo'cal
big

big′a·mist
big′a·mous
big′a·my
big′ger
big′gest
big′horn′
bight
big′ot
big′ot·ed
big′ot·ry
bi′jou
bi·lat′er·al
bile
bilge
bil′i·ar′y
bi·lin′gual
bil′ious
bilk
bill
bill′board′
billed
bil′let
bil′let·ed
bill′fish′
bill′fold′
bill′head′
bil′liards
bil′lings
bil′lion
bil′lion·aire′
bil′low
bill′post′er
bill′stick′er
bi′me·tal′lic
bi·met′al·lism
bi·met′al·list
bi·month′ly
bin
bi′na·ry
bin·au′ral
bind
bind′er
bind′er·y
bind′ing·ly
bind′ings
bind′weed′
bin′go
bin′na·cle
bin·oc′u·lar
bi·no′mi·al
bi·og′ra·pher
bi′o·graph′ic
bi′o·graph′i·cal
bi′o·graph′i·cal·ly
bi·og′ra·phy
bi′o·log′i·cal
bi′o·log′i·cal·ly
bi·ol′o·gist
bi·ol′o·gy
bi′op·sy
bi·par′tite
bi′ped
bi′plane′
bi·po′lar
birch
bird
bird′lime′
bird′man′
birth
birth′day′
birth′mark′
birth′place′
birth′right′
bis′cuit
bi′sect
bish′op
bish′op·ric
bis′muth
bi′son
bisque
bit
bite
bit′er
bit′ing·ly
bit′ten
bit′ter
bit′ter·est
bit′ter·ly
bit′tern
bit′ter·ness
bit′ters
bit′ter·weed′
bi·tu′men
bi·tu′mi·nous
biv′ouac
bi·zarre′

black
black'ball'
black'ber'ry
black'bird'
black'board'
black'en
black'er
black'est
black'fish'
black'guard
black'head'
black'ish
black'jack'
black'leg'
black'mail'
black'mail'er
black'ness
black'smith'
black'strap'
black'thorn'
blad'der
blade
blame
blamed
blame'less
blame'less·ly
blame'less·ness
blame'wor'thy
blanch
blanc·mange'
bland
blan'dish
blan'dish·ing·ly
blan'dish·ment
bland'ly
bland·ness
blank
blanked
blank'er
blank'est
blan'ket
blank'ly
blare
blared
blar'ney
blas·pheme'
blas·phemed'
blas·phem'er
blas'phe·mous
blas'phe·my
blast
blast'ed
blast-off
blaze
blazed
blaz'er
bla'zon
bla'zoned
bleach
bleached
bleach'er
bleak
bleat
bleed
bleed'er
blem'ish
blench
blend
blend'ed
blend'ings
bless
bless'ed·ness
bless'ings
blew
blight
blight'ed
blimp
blind
blind'ed
blind'er
blind'fold'
blind'ly
blind'ness
blink
blinked
blink'er
bliss
bliss'ful
bliss'ful·ly
blis'ter
blis'tered
blis'ter·ing·ly
blis'ter·y
blithe
blithe'ly
blithe'some

bliz'zard
bloat
bloat'ed
block
block·ade'
block·ad'ed
block·ad'er
block'head'
block'house'
blond
blood
blood'ed
blood'hound'
blood'i·est
blood'less
blood'let'ting
blood'line'
blood'root'
blood'shed'
blood'shot'
blood'stain'
blood'wood'
blood'y
bloom
bloomed
bloom'er
blos'som
blos'somed
blot
blotch
blot'ter
blouse
blow
blow'er
blow'fish'
blow'fly'
blow'gun'
blow'hard'
blow'hole'
blown
blow'off'
blow'out'
blow'pipe'
blow'torch'
blow'y
blub'ber
bludg'eon
bludg'eoned
blue
blue'fish'
blue'grass'
blue'nose'
blue'stock'ing
bluff
bluffed
bluff'er
blun'der
blun'dered
blun'der·buss
blun'der·er
blun'der·ing·ly
blunt
blunt'ed
blunt'ly
blunt'ness
blur
blurb
blurred
blurt
blush
blushed
blush'ing·ly
blus'ter
blus'tered
blus'ter·ing·ly
blus'ter·y
bo'a
board
board'ed
board'er
boast
boast'ed
boast'er
boast'ful
boast'ful·ly
boat
boat'load'
boat'man'
boat'swain'
bob'bin
bob'cat'
bob'o·link
bob'tail'
bode
bod'ice
bod'i·ly

bod′kin
bod′y
bod′y·guard′
bod′y·mak′er
bog
bo′gey
bog′gle
bog′gled
bo′gus
bog′wood′
Bo·he′mi·an
boil
boiled
boil′er
bois′ter·ous
bois′ter·ous·ly
bo′la
bold
bold′er
bold′est
bold′face′
bold′ly
bold′ness
bo·le′ro
bole′weed′
bo·liv′i·a
bo·li′via′no
boll
bo′lo
bo·lom′e·ter
bol′she·vik
bol′ster

bol′stered
bolt
bolt′ed
bolt′head′
bo′lus
bomb
bom·bard′
bom·bard′ed
bom′bard·ier′
bom·bard′ment
bom′bast
bom·bas′tic
bombed
bomb′er
bomb′proof′
bomb′shell′
bo·nan′za
bon′bon′
bond
bond′age
bond′ed
bond′hold′er
bond′man
bond′slave′
bonds′man
bone
boned
bone′fish′
bone′less
bone′set′
bon′fire′
bon′go

bo·ni′to
bon′net
bon′net·ed
bo′nus
bon′y
boo′by
boo′dle
book
book′bind′er
booked
book′ings
book′ish
book′keep′er
book′keep′ing
book′let
book′lets
book′mak′er
book′man
book′mark′
book′plate′
book′rack′
book′rest′
book′sell′er
book′shelf
book′stall′
book′stand′
book′worm′
boom
boomed
boom′er·ang
boon
boor

boor′ish
boost
boost′ed
boost′er
boot
boot′black′
boot′ed
boot′ee′
boot′er·y
booth
boot′jack′
boot′leg′
boot′leg′ger
boot′less
boot′strap′
boo′ty
booze
bo·rac′ic
bo′rate
bo′rax
Bor′deaux′
bor′der
bor′de·reau′
bor′dered
bore
bored
bo′re·al
bo′re·a′lis
bore′dom
bor′er
bore′some
bo′ric

bo′rine
bor′ings
born
bo′ron
bor′ough
bor′row
bor′rowed
bor′row·er
bor′row·ings
borsch
bosk′y
Bos′ni·an
bos′om
boss
bossed
boss′ism
boss′y
bo·tan′ic
bo·tan′i·cal
bot′a·nist
bot′a·nize
bot′a·nized
bot′a·ny
botch
botched
bot′fly′
both
both′er
both′ered
both′er·some
Both′ni·an
bot′tle

bot′tle·bird′
bot′tled
bot′tle·head′
bot′tle·hold′er
bot′tle·neck′
bot′tle·nose′
bot′tom
bot′tom·less
bot′tom·ry
bot′u·lism
bou′doir
bough
boughed
bought
bouil′la·baisse′
bouil′lon′
boul′der
bou′le·vard
bounce
bounced
bounc′er
bound
bound′a·ry
bound′ed
bound′en
bound′er
bound′less
boun′te·ous
boun′te·ous·ly
boun′ti·ful
boun′ty
bou·quet′

bour·geois′
bour′geoi′sie′
bourse
bout
bo′va·rysm
bo′vine
bow
bow
bowd′ler·ize
bowed
bowed
bow′el
bow′er
bow′er·bird′
bow′fin′
bow′ie
bow′knot′
bowl
bowled
bow′leg′ged
bowl′er
bow′man
bow′shot′
bow′sprit
bow′string′
box
box′board′
box′car′
boxed
box′er
box′wood′
boy

boy′cott
boy′hood
boy′ish
boy′ish·ness
brace
braced
brace′let
brack′en
brack′et
brack′et·ed
brack′ish
brad′awl′
brag
bragged
brag′ga·do′ci·o
brag′gart
Brah′man
braid
braid′ed
Braille
brain
brained
brain′fag′
brain′less
brain′sick′
brain′work′
brain′y
braise
braised
brake
brake′age
braked

brake′man
bram′ble
bran
branch
branched
branch′ling
brand
brand′ed
bran′died
bran′dish
bran′dished
brand′-new′
bran′dy
brash
brass
bras′sard
brass′bound′
brass′ie
brass′i·ness
brass′y
brat
brat′ling
bra·va′do
brave
brave′ly
brav′er
brav′er·y
brav′est
bra′vo
bra·vu′ra
brawl
brawled

brawl'er
brawn
brawn'y
bray
brayed
braze
brazed
bra'zen
bra'zened
bra'zier
bra·zil'ite
bra·zil'wood'
breach
breached
bread
bread'bas'ket
bread'board'
bread'ed
bread'fruit'
bread'root'
bread'stuff'
breadth
bread'win·ner'
break
break'a·ble
break'age
break'down'
break'er
break'fast
break'neck'
break'off'
break'out'

break'o·ver'
break'-through'
break'up'
break'wa'ter
breast
breast'band'
breast'bone'
breast'ed
breast'-fed'
breast'mark'
breast'pin'
breast'plate'
breast'weed'
breast'work'
breath
breathed
breath'less
bred
breech
breed
breed'er
breeze
breezed
breez'y
breth'ren
breve
bre·vet'
bre'vi·ar'y
bre·vier'
brev'i·ty
brew
brewed

brew'er
brew'er·y
brew'house'
bribe
bribed
brib'er·y
bric'-a-brac'
brick
brick'bat'
bricked
brick'lay'er
brick'ma'son
brick'yard'
brid'al
bride
bride'groom'
brides'maid'
bridge
bridged
bridge'head'
bridge'work'
bri'dle
bri'dled
brief
brief'er
brief'est
brief'ly
brief'ness
bri'er
brig
bri·gade'
brig'a·dier'

brig'and
brig'and·age
brig'an·tine
bright
bright'en
bright'er
bright'est
bright'ly
bright'ness
bright'work'
bril'liance
bril'lian·cy
bril'liant
bril'lian·tine'
bril'liant·ly
bril'liant·ness
brim
brim'ful'
brimmed
brim'stone'
brin'dled
brine
bring
brink
brin'y
bri·oche'
bri·quette'
brisk
brisk'en
bris'ket
brisk'ly
brisk'ness

bris'tle
bris'tled
bris'tli·er
bris'tli·est
bris'tly
Bri·tan'ni·a
Bri·tan'nic
Brit'i·cism
Brit'ish
Brit'ish·er
Brit'on
brit'tle
brit'tle·ness
broach
broached
broad
broad'ax'
broad'bill'
broad'brim'
broad'cast'
broad'cast'er
broad'en
broad'er
broad'est
broad'leaf'
broad'loom'
broad'ly
broad'side'
broad'way'
broad'wise'
bro·cade'
bro·cad'ed

broc'a·tel'
broc'co·li
bro·chette'
bro·chure'
bro'gan
brogue
broil
broiled
broil'er
broke
bro'ken
brok'en·ly
bro'ker
bro'ker·age
bro'mate
bro'mide
bro·mid'ic
bro'mine
bron'chi·al
bron·chi'tis
bron'cho·scope
bron'chus
bron'co
bronze
bronzed
brooch
brood
brood'ed
brood'er
brood'ling
brook
brook'let

broom
broom'weed'
broom'wood'
broth
broth'er
broth'er·hood
broth'er-in-law'
broth'er·li·ness
broth'er·ly
brougham
brought
brow
brown
brown'er
brown'est
brown'out
browse
browsed
bru'in
bruise
bruised
bruit
brum'ma·gem
brunch
bru·net'
bru·nette'
brunt
brush
brushed
brush'ful
brush'less
brush'wood'
brush'work'
brusque
bru'tal
bru·tal'i·ty
bru'tal·i·za'tion
bru'tal·ize
bru'tal·ized
bru'tal·ly
brute
brut'ish
brut'ish·ly
brut'ish·ness
bub'ble
bub'bled
bub'bly
bu·bon'ic
buc'cal
buc'ca·neer'
buck
buck'board'
bucked
buck'et
buck'et·ed
buck'et·ful
buck'le
buck'led
buck'ler
buck'ram
buck'saw'
buck'shot'
buck'skin'
buck'wheat'
bu·col'ic
bud
bud'ded
bud'dy
budge
budged
budg'et
budg'et·ar'y
budg'et·ed
bud'wood'
bud'worm'
buff
buf'fa·lo
buff'er
buff'ered
buf'fet
buf·fet'
buf'fet·ed
buf·foon'
buf·foon'er·y
bug
bug'bear'
bug'ging
bug'gy
bu'gle
bu'gler
bu'gle·weed'
bug'proof'
bug'weed'
build
build'ed
build'er

build′ing
build′ings
built
bulb
bulb′ous
bulge
bulged
bulk
bulk′head′
bulk′i·er
bulk′i·est
bulk′y
bull
bull′doze′
bull′dozed′
bull′doz′er
bul′let
bul′le·tin
bull′fight′
bull′finch′
bull′frog′
bull′head′
bul′lion
bull′ish
bull′ock
bull′weed
bul′ly
bul′ly·rag′
bul′rush′
bul′wark
bum
bum′boat′

bump
bump′er
bump′i·er
bump′i·est
bump′kin
bump′y
bu′na
bunch
bunched
bun′dle
bun′dled
bung
bun′ga·low
bun′gle
bun′gled
bun′gler
bun′ion
bunk′er
bunk′house′
bunt
buoy
buoy′ant
buoy′ant·ly
bur′den
bur′dened
bur′den·some
bu′reau
bu·reauc′ra·cy
bu′reau·crat
bu·rette′
bur′gee
bur′geon

bur′geoned
bur′gess
bur′glar
bur′i·al
bu′rin
bur′lap
bur·lesque′
bur·lesqued′
bur′ly
burn
burned
burn′er
bur′nish
bur′nish·er
burn′out′
burnt
burr
bur′ro
bur′row
bur′rowed
bur′sar
bur·si′tis
burst
bur′y
bus
bus′es
bush
bushed
bush′el
bush′el·er
bush′ings
bus′i·ly

busi′ness
busi′ness·es
busi′ness·like′
bus′kin
bust
bus′tard
bus′tle
bus′tled
bus′y
bus′y·bod′y
but
butch′er
butch′ered
butch′er·y
but′ler
butt
but′ter

but′ter·ball′
but′ter·cup′
but′tered
but′ter·fat′
but′ter·fish′
but′ter·fly′
but′ter·nut′
but′ter·scotch′
but′ter·y
but′ton
but′toned
but′ton·hole′
but′ton·holed′
but′ton·weed′
but′ton·wood′
but′tress
but′tressed

bux′om
buy
buy′er
buzz
buz′zard
buzzed
buzz′er
by
by′gone′
by′pass′
by′path′
by′play′
by′-prod′uct
By·ron′ic
by′stand′er
by′way′
by′word′

cab
ca·bal'
cab'bage
cab'in
cab'i·net
ca'ble
ca'bled
ca'ble·gram
ca·boose'
cab'ri·o·let'
ca·ca'o
cach'a·lot
cache
ca·chet'
cach'in·na'tion
cack'le
cack'led
ca·coph'o·nous
ca·coph'o·ny
cac'ti
cac'toid
cac'tus
cac'tus·es
ca·dav'er
ca·dav'er·ous
cad'die
ca'dence
ca·den'za
ca·det'
cad'mi·um
Cad'mus
ca'dre
ca·du'ce·us
cad'weed
Cae·sar'e·an
cae·su'ra
ca'fé'
caf'e·te'ri·a
caf'fe·ine
cage
caged
cairn
cais'son
cais'soned
cai'tiff
ca·jole'
ca·joled'
ca·jol'er·y
cake
cake'walk'
cal'a·bash
cal'a·mine
ca·lam'i·tous
ca·lam'i·tous·ly
ca·lam'i·ty
cal·car'e·ous
cal'ci·fi·ca'tion
cal'ci·fy
cal'ci·mine
cal'cine
cal·cined'
cal'ci·um
cal'cu·late
cal'cu·lat'ed
cal'cu·la'tion
cal'cu·la'tor

cal′dron
cal′en·dar
cal′en·der
cal′en·dered
calf
calf′skin′
cal′i·ber
cal′i·brate
cal′i·brat′ed
cal′i·bra′tion
cal′i·co
cal′i·per
ca′liph
cal′is·then′ics
calk
calked
calk′er
call
cal′la
call′a·ble
called
cal′ler
cal·lig′ra·phy
cal·li′o·pe
cal·los′i·ty
cal′lous
cal′loused
cal′lous·ly
cal′low
cal′low·ly
cal′lus
calm
calmed
calm′er
calm′est
calm′ly
calm′ness
cal′o·mel
ca·lor′ic
cal′o·rie
cal′u·met
ca·lum′ni·ate
ca·lum′ni·at′ed
ca·lum′ni·a′tion
ca·lum′ni·a′tor
cal′um·ny
Cal′va·ry
calved
ca·lyp′so
ca′lyx
ca′ma·ra′de·rie
cam′ber
cam′bi·um
cam′bric
came
cam′el
cam′el·eer′
Cam′e·lot
Cam′em·bert′
cam′e·o
cam′er·a
cam′er·a·man′
cam′i·sole
cam′o·mile
cam′ou·flage
camp
cam·paign′
cam′pa·ni′le
camp′er
camp′fire′
cam′phor
cam′phor·ate
cam′phor·at′ed
cam′pus
can
ca·nal′
ca·nal′i·za′tion
ca·nar′y
can′can
can′cel
can′celed
can′cel·la′tion
can′cer
can′cer·ous
can′cer·weed′
can′de·la′brum
can′did
can′di·da·cy
can′di·date
can′did·ly
can′died
can′dle
can′dled
can′dle·fish′
can′dle·light′
can′dle·nut′

can'dle·stick'
can'dor
can'dy
can'dy·mak'er
cane
cane'brake'
ca'nine
can'is·ter
can'ker
can'kered
can'ker·ous
can'ker·weed'
can'ker·worm'
canned
can'ner
can'ner·y
can'ni·bal
can'ni·bal·ism
can'ni·ly
can'non
can'non·ade'
can'non·eer'
can'ny
ca·noe'
can'on
ca·non'i·cal
ca·non'i·cals
can'on·i·za'tion
can'on·ize
can'o·py
cant
can't

can'ta·loupe
can·tan'ker·ous
can·ta'ta
can·teen'
cant'er
can'tered
can'ti·cle
can'ti·cles
can'ti·le'ver
can'tle
can'to
can'ton
can·ton'ment
can'tor
can'vas
can'vased
can'vass
can'vassed
can'vass·er
can'yon
caou'tchouc
ca'pa·bil'i·ties
ca'pa·bil'i·ty
ca'pa·ble
ca'pa·bly
ca·pa'cious
ca·pac'i·tance
ca·pac'i·tate
ca·pac'i·tat'ed
ca·pac'i·tor
ca·pac'i·ty
cape

ca'per
ca'pered
ca'per·ings
cap'il·lar'i·ty
cap'il·lar'y
cap'i·tal
cap'i·tal·ism
cap'i·tal·ist
cap'i·tal·is'tic
cap'i·tal·ists
cap'i·tal·i·za'tion
cap'i·tal·ize
cap'i·tal·ized
cap'i·tol
ca·pit'u·late
ca·pit'u·lat'ed
ca·pit'u·lates
ca·pit'u·la'tion
ca'pon
capped
ca·price'
ca·pri'cious
cap·size'
cap·sized'
cap'stan
cap'sule
cap'tain
cap'tain·cy
cap'tion
cap'tious
cap'tious·ly
cap'tious·ness

cap'ti·vate
cap'ti·vat'ed
cap'ti·va'tion
cap'tive
cap·tiv'i·ty
cap'ture
cap'tured
car
ca'ra·ba'o
car'a·bi·neer'
car'a·cal
car'a·cole
ca·rafe'
car'a·mel
car'a·mel·ize
car'a·pace
car'at
car'a·van
car'a·van'sa·ry
car'a·vel
car'a·way
car'bide
car'bine
car'bo·hy'drate
car·bol'ic
car'bon
car'bon·ate
car'bon·at'ed
car·bon'ic
car'bon·if'er·ous
car'bon·ize
car'bon·ized
car'bo·run'dum
car'boy
car'bun·cle
car'bu·ret'or
car'cass
car'ci·no'ma
card
card'board'
card'ed
car'di·ac
car'di·gan
car'di·nal
car'di·nal·ate
car'di·o·gram'
car'di·o·graph'
car'di·ol'o·gy
care
cared
ca·reen'
ca·reened'
ca·reer'
care'free'
care'ful
care'ful·ly
care'less
care'less·ly
care'less·ness
ca·ress'
ca·ressed'
ca·ress'ing·ly
car'et
car'fare'
car'go
car'i·bou
car'i·ca·ture
car'i·es
car'il·lon
car'load·ings'
car·min'a·tive
car'mine
car'nage
car'nal
car'nal·ly
car·na'tion
car·nel'ian
car'ni·val
car·niv'o·rous
car'ol
car'oled
car'om
car'omed
ca·rot'id
ca·rous'al
ca·rouse'
ca·roused'
carp
car'pal
car'pen·ter
car'pet
car'pet·ed
car'riage
car'ried
car'ri·er
car'ri·on

car'rot
car'rou·sel'
car'ry
cart
cart'age
cart'ed
car'tel
car'ti·lage
car'ti·lag'i·nous
car·tog'ra·phy
car'ton
car·toon'
car·touche'
car'tridge
carve
carved
carv'er
carv'ings
car'y·at'id
ca·sa'ba
cas·cade'
cas·cad'ed
cas·car'a
case
ca'se·in
case'ment
case'work'
cash
cash'book'
cash'box'
cashed
ca·shew'

cash·ier'
cash·iered'
cash'mere
ca·si'no
cask
cas'ket
cas·sa'tion
cas·sa'va
cas'se·role
cas·sette'
cas·si'no
cas'sock
cast
cas'ta·net'
caste
cast'er
cas'ti·gate
cas'ti·gat'ed
cas'ti·ga'tion
cas'tle
cast'off'
cas'tor
cas'tra·me·ta'tion
cas'u·al
cas'u·al·ly
cas'u·al·ty
cas'u·ist
cas'u·ist·ry
ca·tab'o·lism
cat'a·clysm
cat'a·comb
cat'a·falque

cat'a·lep'sy
cat'a·lep'tic
cat'a·log
cat'a·loged
ca·tal'pa
ca·tal'y·sis
cat'a·lyst
cat'a·lyt'ic
cat'a·lyze
cat'a·mount
cat'a·pult
cat'a·ract
ca·tarrh'
ca·tarrh'al
ca·tas'tro·phe
cat'a·stroph'ic
cat'a·stroph'i·cal·ly
cat'a·ton'ic
Ca·taw'ba
cat'bird'
cat'boat'
cat'call'
catch
catch'er
catch'weed'
catch'word'
catch'y
cat'e·che'sis
cat'e·chet'i·cal
cat'e·chism
cat'e·chize
cat'e·gor'i·cal

cat′e·go·rize
cat′e·go′ry
cat′e·nar′y
ca′ter
ca′tered
ca′ter·er
cat′er·pil′lar
cat′fish′
cat′gut′
ca·thar′sis
ca·thar′tic
cat′head′
ca·the′dral
cath′e·ter
cath′e·ter·ize
cath′ode
cath′o·lic
ca·thol′i·cism
cath′o·lic′i·ty
ca·thol′i·cize
cat′kin
cat′like′
cat′nip
cat′tail′
cat′tle
cat′walk′
cau′cus
cau′cused
cau′dal
caught
cau′li·flow′er
caus′al
cau·sal′i·ty
cau·sa′tion
caus′a·tive
cause
caused
cause′less
cau′se·rie′
cause′way′
caus′tic
cau′ter·i·za′tion
cau′ter·ize
cau′ter·ized
cau′ter·y
cau′tion
cau′tion·ar′y
cau′tioned
cau′tious
cav′al·cade′
cav′a·lier′
cav′al·ry
ca′va·ti′na
cave
ca′ve·at
cav′ern
cav′ern·ous
cav′i·ar
cav′il
cav′i·ty
ca·vort′
cay·enne′
cease
ceased
cease′less
cease′less·ly
ce′cum
ce′dar
ce′dar·bird′
cede
ced′ed
ce·dil′la
ced′ing
ceil′ings
cel′e·brant
cel′e·brate
cel′e·brat′ed
cel′e·bra′tion
ce·leb′ri·ty
ce·ler′i·ty
cel′er·y
ce·les′ta
ce·les′tial
ce·les′tial·ly
cel′i·ba·cy
cel′i·bate
cell
cel′lar
cel′lar·er
cel′lar·et′
cel′list
cel′lo
cel′lo·phane
cel′lu·lar
cel′lu·li′tis
cel′lu·loid

cel′lu·lose
Celt′ic
ce·ment′
ce′men·ta′tion
cem′e·ter′y
cen′a·cle
cen′o·bite
cen′o·taph
cen′ser
cen′sor
cen′sored
cen·so′ri·al
cen·so′ri·ous
cen′sor·ship
cen′sur·a·ble
cen′sure
cen′sured
cen′sus
cent
cen′taur
cen′te·nar′i·an
cen′te·nar′y
cen·ten′ni·al
cen′ter
cen′ter·board′
cen′tered
cen′ter·piece′
cen′ti·grade
cen′ti·me′ter
cen′ti·pede
cen′tral
cen′tral·i·za′tion
cen′tral·ize
cen′tral·ized
cen·trif′u·gal
cen′tri·fuge
cen·trip′e·tal
cen′trist
cen·tu′ri·on
cen′tu·ry
ce·phal′ic
ce·ram′ic
ce′re·al
cer′e·bel′lum
cer′e·bral
cer′e·bra′tion
cer′e·brum
cere′ment
cer′e·mo′ni·al
cer′e·mo′ni·al·ly
cer′e·mo′ni·ous
cer′e·mo′ni·ous·ly
cer′e·mo′ni·ous·ness
cer′e·mo′ny
ce·rise′
ce′ri·um
cer′tain
cer′tain·ly
cer′tain·ty
cer·tif′i·cate
cer·tif′i·cat′ed
cer′ti·fi·ca′tion
cer′ti·fied
cer′ti·fy
cer′ti·o·ra′ri
cer′ti·tude
cer′vi·cal
cer′vix
ce′si·um
ces·sa′tion
ces′sion
cess′pool′
ces′tus
ce·ta′cean
chafe
chaf′fer
chaf′fered
chaf′finch
chaff′weed′
cha·grin′
cha·grined′
chain
chained
chain′work′
chair
chair′man
chaise
chal·ced′o·ny
cha·let′
chal′ice
chalk
chalk′i·ness
chal′lenge
chal′lenged
cham′ber
cham′bered

cham'ber·lain
cham'ber·maid'
cha·me'le·on
cham'ois
cham·pagne'
cham'per·ty
cham'pi·on
cham'pi·on·ship'
chance
chanced
chan'cel
chan'cel·ler·y
chan'cel·lor
chan'cer·y
chan'de·lier'
chan'dler
chan'dler·y
change
change'a·ble
changed
change'less
change'ling
chan'nel
chan'neled
chant
chant'ed
cha'os
cha·ot'ic
cha·ot'i·cal·ly
chap'ar·ral'
chap'el
chap'er·on
chap'lain
chap'let
chap'ter
char
char'ac·ter
char'ac·ter·is'tic
char'ac·ter·is'ti·cal·ly
char'ac·ter·i·za'tion
char'ac·ter·ize
char'ac·ter·ized
cha·rade'
char'coal'
cha·ris'ma
charge
charge'a·ble
charged
charg'er
char'i·ly
char'i·ness
char'i·ot
char'i·ot·eer'
char'i·ta·ble
char'i·ta·bly
char'i·ty
char'la·tan
charm
charmed
charm'ing·ly
char'nel
charred
chart
chart'ed
char'ter
char'tered
char·treuse'
char'y
chase
chased
chasm
chas'sis
chaste
chas'ten
chas'tened
chas'ten·ing·ly
chas·tise'
chas·tised'
chas'tise·ment
chas'ti·ty
chas'u·ble
châ·teau'
chat'e·laine
chat'tel
chat'ter
chat'tered
chat'ter·er
chat'ty
chauf·feur'
chau'vin·ism
cheap
cheap'en
cheap'ened
cheap'er
cheap'est
cheap'ly

cheap'ness
cheat
cheat'ed
cheat'er
check
check'book'
checked
check'er
check'er·board'
check'ered
check'mate'
check'mat'ed
check'off'
check'rein'
cheek'y
cheer
cheered
cheer'ful
cheer'ful·ly
cheer'ful·ness
cheer'i·ly
cheer'less
cheer'less·ly
cheer'y
cheese
cheese'cake'
cheese'cloth'
chef
chem'i·cal
chem'i·cal·ly
che·mise'
chem'ist

chem'is·try
che·nille'
cher'ish
che·root'
cher'ry
cher'ub
che·ru'bic
cher'u·bim
cher'vil
chess
chess'board'
chess'man
chest
ches'ter·field'
chest'nut
chev'ron
chew
chic
chi·can'er·y
chick'a·dee
chick'en
chick'weed'
chic'le
chic'o·ry
chide
chief
chief'ly
chief'tain
chif'fon
chif'fo·nier'
chig'ger
chil'blain'

child
child'hood
child'ish
child'ish·ly
child'ish·ness
child'less
child'like'
chil'dren
chil'i
chill
chilled
chill'i·er
chill'i·est
chill'ing·ly
chill'y
chime
chimed
chi·me'ra
chi·mer'i·cal
chim'ney
chim'pan·zee'
chin
chi'na
chinch
chin·chil'la
chine
Chi'nese'
chink
chintz
chip
chip'munk
chipped

chip′per
chi·rog′ra·phy
chi·rop′o·dist
chi′ro·prac′tor
chirp
chis′el
chis′eled
chit′chat′
chit′ter·ling
chiv′al·ric
chiv′al·rous
chiv′al·ry
chive
chlo′ral
chlo′rate
chlo′ride
chlo′rin·ate
chlo′rine
chlo′rite
chlo′ro·form
chlo′ro·phyll
chlo·ro′sis
choc′o·late
choice
choir
choir′boy′
choke
chok′er
chol′er
chol′er·a
chol′er·ic
choose

chop
chop′house′
chopped
chop′per
cho·ral′
chord
cho·re′a
cho′re·og′ra·phy
chor′is·ter
chor′tle
cho′rus
chose
cho′sen
chow
chow′der
chrism
chris′ten
Chris′ten·dom
chris′tened
chris′ten·ings
Chris′tian
Chris′ti·an′i·ty
Christ′mas
chro′mate
chro·mat′ics
chrome
chro′mic
chro′mite
chro′mi·um
chro′mo·some
chron′ic
chron′i·cal·ly

chron′i·cle
chron′i·cled
chron′i·cler
chron′i·cles
chron′o·graph
chron′o·log′i·cal
chron′o·log′i·cal·ly
chro·nol′o·gy
chro·nom′e·ter
chron′o·met′ric
chrys′a·lis
chrys·an′the·mum
chrys′o·lite
chub′bi·ness
chub′by
chuck
chuck′le
chuck′led
chuck′le·head′
chuck′ling·ly
chum
chum′my
chump
chunk
chunk′i·ness
chunk′y
church
church′man
churl
churl′ish
churl′ish·ly
churl′ish·ness

churn
churned
chute
chut′ney
chyle
ci·ca′da
cic′a·trix
ci′der
ci·gar′
cig′a·rette′
cinch
cinc′ture
cinc′tured
cin′der
cin′e·ma
cin′e·mat′o·graph
cin′na·bar
cin′na·mon
cinque′foil′
ci′on
ci′pher
ci′phered
cir′cle
cir′cled
cir′cuit
cir·cu′i·tous
cir·cu′i·tous·ly
cir′cuit·ry
cir′cu·lar
cir′cu·lar·i·za′tion
cir′cu·lar·ize
cir′cu·late
cir′cu·lat′ed
cir′cu·la′tion
cir′cu·la·to′ry
cir′cum·am′bi·ent
cir·cum′fer·ence
cir·cum′fer·en′tial
cir′cum·flex
cir′cum·lo·cu′tion
cir′cum·loc′u·to′ry
cir′cum·nav′i·gate
cir′cum·scribe′
cir′cum·scribed′
cir′cum·spect
cir′cum·spec′tion
cir′cum·spect′ly
cir′cum·spect′ness
cir′cum·stance
cir′cum·stanc·es
cir′cum·stan′tial
cir′cum·stan′ti·al′i·ty
cir′cum·stan′ti·ate
cir′cum·stan′ti·at′ed
cir′cum·vent′
cir′cum·vent′ed
cir′cum·ven′tion
cir′cus
cir·rho′sis
cir·rhot′ic
cir′rus
cis′tern
cit′a·del
ci·ta′tion
cite
cit′ed
cit′i·zen
cit′i·zen·ry
cit′i·zen·ship′
cit′rate
cit′ric
cit′ron
cit′y
civ′ic
civ′il
ci·vil′ian
ci·vil′i·ty
civ′i·li·za′tion
civ′i·lize
civ′i·lized
civ′il·ly
clack
claim
claim′ant
claimed
clair·voy′ance
clair·voy′ant
cla′mant
clam′bake′
clam′ber
clam′bered
clam′my
clam′or
clam′ored
clam′or·ous
clamp

clam′shell′
clan
clan·des′tine
clang
clanged
clang′or
clank
clanked
clan′nish
clan′ship
clans′man
clap
clapped
clap′per
clap′trap′
claque
clar′et
clar′i·fi·ca′tion
clar′i·fied
clar′i·fy
clar′i·net′
clar′i·on
clar′i·ty
clash
clasp
class
clas′sic
clas′si·cal
clas′si·cal·ism
clas′si·cal·ist
clas′si·cal·ly
clas′si·cist
clas′si·fi·ca′tion
clas′si·fied
clas′si·fi′er
clas′si·fy
class′mate′
class′room′
class′work′
clat′ter
clat′tered
clause
claus′tro·pho′bi·a
clav′i·chord
clav′i·cle
claw
clay
clean
cleaned
clean′er
clean′est
clean′li·ness
clean′ly
clean′ness
cleanse
cleans′er
clean′up′
clear
clear′ance
cleared
clear′er
clear′est
clear′head′ed
clear′ing·house′
clear′ly
clear′ness
cleat
cleat′ed
cleav′age
cleave
cleav′er
clef
cleft
clem′a·tis
clem′en·cy
clem′ent
clench
clere′sto′ry
cler′gy
cler′gy·man
cler′i·cal
cler′i·cal·ism
clerk
clev′er
clev′er·er
clev′er·est
clev′er·ness
clew
cli·ché′
click
cli′ent
cli′en·tele′
cliff
cli·mac′ter·ic
cli·mac′tic
cli′mate

cli·mat′ic
cli′max
climb
climbed
climb′er
clinch
clinch′er
cling
cling′ing·ly
clin′ic
clin′i·cal
cli·ni′cian
clink
clinked
clink′er
clip
clip′per
clip′pings
clique
cloak
clock
clock′wise′
clock′work′
clod
clog
cloi′son′né′
clois′ter
clois′tered
clon′ic
close
closed
close′ly
close′ness
clos′er
clos′est
clos′et
clos′et·ed
clo′sure
clot
cloth
clothed
clothes
clothes′pin′
cloth′ier
clot′ted
cloud
cloud′i·er
cloud′i·est
cloud′i·ness
cloud′less
cloud′y
clout
clout′ed
clove
clo′ven
clo′ver
clown
clowned
clown′ish
cloy
cloyed
club
clubbed
club′house′
club′man
cluck
clump
clum′si·er
clum′si·est
clum′si·ly
clum′si·ness
clum′sy
clus′ter
clus′tered
clutch
clut′ter
clut′tered
coach
coach′man
co·ad′ju·tor
co·ag′u·late
co·ag′u·lat′ed
co·ag′u·lates
co·ag′u·la′tion
co·ag′u·la′tive
coal
co′a·lesce′
co′a·lesced′
co′a·les′cence
co′a·les′cent
co′a·li′tion
coal′sack′
coarse
coars′en
coars′ened
coars′er

coars'est
coast
coast'al
coast'er
coast'wise'
coat
coat'ed
coat'ings
co·au'thor
coax
coaxed
co·ax'i·al
coax'ing·ly
co'balt
cob'ble
cob'bled
Co'bol
cob'web'
co·caine'
coc'cyx
coch'i·neal'
cock·ade'
cock'a·too'
cock'le
cock'le·shell'
cock'ney
cock'pit'
cock'roach'
cock'sure'
cock'sure'ness
cock'tail'
co'coa

co'co·nut'
co·coon'
co'da
code
cod'ed
co'de·fend'ant
co'de·ine
co'dex
cod'fish'
cod'i·cil
cod'i·fi·ca'tion
cod'i·fy
co'ed'
co'ed'u·ca'tion
co'ef·fi'cient
co·erce'
co·erced'
co·er'cion
co·er'cive
co·e'val
co'ex·ec'u·tor
cof'fee
cof'fer
cof'fin
cog
co'gen·cy
co'gent
cog'i·tate
cog'i·tat'ed
cog'i·ta'tion
cog'i·ta'tive
co'gnac

cog'nate
cog·ni'tion
cog'ni·zance
cog'ni·zant
cog·no'men
co·hab'it
co·here'
co·hered'
co·her'ence
co·her'ent
co·her'ent·ly
co·her'er
co·he'sion
co·he'sive
co'hort
coif
coif·fure'
coign
coil
coiled
coin
coin'age
co'in·cide'
co'in·cid'ed
co·in'ci·dence
co·in'ci·den'tal
coined
coin'er
co'in·sur'ance
co'in·sure'
co'in·sur'er
coke

col′an·der
cold
cold′er
cold′est
cold′ly
cole′slaw′
col′ic
col′i·se′um
co·li′tis
col·lab′o·rate
col·lab′o·rat′ed
col·lab′o·ra′tion
col·lapse′
col·lapsed′
col·laps′i·ble
col′lar
col′lar·band′
col′lar·bone′
col·late′
col·lat′ed
col·lat′er·al
col·la′tion
col·la′tor
col·league′
col′lect
col·lect′ed
col·lect′i·ble
col·lec′tion
col·lec′tive
col·lec′tiv·ism
col·lec′tiv·ist
col·lec′tor
col·lec′tor·ship
col′lege
col·le′gi·ate
col·lide′
col·lid′ed
col′lie
col′lier
col·li′sion
col′lo·ca′tion
col·lo′di·on
col′loid
col·loi′dal
col·lo′qui·al
col′lo·quy
col′lo·type
col·lu′sion
col·lu′sive
co·logne′
co′lon
colo′nel
co·lo′ni·al
col′o·nist
col′o·ni·za′tion
col′o·nize
col′o·nized
col′on·nade′
col′o·ny
col′o·phon
col′or
col′or·a′tion
col′o·ra·tu′ra
col′ored
col′or·less
co·los′sal
Col′os·se′um
co·los′sus
col′por′teur
colt
col′um·bine
col′umn
co·lum′nar
co′ma
com′a·tose
comb
com′bat
com′bat·ant
com′ba·tive
com·bat′ive·ness
combed
com′bi·na′tion
com′bine
com·bined′
comb′ings
com·bust′
com·bus′ti·ble
com·bus′tion
come
co·me′di·an
com′e·dy
come′li·ness
come′ly
co·mes′ti·ble
com′et
com′fit

com'fort
com'fort·a·ble
com'fort·a·bly
com'fort·ed
com'fort·er
com'fort·less
com'ic
com'i·cal
com'ings
com'ma
com·mand'
com'man·dant'
com·mand'ed
com'man·deer'
com·mand'er
com·mand'er·y
com·mand'ing·ly
com·mand'ment
com·man'do
com·mem'o·rate
com·mem'o·rat'ed
com·mem'o·ra'tion
com·mem'o·ra'tive
com·mence'
com·menced'
com·mence'ment
com·mend'
com·mend'a·ble
com'men·da'tion
com·mend'a·to'ry
com·mend'ed
com·men'su·ra·ble
com·men'su·rate
com'ment
com'men·tar'y
com'men·ta'tor
com'ment·ed
com'merce
com·mer'cial
com·mer'cial·ism
com·mer'cial·i·za'tion
com·mer'cial·ize
com·min'a·to'ry
com·min'gle
com·min'gled
com'mi·nute
com'mi·nut'ed
com'mi·nu'tion
com·mis'er·ate
com·mis'er·a'tion
com'mis·sar'
com'mis·sar'i·at
com'mis·sar'y
com·mis'sion
com·mis'sioned
com·mis'sion·er
com·mit'
com·mit'ment
com·mit'ted
com·mit'tee
com·mo'di·ous
com·mod'i·ty
com'mo·dore'
com'mon
com'mon·al·ty
com'mon·er
com'mon·est
com'mon·ly
com'mon·place'
com'mon·wealth'
com·mo'tion
com'mu·nal
com·mune'
com·mu'ni·ca·ble
com·mu'ni·cant
com·mu'ni·cate
com·mu'ni·cat'ed
com·mu'ni·ca'tion
com·mu'ni·ca'tive
com·mun'ion
com·mu'ni·qué'
com'mu·nism
com'mu·nist
com·mu·nis'tic
com·mu'ni·ty
com'mu·ni·za'tion
com'mu·nize
com'mu·ta'tion
com'mu·ta'tor
com·mute'
com·mut'ed
com·mut'er
com·pact'
com·pan'ion
com·pan'ion·a·ble
com·pan'ion·ship

com·pan′ion·way′
com′pa·ny
com′pa·ra·bil′i·ty
com′pa·ra·ble
com·par′a·tive
com·pare′
com·pared′
com·par′i·son
com·part′ment
com′pass
com·pas′sion
com·pas′sion·ate
com·pas′sion·ate·ly
com·pat′i·bil′i·ty
com·pat′i·ble
com·pa′tri·ot
com·peer′
com·pel′
com·pelled′
com·pel′ling·ly
com′pend
com·pen′di·ous
com·pen′di·um
com′pen·sate
com′pen·sat′ed
com′pen·sa′tion
com′pen·sa′tor
com·pen′sa·to′ry
com·pete′
com·pet′ed
com′pe·tence
com′pe·ten·cy

com′pe·tent·ly
com′pe·ti′tion
com·pet′i·tive
com·pet′i·tor
com′pi·la′tion
com·pile′
com·piled′
com·pil′er
com·pla′cence
com·pla′cen·cy
com·pla′cent
com·plain′
com·plain′ant
com·plained′
com·plain′ing·ly
com·plaint′
com·plai′sance
com·plai′sant
com′ple·ment
com′ple·men′tal
com′ple·men′ta·ry
com′ple·ment·ed
com·plete′
com·plet′ed
com·ple′tion
com·plex′
com·plex′ion
com·plex′i·ty
com·pli′ance
com·pli′ant
com′pli·cate
com′pli·cat′ed

com′pli·ca′tion
com·plic′i·ty
com·plied′
com′pli·ment
com′pli·men′ta·ry
com′plin
com·ply′
com·po′nent
com·port′
com·pose′
com·posed′
com·pos′er
com·pos′ite
com·po·si′tion
com·pos′i·tor
com′post
com·po′sure
com′pote
com′pound
com′pre·hend′
com′pre·hend′ed
com′pre·hen′si·bil′i·ty
com′pre·hen′si·ble
com′pre·hen′sion
com′pre·hen′sive
com·press′
com·press′i·bil′i·ty
com·press′ible
com·pres′sion
com·pres′sor
com·prise′
com′pro·mise

com′pro·mis′ing·ly
Comp·tom′e·ter
comp·trol′ler
com·pul′sion
com·pul′sive
com·pul′so·ry
com·punc′tion
com′pu·ta′tion
com·pute′
com·put′er
com·put′er·ized
com′rade
con′cave
con·cav′i·ty
con·ceal′
con·cealed′
con·ceal′ment
con·cede′
con·ced′ed
con·ceit′
con·ceit′ed
con·ceit′ed·ly
con·ceiv′a·ble
con·ceiv′a·bly
con·ceive′
con·ceived′
con′cen·trate
con′cen·trat′ed
con′cen·tra′tion
con·cen′tric
con′cept
con·cep′tion
con·cep′tu·al
con·cern′
con·cerned′
con′cert
con·cert′ed
con′cer·ti′na
con·ces′sion
con·ces′sion·aire′
conch
con·cil′i·ate
con·cil′i·at′ed
con·cil′i·a′tion
con·cil′i·a·to′ry
con·cise′
con·cise′ness
con′clave
con·clude′
con·clud′ed
con·clu′sion
con·clu′sive
con·clu′sive·ly
con·coct′
con·coct′ed
con·coc′tion
con·com′i·tant
con′cord
con·cord′ance
con′course
con·crete′
con·cur′
con·curred′
con·cur′rence
con·cur′rent
con·cus′sion
con·demn′
con·dem·na′tion
con·dem′na·to′ry
con·demned′
con′den·sa′tion
con·dense′
con·densed′
con·dens′er
con′de·scend′
con′de·scend′ing·ly
con′de·scen′sion
con·dign′
con′di·ment
con·di′tion
con·di′tion·al
con·di′tion·al·ly
con·di′tioned
con·dole′
con·do′lence
con′do·min′i·um
con′do·na′tion
con·done′
con·doned′
con′dor
con·du′cive
con·duct′
con·duct′ed
con·duc′tion
con′duc·tiv′i·ty
con·duc′tor

con'duit
con'dyle
cone
con·fec'tion
con·fec'tion·er
con·fec'tion·er'y
con·fed'er·a·cy
con·fed'er·ate
con·fed'er·a'tion
con·fer'
con'fer·ee'
con'fer·ence
con·ferred'
con·fess'
con·fess'ed·ly
con·fes'sion
con·fes'sion·al
con·fes'sor
con·fide'
con·fid'ed
con'fi·dence
con'fi·dent
con'fi·den'tial
con'fi·den'tial·ly
con'fi·dent·ly
con·fid'ing·ly
con·fig'u·ra'tion
con·fine'
con·fined'
con·fine'ment
con·firm'
con'fir·ma'tion
con·firmed'
con'fis·cate
con'fis·cat'ed
con'fis·ca'tion
con·fis'ca·to'ry
con'fla·gra'tion
con·flict'
con·flict'ed
con·flic'tion
con'flu·ence
con'flu·ent
con·form'
con·form'a·ble
con'for·ma'tion
con·formed'
con·form'er
con·form'i·ty
con·found'
con·found'ed
con'frere
con·front'
con'fron·ta'tion
con·front'ed
con·fuse'
con·fused'
con·fus'ed·ly
con·fus'ing·ly
con·fu'sion
con'fu·ta'tion
con·fute'
con·fut'ed
con·geal'
con·gealed'
con'ge·la'tion
con'ge·ner
con·gen'ial
con·ge'ni·al'i·ty
con·gen'i·tal
con·gest'
con·gest'ed
con·ges'tion
con·glom'er·ate
con·glom'er·a'tion
con·grat'u·late
con·grat'u·lat'ed
con·grat'u·lates
con·grat'u·la'tion
con·grat'u·la·to'ry
con'gre·gate
con'gre·gat'ed
con'gre·ga'tion
con'gre·ga'tion·al
con'gress
con·gres'sion·al
con'gru·ence
con'gru·ent
con·gru'i·ty
con'gru·ous
con'ic
con'i·cal
co'ni·fer
co·nif'er·ous
con·jec'tur·al
con·jec'ture

con·jec′tured
con′ju·gal
con′ju·gate
con′ju·gat′ed
con′ju·ga′tion
con·junc′tion
con·junc′tive
con·junc′ti·vi′tis
con′ju·ra′tion
con·jure′
con·jured′
con′jur·er
con·nect′
con·nect′ed·ly
con·nec′tion
con·nec′tive
con·nec′tor
con·niv′ance
con·nive′
con·nived′
con′nois·seur′
con′no·ta′tion
con·note′
con·not′ed
con·nu′bi·al
con′quer
con′quered
con′quer·or
con′quest
con′san·guin′i·ty
con′science
con′sci·en′tious
con′sci·en′tious·ly
con′scious
con′scious·ly
con′scious·ness
con′script
con·scrip′tion
con′se·crate
con′se·crat′ed
con′se·cra′tion
con′se·cra′tive
con·sec′u·tive
con·sen′sus
con·sent′
con·sent′ed
con′se·quence
con′se·quent
con′se·quen′tial
con′se·quent·ly
con′ser·va′tion
con·serv′a·tism
con·serv′a·tive
con·serv′a·to′ry
con·serve′
con·served′
con·sid′er
con·sid′er·a·ble
con·sid′er·ate
con·sid′er·a′tion
con·sid′ered
con·sign′
con·signed′
con′sign·ee′
con·sign′ment
con·sign′or
con·sist′
con·sist′en·cy
con·sist′ent
con·sis′to·ry
con·so·la′tion
con·sole′
con·soled′
con·sol′i·date
con·sol′i·dat′ed
con·sol′i·da′tion
con·sol′ing·ly
con′sols
con′som·mé′
con′so·nance
con′so·nant
con′so·nan′tal
con·sort′
con·sort′ed
con·spic′u·ous
con·spic′u·ous·ly
con·spir′a·cy
con·spir′a·tor
con·spir′a·to′ri·al
con·spire′
con·spired′
con′sta·ble
con·stab′u·lar′y
con′stan·cy
con′stant
con′stant·ly

con′stel·la′tion
con′ster·na′tion
con′sti·pa′tion
con·stit′u·en·cy
con·stit′u·ent
con′sti·tute
con′sti·tut′ed
con′sti·tu′tion
con′sti·tu′tion·al
con′sti·tu′tion·al′i·ty
con′sti·tu′tion·al·ly
con·strain′
con·strained′
con·straint′
con·strict′
con·strict′ed
con·stric′tion
con·struct′
con·struct′ed
con·struc′tive
con·strue′
con·strued′
con′sul
con′su·lar
con′su·late
con′su·lates
con·sult′
con·sult′ant
con′sul·ta′tion
con·sult′a·tive
con·sult′ed
con·sum′a·ble
con·sume′
con·sumed′
con·sum′er·ism
con′sum·mate
con′sum·ma′tion
con·sump′tion
con·sump′tive
con′tact
con·ta′gion
con·ta′gious
con·tain′
con·tained′
con·tain′er·ize
con·tam′i·nate
con·tam′i·nat′ed
con·tam′i·na′tion
con′tem·plate
con′tem·plat′ed
con′tem·pla′tion
con·tem′pla·tive
con·tem′po·ra′ne·ous
con·tem′po·rar′y
con·tempt′
con·tempt′i·ble
con·temp′tu·ous
con·tend′
con·tend′ed
con·tend′er
con·tent′
con·tent′ed
con·ten′tion
con·ten′tious
con·tent′ment
con′test
con·test′ant
con′tes·ta′tion
con′text
con·tex′tu·al
con′ti·gu′i·ty
con·tig′u·ous
con′ti·nence
con′ti·nent
con′ti·nen′tal
con·tin′gen·cy
con·tin′gent
con·tin′u·al
con·tin′u·al·ly
con·tin′u·ance
con·tin′u·ant
con·tin′u·a′tion
con·tin′ue
con·tin′ued
con′ti·nu′i·ty
con·tin′u·ous
con·tin′u·ous·ly
con·tin′u·um
con·tort′
con·tort′ed
con·tor′tion
con·tor′tion·ist
con′tour
con′tra·band
con′tra·bass′
con′tract

con·tract'ed
con·trac'tile
con·trac'tion
con·trac'tor
con·trac'tu·al
con'tra·dict'
con'tra·dic'tion
con'tra·dic'to·ry
con'tra·dis·tinc'tion
con'tra·in'di·cate
con'tra·in'di·ca'tion
con·tral'to
con·trap'tion
con'tra·ri·ly
con'tra·ri·ness
con'tra·ri·wise'
con'tra·ry
con'trast
con'tra·vene'
con'tra·ven'tion
con·trib'ute
con'tri·bu'tion
con·trib'u·tive
con·trib'u·tor
con·trib'u·to'ry
con'trite
con'trite·ly
con·tri'tion
con·triv'ance
con·trive'
con·trol'
con·trol'la·ble

con·trolled'
con·trol'ler
con'tro·ver'sial
con'tro·ver'sy
con'tro·vert
con'tu·ma'cious
con'tu·ma·cy
con'tu·me'li·ous
con'tu·me'ly
con·tuse'
con·tused'
con·tu'sion
co·nun'drum
con'va·lesce'
con'va·les'cence
con'va·les'cent
con·vec'tion
con·vene'
con·vened'
con·ven'ience
con·ven'ienc·es
con·ven'ient
con·ven'ient·ly
con·vent'
con·ven'tion
con·ven'tion·al
con·ven'tion·al'i·ty
con·ven'tion·al·ize
con·ven'tion·al·ly
con·ven'tu·al
con·ven'tu·al·ly
con·verge'

con·verged'
con·ver'gence
con·ver'gent
con'ver·sant
con'ver·sa'tion
con'ver·sa'tion·al
con'ver·sa'tion·al·ist
con·verse'
con·ver'sion
con·vert'
con·vert'ed
con·vert'i·bil'i·ty
con·vert'i·ble
con'vex
con·vex'i·ty
con·vey'
con·vey'ance
con·veyed'
con·vey'er
con·vict'
con·vict'ed
con·vic'tion
con·vince'
con·vinc'ing·ly
con·viv'i·al
con·viv'i·al'i·ty
con·viv'i·al·ly
con'vo·ca'tion
con·voke'
con·voked'
con'vo·lute
con'vo·lut'ed

con′vo·lu′tion
con·voy′
con·voyed′
con·vulse′
con·vul′sion
con·vul′sive
cook′book′
cook′er
cook′er·y
cook′house′
cool
cooled
cool′er
cool′est
cool′head′ed
cool′house′
coo′lie
cool′ly
cool′ness
coop
co-op
coop′er·age
co-op′er·ate
co-op′er·at′ed
co-op′er·a′tion
co-op′er·a′tive
co-opt′
co-opt′ed
co-or′di·nate
co-or′di·nat′ed
co-or′di·na′tion
co-or′di·na′tor
coot
co′pal
co·part′ner
co·part′ner·ship
cope
coped
Co·per′ni·can
cop′ied
cop′i·er
cop′ing
co′pi·ous
co′pi·ous·ly
co′pi·ous·ness
cop′per
cop′per·head′
cop′per·plate′
cop′per·smith′
cop′pice
cop′ra
cop′y
cop′y·hold′er
cop′y·ist
cop′y·read′er
cop′y·right′
co′quet·ry
co·quette′
co·quet′tish
cor′a·cle
cor′a·coid
cor′al
cor′al·line
cord
cord′age
cord′ed
cor′dial
cor·dial′i·ty
cor′dial·ly
cord′ite
cor′don
Cor′do·van
cor′du·roy
cord′wood′
core
cored
co′re·spond′ent
co′ri·an′der
Co·rin′thi·an
cork
cork′age
cork′screw′
cork′wood′
cor′mo·rant
corn
cor′ne·a
cor′ner
cor′nered
cor′ner·stone′
cor′net
corn′field′
corn′flow′er
cor′nice
corn′stalk′
cor′nu·co′pi·a
cor′ol·lar′y

co·ro′na
cor′o·nar′y
cor′o·na′tion
cor′o·ner
cor′o·net
cor′po·ral
cor′po·rate
cor′po·rate·ly
cor′po·ra′tion
cor′po·ra′tive
cor·po′re·al
corps
corpse
cor′pu·lence
cor′pu·lent
cor′pus
cor′pus·cle
cor·pus′cu·lar
cor·ral′
cor·rect′
cor·rect′ed
cor·rec′tion
cor·rec′tion·al
cor·rec′tive
cor·rect′ly
cor·rect′ness
cor·rec′tor
cor′re·late
cor′re·lat′ed
cor′re·la′tion
cor·rel′a·tive
cor′re·spond′
cor′re·spond′ed
cor′re·spond′ence
cor′re·spond′ent
cor·re·spond′ing·ly
cor′re·sponds′
cor′ri·dor
cor·rob′o·rate
cor·rob′o·ra′tion
cor·rob′o·ra′tive
cor·rob′o·ra·to′ry
cor·rode′
cor·rod′ed
cor·ro′si·ble
cor·ro′sion
cor·ro′sive
cor′ru·gate
cor′ru·gat′ed
cor′ru·ga′tion
cor·rupt′
cor·rupt′ed
cor·rupt′i·bil′i·ty
cor·rupt′i·ble
cor·rup′tion
cor·rupt′ly
cor·sage′
cor′sair
corse′let
cor′set
cor·tege′
cor′tex
cor′ti·cal
co·run′dum
cor′us·cate
cor′us·cat′ed
cor′us·ca′tion
cor·vette′
co·ry′za
co·sig′na·to′ry
co·sign′er
cos′i·ly
co′sine
cos·met′ic
cos′me·ti′cian
cos′mic
cos·mog′o·ny
cos·mol′o·gy
cos′mo·naut
cos′mo·pol′i·tan
cos·mop′o·lite
cos′mos
Cos′sack
cost
cos′tal
cos′tive
cost′li·ness
cost′ly
cos′tume
cos·tum′er
co′sy
cot
co′te·rie
co·ter′mi·nous
co·til′lion
cot′tage

cot'ter
cot'ton
cot'ton·tail'
cot'ton·wood'
couch
cou'gar
cough
could
coun'cil
coun'ci·lor
coun'sel
coun'seled
count
count'down
coun'te·nance
count'er
coun'ter·act'
coun'ter·at·tack'
coun'ter·bal'ance
coun'ter·blast'
coun'ter·change'
coun'ter·check'
coun'ter·claim'
coun'ter·clock'wise'
count'ered
coun'ter·feit
coun'ter·feit'er
coun'ter·foil'
coun'ter·ir'ri·tant
coun'ter·mand'
coun'ter·march'
coun'ter·mine'
coun'ter·of·fen'sive
coun'ter·pane'
coun'ter·part'
coun'ter·plot'
coun'ter·point'
coun'ter·shaft'
coun'ter·sign'
coun'ter·sink'
coun'ter·vail'
coun'ter·weight'
count'ess
count'less
coun'try
coun'try·man
coun'try·side'
coun'ty
coup
cou'pé'
cou'ple
cou'pler
cou'plet
cou'pling
cou'pon
cour'age
cou·ra'geous
cour'i·er
course
coursed
cours'er
court
court'ed
cour'te·ous
cour'te·sy
court'house'
cour'ti·er
court'li·ness
court'ly
court'-mar'tial
court'ship
court'yard'
cous'in
cove
cov'e·nant
cov'er
cov'er·age
cov'ered
cov'er·let
cov'ert
cov'et
cov'et·ed
cov'et·ous
cov'ey
cow'ard
cow'ard·ice
cow'ard·ly
cow'bell'
cow'boy'
cow'catch'er
cow'er
cowl
cow'lick'
co-work'er
cow'slip
cox'comb'

cox'swain
coy
coy'ly
coy'ness
coy'ote
coz'en
co'zi·er
co'zi·est
co'zi·ly
co'zi·ness
co'zy
crab
crack
cracked
crack'er
crack'le
crack'led
cra'dle
cra'dled
craft
craft'i·er
craft'i·est
craft'i·ly
craft'i·ness
crafts'man
craft'y
crag
cram
crammed
cramp
cram'pon
cran'ber'ry

crane
craned
cra'ni·al
cra'ni·om'e·try
cra'ni·ot'o·my
cra'ni·um
crank
crank'case'
cranked
crank'i·ly
crank'i·ness
crank'y
cran'ny
crape
crash
crass
crass'ly
crass'ness
crate
crat'ed
cra'ter
cra·vat'
crave
craved
cra'ven
cra'ven·ette'
crav'ings
craw'fish'
crawl
crawled
cray'fish'
cray'on

craze
cra'zi·er
cra'zi·est
cra'zi·ly
cra'zi·ness
cra'zy
creak
creak'ing·ly
cream
creamed
cream'er·y
cream'i·er
cream'i·est
cream'y
crease
cre·ate'
cre·at'ed
cre·a'tion
cre·a'tive
cre·a'tive·ly
cre·a'tive·ness
cre'a·tiv'i·ty
cre·a'tor
crea'ture
crèche
cre'dence
cre·den'tial
cre·den'za
cred'i·bil'i·ty
cred'i·ble
cred'it
cred'it·a·bil'i·ty

cred′it·a·ble
cred′it·ed
cred′i·tor
cre′do
cre·du′li·ty
cred′u·lous
cred′u·lous·ness
creed
creek
creel
creep
creep′er
creep′i·ness
cre′mate
cre′mat·ed
cre·ma′tion
cre′ma·to′ry
Cre·mo′na
cre′ole
cre′o·sote
crepe
crep′i·tant
crep′i·tate
crep′i·ta′tion
cre·scen′do
cres′cent
crest
crest′ed
crest′fall′en
cre′tin
cre′tin·ism
cre′tin·oid
cre′tin·ous
cre·tonne′
cre·vasse′
crev′ice
crew
crew′el
crib
crib′bage
crib′work′
crick′et
crime
crim′i·nal
crim′i·nal′i·ty
crim′i·nal·ly
crim′i·nol′o·gist
crim′i·nol′o·gy
crimp
crim′son
cringe
cringed
crin′kle
crin′kled
crin′o·line
crip′ple
crip′pled
cri′ses
cri′sis
crisp
crisp′er
crisp′est
crisp′ly
crisp′ness
criss′cross′
cri·te′ri·a
cri·te′ri·on
crit′ic
crit′i·cal
crit′i·cal·ly
crit′i·cism
crit′i·cize
crit′i·cized
cri·tique′
croak
croaked
croak′er
croak′ing·ly
croch′et
crock
crock′er·y
croc′o·dile
cro′cus
crook
crook′ed
crook′ed·ness
croon
crooned
croon′er
crop
cro·quet′
cro·quette′
cro′sier
cross
cross′bar′
cross′bow′

cross'bow'man
cross'bred'
cross'cut'
cross'hatch'
cross'ings
cross'o'ver
cross'road'
cross'walk'
cross'wise'
cross'word'
crotch'et
crouch
crouched
croup
crou'pi·er
crow
crow'bar'
crowd
crowd'ed
crown
crowned
crown'work'
cru'cial
cru'cial·ly
cru'ci·ble
cru'ci·fied
cru'ci·fix
cru'ci·fix'ion
cru'ci·form
cru'ci·fy
crude
crud'er

crud'est
cru'di·ty
cru'el
cru'el·ly
cru'el·ty
cru'et
cruise
cruis'er
crul'ler
crumb
crum'ble
crum'bled
crump
crum'pet
crum'ple
crum'pled
crunch
crup'per
cru·sade'
cru·sad'er
cruse
crush
crushed
crush'er
crush'ing·ly
crust
crust'ed
crust'i·er
crust'i·est
crust'y
crutch
crux

cry
cry'o·lite
crypt
cryp'tic
cryp'ti·cal
cryp'ti·cal·ly
cryp'to·gram
cryp'to·graph
cryp·tog'ra·phy
crys'tal
crys'tal·line
crys'tal·li·za'tion
crys'tal·lize
crys'tal·lized
crys'tal·loid
cub
cub'by·hole'
cube
cu'beb
cu'bic
cu'bi·cle
cub'ism
cu'bit
cuck'oo
cu'cum·ber
cud'dle
cud'dled
cudg'el
cudg'eled
cue
cuff
cuffed

cui·rass′
cui·sine′
cu′li·nar′y
cull
culled
cul′mi·nate
cul′mi·nat′ed
cul′mi·na′tion
cul′pa·bil′i·ty
cul′pa·ble
cul′prit
cult
cul′ti·vate
cul′ti·vat′ed
cul′ti·va′tion
cul′ti·va′tor
cul′tur·al
cul′tur·al·ly
cul′ture
cul′tured
cul′vert
cum′ber
cum′bered
cum′ber·some
cum′brous
cum′mer·bund′
cu′mu·la′tive
cu′mu·lus
cu·ne′i·form
cun′ning
cun′ning·ly
cup
cup′board
cup′cake′
cu′pel
cu′pel·la′tion
cup′ful
Cu′pid
cu·pid′i·ty
cu′po·la
cupped
cu′pric
cu′prous
cur
cur′a·ble
cu′ra·çao′
cu′ra·cy
cu·ra′re
cu′rate
cur′a·tive
cu·ra′tor
curb
curbed
curd
cure
cured
cu·ret′tage
cu·rette′
cur′few
cu′rie
cu′ri·o
cu′ri·os′i·ties
cu′ri·os′i·ty
cu′ri·ous
cu′ri·ous·ly
curl
curled
curl′er
cur′lew
curl′i·cue
curl′y
cur·mudg′eon
cur′rant
cur′ren·cy
cur′rent
cur′rent·ly
cur·ric′u·la
cur·ric′u·lar
cur·ric′u·lum
cur′ry
curse
curs′ed
cur′sive
cur′so·ry
curt
cur·tail′
cur·tailed′
cur′tain
cur′te·sy
curt′ly
cur′va·ture
curve
curved
cur′vi·lin′e·ar
cush′ion
cush′ioned

cusp
cus′pi·dor
cuss′ed·ness
cus′tard
cus·to′di·al
cus·to′di·an
cus′to·dy
cus′tom
cus′tom·ar′i·ly
cus′tom·ar′y
cus′tom·er
cut
cu·ta′ne·ous
cut′a·way′
cut′back′
cute
cu′ti·cle
cut′lass
cut′ler·y
cut′let
cut′off′
cut′out′
cut′purse′
cut′ter
cut′tings
cut′tle·fish′
cut′weed′
cut′worm
cy′a·nate
cy·an′ic
cy′a·nide
cy′a·nite
cy·an′o·gen
cy′a·no′sis
cy′ber·net′ics
cy′cla·mate
cy′cle
cy′clic
cy′cloid
cy·clom′e·ter
cy′clone
cy·clon′ic
cy′clo·pe′dic
Cy′clops
cy′clo·ra′ma
cyg′net
cyl′in·der
cy·lin′dric
cy·lin′dri·cal
cym′bal
cyn′ic
cyn′i·cal
cyn′i·cal·ly
cyn′i·cism
cy′no·sure
cy′press
Cy·ril′lic
cyst
cys·ti′tis
cyst′oid
cys′to·lith
czar
Czech

dab'ble
dachs'hund'
da·coit'
dae'dal
dae'mon
daf'fo·dil
daft
dag'ger
da·guerre'o·type
dahl'ia
dai'ly
dain'ti·er
dain'ti·est
dain'ti·ly
dain'ti·ness
dain'ty
dair'y
dair'y·maid'
dair'y·man
da'is
dai'sy
dal'li·ance
dal'ly
dal·ma'tian
dam
dam'age
dam'aged
dam'a·scene'
dam'a·scened'
da·mas'cus
dam'ask
dammed
dam'na·ble
dam·na'tion
damp
damp'en
damp'ened
damp'er
damp'est
damp'ness
dam'sel
dance
danc'er
dan'de·li'on
dan'dle
dan'dled
dan'druff
dan'dy
dan'ger
dan'ger·ous
dan'ger·ous·ly
dan'gle
dan'gled
Dan'ish
dank
dap'per
dap'ple
dap'pled
dare
dared
dar'ing·ly
dark
dark'en
dark'er
dark'est
dark'ly

dark'ness
dar'ling
darned
dart
dart'ed
dash
dash'board'
dashed
dash'ing·ly
das'tard·ly
da'ta
date
dat'ed
da'tive
da'tum
daub
daubed
daugh'ter
daugh'ter-in-law'
daunt
daunt'ed
daunt'less
dau'phin
dav'en·port
dav'it
daw'dle
daw'dled
dawn
dawned
day
day'book'
day'break'

day'dream'
day'light'
day'time'
daz'zle
daz'zled
dea'con
dead
dead'en
dead'ened
dead'fall'
dead'head'
dead'light'
dead'li·ness
dead'lock
dead'ly
deaf
deaf'en
deaf'ened
deaf'en·ing·ly
deaf'er
deaf'est
deal
deal'er
deal'ings
dean
dean'er·y
dear
dear'er
dear'est
dear'ly
dear'ness
dearth

death
death'bed'
death'blow'
death'less
death'like'
death'ly
de·ba'cle
de·bar'
de·bark'
de·barred'
de·base'
de·based'
de·base'ment
de·bat'a·ble
de·bate'
de·bat'ed
de·bat'er
de·bauch'
de·bauched'
de·bauch'er·y
de·ben'ture
de·bil'i·tate
de·bil'i·tat'ed
de·bil'i·ty
deb'it
deb'it·ed
de·bris'
debt
debt'or
de·bug'ging
de'but
deb'u·tante'

dec′ade
de·ca′dence
de·ca′dent
de·cal′co·ma′ni·a
de·camp′
de·cant′
de·cant′er
de·cap′i·tate
de·cap′i·ta′tion
de·car′bon·ize
de·cath′lon
de·cay′
de·cayed′
de·cease′
de·ceased′
de·ce′dent
de·ceit′
de·ceit′ful
de·ceit′ful·ness
de·ceive′
de·ceived′
de·cel′er·a′tion
De·cem′ber
de′cen·cy
de·cen′ni·al
de′cent
de′cent·ly
de·cen′tral·i·za′tion
de·cen′tral·ize
de·cep′tion
de·cep′tive
de·cep′tive·ly
de·cep′tive·ness
de·cide′
de·cid′ed·ly
de·cid′u·ous
dec′i·mal
dec′i·mate
dec′i·mat′ed
dec′i·ma′tion
de·ci′pher
de·ci′pher·a·ble
de·ci′phered
de·ci′sion
de·ci′sive
de·ci′sive·ly
de·ci′sive·ness
deck
decked
deck′house′
deck′le
de·claim′
de·claimed′
dec′la·ma′tion
de·clam′a·to′ry
dec′la·ra′tion
de·clar′a·tive
de·clar′a·to′ry
de·clare′
de·clared′
de·clen′sion
dec′li·na′tion
de·cline′
de·clined′
de·cliv′i·ty
de·coc′tion
dé·col′le·tage
dé·col′le·té
de·com′pen·sate
de·com′pen·sa′tion
de′com·pose′
de·com·posed′
de′com·po·si′tion
dec′o·rate
dec′o·rat′ed
dec′o·ra′tion
dec′o·ra′tive
dec′o·ra′tor
dec′o·rous
dec′o·rous·ly
dec′o·rous·ness
de·co′rum
de·coy′
de·crease′
de·creased′
de·creas′ing·ly
de·cree′
de·creed′
de·crep′it
de·crep′i·tude
de·cre′tal
de·cried′
de·cry′
ded′i·cate
ded′i·cat′ed
ded′i·ca′tion

ded′i·ca·to′ry
de·duce′
de·duced′
de·duc′i·ble
de·duct′
de·duct′ed
de·duct′i·ble
de·duc′tion
de·duc′tive·ly
deed
deed′ed
deem
deemed
deep
deep′en
deep′ened
deep′er
deep′est
deep′ly
deep′ness
deer
deer′hound′
deer′skin′
deer′stalk′er
deer′weed′
de·face′
de·faced′
de·fal′cate
de·fal′cat·ed
de′fal·ca′tion
def′a·ma′tion
de·fam′a·to′ry

de·fame′
de·famed′
de·fault′
de·fault′ed
de·fault′er
de·fea′si·ble
de·feat′
de·feat′ed
de·feat′ism
de·fect′
de·fec′tion
de·fec′tive
de·fec′tor
de·fend′
de·fend′ant
de·fend′ed
de·fend′er
de·fense′
de·fen′si·ble
de-fen′sive
de·fen′sive·ly
de·fen′sive·ness
de·fer′
def′er·ence
def′er·en′tial
def′er·en′tial·ly
de·fer′ment
de·fer′ral
de·ferred′
de·fi′ance
de·fi′ant
de·fi′ant·ly

de·fi′cien·cy
de·fi′cient
def′i·cit
def′i·lade′
def′i·lad′ed
de·file′
de·filed′
de·file′ment
de·fin′a·ble
de·fine′
de·fined′
def′i·nite
def′i·nite·ly
def′i·nite·ness
def′i·ni′tion
de·fin′i·tive
de·fin′i·tive·ly
de·fin′i·tive·ness
de·fin′i·tize
de·flate′
de·flat′ed
de·fla′tion
de·fla′tion·ar′y
de·flect′
de·flect′ed
de·flec′tion
de·for′est·a′tion
de·form′
de′for·ma′tion
de·formed′
de·form′i·ty
de·fraud′

de·fraud′ed
de·fray′
de·frayed′
deft
deft′ly
deft′ness
de·funct′
de·fied′
de·fy′
de·gen′er·a·cy
de·gen′er·ate
de·gen′er·at′ed
de′gen·er·a′tion
deg′ra·da′tion
de·grade′
de·grad′ed
de·grad′ing·ly
de·gree′
de·hy′drate
de·hy′drat·ed
de′i·fi·ca′tion
de′i·fied
de′i·fy
deign
deigned
de′ism
de′ist
de′i·ty
de·ject′ed
de·ject′ed·ly
de·jec′tion
de·lay′
de·layed′
de·lec′ta·bil′i·ty
de·lec′ta·ble
de′lec·ta′tion
del′e·gate
del′e·gat′ed
del′e·ga′tion
de·lete′
de·let′ed
del′e·te′ri·ous
del′e·te′ri·ous·ly
de·le′tion
delft′ware′
de·lib′er·ate
de·lib′er·at′ed
de·lib′er·a′tion
de·lib′er·a′tive
del′i·ca·cy
del′i·cate
del′i·cate·ly
del′i·ca·tes′sen
de·li′cious
de·li′cious·ly
de·light′
de·light′ed
de·light′ful
de·light′ful·ly
de·lim′it
de·lim′i·ta′tion
de·lin′e·ate
de·lin′e·at′ed
de·lin′e·a′tion
de·lin′e·a′tive
de·lin′e·a′tor
de·lin′quen·cy
de·lin′quent
del′i·quesce′
del′i·ques′cence
del′i·ques′cent
de·lir′i·ous
de·lir′i·um
de·liv′er
de·liv′er·ance
de·liv′ered
de·liv′er·er
de·liv′er·y
del·phin′i·um
del′ta
del′toid
de·lude′
de·lud′ed
del′uge
del′uged
de·lu′sion
de·lu′sive
de luxe′
delve
de·mag′net·ize
dem′a·gog′ic
dem′a·gogue
de·mand′
de·mand′ed
de·mand′ing·ly
de′mar·ca′tion

de·mean'
de·meaned'
de·mean'or
de·ment'ed
de·men'ti·a
de·mer'it
dem'i·god'
de·mil'i·ta·rize
de·mise'
de·mo'bi·li·za'tion
de·mo'bi·lize
de·mo'bi·lized
de·moc'ra·cy
dem'o·crat
dem'o·crat'ic
dem'o·crat'i·cal·ly
de·moc'ra·ti·za'tion
de·moc'ra·tize
de·mol'ish
de·mol'ished
dem'o·li'tion
de'mon
de·mon'e·ti·za'tion
de·mon'e·tize
de'mo·ni'a·cal
de·mon'stra·ble
dem'on·strate
dem'on·strat'ed
dem'on·stra'tion
de·mon'stra·tive
dem'on·stra'tor
de·mor'al·i·za'tion

de·mor'al·ize
de·mor'al·ized
de·mot'ic
de·mount'able
de·mur'
de·mure'
de·mure'ly
de·mur'rage
de·murred'
de·mur'rer
den
de·na'ture
de·na'tured
den·drol'o·gy
de·ni'al
de·nied'
den'i·grate
den'i·zen
de·nom'i·nate
de·nom'i·nat'ed
de·nom'i·na'tion
de·nom'i·na'tion·al
de·nom'i·na'tor
de'no·ta'tion
de·note'
de·not'ed
de·noue'ment
de·nounce'
de·nounced'
dense
dens'er
dens'est

den'si·ty
dent
den'tal
den·tal'gi·a
dent'ed
den'ti·frice
den'tine
den'tist
den'tist·ry
den·ti'tion
den'u·da'tion
de·nude'
de·nun'ci·a'tion
de·nun'ci·a·to'ry
de·ny'
de·o'dor·ant
de·o'dor·ize
de·o'dor·ized
de·part'
de·part'ed
de·part'ment
de'part·men'tal
de'part·men'tal·ize
de·par'ture
de·pend'
de·pend'ed
de·pend'en·cy
de·pend'ent
de·per'son·al·ize
de·pict'
de·pict'ed
de·pic'tion

de·pil′a·to′ry
de·plete′
de·plet′ed
de·ple′tion
de·plor′a·ble
de·plore′
de·plored′
de·ploy′
de·ployed′
de·ploy′ment
de·po′lar·i·za′tion
de·po′lar·ize
de·po′nent
de·pop′u·late
de·pop′u·lat′ed
de·port′
de′por·ta′tion
de·port′ed
de·port′ment
de·pose′
de·posed′
de·pos′it
de·pos′i·tar′y
de·pos′it·ed
dep′o·si′tion
de·pos′i·tor
de·pos′i·to′ry
de′pot
dep′ra·va′tion
de·prave′
de·praved′
de·prav′i·ty

dep′re·cate
dep′re·cat′ed
dep′re·ca′tion
dep′re·ca·to′ry
de·pre′ci·ate
de·pre′ci·at′ed
de·pre′ci·a′tion
dep′re·da′tion
de·press′
de·pres′sant
de·pressed′
de·press′ing·ly
de·pres′sion
de·pres′sive
dep′ri·va′tion
de·prive′
de·prived′
depth
dep′u·ta′tion
de·pute′
de·put′ed
dep′u·tize
dep′u·tized
dep′u·ty
de·rail′
de·railed′
de·rail′ment
de·range′
de·ranged′
de·range′ment
der′by
der′e·lict

der′e·lic′tion
de·ride′
de·rid′ed
de·ri′sion
de·ri′sive
de·riv′a·ble
der′i·va′tion
de·riv′a·tive
de·rive′
de·rived′
der′mal
der′ma·ti′tis
der′ma·tol′o·gy
der′ma·to′sis
der′o·gate
der′o·gat′ed
der′o·ga′tion
de·rog′a·to′ry
der′rick
der′vish
des′cant
de·scend′
de·scend′ant
de·scent′
de·scribe′
de·scribed′
de·scrip′tion
de·scrip′tive
de·scry′
des′e·crate
des′e·crat′ed
des′e·cra′tion

de·sen′si·tize
de·sen′si·tiz′er
de·sert′
de·sert′ed
de·sert′er
de·ser′tion
de·serve′
de·served′
des′ic·cant
des′ic·cate
des′ic·cat′ed
des′ic·ca′tion
des′ic·ca′tive
de·sid′er·a′ta
de·sid′er·a′tum
de·sign′
des′ig·nate
des′ig·nat′ed
des′ig·na′tion
de·signed′
de·sign′ed·ly
de·sign′er
de·sir′a·bil′i·ty
de·sir′a·ble
de·sire′
de·sired′
de·sires′
de·sir′ous
de·sist′
de·sists′
desk
des′o·late

des′o·lat′ed
des′o·late·ly
des′o·la′tion
de·spair′
de·spaired′
de·spair′ing·ly
des′per·a′do
des′per·ate
des′per·ate·ly
des′per·a′tion
des′pi·ca·ble
de·spise′
de·spised′
de·spite′
de·spoil′
de·spoiled′
de·spond′en·cy
de·spond′ent
de·spond′ing·ly
des′pot
des·pot′ic
des′pot·ism
des′qua·ma′tion
des·sert′
des′ti·na′tion
des′tine
des′tined
des′ti·ny
des′ti·tute
des′ti·tu′tion
de·stroy′
de·stroyed′

de·stroy′er
de·struct′i·ble
de·struc′tion
de·struc′tive
des′ue·tude
des′ul·to′ri·ly
des′ul·to′ry
de·tach′
de·tach′a·ble
de·tached′
de·tach′ment
de·tail′
de·tailed′
de·tain′
de·tained′
de·tect′
de·tect′ed
de·tec′tion
de·tec′tive
de·tec′tor
de·ten′tion
de·ter′
de·ter′gent
de·te′ri·o·rate
de·te′ri·o·rat′ed
de·te′ri·o·ra′tion
de·ter′mi·na·ble
de·ter′mi·nant
de·ter′mi·na′tion
de·ter′mi·na′tive
de·ter′mine
de·ter′mined

de·ter′min·ism
de·terred′
de·ter′rent
de·test′
de·test′a·ble
de′tes·ta′tion
de·test′ed
de·throne′
de·throned′
det′o·nate
det′o·nat′ed
det′o·na′tion
det′o·na′tor
de·tour′
de·toured′
de·tract′
de·tract′ed
de·trac′tion
de·trac′tor
det′ri·ment
det′ri·men′tal
de·tri′tus
de·val′u·ate
de·val′u·at′ed
de·val′u·a′tion
dev′as·tate
dev′as·tat′ed
dev′as·tat′ing·ly
dev′as·ta′tion
de·vel′op
de·vel′oped
de·vel′op·ment

de·vel′op·men′tal
de′vi·ate
de′vi·at′ed
de′vi·a′tion
de·vice′
dev′il
dev′il·try
de′vi·ous
de′vi·ous·ness
de·vise′
de·vised′
de·vi′tal·ize
de·void′
de·volve′
de·volved′
de·vote′
de·vot′ed
de·vot′ed·ly
dev′o·tee′
de·vo′tion
de·vo′tion·al
de·vour′
de·voured′
de·vout′ly
dew
dew′y
dex′ter
dex·ter′i·ty
dex′ter·ous
dex′ter·ous·ly
dex′trose
di′a·be′tes

di′a·bet′ic
di′a·bol′ic
di′a·bol′i·cal
di·ac′o·nal
di′a·crit′i·cal
di′a·dem
di·aer′e·sis
di′ag·nose′
di′ag·nosed′
di′ag·no′ses
di′ag·no′sis
di′ag·nos′tic
di′ag·nos·ti′cian
di·ag′o·nal
di·ag′o·nal·ly
di′a·gram
di′al
di′a·lect
di′a·lec′tic
di′aled
di′a·logue
di·al′y·sis
di·am′e·ter
di′a·met′ric
di′a·met′ri·cal·ly
di′a·mond
di′a·pa′son
di′a·per
di·aph′a·nous
di′a·phragm
di′a·rist
di′a·ry

Di·as′po·ra
di·as′to·le
di′as·tol′ic
di′a·ther′mic
di′a·tom
di′a·tom′ic
di′a·tribe
dice
di·chot′o·mous
di·chot′o·my
Dic′ta·phone
dic′tate
dic′tat·ed
dic·ta′tion
dic·ta′tor
dic′ta·to′ri·al
dic′ta·to′ri·al·ly
dic·ta′tor·ship
dic′tion
dic′tion·ar′y
Dic′to·graph
dic′tum
did
di·dac′tic
die
died
die′stock′
di′et
di′e·tar′y
di′e·tet′ics
dif′fer
dif′fered
dif′fer·ence
dif′fer·ent
dif′fer·en′tial
dif′fer·en′ti·ate
dif′fer·en′ti·at′ed
dif′fer·en′ti·a′tion
dif′fi·cult
dif′fi·cul·ty
dif′fi·dence
dif′fi·dent
dif·fract′
dif·frac′tion
dif·fuse′
dif·fused′
dif·fu′sion
dig
di·gest′
di·gest′ed
di·gest′i·ble
di·ges′tion
di·ges′tive
dig′gings
dig′it
dig′i·tal′is
dig′ni·fied
dig′ni·fy
dig′ni·tar′y
dig′ni·ty
di·gress′
di·gres′sion
dike
di·lap′i·date
di·lap′i·dat′ed
di·lap′i·da′tion
dil′a·ta′tion
di·late′
di·lat′ed
di·la′tion
dil′a·to′ry
di·lem′ma
dil′et·tan′te
dil′i·gence
dil′i·gent
dil′i·gent·ly
di·lute′
di·lut′ed
di·lu′tion
dim
dime
di·men′sion
di·men′sion·al
di·min′ish
di·min′u·en′do
dim′i·nu′tion
di·min′u·tive
dim′i·ty
dim′ly
dimmed
dim′mer
dim′mest
dim′ness
dim′ple
dine
dined

din′er
din′gy
din′ner
di′no·saur
dint
di·oc′e·san
di′o·cese
di′o·ra′ma
diph·the′ri·a
diph′thong
di·plo′ma
di·plo′ma·cy
dip′lo·mat
dip′lo·mat′ic
dip′lo·mat′i·cal·ly
di·plo′ma·tist
di·plo′pi·a
dip′per
dip′so·ma′ni·a
dip′so·ma′ni·ac
di·rect′
di·rect′ed
di·rec′tion
di·rec′tion·al
di·rec′tive
di·rect′ly
di·rect′ness
di·rec′tor
di·rec′to·ry
dire′ful
dir′est
dirge

dir′i·gi·ble
dirt
dirt′i·ly
dirt′y
dis′a·bil′i·ty
dis·a′ble
dis·a′bled
dis′a·buse′
dis′ad·van′tage
dis′ad·van′taged
dis·ad′van·ta′geous
dis′af·fec′tion
dis′af·firm′
dis′af·firmed′
dis′a·gree′
dis′a·gree′a·ble
dis′a·gree′ment
dis′al·low′
dis′al·lowed′
dis′ap·pear′
dis′ap·pear′ance
dis′ap·peared′
dis′ap·point′
dis′ap·point′ment
dis′ap·pro·ba′tion
dis′ap·prov′al
dis′ap·prove′
dis·arm′
dis·ar′ma·ment
dis·armed′
dis·arm′ing·ly
dis′ar·range′

dis′ar·ranged′
dis′ar·ray′
dis′ar·tic′u·late
dis′as·so′ci·a′tion
dis·as′ter
dis·as′trous
dis′a·vow′
dis′a·vow′al
dis·band′
dis·band′ed
dis·bar′
dis·bar′ment
dis·barred′
dis′be·lieve′
dis′be·lieved′
dis′be·liev′er
dis′be·liev′ing·ly
dis·burse′
dis·burse′ment
disc
dis′card
dis·card′ed
dis·cern′
dis·cerned′
dis·cern′i·ble
dis·cern′ing·ly
dis·cern′ment
dis·charge′
dis·charged′
dis·ci′ple
dis·ci′ple·ship
dis′ci·pli·nar′y

dis′ci·pline
dis′ci·plined
dis·claim′
dis·claimed′
dis·close′
dis·clo′sure
dis·col′or
dis·col′or·a′tion
dis·col′ored
dis·com′fit
dis·com′fi·ture
dis·com′fort
dis′com·pose′
dis′com·posed′
dis′com·po′sure
dis′con·cert′
dis′con·nect′
dis′con·nect′ed
dis·con′so·late
dis′con·tent′
dis·con·tent′ed
dis′con·tin′u·ance
dis′con·tin′ue
dis′con·tin′ued
dis′cord
dis·cord′ance
dis·cord′ant
dis′count
dis′count·ed
dis·coun′te·nance
dis·cour′age
dis·cour′aged

dis·cour′age·ment
dis·cour′ag·ing·ly
dis·course′
dis·cour′te·ous
dis·cour′te·sy
dis·cov′er
dis·cov′ered
dis·cov′er·er
dis·cov′er·y
dis·cred′it
dis·cred′it·a·ble
dis·cred′it·ed
dis·creet′
dis·crep′an·cy
dis·crete′
dis·cre′tion
dis·cre′tion·ar′y
dis·crim′i·nate
dis·crim′i·nat′ed
dis·crim′i·na′tion
dis·crim′i·na′tive
dis·crim′i·na·to′ry
dis·cur′sive
dis′cus
dis·cuss′
dis·cuss′es
dis·dain′
dis·dained′
dis·dain′ful
dis·ease′
dis·eased′
dis·em′bar·ka′tion

dis′em·bar′rass
dis′em·bod′y
dis′en·chant′
dis′en·gage′
dis′es·tab′lish
dis′es·teem′
dis·fa′vor
dis·fea′ture
dis·fig′ure
dis·fig′ured
dis·fig′ure·ment
dis·fran′chise
dis·gorge′
dis·grace′
dis·grace′ful
dis·grun′tle
dis·guise′
dis·gust′
dis·gust′ed
dis·gust′ed·ly
dis·gust′ing·ly
dish
dis′ha·bille′
dis·har′mo·ny
dis·heart′en
di·shev′el
di·shev′eled
dis·hon′est
dis·hon′est·ly
dis·hon′or
dis·hon′or·a·ble
dis·hon′ored

dis′il·lu′sion
dis·in′cli·na′tion
dis′in·cline′
dis′in·clined′
dis′in·fect′
dis′in·fect′ant
dis′in·gen′u·ous
dis′in·her′it
dis·in′te·grate
dis·in′te·gra′tion
dis·in′ter·est·ed
dis·join′
dis·joined′
dis·join′ings
dis·joint′ed
dis·junc′tion
dis·junc′tive
disk
dis·like′
dis′lo·cate
dis′lo·cat′ed
dis′lo·ca′tion
dis·lodge′
dis·loy′al
dis·loy′al·ty
dis′mal
dis′mal·ly
dis·man′tle
dis·man′tled
dis·mast′
dis·mast′ed
dis·may′
dis·mayed′
dis·mem′ber
dis·mem′bered
dis·mem′ber·ment
dis·miss′
dis·miss′al
dis·mount′
dis·mount′ed
dis′o·be′di·ence
dis′o·be′di·ent
dis′o·bey′
dis′o·beyed′
dis′o·blige′
dis′o·blig′ing·ly
dis·or′der
dis·or′dered
dis·or′der·ly
dis·or′gan·ize
dis·or′gan·ized
dis·own′
dis·par′age
dis·par′age·ment
dis·par′ag·ing·ly
dis′pa·rate
dis·par′i·ty
dis·pas′sion·ate
dis·patch′
dis·patched′
dis·patch′er
dis·pel′
dis·pelled′
dis·pen′sa·ble
dis·pen′sa·ry
dis′pen·sa′tion
dis·pense′
dis·pensed′
dis·per′sal
dis·perse′
dis·persed′
dis·per′sion
dis·pir′it·ed
dis·place′
dis·place′ment
dis·play′
dis·please′
dis·pleas′ure
dis·port′
dis·pos′al
dis·pose′
dis·posed′
dis′po·si′tion
dis′pos·sess′
dis′pos·sessed′
dis·po′sure
dis·praise′
dis·proof′
dis′pro·por′tion
dis′pro·por′tion·ate
dis′pu·ta·ble
dis′pu·tant
dis′pu·ta′tion
dis′pu·ta′tious
dis·pute′
dis·put′ed

dis·qual′i·fi·ca′tion
dis·qual′i·fy
dis·qui′et·ed
dis·qui′e·tude
dis′qui·si′tion
dis′re·gard′
dis·re·pair′
dis·rep′u·ta·ble
dis′re·pute′
dis′re·spect′
dis′re·spect′ful
dis·robe′
dis·root′
dis·rupt′
dis·rup′tion
dis·rup′tive
dis′sat·is·fac′tion
dis·sat′is·fied
dis·sect′
dis·sect′ed
dis·sem′ble
dis·sem′i·nate
dis·sem′i·nat′ed
dis·sem′i·na′tion
dis·sen′sion
dis·sent′
dis·sent′er
dis·sen′tient
dis′ser·ta′tion
dis·serv′ice
dis′si·dence
dis′si·dent

dis·sim′i·lar
dis·sim′i·lar′i·ty
dis·sim′u·late
dis·sim′u·lat′ed
dis·sim′u·la′tion
dis′si·pate
dis′si·pat′ed
dis′si·pa′tion
dis·so′ci·ate
dis·so′ci·at′ed
dis·so′ci·a′tion
dis′so·lute
dis′so·lu′tion
dis·solv′a·ble·ness
dis·solve′
dis·solved′
dis′so·nance
dis′so·nant
dis·suade′
dis·sua′sion
dis′taff
dis′tal
dis′tance
dis′tant
dis·taste′
dis·taste′ful
dis·tem′per
dis·tend′
dis·ten′si·ble
dis·till′
dis′til·late
dis′til·la′tion

dis·tilled′
dis·till′er
dis·till′er·y
dis·tinct′
dis·tinc′tion
dis·tinc′tive
dis·tinct′ly
dis·tinct′ness
dis·tin′guish
dis·tin′guished
dis·tort′
dis·tort′ed
dis·tor′tion
dis·tract′
dis·tract′ing·ly
dis·trac′tion
dis·train′
dis·trained′
dis·traught′
dis·tress′
dis·trib′ute
dis′tri·bu′tion
dis·trib′u·tive
dis·trib′u·tor
dis′trict
dis·trust′
dis·trust′ful
dis·turb′
dis·turb′ance
dis·turbed′
dis·turb′er
dis·un′ion

dis'u·nite'
dis·use'
ditch
ditched
dith'y·ram'bic
dit'to
dit'ty
di·ur'nal
di'va·gate
di'van
dive
dived
div'er
di·verge'
di·verged'
di·ver'gence
di·ver'gent
di·verg'ing·ly
di·verse'
di·ver'si·fi·ca'tion
di·ver'si·fy
di·ver'sion
di·ver'sion·ar·y
di·ver'si·ty
di·vert'
di·vest'
di·vide'
di·vid'ed
div'i·dend
di·vid'er
di·vine'
di·vined'
di·vine'ly
di·vin'i·ty
di·vis'i·bil'i·ty
di·vis'i·ble
di·vi'sion
di·vi'sor
di·vorce'
di·vor'cee'
di·vorce'ment
di·vulge'
di·vulged'
diz'zi·er
diz'zi·est
diz'zi·ly
diz'zi·ness
diz'zy
do
doc'ile
do·cil'i·ty
dock
dock'et
dock'yard'
doc'tor
doc'tor·ate
doc'tri·naire'
doc'tri·nal
doc'trine
doc'u·ment
doc'u·men'ta·ry
doc'u·men·ta'tion
doc'u·ment'ed
dod'der
dodge
dodged
do'do
doe
doe'skin'
doff
dog
dog'cart'
doge
dog'ged
dog'ger·el
dog'ma
dog·mat'ic
dog'ma·tism
dog'ma·tize
dog'trot'
dog'wood'
doi'ly
do'ings
dol'drums
dole
doled
dole'ful
doll
dol'lar
dol'man
dol'phin
dolt
do·main'
dome
domed
do·mes'tic

do·mes′ti·cal·ly
do·mes′ti·cate
do·mes′ti·cat′ed
do′mes·tic′i·ty
dom′i·cile
dom′i·cil′i·ar′y
dom′i·nance
dom′i·nant
dom′i·nate
dom′i·nat′ed
dom′i·na′tion
dom′i·neer′
dom′i·neered′
dom′i·neer′ing·ly
dom′i·nie
do·min′ion
dom′i·no
do′nate
do′nat·ed
do·na′tion
don′a·tive
done
don′key
do′nor
doom
doomed
door
door′bell′
door′frame′
door′knob′
door′nail′
door′sill′
door′stop′
door′way′
door′yard′
dope
dor′mant
dor′mer
dor′mi·to′ry
dor′mouse′
dor′sal
do′ry
dos′age
dose
dos′si·er
dot
dot′age
do′tard
dote
dot′ing·ly
dot′ted
dou′ble
dou′bled
dou′ble·knit
doubt
doubt′ed
doubt′ful
doubt′ful·ly
doubt′ing·ly
doubt′less
dough
dough′boy′
dough′nut′
dough′ty
dough′y
dour
dove
dove
dove′cot′
dove′tail′
dow′a·ger
dow′di·er
dow′di·est
dow′di·ly
dow′dy
dow′el
dow′eled
dow′er
down
down′cast′
down′fall′
down′heart′ed
down′hill′
down′pour′
down′right′
down′stairs′
down′town′
down′ward
down′y
dow′ry
dows′er
dox·ol′o·gy
doze
doz′en
drab
drach′ma

draft
draft'ed
draft'ee'
draft'i·er
draft'i·est
draft'i·ly
draft'y
drag
drag'gle
drag'gled
drag'net'
drag'on
drag'on·fly'
dra·goon'
dra·gooned'
drain
drain'age
drained
drain'er
drake
dra'ma
dra·mat'ic
dra·mat'i·cal·ly
dra·mat'ics
dram'a·tist
dram'a·ti·za'tion
dram'a·tize
dram'a·tized
dram'a·tur'gy
drank
drape
drap'er
dra'per·y
dras'tic
draught
draw
draw'back'
draw'bar'
draw'bridge'
draw'ee'
draw'er
draw'ings
drawl
drawled
drawn
draw'plate'
draw'string'
dray
dray'age
dray'man
dread
dread'ed
dread'ful
dream
dreamed
dream'er
dream'i·er
dream'i·est
dream'i·ly
dream'i·ness
dream'land
dream'less
dream'like
dream'y
drear'i·er
drear'i·est
drear'i·ly
drear'i·ness
drear'y
dredge
dredged
dreg
drench
drenched
dress
dressed
dress'er
dress'ings
dress'mak'er
dress'y
drew
drib'ble
drib'bled
dried
dri'er
dri'est
drift
drift'wood'
drill
drilled
drill'er
drink
drink'a·ble
drink'er
drip
drip'pings

drive
driv′el
driv′en
driv′er
drive′way′
driz′zle
driz′zled
droll
droll′er·y
drom′e·dar′y
drone
dron′ing·ly
drool
drool′ings
droop
drop
drop′out′
drop′per
drop′pings
drop′si·cal
drop′sy
dross
drought
drove
drown
drowned
drown′ings
drowse
drow′si·ly
drow′si·ness
drow′sy
drudge

drudg′er·y
drug
drug′gist
drug′store′
dru′id
dru·id′i·cal
drum
drum′head′
drummed
drum′mer
drum′stick′
drunk
drunk′ard
drunk′en
dry
dry′ly
dry′ness
du′al
du′al·ism
du′al·is′tic
du·al′i·ty
du·bi′e·ty
du′bi·ous
du′cal
duc′at
duch′ess
duch′y
duck
duck′ling
duck′pin′
duck′weed′
duct

duc′tile
duc·til′i·ty
dudg′eon
due
du′el
du′el·ist
du·en′na
du·et′
duf′fel
duff′er
dug
du′gong
dug′out′
duke
duke′dom
dul′cet
dul′ci·mer
dull
dull′ard
dull′er
dull′est
dull′ness
du′ly
dumb
dumb′bell′
dum′my
dump
dump′ing
dump′ling
dun
dunce
dune

dun′ga·ree′
dun′geon
dun′nage
dunned
dupe
du′plex
du′pli·cate
du′pli·cat′ed
du′pli·ca′tion
du′pli·ca′tor
du·plic′i·ty
du′ra·bil′i·ty
du′ra·ble
du·ral′u·min
dur′ance
du·ra′tion
du′ress
dur′ing
dusk′y
dust
dust′ed
dust′er
dust′i·er
dust′i·est
dust′y
du′te·ous
du′ties
du′ti·ful
du′ty
dwarf
dwarf′ish
dwell
dwel′lings
dwelt
dwin′dle
dwin′dled
dy·nam′ic
dy′na·mism
dy′na·mite
dy′na·mit′ed
dy′na·mo
dy′nas·ty
dys′en·ter′y
dys·func′tion
dys·pep′si·a
dys·pep′tic
dys′tro·phy

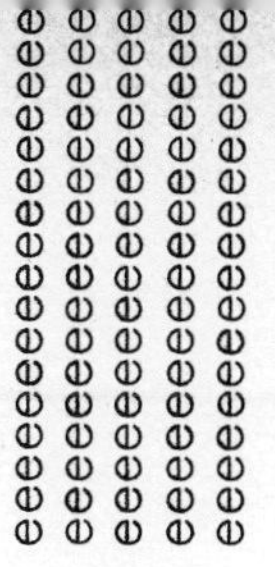

# E

each
ea'ger
ea'ger·ly
ea'ger·ness
ea'gle
ea'glet
ear
earl
earl'dom
ear'li·er
ear'li·est
ear'ly
ear'mark'
earn
earned
earn'er
ear'nest
ear'nest·ly
ear'nest·ness
earn'ings
ear'ring'
ear'rings'
ear'shot'
earth
earth'en
earth'en·ware'
earth'li·ness
earth'ly
earth'men
earth'quake'
earth'ward
earth'work'
earth'worm'
ear'wax'
ear'wig'
ease
eased
ea'sel
ease'ment
eas'i·er
eas'i·est
eas'i·ly
eas'i·ness
east
East'er
east'er·ly
east'ern
east'ern·er
east'ward
east'ward·ly
eas'y
eas'y·go'ing
eat
eat'a·ble
eat'en
eat'er
eaves'drop'
ebb
ebbed
eb'on·ize
eb'on·ized
eb'on·y
e·bul'li·ence
e·bul'li·ent
eb'ul·li'tion
ec·cen'tric

ec′cen·tric′i·ty
ec′chy·mo′sis
ec·cle′si·as′tic
ec·cle′si·as′ti·cal
ech′e·lon
ech′o
ech′oed
é·clair′
é·clat′
ec·lec′tic
ec·lec′ti·cism
e·clipse′
e·col′o·gy
e′co·nom′ic
e′co·nom′i·cal
e′co·nom′i·cal·ly
e·con′o·mist
e·con′o·mize
econ′omized
econ′omy
ec′ru
ec′sta·sy
ec·stat′ic
ec·stat′i·cal·ly
ec′ze·ma
ed′dy
e′del·weiss
e·de′ma
edge
edged
edg′er
edge′ways′
edge′wise′
ed′i·bil′i·ty
ed′i·ble
e′dict
ed′i·fi·ca′tion
ed′i·fice
ed′i·fied
ed′i·fy
ed′it
ed′it·ed
e·di′tion
ed′i·tor
ed′i·to′ri·al
ed′i·to′ri·al·ize
ed′i·to′ri·al·ly
ed′u·ca·ble
ed′u·cate
ed′u·cat′ed
ed′u·ca′tion
ed′u·ca′tion·al
ed′u·ca′tion·al·ly
ed′u·ca′tor
e·duce′
eel
eel′pot′
eel′worm′
ee′rie
ef·face′
ef·face′ment
ef·fect′
ef·fect′ed
ef·fec′tive
ef·fec′tu·al
ef·fec′tu·al·ly
ef·fec′tu·ate
ef·fem′i·na·cy
ef·fem′i·nate
ef′fer·ent
ef′fer·vesce′
ef′fer·ves′cence
ef·fer·ves′cent
ef·fete′
ef′fi·ca′cious
ef′fi·ca·cy
ef·fi′cien·cy
ef·fi′cient
ef′fi·gies
ef′fi·gy
ef′flo·resce′
ef′flo·res′cence
ef′flo·res′cent
ef·flu′vi·a
ef·flu′vi·um
ef′flux
ef′fort
ef′fort·less
ef·fron′ter·y
ef·ful′gence
ef·ful′gent
ef·fu′sion
ef·fu′sive
ef·fu′sive·ly
ef·fu′sive·ness
e·gal′i·tar′i·an

egg′nog′
egg′plant′
egg′shell′
eg′lan·tine
e′go
e′go·cen′tric
e′go·cen·tric′i·ty
e′go·ism
e′go·is′tic
e′go·tism
e′go·tis′tic
e′go·tis′ti·cal
e·gre′gious
e′gress
e′gret
E·gyp′tian
ei′der
ei′ther
e·jac′u·late
e·jac′u·la′tion
e·ject′
e·jec′tion
e·ject′ment
e·jec′tor
e·lab′o·rate
e·lab′o·rate·ly
e·lab′o·ra′tion
e·lapse′
e·lapsed′
e·las′tic
e·las′tic′i·ty
e·lat′ed
e·la′tion
el′bow
el′bowed
el′bow·room′
eld′er
el′der·ber′ry
eld′er·ly
eld′est
e·lect′
e·lect′ed
e·lec′tion
e·lec′tion·eer′
e·lec′tive
e·lec′tor
e·lec′tor·al
e·lec′tor·ate
e·lec′tric
e·lec′tri·cal
e·lec′tri·cal·ly
e·lec′tri′cian
e·lec′tric′i·ty
e·lec′tri·fi·ca′tion
e·lec′tri·fy
e·lec′tro·cute
e·lec′tro·cu′tion
e·lec′trode
e·lec′tro·lier′
e·lec′trol′y·sis
e·lec′tro·lyt′ic
e·lec′tro·lyt′i·cal
e·lec′tro·lyze
e·lec′tro·mag′net
e·lec′trom′e·ter
e·lec′tro·mo′tive
e·lec′tron
e·lec′tron′ic
e·lec′tro·plate′
e·lec′tro·pos′i·tive
e·lec′tro·scope
e·lec′tro·type
e·lec′tro·typ′er
el′ee·mos′y·nar′y
el′e·gance
el′e·gant
el′e·gy
el′e·ment
el′e·men′tal
el′e·men′tal·ly
el′e·men′ta·ry
el′e·phant
el′e·phan·ti′a·sis
el′e·phan′tine
el′e·vate
el′e·vat′ed
el′e·va′tion
el′e·va′tor
elf′in
e·lic′it
e·lic′it·ed
e·lide′
el′i·gi·bil′i·ty
el′i·gi·ble
e·lim′i·nate
e·lim′i·nat′ed

e·lim′i·na′tion
e·lim′i·na′tive
e·li′sion
e·lite′
e·lix′ir
E·liz′a·be′than
elk
el·lip′sis
el·lips′oid
el·lip′tic
el·lip′ti·cal
elm
el′o·cu′tion
el′o·cu′tion·ist
e·lon′gate
e·lon′gat·ed
e·lon′ga′tion
e·lope′
e·lope′ment
el′o·quence
el′o·quent
el′o·quent·ly
else
else′where
else′wise
e·lu′ci·date
e·lu′ci·dat′ed
e·lu′ci·da′tion
e·lude′
e·lud′ed
e·lu′sive
e·lu′sive·ness

e·lu′so·ry
e·ma′ci·ate
e·ma′ci·at′ed
e·ma′ci·a′tion
em′a·nate
em′a·nat′ed
e·man′ci·pate
e·man′ci·pat′ed
e·man′ci·pa′tion
e·man′ci·pa′tor
e·mas′cu·late
e·mas′cu·la′tion
em·balm′
em·balmed′
em·balm′er
em·bank′ment
em·bar′go
em·bar′goed
em·bark′
em′bar·ka′tion
em·bar′rass
em·bar′rassed
em·bar′rass·ment
em′bas·sy
em·bat′tle
em·bat′tled
em·bel′lish
em·bel′lished
em·bel′lish·ment
em′ber
em·bez′zle
em·bez′zled

em·bez′zle·ment
em·bez′zler
em·bit′ter
em·bit′tered
em·bla′zon
em′blem
em′blem·at′ic
em′blem·at′i·cal
em·bod′ied
em·bod′i·ment
em·bod′y
em·bold′en
em·bold′ened
em′bo·lism
em′bo·lus
em·boss′
em·bossed′
em·brace′
em·braced′
em·bra′sure
em′bro·cate
em′bro·ca′tion
em·broi′der
em·broi′dered
em·broi′der·y
em·broil′
em·broiled′
em′bry·o
em′bry·ol′o·gy
em′bry·on′ic
e·mend′
e′men·da′tion

e·mend'ed
em'er·ald
e·merge'
e·merged'
e·mer'gence
e·mer'gen·cy
e·mer'gent
e·mer'i·tus
em'er·y
e·met'ic
em'i·grant
em'i·grate
em'i·grat'ed
em'i·gra'tion
em'i·nence
em'i·nent
em'is·sar'y
e·mis'sion
e·mit'
e·mit'ted
e·mol'li·ent
e·mol'u·ment
e·mo'tion
e·mo'tion·al
e·mo'tion·al·ly
em·pan'el
em'per·or
em'pha·ses
em'pha·sis
em'pha·size
em'pha·sized
em·phat'ic

em·phat'i·cal·ly
em'pire
em·pir'ic
em·pir'i·cal
em·pir'i·cism
em·place'ment
em·ploy'
em·ployed'
em·ploy'ee
em·ploy'er
em·ploy'ment
em·po'ri·um
em·pow'er
em·pow'ered
em'press
emp'tied
emp'ti·ly
emp'ti·ness
emp'ty
em'py·re'an
e'mu
em'u·late
em'u·lat'ed
em'u·lates
em'u·la'tion
em'u·la'tive
em'u·la·to'ry
em'u·lous
e·mul'si·fi·ca'tion
e·mul'si·fi'er
e·mul'si·fy
e·mul'sion

en·a'ble
en·a'bled
en·act'
en·act'ed
en·act'ment
en·am'el
en·am'eled
en·am'ored
en·camp'
en·camp'ment
en·cap'su·late
en·caus'tic
en'ce·phal'ic
en·ceph'a·li'tis
en·chant'
en·chant'ed
en·chant'ing·ly
en·chant'ment
en·cir'cle
en·cir'cled
en·cir'cle·ment
en'clave
en·close'
en·closed'
en·clo'sure
en·co'mi·a
en·co'mi·as'tic
en·co'mi·um
en·com'pass
en·core'
en·coun'ter
en·coun'tered

en·cour′age
en·cour′aged
en·cour′age·ment
en·cour′ag·ing·ly
en·croach′
en·croached′
en·croach′ment
en·cum′ber
en·cum′bered
en·cum′brance
en·cy′cli·cal
en·cy′clo·pe′di·a
en·cy′clo·pe′dic
en·cyst′
en·cyst′ed
end
en·dan′ger
en·dan′gered
en·dear′
en·deared′
en·deav′or
en·deav′ored
end′ed
en·dem′ic
end′ings
en′dive
end′less
end′less·ly
end′long′
en′do·crine
en′do·cri·nol′o·gy
en′do·derm
en·dog′e·nous
en·dorse′
en·dorse′ment
en·dow′
en·dowed′
en·dow′ment
en·due′
en·dued′
en·dur′a·ble
en·dur′ance
en·dure′
en·dured′
en·dur′ing·ly
end′ways
end′wise
en′e·my
en′er·get′ic
en′er·gize
en′er·gized
en′er·vate
en′er·va′tion
en·fee′ble
en·fee′bled
en′fi·lade′
en·fold′
en·force′
en·force′a·ble
en·forced′
en·force′ment
en·forc′er
en·fran′chise
en·fran′chised
en·gage′
en·gaged′
en·gage′ment
en·gag′ing·ly
en·gen′der
en·gen′dered
en′gine
en′gi·neer′
Eng′lish
Eng′lish·man
en·gorge′
en·gorge′ment
en·grain′
en·grained′
en·grave′
en·graved′
en·grav′er
en·gross′
en·grossed′
en·gross′er
en·gulf′
en·hance′
en·hanced′
en·hance′ment
en′har·mon′ic
e·nig′ma
e′nig·mat′ic
e′nig·mat′i·cal
en·join′
en·joined′
en·joy′
en·joy′a·ble

en·joyed'
en·joy'ment
en·large'
en·larged'
en·large'ment
en·larg'er
en·light'en
en·light'ened
en·light'en·ing·ly
en·light'en·ment
en·list'
en·list'ed
en·list'ment
en·liv'en
en·liv'ened
en·mesh'
en'mi·ty
en·no'ble
en·no'bled
e·nor'mi·ty
e·nor'mous
e·nough'
en·rage'
en·raged'
en·rap'ture
en·rap'tured
en·rich'
en·riched'
en·rich'ment
en·roll'
en·rolled'
en·roll'ment

en·shrine'
en·shrined'
en'sign
en'si·lage
en-slave'
en·slave'ment
en·sue'
en·sued'
en·sure'
en·sured'
en·tab'la·ture
en·tail'
en·tailed'
en·tan'gle
en·tan'gled
en·tan'gle·ment
en'ter
en'tered
en'ter·i'tis
en'ter·prise
en'ter·tain'
en'ter·tained'
en'ter·tain'er
en'ter·tain'ing·ly
en'ter·tain'ment
en·thrall'
en·thralled'
en·throne'
en·throned'
en·thu'si·asm
en·thu'si·ast
en·thu'si·as'tic

en·thu'si·as'ti·cal·ly
en·tice'
en·ticed'
en·tice'ment
en·tic'ing·ly
en·tire'
en·tire'ly
en·tire'ty
en·ti'tle
en·ti'tled
en'ti·ty
en·tomb'
en·tombed'
en·tomb'ment
en'to·mol'o·gist
en'to·mol'o·gy
en'trails
en'trance
en·tranc'ing·ly
en'trant
en·trap'
en·treat'
en·treat'ed
en·treat'y
en·trench'
en·trust'
en'try
en'try·way'
en·twine'
e·nu'cle·ate
e·nu'cle·a'tion
e·nu'mer·ate

e·nu′mer·at′ed
e·nu′mer·a′tion
e·nu′mer·a′tor
e·nun′ci·ate
e·nun′ci·at′ed
e·nun′ci·a′tion
e·nun′ci·a′tor
en·vel′op
en′ve·lope
en·ven′om
en′vi·a·ble
en′vi·ous
en·vi′ron·ment
en·vi′ron·men′tal
en·vi′ron·men′tal·ly
en·vi′rons
en·vis′age
en·vis′aged
en′voy
en′voys
en′vy
en′zyme
e′on
e·phem′er·al
ep′ic
ep′i·cure
ep′i·cu·re′an
ep′i·dem′ic
ep′i·der′mal
ep′i·der′mic
ep′i·der′mis
ep′i·der′moid
ep′i·gas′tric
ep′i·glot′tis
ep′i·gram
ep′i·gram·mat′ic
ep′i·graph
ep′i·lep′sy
ep′i·lep′tic
ep′i·lep′toid
ep′i·logue
e·piph′y·sis
e·pis′co·pa·cy
e·pis′co·pal
e·pis′co·pa′li·an
e·pis′co·pate
ep′i·sode
ep′i·sod′ic
e·pis′te·mol′o·gy
e·pis′tle
e·pis′to·lar′y
e·pis′to·la·to′ry
ep′i·taph
ep′i·tha·la′mi·um
ep′i·the′li·um
ep′i·thet
e·pit′o·me
e·pit′o·mize
ep′i·zo·ot′ic
ep′och
ep′och·al
ep′o·nym
ep·ox′y
eq′ua·ble
eq′ua·bly
e′qual
e′qualed
e·qual′i·tar′i·an
e·qual′i·ty
e′qual·i·za′tion
e′qual·ize
e′qual·ized
e′qual·iz′er
e′qual·ly
e′qua·nim′i·ty
e·quate′
e·quat′ed
e·qua′tion
e·qua′tor
e′qua·to′ri·al
eq′uer·ry
e·ques′tri·an
e·ques′tri·enne′
e′qui·an′gu·lar
e′qui·dis′tance
e′qui·dis′tant
e′qui·lat′er·al
e′qui·lib′ri·um
e′quine
e′qui·noc′tial
e′qui·nox
e·quip′
eq′ui·page
e·quip′ment
e′qui·poise
eq′ui·ta·ble

eq′ui·ta′tion
eq′ui·ty
e·quiv′a·lence
e·quiv′a·len·cy
e·quiv′a·lent
e·quiv′o·cal
e·quiv′o·cal·ly
e·quiv′o·cate
e·quiv′o·ca′tion
e′ra
e·rad′i·cate
e·rad′i·cat′ed
e·rad′i·ca′tion
e·rase′
e·rased′
e·ras′er
e·ra′sure
e·rect′
e·rect′ed
e·rec′tile
e·rec′tion
e·rect′ness
erg
er′go
er′got
er′mine
e·rode′
e·ro′sion
e·rot′ic
err
er′rand
er·ra′ta

er·rat′ic
er·rat′i·cal·ly
er·ra′tum
erred
er·ro′ne·ous
er′ror
erst′while′
er′u·dite
er′u·di′tion
e·rupt′
e·rup′tion
e·rup′tive
er′y·sip′e·las
es′ca·lade′
es′ca·la′tor
es′ca·pade′
es·cape′
es·cape′ment
es·cap′ist
es·carp′ment
es·cheat′
es·chew′
es′cort
es·cort′ed
es′cri·toire′
es′crow′
es·cutch′eon
Es′ki·mo
e·soph′a·gus
es′o·ter′ic
es·par′to
es·pe′cial

es·pe′cial·ly
Es′pe·ran′to
es′pi·o·nage
es′pla·nade′
es·pous′al
es·pouse′
es′prit′
es·py′
es·quire′
es·say′
es·sayed′
es′say·ist
es′sence
es·sen′tial
es·sen′tial·ly
es·tab′lish
es·tab′lished
es·tab′lish·ment
es·tate′
es·teem′
es·teemed′
es′ter
es·thet′ic
es′ti·ma·ble
es′ti·mate
es′ti·mat′ed
es′ti·ma′tion
es′ti·ma′tor
es′ti·vate
es·top′pel
es·trange′
es·tranged′

es·trange′ment
es′tu·ar′y
e·su′ri·ent
etch
etch′er
etch′ings
e·ter′nal
e·ter′nal·ly
e·ter′ni·ty
eth′ane
e′ther
e·the′re·al
e·the′re·al·ly
eth′i·cal
eth′ics
eth′nic
eth·nol′o·gy
eth′yl
e′ti·ol′o·gy
et′i·quette
e′tude
et′y·mo·log′i·cal
et′y·mol′o·gy
eu′ca·lyp′tus
Eu′cha·rist
eu′chre
Eu·clid′e·an
eu·gen′ics
eu′lo·gis′tic
eu′lo·gize
eu′lo·gy
eu′phe·mism
eu′phe·mis′tic
eu·pho′ni·ous
eu′pho·ny
Eur·a′sian
eu·re′ka
Eu′ro·pe′an
Eu·sta′chi·an
eu·tec′tic
eu′tha·na′si·a
e·vac′u·ate
e·vac′u·at′ed
e·vac′u·a′tion
e·vade′
e·vad′ed
e·val′u·ate
e·val′u·a′tion
ev′a·nesce′
ev′a·nes′cence
ev′a·nes′cent
e′van·gel′i·cal
e·van′ge·list
e·vap′o·rate
e·vap′o·rat′ed
e·vap′o·ra′tion
e·vap′o·ra′tor
e·va′sion
e·va′sive
e·va′sive·ly
e·va′sive·ness
e′ven
eve′ning
eve′nings
e′ven·ly
e′ven·ness
e·vent′
e·vent′ful
e·vent′ful·ly
e·ven′tu·al
e·ven′tu·al′i·ty
e·ven′tu·al·ly
e·ven′tu·ate
ev′er
ev′er·glade
ev′er·green′
ev′er·last′ing
ev′er·last′ing·ly
ev′er·y
ev′er·y·bod′y
ev′er·y·day′
ev′er·y·one′
ev′er·y·thing′
ev′er·y·where′
e·vict′
e·vict′ed
e·vic′tion
ev′i·dence
ev′i·dent
ev′i·den′tial
ev′i·den′tial·ly
e′vil
e′vil·ly
e·vince′
e·vinced′
e·vis′cer·ate

ev′o·ca′tion
e·voc′a·tive
e·voke′
e·voked′
ev′o·lu′tion
ev′o·lu′tion·ar′y
ev′o·lu′tion·ist
e·volve′
ewe
ew′er
ex·ac′er·bate
ex·ac′er·ba′tion
ex·act′
ex·act′ed
ex·ac′tion
ex·act′i·tude
ex·act′ly
ex·act′ness
ex·ag′ger·ate
ex·ag′ger·at′ed
ex·ag′ger·a′tion
ex·alt′
ex′al·ta′tion
ex·alt′ed
ex·a′men
ex·am′i·na′tion
ex·am′ine
ex·am′ined
ex·am′in·er
ex·am′ple
ex·as′per·ate
ex·as′per·at′ed
ex·as′per·a′tion
ex′ca·vate
ex′ca·vat′ed
ex′ca·va′tion
ex′ca·va′tor
ex·ceed′
ex·ceed′ed
ex·ceed′ing·ly
ex·cel′
ex·celled′
ex′cel·lence
ex′cel·len·cy
ex′cel·lent
ex·cel′si·or
ex·cept′
ex·cept′ed
ex·cep′tion
ex·cep′tion·al
ex·cep′tion·al·ly
ex·cerpt′
ex·cess′
ex·cess′es
ex·ces′sive
ex·ces′sive·ly
ex·change′
ex·change′a·ble
ex·cheq′uer
ex·cip′i·ent
ex′cise
ex·ci′sion
ex·cit′a·bil′i·ty
ex·cit′a·ble
ex·cit′ant
ex′ci·ta′tion
ex·cite′
ex·cit′ed·ly
ex·cite′ment
ex·claim′
ex·claimed′
ex′cla·ma′tion
ex·clam′a·to′ry
ex·clude′
ex·clud′ed
ex·clu′sion
ex·clu′sive
ex′com·mu′ni·cate
ex′com·mu′ni·ca′tion
ex·co′ri·ate
ex·co′ri·at′ed
ex·co′ri·a′tion
ex·cres′cence
ex·cres′cent
ex·crete′
ex·cret′ed
ex·cre′tion
ex′cre·to′ry
ex·cru′ci·ate
ex·cru′ci·at′ing·ly
ex·cru′ci·a′tion
ex′cul·pate
ex′cul·pat′ed
ex′cul·pa′tion
ex·cur′sion
ex·cus′a·ble

ex·cuse′
ex·cused′
ex·cus′es
ex′e·cra·ble
ex′e·crate
ex′e·crat′ed
ex′e·cra′tion
ex·ec′u·tant
ex′e·cute
ex′e·cut′ed
ex′e·cu′tion
ex′e·cu′tion·er
ex·ec′u·tive
ex·ec′u·tor
ex·ec′u·trix
ex′e·ge′sis
ex·em′plar
ex′em·pla·ry
ex·em′pli·fi·ca′tion
ex·em′pli·fy
ex·empt′
ex·empt′ed
ex·emp′tion
ex′e·qua′tur
ex′er·cise
ex′er·cised
ex′er·cis′er
ex·ert′
ex·ert′ed
ex·er′tion
ex′ha·la′tion
ex·hale′
ex·haled′
ex·haust′
ex·haus′tion
ex·haus′tive
ex·haust′less
ex·hib′it
ex·hib′it·ed
ex′hi·bi′tion
ex·hib′i·tor
ex·hil′a·rate
ex·hil′a·rat′ed
ex·hil′a·ra′tion
ex·hort′
ex′hor·ta′tion
ex·hort′ed
ex·hu·ma′tion
ex·hume′
ex·humed′
ex′i·gen·cy
ex′i·gent
ex·ig′u·ous
ex′ile
ex′iled
ex·ist′
ex·ist′ed
ex·ist′ence
ex·ist′ent
ex′it
ex′o·dus
ex·on′er·ate
ex·on′er·at′ed
ex·on′er·a′tion
ex·or′bi·tant
ex·or′bi·tant·ly
ex′or·cise
ex′or·cised
ex′or·cism
ex·or′di·um
ex′o·ter′ic
ex·ot′ic
ex·ot′i·cism
ex·pand′
ex·pand′ed
ex·panse′
ex·pan′sion
ex·pan′sive
ex·pa′ti·ate
ex·pa′ti·at′ed
ex·pa′tri·ate
ex·pa′tri·a′tion
ex·pect′
ex·pect′an·cy
ex·pect′ant
ex′pec·ta′tion
ex·pect′ed
ex·pec′to·rant
ex·pec′to·rate
ex·pec′to·ra′tion
ex·pe′di·en·cy
ex·pe′di·ent
ex′pe·dite
ex′pe·dit′ed
ex′pe·di′tion
ex′pe·di′tion·ar′y

ex′pe·di′tious
ex′pe·di′tious·ly
ex·pel′
ex·pelled′
ex·pend′
ex·pend′ed
ex·pend′i·ture
ex·pense′
ex·pen′sive·ly
ex·pe′ri·ence
ex·pe′ri·enced
ex·pe′ri·enc·es
ex·per′i·ment
ex·per′i·men′tal
ex·per′i·men′tal·ly
ex·per′i·men·ta′tion
ex·per′i·ment·er
ex·pert′
ex·pert′ly
ex·pert′ness
ex′per·tise′
ex′pi·ate
ex′pi·a′tion
ex′pi·ra′tion
ex·pire′
ex·pired′
ex·plain′
ex·plained′
ex′pla·na′tion
ex·plan′a·to′ry
ex′ple·tive
ex′pli·ca·ble

ex′pli·cate
ex·plic′it
ex·plic′it·ly
ex·plode′
ex·plod′ed
ex′ploit
ex′ploi·ta′tion
ex·ploit′ed
ex′plo·ra′tion
ex·plor′a·to′ry
ex·plore′
ex·plored′
ex·plor′er
ex·plor′ing·ly
ex·plo′sion
ex·plo′sive
ex·po′nent
ex′po·nen′tial
ex·port′
ex′por·ta′tion
ex·pose′
ex·posed′
ex′po·si′tion
ex·pos′i·to′ry
ex·pos′tu·late
ex·pos′tu·lat′ed
ex·pos′tu·la′tion
ex·po′sure
ex·pound′
ex·press′
ex·pres′sion
ex·pres′sive

ex·pres′sive·ly
ex·press′ly
ex·press′man
ex·pro′pri·ate
ex·pro′pri·a′tion
ex·pul′sion
ex·punge′
ex·punged′
ex′pur·gate
ex′pur·gat′ed
ex′pur·ga′tion
ex′qui·site
ex′tant
ex·tem′po·ra′ne·ous
ex·tem′po·rar′y
ex·tem′po·re
ex·tem′po·ri·za′tion
ex·tem′po·rize
ex·tend′
ex·tend′ed
ex·ten′si·ble
ex·ten′sion
ex·ten′sive
ex·tent′
ex·ten′u·ate
ex·ten′u·at′ed
ex·ten′u·a′tion
ex·te′ri·or
ex·ter′mi·nate
ex·ter′mi·nat′ed
ex·ter′mi·na′tion
ex·ter′mi·na′tor

ex·ter′nal
ex·ter′nal·i·za′tion
ex·ter′nal·ly
ex·tinct′
ex·tinc′tion
ex·tin′guish
ex·tin′guished
ex·tin′guish·er
ex′tir·pate
ex′tir·pat′ed
ex′tir·pa′tion
ex·tol′
ex·tolled′
ex·tort′
ex·tort′ed
ex·tor′tion
ex·tor′tion·ate
ex′tra
ex·tract′
ex·tract′ed
ex·trac′tion
ex·trac′tive
ex′tra·cur·ric′u·lar
ex′tra·dite
ex′tra·dit′ed
ex′tra·di′tion
ex·tra′ne·ous
ex·traor′di·nar′i·ly
ex·traor′di·nar′y
ex·trap′o·late
ex′tra·ter′ri·to′ri·al′i·ty
ex·trav′a·gance
ex·trav′a·gant
ex·trav′a·gan′za
ex·trav′a·sate
ex·trav′a·sa′tion
ex·treme′
ex·trem′ist
ex·trem′i·ty
ex′tri·cate
ex′tri·cat′ed
ex′tri·ca′tion
ex·trin′sic
ex′tro·ver′sion
ex′tro·vert′
ex·trude′
ex·trud′ed
ex·tru′sion
ex·u′ber·ance
ex·u′ber·ant
ex′u·date
ex′u·da′tion
ex·ude′
ex·ud′ed
ex·ult′
ex·ult′ant
ex′ul·ta′tion
ex·ult′ed
ex·ult′ing·ly
eye
eye′ball′
eye′brow′
eye′cup′
eyed
eye′lash′
eye′let
eye′lid′
eye′piece′
eyes
eye′shot′
eye′sight′
eye′strain′
eye′tooth′
eye′wash′
eye′wit′ness

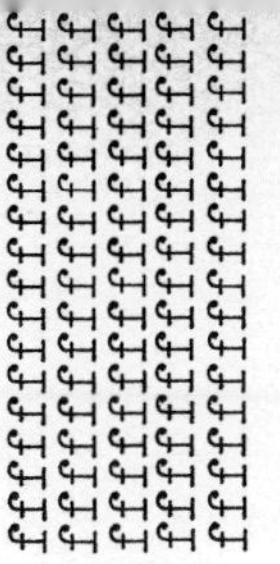

Fa′bi·an
fa′ble
fa′bled
fab′ric
fab′ri·cate
fab′ri·cat′ed
fab′ri·ca′tion
fab′u·lous
fa·çade′
face
faced
fac′et
fa·ce′tious
fa′cial
fac′ile
fa·cil′i·tate
fa·cil′i·tat′ed
fa·cil′i·ty
fac′ings
fac·sim′i·le
fact
fac′tion
fac′tion·al
fac′tious
fac·ti′tious
fac′tor
fac′to·ry
fac·to′tum
fac′tu·al
fac′tu·al·ly
fac′ul·ta′tive
fac′ul·ty
fad′dist
fade
fad′ed
fad′ing·ly
Fahr′en·heit
fail
failed
fail′ing·ly
fail′ings
faille
fail′ure
faint
faint′ed
faint′heart′ed
faint′ly
faint′ness
fair
fair′er
fair′est
fair′ly
fair′ness
fair′way′
fair′y
fair′y·land′
faith
faith′ful
faith′less
faith′less·ly
fake
fak′er
fal′con
fall
fal·la′cious
fal′la·cy

fall'en
fal'li·bil'i·ty
fal'li·ble
fall'out
false
false'hood
false'ly
false'ness
fal·set'to
fal'si·fi·ca'tion
fal'si·fi'er
fal'si·fy
fal'si·ty
fal'ter
fal'tered
fal'ter·ing·ly
fame
famed
fa·mil'ial
fa·mil'iar
fa·mil'i·ar'i·ty
fa·mil'iar·ize
fa·mil'iar·ly
fam'i·lies
fam'i·ly
fam'ine
fam'ish
fa'mous
fa'mous·ly
fan
fa·nat'ic
fa·nat'i·cal
fa·nat'i·cism
fan'cied
fan'ci·er
fan'ci·est
fan'ci·ful
fan'cy
fan'fare
fang
fanged
fan'light'
fanned
fan'tail'
fan·ta'sia
fan·tas'tic
fan'ta·sy
far
far'ad
farce
far'cial
far'ci·cal
far'cy
fare
fared
fare'well'
far'fetched'
fa·ri'na
far'i·na'ceous
farm
farmed
farm'er
farm'house'
farm'yard'
far'o
far'ri·er
far'see'ing
far'sight'ed
far'ther
far'thest
far'thing
fas'ci·nate
fas'ci·nat'ed
fas'ci·na'tion
fas'ci·nat'ing·ly
fas'ci·na'tor
fas'cism
fas'cist
fash'ion
fash'ion·a·ble
fash'ioned
fast
fas'ten
fas'tened
fas'ten·ings
fast'er
fast'est
fas·tid'i·ous
fast'ness
fat
fa'tal
fa'tal·ism
fa'tal·ist
fa'tal·is'tic
fa'tal'i·ty
fa'tal·ly

fate
fat'ed
fate'ful
fa'ther
fa'thered
fa'ther·hood
fa'ther-in-law'
fa'ther·land'
fa'ther·less
fa'ther·li·ness
fa'ther·ly
fath'om
fath'omed
fath'om·less
fa·tigue'
fat'ness
fat'ten
fat'tened
fat'ter
fat'test
fat'ty
fa·tu'i·ty
fat'u·ous
fau'cet
fault
fault'i·ly
fault'less
fault'less·ly
fault'y
fau'na
fa'vor
fa'vor·a·ble
fa'vored
fa'vor·ite
fa'vor·it·ism
fawn
fawned
fe'al·ty
fear
feared
fear'ful
fear'less
fear'less·ly
fear'some
fea'si·bil'i·ty
fea'si·ble
feast
feat
feath'er
feath'ered
feath'er·edge'
feath'er·weight'
feath'er·y
fea'ture
fea'tured
fe'brile
Feb'ru·ar'y
fe'cund
fe'cun·date
fe·cun'di·ty
fed'er·al
fed'er·al·ism
fed'er·al·ist
fed'er·al·i·za'tion
fed'er·al·ize
fed'er·al·ized
fed'er·ate
fed'er·at'ed
fed'er·a'tion
fed'er·a'tive
fe·do'ra
fee
fee'ble
fee'ble·ness
fee'blest
fee'bly
feed
feed'-back'
feed'ings
feel
feel'er
feel'ing·ly
feel'ings
feer
feered
feet
feign
feigned
feint
feld'spar'
fe·lic'i·tate
fe·lic'i·tat'ed
fe·lic'i·ta'tion
fe·lic'i·tous
fe·lic'i·tous·ly
fe·lic'i·ty

fe'line
fel'low
fel'low·ship
fel'on
fe·lo'ni·ous
fel'o·ny
felt
fe·luc'ca
fe'male
fem'i·nine
fem'i·nin'i·ty
fem'i·nism
fem'i·nist
fem'o·ral
fe'mur
fen
fence
fenc'er
fend
fend'ed
fend'er
fe·nes'trat·ed
fen'es·tra'tion
Fe'ni·an
fen'nel
fe'ral
fer·ment'
fer'men·ta'tion
fer·ment'ed
fern
fe·ro'cious
fe·ro'cious·ly
fe·roc'i·ty
fer'ret
fer'ret·ed
fer'ric
fer'ro·chrome
fer'ro·type
fer'rous
fer'rule
fer'ry
fer'ry·boat'
fer'tile
fer·til'i·ty
fer'ti·li·za'tion
fer'ti·lize
fer'ti·lized
fer'ti·liz'er
fer'ule
fer'vent
fer'vent·ly
fer'vid
fer'vid·ly
fer'vor
fes'cue
fes'tal
fes'ter
fes'tered
fes'ti·val
fes'tive
fes·tiv'i·ty
fes·toon'
fes·tooned'
fetch
fet'id
fe'tish
fe'tish·ism
fet'lock
fet'ter
fet'tered
fet'tle
feud
feu'dal
feu'dal·ism
feu'da·to'ry
fe'ver
fe'ver·ish
fe'ver·ish·ly
few
few'er
few'est
fez
fi·as'co
fi'at
fib
fi'ber
fi'broid
fib'u·la
fick'le
fic'tion
fic'tion·al
fic·ti'tious
fid'dle
fid'dled
fid'dler
fi·del'i·ty

fidg'et
fi·du'ci·ar'y
fief
field
field'ed
field'piece'
fiend
fiend'ish
fiend'ish·ly
fierce
fierce'ness
fierc'er
fierc'est
fi'er·y
fife
fig
fight
fig'ment
fig'u·ra'tion
fig'ur·a·tive
fig'ur·a·tive·ly
fig'ure
fig'ured
fig'ure·head'
fig'u·rine'
fil'a·ment
fil'a·ri'a·sis
fil'a·ture
fil'bert
filch
filched
file

filed
fil'i·al
fil'i·bus'ter
fil'i·gree
fil'ings
fill
filled
fill'er
fil'let
fill'ings
film
filmed
film'strip
fil'ter
fil'tered
filth
filth'i·er
filth'i·est
filth'i·ness
filth'y
fil'trate
fil·tra'tion
fin
fi'nal
fi'nal·ist
fi·nal'i·ty
fi'nal·ly
fi·nance'
fi·nan'cial
fi·nan'cial·ly
fin'an·cier'
finch

find
find'er
find'ings
fine
fined
fine'ly
fine'ness
fin'er
fin'er·y
fine'spun'
fi·nesse'
fin'est
fin'ger
fin'gered
fin'ger·print'
fin'i·al
fi'nis
fin'ish
fin'ished
fin'ish·er
fi'nite
fiord
fir
fire
fire'arm'
fire'boat'
fire'box'
fire'brand'
fire'break'
fire'brick'
fired
fire'fly'

fire′man
fire′place′
fire′proof′
fire′side′
fire′weed′
fire′wood′
fire′works′
fir′kin
firm
fir′ma·ment
firm′er
firm′est
firm′ly
firm′ness
first
first′ly
firth
fis′cal
fish
fish′er·man
fish′er·y
fish′hook′
fish′wife′
fish′y
fis′sile
fis′sion
fis′sure
fist
fist′ic
fist′i·cuffs
fis′tu·la
fit

fit′ful
fit′ful·ly
fit′ness
fit′ted
fit′ter
fit′ting·ly
fit′tings
fix
fix·a′tion
fix′a·tive
fixed
fix′er
fix′ings
fix′i·ty
fix′ture
fiz′zle
fiz′zled
flab′bi·er
flab′bi·est
flab′bi·ness
flab′by
flac′cid
flag
flag′el·lant
flag′el·late
flag′el·la′tion
flag′eo·let′
flag′eo·lets′
fla·gi′tious
flag′on
flag′pole′
fla′grance

fla′grant
fla′grant·ly
flag′ship′
flag′staff′
flag′stone′
flail
flailed
flair
flake
flak′i·ness
flak′y
flam′beau
flam·boy′ant
flame
flamed
fla·men′co
flame′proof′
flam′ing·ly
fla·min′go
flan
flange
flanged
flank
flanked
flan′nel
flan′nel·ette′
flap
flap′jack′
flare
flare′back′
flared
flash

flash'board'
flash'er
flash'i·ly
flash'i·ness
flash'ing·ly
flash'light'
flash'y
flask
flat
flat'-bed'
flat'boat'
flat'fish'
flat'-foot'ed
flat'head'
flat'i'ron
flat'ly
flat'ness
flat'ten
flat'tened
flat'ter
flat'tered
flat'ter·er
flat'ter·ing·ly
flat'ter·y
flat'test
flat'u·lence
flat'u·lent
flat'ware'
flat'wise'
flat'work'
flat'worm'
flaunt

flaunt'ed
flaunt'ing·ly
flau'tist
fla'vor
fla'vored
fla'vor·ings
fla'vors
flaw
flawed
flax
flax'en
flax'seed'
flay
flea
flea'bite'
fleck
fledge
fledg'ling
flee
fleece
fleeced
fleec'i·ness
fleec'y
fleet
fleet'ing·ly
Flem'ish
flesh
flesh'i·ness
flesh'ings
flesh'pot'
flesh'y
Fletch'er·ism

fleur'-de-lis'
flew
flex
flexed
flex'i·bil'i·ty
flex'i·ble
flex'ure
flick
flicked
flick'er
flick'er·ing·ly
fli'er
flight
flight'i·ness
flight'y
flim'si·er
flim'si·est
flim'si·ly
flim'si·ness
flim'sy
flinch
flinched
flinch'ing·ly
fling
flint
flint'i·ness
flint'lock'
flint'y
flip'pan·cy
flip'pant
flip'pant·ly
flip'per

flirt
flir·ta′tion
flir·ta′tious
flirt′ed
flit
flitch
fliv′ver
float
float′ed
float′er
floc′cu·lence
floc′cu·lent
flock
floe
flog
flogged
flog′gings
flood
flood′ed
flood′gate′
flood′light′
flood′wa′ter
floor
floor′walk′er
flop′pi·ness
flop′py
flo′ral
Flor′en·tine
flo′ret
flo′ri·cul′ture
flor′id
flo·rid′i·ty
flor′id·ly
flor′in
flo′rist
floss
floss′i·er
floss′i·est
floss′y
flo·ta′tion
flo·til′la
flot′sam
flounce
floun′der
floun′dered
floun′der·ing·ly
flour
flour′ish
flour′ish·ing·ly
flour′y
flout
flout′ed
flow
flowed
flow′er
flow′ered
flow′er·i·ness
flow′er·pot′
flow′er·y
flow′ing·ly
flown
fluc′tu·ate
fluc′tu·at′ed
fluc′tu·a′tion
flue
flu′en·cy
flu′ent
flu′ent·ly
fluff
fluff′i·ness
fluff′y
flu′id
flu′id·ly
flu′id·ex′tract
flu·id′i·ty
fluke
flume
flung
flunk
flunked
flunk′y
flu′o·res′cence
flu′o·res′cent
flu·or′ic
flu′o·ri·date
flu′o·ri·da′tion
flu′o·ride
flu′o·ri·nate
flu′o·rine
flu′o·ro·scope
flu′or·os′co·py
flur′ry
flush
flushed
flus′ter
flus′tered

flute
flut'ed
flut'ings
flut'ist
flut'ter
flut'tered
flut'ter·ing·ly
flut'ter·y
flux
flux'ion
fly
fly'er
fly'leaf'
fly'trap'
fly'wheel'
foal
foaled
foam
foamed
foam'i·er
foam'i·est
foam'i·ness
foam'y
fob
fobbed
fo'cal
fo'cal·i·za'tion
fo'cal·ize
fo'cal·ized
fo'cus
fo'cused
fod'der

foe
foe'man
fog
fog'gi·er
fog'gi·est
fog'gy
fog'horn'
foi'ble
foil
foiled
foist
foist'ed
fold
fold'ed
fold'er
fo'li·age
fo'li·ate
fo'li·a'tion
fo'li·o
folk
folk'way'
fol'li·cle
fol·lic'u·lar
fol'low
fol'lowed
fol'low·er
fol'ly
fo·ment'
fo'men·ta'tion
fo·ment'ed
fond
fon'dant

fond'er
fond'est
fon'dle
fon'dled
fond'ly
fond'ness
fon·due'
font
food
fool
fooled
fool'har'di·ness
fool'har'dy
fool'ish
fool'ish·ly
fool'ish·ness
fool'proof'
fools'cap'
foot
foot'age
foot'ball'
foot'board'
foot'bridge'
foot'ed
foot'fall'
foot'gear'
foot'hill'
foot'hold'
foot'ings
foot'less
foot'lights'
foot'-loose'

foot′man
foot′mark′
foot′note′
foot′pace′
foot′pad′
foot′path′
foot′print′
foot′rest′
foot′sore′
foot′step′
foot′stool′
foot′wear′
foot′work′
foot′worn′
foo′zle
foo′zled
fop′per·y
fop′pish
for
for′age
fo·ra′men
for′as·much′
for′ay
for·bear′
for·bear′ance
for·bid′
for·bid′den
for·bid′ding·ly
force
force′ful
force′meat′
for′ceps
for′ci·ble
ford
ford′ed
fore′arm′
fore′bear
fore·bode′
fore·bod′ing·ly
fore·bod′ings
fore·bore′
fore-cast′
fore′cas·tle
fore·close′
fore·closed′
fore·clo′sure
fore′deck′
fore·doom′
fore·doomed′
fore′fa′ther
fore′fin′ger
fore′foot′
fore′front′
fore·gone′
fore′ground′
fore′hand′ed
fore′head
for′eign
for′eign·er
for′eign·ism
fore·knowl′edge
fore′leg′
fore′lock′
fore′man
fore′mast′
fore′most
fore′name′
fore′noon′
fo·ren′sic
fore′or·dain′
fore′or·dained′
fore′quar′ter
fore·run′ner
fore·saw′
fore·see′
fore·see′ing·ly
fore·shad′ow
fore′shore′
fore·short′en
fore′sight′
fore′sight′ed·ness
for′est
fore·stall′
fore·stalled′
for′est·a′tion
for′est·ed
for′est·er
for′est·ry
fore·taste′
fore·tell′
fore′thought′
fore·told′
for·ev′er
fore·warn′
fore·warned′
fore′wom′an

fore'word'
for'feit
for'feit·ed
for'fei·ture
for·gath'er
for·gave'
forge
forged
for'ger
for'ger·y
for·get'
for·get'ful
for·get'ful·ly
for·get'ful·ness
for·give'
for·giv'en
for·give'ness
for·giv'ing·ly
for·go'
for·got'
for·got'ten
fork
forked
for·lorn'
form
for'mal
form·al'de·hyde
for'mal·ism
for·mal'i·ty
for'mal·i·za'tion
for'mal·ize
for'mal·ly
for'mat
for·ma'tion
form'a·tive
formed
form'er
for'mer·ly
for'mic
for'mi·da·ble
form'less
for'mu·la
for'mu·lar'y
for'mu·late
for'mu·lat'ed
for'mu·la'tion
for·sake'
for·sak'en
for·sook'
for·sooth'
for·swear'
for·syth'i·a
fort
for'ta·lice
forte
for'te
forth
forth'com'ing
forth'right'
forth'right'ness
forth'with'
for'ti·fi·ca'tion
for'ti·fy
for·tis'si·mo
for'ti·tude
fort'night
fort'night·ly
For'tran
for·tu'i·tous
for·tu'i·ty
for'tu·nate
for'tune
for'tune·tell'er
fo'rum
for'ward
for'ward·ed
for'ward·er
for'ward·ness
fos'sil
fos'sil·if'er·ous
fos'sil·i·za'tion
fos'sil·ize
fos'sil·ized
fos'ter
fos'tered
fought
foul
fou·lard'
foul'er
foul'est
foul'ly
foul'ness
found
foun·da'tion
found'ed
found'er

found′ling
found′lings
found′ry
fount
foun′tain
foun′tain·head′
four′some
four′square′
fourth
fowl
fox
foxes
fox′glove′
fox′i·er
fox′i·est
fox′y
fra′cas
frac′tion
frac′tion·al
frac′tion·al·ly
frac′tion·ate
frac′tion·a′tion
frac′tious
frac′ture
frac′tured
frag′ile
frag′ile·ly
fra·gil′i·ty
frag′ment
frag′men·tar′i·ly
frag′men·tar′y
frag′men·ta′tion
frag′ment·ed
fra′grance
fra′grant
fra′grant·ly
frail
frail′er
frail′est
frail′ty
frame
framed
frame′work′
franc
fran′chise
Fran·cis′can
frank
frank′er
frank′est
frank′furt·er
frank′ly
frank′ness
fran′tic
frap′pé′
fra·ter′nal
fra·ter′nal·ly
fra·ter′ni·ty
frat′er·ni·za′tion
frat′er·nize
frat′er·nized
frat′ri·cid′al
frat′ri·cide
fraud
fraud′u·lent
fraught
fray
fraz′zle
fraz′zled
freak
freak′ish
freck′le
freck′led
free
free′board′
free′born′
free′dom
free′hand′
free′hold′
free′ly
free′man
free′ma′son
free′ma′son·ry
fre′er
fre′est
free′stone′
free′think′er
free′wheel′ing
freeze
freez′er
freight
freight′er
French
fren′zied
fren′zy
fre′quen·cy
fre′quent

fre'quent·ly
fres'co
fresh
fresh'en
fresh'en·er
fresh'er
fresh'est
fresh'ly
fresh'man
fresh'ness
fret
fret'ful
fret'ted
fret'work'
fri'a·bil'i·ty
fri'a·ble
fri'ar
fric'as·see'
fric'tion
fric'tion·al
Fri'day
fried
friend
friend'less
friend'li·er
friend'li·est
friend'li·ness
friend'ly
friend'ship
frieze
frig'ate
fright

fright'en
fright'ened
fright'en·ing·ly
fright'ful
fright'ful·ly
fright'ful·ness
frig'id
Frig'id·aire'
fri·gid'i·ty
frig'id·ly
frill
frilled
frill'i·ness
frill'y
fringe
fringed
frip'per·y
frisk
frit'ter
frit'tered
fri·vol'i·ty
friv'o·lous
friv'o·lous·ly
friz'zi·ness
friz'zle
friz'zled
frock
frog
frog'fish'
frol'ic
frol'icked
from

frond
frond'ed
front
front'age
fron'tal
front'ed
fron·tier'
fron'tis·piece
frost
frost'bite'
frost'ed
frost'fish'
frost'i·er
frost'i·est
frost'i·ly
frost'i·ness
frost'work'
frost'y
froth
frothed
froth'y
fro'ward
frown
frowned
frown'ing·ly
frowz'i·ly
frowz'y
froze
fro'zen
fruc·tif'er·ous
fruc'ti·fy
fru'gal

fru·gal′i·ty
fru′gal·ly
fruit
fruit′er·er
fruit′ful
fruit′ful·ly
fruit′i·ness
fru·i′tion
fruit′less
fruit′less·ly
fruit′less·ness
fruit′worm′
fruit′y
frump
frus′trate
frus·tra′tion
fry
fry′er
fuch′sia
fud′dle
fud′dled
fudge
fu′el
fu′eled
fu·ga′cious
fu′gi·tive
fugue
ful′crum
ful·fill′
ful·filled′
ful·fill′ment
full
full′er
full′est
full′ness
ful′ly
ful′mi·nate
ful′mi·nat′ed
ful′mi·na′tion
ful′some
fum′ble
fum′bling
fume
fumed
fu′mi·gate
fu′mi·gat′ed
fu′mi·ga′tion
fu′mi·ga′tor
fun
func′tion
func′tion·al
func′tion·al·ly
func′tion·ar′y
fund
fun′da·men′tal
fun′da·men′tal·ly
fund′ed
fu′ner·al
fu·ne′re·al
fu·ne′re·al·ly
fun′gi
fun′gi·ble
fun′gi·cide
fun′goid
fun′gus
fu·nic′u·lar
fun′nel
fun′ni·er
fun′ni·est
fun′ny
fur
fur′be·low
fur′bish
fu′ri·ous
fu′ri·ous·ly
furl
furled
fur′long
fur′lough
fur′loughed
fur′nace
fur′nish
fur′nished
fur′nish·ings
fur′ni·ture
fu′ror
fur′ri·er
fur′ri·est
fur′row
fur′rowed
fur′ry
fur′ther
fur′ther·ance
fur′ther·more′
fur′thest
fur′tive

fur'tive·ly
fu'run·cle
fu'ry
furze
fuse
fused
fu'sel
fu'se·lage
fus'es
fu'si·bil'i·ty
fu'si·ble
fu'sil·lade'
fu'sion
fuss
fussed
fuss'i·er
fuss'y
fus'tian
fu'tile
fu'tile·ly
fu·til'i·ty
fu'ture
fu'tur·is'tic
fu·tu'ri·ty
fuzz
fuzz'i·ly
fuzz'i·ness

# G

gab'ar·dine'
ga'ble
gad'fly'
gad'o·lin'i·um
ga·droon'
gaff
gag
gage
gagged
gag'gle
gai'e·ty
gai'ly
gain
gained
gain'er
gain'ful
gain'ful·ly
gain'say'
gait'ed
gai'ter
ga'la
gal'an·tine

gal'ax·y
gale
ga·le'na
gall
gal'lant
gal'lant·ry
galled
gal'ler·y
gal'ley
Gal'lic
gall'ing·ly
gal'li·um
gal'lon
gal'lop
gal'lows
gall'stone'
ga·lore'
gal'va·nism
gal'va·ni·za'tion
gal'va·nize
gal'va·nized
gal'va·nom'e·ter

gam'bit
gam'ble
gam'bled
gam'bler
gam·boge'
gam'bol
gam'brel
game
game'ness
gam'mon
gam'ut
gan'der
gang
ganged
gan'gli·a
gan'gli·on
gang'plank'
gan'grene
gan'gre·nous
gang'ster
gang'way'
gan'try

gap
gaped
ga·rage'
garb
gar'bage
gar'ble
gar'den
gar'den·er
gar·de'ni·a
gar'gle
gar'goyle
gar'ish
gar'land
gar'lic
gar'ment
gar'ner
gar'nered
gar'net
gar'nish
gar'nished
gar'nish·ee'
gar'nish·er
gar'nish·ment
gar'ni·ture
gar'ret
gar'ri·son
gar'ri·soned
gar'ru·lous
gar'ter
gas
gas'e·ous
gash

gashed
gas'house'
gas'ket
gas'o·line
gasp
gas'tight'
gas·tral'gi·a
gas'tric
gas·tri'tis
gas'tro·nom'ic
gas·tron'o·my
gate
gate'house'
gate'post'
gate'way'
gath'er
gath'ered
gath'er·er
gau'che·rie'
gaud'i·er
gaud'i·est
gaud'y
gauge
gauged
gaunt'let
gauze
gave
gav'el
ga·votte'
gawk'y
gay
gay'e·ty

gay'ly
gay'ness
gaze
ga·ze'bo
ga·zelle'
ga·zette'
ga·zet'ted
gaz'et·teer'
gear
geared
gear'shift'
gei'sha
gel'a·tin
ge·lat'i·nize
ge·lat'i·noid
ge·lat'i·nous
gem
gen'der
gen'e·a·log'i·cal
gen'e·al'o·gist
gen'e·al'o·gy
gen'er·al
gen'er·al·is'si·mo
gen'er·al·ist
gen'er·al'i·ty
gen'er·al·i·za'tion
gen'er·al·ize
gen'er·al·ized
gen'er·al·ly
gen'er·al·ship'
gen'er·ate
gen'er·at'ed

gen′er·a′tion
gen′er·a′tive
gen′er·a′tor
ge·ner′ic
gen′er·os′i·ty
gen′er·ous
gen′er·ous·ly
gen′e·sis
ge·net′ics
ge·ni′al
ge′ni·al′i·ty
gen′ial·ly
gen′i·tive
gen′ius
gen·teel′
gen·teel′ly
gen′tian
gen′tile
gen·til′i·ty
gen′tle
gen′tle·man
gen′tle·men
gen′tle·ness
gen′tler
gen′tlest
gen′tly
gen′try
gen′u·flect
gen′u·flec′tion
gen′u·ine
gen′u·ine·ly
gen′u·ine·ness

ge′nus
ge·od′e·sy
ge′o·det′ic
ge·og′ra·pher
ge·og′ra·phy
ge′o·log′i·cal
ge·ol′o·gist
ge·ol′o·gy
ge′o·met′ric
ge′o·met′ri·cal
ge·om′e·try
ge·ra′ni·um
ge′rent
ger′i·a·tri′cian
ger′i·at′rics
germ
Ger′man
ger·mane′
ger′mi·cide
ger′mi·nal
ger′mi·nant
ger′mi·nate
ger′mi·nat′ed
ger′mi·na′tion
ger′mi·na′tive
ger′und
ge·run′di·al
ge·run′dive
ges′so
Ge·stalt′
ges·tic′u·late
ges·tic′u·la′tion

ges′ture
ges′tured
get
gew′gaw
gey′ser
ghast′li·ness
ghast′ly
gher′kin
ghet′to
ghost
ghost′li·ness
ghost′ly
ghoul
gi′ant
gi′ant·ism
gib′ber
gib′ber·ish
gib′bet
gib′bon
gibe
gib′let
gid′di·ly
gid′di·ness
gid′dy
gift
gift′ed
gig
gi·gan′tic
gi·gan′ti·cal·ly
gi·gan′tism
gig′gle
gig′gled

gild
gild′ed
gild′er
gill
gill
gilt
gim′bals
gim′crack′
gim′let
gin
gin′ger
gin′ger·ly
ging′ham
gin′gi·vi′tis
gi·raffe′
gir′an·dole
gird
gird′er
gir′dle
gir′dled
gir′dler
girl
girl′hood
girl′ish
girt
girth
gist
give
giv′en
giv′er
giz′zard
gla′cial
gla′cier
glad
glad′den
glad′dened
glade
glad′i·a′tor
glad′i·a·to′ri·al
glad′i·o′lus
glad′ly
glad′ness
Glad′stone
glam′or·ous
glam′our
glance
gland
glan′dered
glan′ders
glan′du·lar
glare
glared
glar′ing·ly
glass
glass′ful
glass′house′
glass′i·ly
glass′i·ness
glass′ware′
glass′y
glau·co′ma
glaze
glazed
gla′zier
gleam
gleamed
glean
glean′er
glean′ings
glee′ful
glib
glib′ly
glide
glid′ed
glid′er
glim′mer
glim′mered
glim′mer·ings
glimpse
glimpsed
glint
glint′ed
gli·o′ma
glis·san′do
glis′ten
glis′tened
glis′ter
glit′ter
glit′tered
gloat
gloat′ed
glob′al
glob′al·ly
globe
glob′u·lar
glob′ule

glock'en·spiel'
gloom
gloom'i·ly
gloom'i·ness
glo'ri·fi·ca'tion
glo'ri·fy
glo'ri·ous
glo'ry
gloss
glos'sal
glos'sa·ry
gloss'i·ly
gloss'i·ness
glos·si'tis
gloss'y
glot'tis
glove
glov'er
glow
glowed
glow'er
glow'ered
glow'ing·ly
glow'worm'
glu·ci'num
glu'cose
glue
glued
glue'y
glum
glut
glut'ted
glut'ton
glut'ton·ize
glut'ton·ous
glut'ton·y
glyc'er·in
gnarl
gnarled
gnash
gnashed
gnat
gnath'ic
gnaw
gnawed
gnaw'ings
gneiss
gnome
gno'mic
gno'mon
gnu
go
goad
goal
goat
goat'fish'
goat'herd'
goat'skin'
goat'weed'
gob'ble
gob'bled
gob'let
gob'lin
go'cart'
god
god'child'
god'dess
god'fa'ther
god'head
god'hood
god'less
god'like'
god'li·ness
god'ly
god'moth'er
god'par'ent
god'send'
god'son'
gog'gle
go'ings
goi'ter
gold
gold'en
gold'en·rod'
gold'finch'
gold'smith'
gold'weed'
golf
golf'er
gon'do·la
gon'do·lier'
gone
gong
goo'ber
good
good'-by'

good'ly
good'-na'tured
good'ness
goose
goose'ber'ry
goose'neck'
go'pher
Gor'di·an
gore
gored
gorge
gorged
gor'geous
gor'get
gor'gon
go·ril'la
gos'hawk'
gos'ling
gos'pel
gos'sa·mer
gos'sip
got
Goth'ic
got'ten
gouache
gouge
gouged
gou'lash
gourd
gour'mand
gour'met
gout
gov'ern
gov'ern·ance
gov'erned
gov'ern·ess
gov'ern·ment
gov'ern·men'tal
gov'er·nor
gown
grab
grabbed
grace
grace'ful
grace'less
gra'cious
gra'cious·ly
grack'le
gra·da'tion
grade
grad'ed
gra'di·ent
grad'u·al
grad'u·al·ly
grad'u·ate
grad'u·at'ed
grad'u·a'tion
graf·fi'ti
graft'ed
graft'er
grail
grain
grained
grain'field'
gram'mar
gram·mar'i·an
gram·mat'i·cal
gram·mat'i·cal·ly
gram'pus
gran'a·ry
grand
grand'child'
gran·dee'
gran'deur
grand'fa'ther
gran·dil'o·quence
gran·dil'o·quent
gran'di·ose
grand'ly
grand'moth'er
grand'ness
grand'par'ent
grand'sire'
grand'son'
grand'stand'
grange
gran'ite
gran'it·oid
gra·niv'o·rous
grant
grant'ed
gran'u·lar
gran'u·late
gran'u·lat'ed
gran'u·la'tion
gran'ule

grape
grape′shot′
graph
graph′ic
graph′ics
graph′ite
grap′nel
grap′ple
grap′pled
grasp
grasp′ing·ly
grass
grass′hop′per
grass′plot′
grate
grat′ed
grate′ful
grat′er
grat′i·fi·ca′tion
grat′i·fy
grat′i·fy′ing·ly
grat′i·nate
grat′ings
gra′tis
grat′i·tude
gra·tu′i·tous
gra·tu′i·ty
gra·va′men
grave
grave′dig′ger
grav′el
grav′el·ly
grav′en
grav′er
grav′est
grave′stone′
grave′yard′
grav′i·tate
grav′i·tat′ed
grav′i·ta′tion
grav′i·ta′tion·al
grav′i·ty
gra·vure′
gra′vy
gray
gray′beard′
gray′ish
gray′ness
graze
grazed
gra′zier
grease
greased
grease′wood′
greas′i·er
greas′i·est
greas′i·ly
greas′i·ness
greas′y
great
great′er
great′est
great′ly
great′ness
greed
greed′i·er
greed′i·est
greed′i·ly
greed′i·ness
greed′y
Greek
green
green′back′
green′er
green′er·y
green′est
green′horn′
green′house′
green′ish
green′ness
green′room′
green′stick′
green′sward′
green′wood′
greet
greet′ed
greet′ings
gre·gar′i·ous
Gre·go′ri·an
gre·nade′
gren′a·dier′
gren′a·dine′
grew
grey′hound′
grid
grid′dle

grid′i′ron
grief
griev′ance
grieve
grieved
griev′ous
griev′ous·ly
grif′fin
grill
grilled
grim
gri·mace′
grime
grim′i·er
grim′i·est
grim′i·ly
grim′i·ness
grim′y
grin
grind
grind′er
grind′ing·ly
grind′stone′
grinned
grip
gripe
grip′per
gris′ly
grist
gris′tle
grist′mill′
grit

grit′ti·ness
grit′ty
griz′zle
griz′zled
griz′zly
groan
groaned
groan′ing·ly
gro′cer
gro′cer·y
grog
grog′gy
groin
grom′met
groom
groomed
groove
grooved
grope
grop′ing·ly
gros′beak′
gros′grain′
gross
gross′er
gross′est
gross′ly
gross′ness
gro·tesque′
gro·tesque′ly
grot′to
grouch
grouch′i·ly

grouch′y
ground
ground′ed
ground′less
ground′lings
ground′work′
group
group′ings
grouse
grout
grout′ed
grove
grov′el
grov′eled
grow
grow′er
growl
growled
grown
growth
grub
grubbed
grub′bi·ness
grub′by
grudge
grudg′ing·ly
gru′el
grue′some
gruff
gruff′er
gruff′est
gruff′ly

grum'ble
grum'bled
grump'i·ly
grump'i·ness
grump'y
grunt
grunt'ed
guar'an·tee'
guar'an·tor
guar'an·ty
guard
guard'ed
guard'i·an
guard'i·an·ship'
guard'room'
guards'man
gua'va
gu'ber·na·to'ri·al
gudg'eon
guer'don
guer·ril'la
guess
guess'work'
guest
guid'ance
guide
guide'book'
guid'ed
guide'line'
gui'don
guild
guile
guile'ful
guile'less
guil'lo·tine
guilt
guilt'i·er
guilt'i·est
guilt'i·ly
guilt'i·ness
guilt'y
guin'ea
guise
guis'es
gui·tar'
gulch
gul'den
gulf
gull
gul'let
gul'li·bil'i·ty
gul'li·ble
gul'ly
gulp
gum
gum'bo
gum'boil'
gummed
gum·mo'sis
gum'my
gump'tion
gum'shoe'
gum'weed'
gum'wood'
gun
gun'boat'
gun'cot'ton
gun'fire'
gun'lock'
gun'man
gun'ner
gun'ner·y
gun'ny
gun'pa'per
gun'pow'der
gun'run'ning
gun'shot'
gun'smith'
gun'stock'
gun'wale
gur'gle
gu'ru
gush
gush'er
gush'y
gus'set
gust
gus'ta·to'ry
gust'i·ly
gus'to
gust'y
gut'ter
gut'ter·snipe'
gut'tur·al
gut'tur·al·ly
guy

guz′zle
guz′zled
guz′zler
gym·kha′na
gym·na′si·um
gym′nast
gym·nas′tic
gyn′e·col′o·gist
gyn′e·col′o·gy
gyp′sum
gyp′sy
gy′rate
gy′rat·ed
gy·ra′tion
gy′ra·to′ry
gyr′fal′con
gy′ro
gy′ro·com′pass
gy′ro·scope
gy′ro·stat
gyves

hab′er·dash'er
hab′er·dash'er·y
ha·bil′i·ment
hab′it
hab′it·a·ble
hab′i·tat
hab'i·ta′tion
hab′it·ed
ha·bit′u·al
ha·bit′u·al·ly
ha·bit′u·ate
ha·bit′u·at'ed
hab′i·tude
hack′le
hack′man
hack′ney
hack′neyed
hack saw
had
had′dock
haft
hag

hag′gard
hag′gle
hag′gled
hail
hailed
hail′stone'
hail′storm'
hair
hair′breadth'
hair′brush'
hair′cut'
hair′line'
hair′pin'
hair′split'ter
hair′spring'
hair′y
hake
ha·la′tion
hal′berd
hal′cy·on
hale
half

half′heart'ed
half′tone'
half′way'
half′-wit′ted
hal'i·but
hal′ide
hal′ite
hal'i·to′sis
hall
hall′mark'
hal′low
hal′lowed
Hal'low·een′
hal·lu'ci·na′tion
hal·lu'ci·na·to'ry
hal·lu'ci·no′sis
ha′lo
hal′o·gen
halt
halt′ed
hal′ter
halt′ing·ly

halves
hal'yard
ham
ham'let
ham'mer
ham'mered
ham'mer·less
ham'mock
ham'per
ham'pered
ham'ster
ham'string'
ham'strung'
hand
hand'bag'
hand'ball'
hand'bill'
hand'book'
hand'cuff'
hand'ed
hand'ful
hand'i·cap
hand'i·capped
hand'i·craft
hand'i·er
hand'i·est
hand'i·ly
hand'i·ness
hand'ker·chief
han'dle
han'dled
hand'rail

hand'some
hand'spring'
hand'work'
hand'writ'ing
hand'y
hang
hang'ar
hanged
hang'er
hang'ings
hang'man
han'ker
han'kered
han'som
hap'haz'ard
hap'less
hap'loid
hap'pen
hap'pened
hap'pen·ings
hap'pi·er
hap'pi·est
hap'pi·ly
hap'pi·ness
hap'py
ha·rangue'
ha·rangued'
har'ass
har'ass·ment
har'bin·ger
har'bor
har'bored

hard
hard'en
hard'ened
hard'en·er
hard'er
hard'est
hard'hat
hard'head'ed
har'di·hood
har'di·ness
hard'ly
hard'ness
hard'pan'
hard'ship
hard'ware'
har'dy
hare
hare'brained'
hare'lip'
ha'rem
hark
har'le·quin
har'le·quin·ade'
harm
harmed
harm'ful
harm'ful·ly
harm'ful·ness
harm'less
harm'less·ly
harm'less·ness
har·mon'ic

har·mon′i·ca
har·mo′ni·ous
har·mo′ni·ous·ly
har·mo′ni·ous·ness
har·mo′ni·um
har′mo·ni·za′tion
har′mo·nize
har′mo·nized
har′mo·ny
har′ness
har′nessed
harp
harp′er
harp′ist
har·poon′
har·pooned′
harp′si·chord
har′ri·er
har′row
harsh
harsh′er
harsh′est
harsh′ly
harsh′ness
har′te·beest′
har′vest
har′vest·ed
har′vest·er
has
hash
hashed
hash′ish
hasp
has′sock
haste
has′ten
has′tened
hast′i·er
hast′i·est
hast′i·ly
hast′i·ness
hast′y
hat
hat′band′
hatch
hatched
hatch′er·y
hatch′et
hatch′ment
hatch′way′
hate
hat′ed
hate′ful
hate′ful·ly
hate′ful·ness
hat′pin′
ha′tred
hat′ter
haugh′ti·er
haugh′ti·est
haugh′ti·ly
haugh′ty
haul
haul′age
hauled
haunch
haunt
haunt′ed
haunt′ing·ly
haut′boy
hau·teur′
have
ha′ven
hav′er·sack
hav′oc
Ha·wai′ian
hawk
hawk′er
hawk′weed′
hawse
haw′ser
haw′thorn
hay
hay′cock′
hay′fork′
hay′loft′
hay′mow′
hay′rack′
hay′seed′
hay′stack′
haz′ard
haz′ard·ed
haz′ard·ous
haz′ard·ous·ly
haze
ha′zel

ha'zel·nut'
ha'zi·er
ha'zi·est
ha'zi·ly
ha'zi·ness
ha'zy
he
head
head'ache'
head'band'
head'board'
head'cheese'
head'dress'
head'ed
head'er
head'first'
head'fore'most
head'gear'
head'i·ly
head'ings
head'land'
head'less
head'light'
head'line'
head'lock'
head'long
head'mas'ter
head'phone'
head'piece'
head'quar'ters
heads'man
head'spring'

head'stone'
head'strong
head'wa'ter
head'way'
head'work'
head'y
heal
healed
heal'er
health
health'ful
health'ful·ness
health'i·er
health'i·est
health'i·ly
health'y
heap
heaped
hear
heard
hear'er
hear'ings
heark'en
heark'ened
hear'say'
hearse
heart
heart'ache'
heart'beat'
heart'break'
heart'bro'ken
heart'burn'

heart'en
heart'ened
heart'felt'
hearth
hearth'stone'
heart'i·er
heart'i·est
heart'i·ly
heart'less
heart'sick'
heart'sore'
heart'string'
heart'wood'
heart'y
heat
heat'ed
heat'er
heath
hea'then
hea'then·ish
hea'then·ish·ly
heath'er
heat'stroke'
heave
heav'en
heav'en·ly
heav'en·ward
heav'i·er
heav'i·est
heav'i·ly
heav'i·ness
heav'y

He·bra′ic
He′brew
hec′a·tomb
heck′le
heck′led
heck′ler
hec′tic
hec′to·graph
hedge
hedged
hedge′hog′
hedge′row′
he′don·ism
heed
heed′ed
heed′ful·ly
heed′ful·ness
heed′less
heed′less·ness
heel
heft
he·gem′o·ny
he·gi′ra
heif′er
height
height′en
height′ened
hei′nous
heir
heir′ess
heir′loom′
hel′i·cal

hel′i·coid
hel′i·cop′ter
he′li·o·trope
he′li·um
he′lix
helm
hel′met
hel′met·ed
helms′man
help
help′er
help′ful
help′ful·ly
help′ful·ness
help′ing
help′less
help′less·ly
help′less·ness
help′mate′
hem
hem′a·tite
hem′i·cy′cle
hem′i·ple′gi·a
hem′i·sphere
hem′i·spher′i·cal
hem′lock
hemmed
hem′or·rhage
hemp
hemp′en
hem′stitch′
hem′stitched′

hence
hence′forth′
hence′for′ward
hench′man
hen′e·quen
hen′na
he·pat′ic
he·pat′i·ca
hep′a·ti′tis
hep′ta·gon
hep·tam′e·ter
her
her′ald
her′ald·ed
he·ral′dic
her′ald·ry
herb
her·ba′ceous
herb′age
herb′al
her·bar′i·um
her′bi·cide
her·biv′o·rous
Her·cu′le·an
herd
herd′ed
here
here′a·bouts′
here·aft′er
here·by′
he·red′i·ta·bil′i·ty
he·red′i·ta·ble

he·red'i·ta·bly
her'e·dit'a·ment
he·red'i·tar'y
he·red'i·ty
here'in·aft'er
here·in'be·fore'
here·on'
her'e·sy
her'e·tic
he·ret'i·cal
here·to'
here'to·fore'
here'un·to'
here'up·on'
here·with'
her'it·a·bil'i·ty
her'it·a·ble
her'it·a·bly
her'it·age
her·met'ic
her·met'i·cal·ly
her'mit
her'mit·age
her'ni·a
he'ro
he·ro'ic
he·ro'i·cal
her'o·ine
her'o·ism
her'on
her'pes
her'pe·tol'o·gy
her'ring
her'ring·bone'
hers
her·self'
hes'i·tance
hes'i·tan·cy
hes'i·tant
hes'i·tate
hes'i·tat'ed
hes'i·tat'ing·ly
hes'i·ta'tion
hes'i·ta'tive·ly
het'er·o·dox
het'er·o·ge·ne'i·ty
het'er·o·ge'ne·ous
het'er·o·nym'
heu·ris'tic
hew
hewed
hew'er
hewn
hex'a·gon
hex·ag'o·nal
hex·am'e·ter
hex·an'gu·lar
hex'a·pod
hey'day'
hi·a'tus
hi'ber·nate
hi'ber·na'tion
hi·bis'cus
hick'o·ry
hid
hid'den
hide
hide'bound'
hid'e·ous
hid'e·ous·ly
hid'e·ous·ness
hi'er·arch'y
hi'er·at'ic
hi'er·o·glyph'ic
high
high'born'
high'boy'
high'er
high'est
high'land
high'land·er
high'ly
high'ness
high'road'
high'way'
high'way'man
hi'jack'
hi'jack'er
hik'er
hi·lar'i·ous
hi·lar'i·ty
hill
hill'i·er
hill'i·est
hill'i·ness
hill'ock

hill'side'
hilt
him
him·self'
hind
hin'der
hin'dered
hin'drance
hinge
hinged
hint
hint'ed
hin'ter·land'
hip'po·drome
hip'po·pot'a·mus
hire
hired
hire'ling
hir'sute
his
His·pan'ic
his·tol'o·gist
his·tol'o·gy
his·to'ri·an
his·tor'ic
his·tor'i·cal
his'to·ry
his'tri·on'ic
hit
hitch
hitched
hitch'hike'
hith'er
hith'er·to'
hive
hoar
hoard
hoard'ed
hoard'er
hoar'frost'
hoarse
hoars'er
hoars'est
hoax
hob'ble
hob'bled
hob'by
hob'gob'lin
hob'nail'
hob'nailed'
hob'nob'
ho'bo
hock
hock'ey
hod
hoe
hog
hog'back'
hog'fish'
hog'gish
hogs'head
hog'weed'
hoist
hoist'ed
hoist'way'
ho'kum
hold
hold'er
hold'ings
hole
hol'i·day
ho'li·ly
ho'li·ness
Hol'land
hol'low
hol'lowed
hol'ly
hol'ly·hock
hol'o·caust
hol'o·graph
hol'o·graph'ic
hol'ster
ho'ly
ho'ly·stone'
hom'age
home
home'land'
home'like'
home'li·ness
home'ly
ho'me·o·path'ic
ho'me·op'a·thy
home'sick'ness
home'site'
home'spun'
home'stead

home′ward
home′work′
hom′i·cid′al
hom′i·cide
hom′i·let′ics
hom′i·lies
hom′i·ly
hom′i·ny
ho′mo·ge·ne′i·ty
ho′mo·ge′ne·ous
ho′mo·ge′ne·ous·ly
ho·mog′e·nize
ho·mol′o·gous
hom′o·nym
ho·mun′cu·lus
hone
honed
hon′est
hon′est·ly
hon′es·ty
hon′ey
hon′ey·bee′
hon′ey·comb′
hon′ey·dew′
hon′eyed
hon′ey·moon′
hon′ey·suck′le
honk
hon′or
hon′or·a·ble
hon′or·a·bly
hon′o·rar′i·um

hon′or·ar′y
hon′ored
hood
hood′ed
hood′lum
hoo′doo
hood′wink
hoof
hook
hooked
hook′er
hook′worm′
hoop
Hoo′sier
hope
hope′ful
hope′ful·ly
hope′ful·ness
hope′less
hope′less·ly
hope′less·ness
hop′lite
hop′per
hop′scotch′
horde
hore′hound′
ho·ri′zon
hor′i·zon′tal
hor′mone
horn
horn′book′
horned

hor′net
horn′pipe′
ho·rol′o·gy
hor′o·scope
hor·ren′dous
hor′ri·ble
hor′rid
hor′ri·fi·ca′tion
hor′ri·fied
hor′ri·fy
hor′ror
horse
horse′back′
horse chest′nut
horse′hair′
horse′man
horse′man·ship
horse′pow′er
horse′shoe′
horse′weed′
horse′whip′
horse′wom′an
hor′ta·tive
hor′ta·to′ry
hor′ti·cul′ture
hose
ho′sier
ho′sier·y
hos′pice
hos′pi·ta·ble
hos′pi·tal
hos′pi·tal′i·ty

hos′pi·tal·i·za′tion
hos′pi·tal·ize
host
hos′tage
hos′tel
host′ess
hos′tile
hos′tile·ly
hos·til′i·ty
hot
hot′bed′
hot′box′
ho·tel′
hot′head′ed
hot′house′
hot′ly
hot′ness
hot′ter
hot′test
hound
hound′ed
hour
hour′ly
house
housed
house′fly′
house′fur′nish·ings
house′hold
house′hold′er
house′keep′er
house′maid′
house′man
house′moth′er
house′room′
house′wares′
house′warm′ing
house′wife′
house′work′
hous′ing
hov′er
hov′ered
hov′er·ing·ly
how
how·ev′er
how′itz·er
howl
how′so·ev′er
hoy′den
hub
hub′bub
huck′le·ber′ry
huck′ster
hud′dle
hud′dled
hue
huff
hug
huge
hug′er
hug′est
Hu′gue·not
hulk
hull
hulled
hum
hu′man
hu·mane′
hu·mane′ly
hu·mane′ness
hu′man·ism
hu′man·ist
hu′man·is′tic
hu·man′i·tar′i·an
hu·man′i·tar′i·an·ism
hu·man′i·ty
hu′man·i·za′tion
hu′man·ize
hu′man·ized
hu′man·kind′
hu′man·ly
hum′ble
hum′bled
hum′ble·ness
hum′bler
hum′blest
hum′bly
hum′bug′
hum′drum′
hu′mer·us
hu′mid
hu·mid′i·fi·ca′tion
hu·mid′i·fied
hu·mid′i·fi′er
hu·mid′i·fy
hu·mid′i·ty
hu′mi·dor

hu·mil′i·ate
hu·mil′i·at′ed
hu·mil′i·a′tion
hu·mil′i·ty
hummed
hum′ming·bird′
hum′mock
hu′mor
hu′mored
hu′mor·esque′
hu′mor·ist
hu′mor·ous
hu′mor·ous·ness
hump
hu′mus
hunch
hun′dred
hun′dred·fold′
hun′dredth
Hun·gar′i·an
hun′ger
hun′gered
hun′gri·er
hun′gri·est
hun′gry
hunk
hunt
hunt′ed
hunt′er
hunts′man
hur′dle
hur′dled

hurl
hurled
hur′ri·cane
hur′ry
hurt
hurt′ful
hurt′ful·ly
hurt′ful·ness
hur′tle
hur′tled
hus′band
hus′band·ry
hush
hushed
husk
husk′i·ly
husk′i·ness
hus′ky
hus′sy
hus′tings
hus′tle
hus′tled
hus′tler
hut
hutch
hy′a·cinth
hy′a·loid
hy′brid
hy′brid·ism
hy′brid·i·za′tion
hy′brid·ize
hy·dran′ge·a

hy′drant
hy′drate
hy·drau′lic
hy′dro·car′bon
hy′dro·chlo′ric
hy′dro·cy·an′ic
hy′dro·e·lec′tric
hy′dro·flu·or′ic
hy′dro·foil′
hy′dro·gen
hy·drom′e·ter
hy′dro·pho′bi·a
hy′dro·plane
hy′dro·stat′ics
hy·drox′ide
hy·e′na
hy′giene
hy′gi·en′ic
hy′gi·en′i·cal·ly
hy′gi·en·ist
hy·grom′e·ter
hy′gro·scop′ic
hymn
hym′nal
hymn′book′
hy·per′bo·la
hy·per′bo·le
hy′per·bol′ic
hy′per·crit′i·cal
hy′per·e′mi·a
hy′per·o′pi·a
hy′per·sen′si·tive

hy′per·thy′roid
hy·per′tro·phy
hy′phen
hy′phen·ate
hy′phen·at′ed
hy′phen·a′tion
hyp·no′sis
hyp·not′ic
hyp′no·tist
hyp′no·tize
hyp′no·tized
hy′po·chon′dri·a
hy′po·chon′dri·ac
hy·poc′ri·sy
hyp′o·crite
hyp′o·crit′i·cal
hy′po·der′mic
hy′po·der′mi·cal·ly
hy·pot′e·nuse
hy·poth′e·cate
hy·poth′e·ca′tion
hy·poth′e·ses
hy·poth′e·sis
hy·poth′e·size
hy′po·thet′i·cal
hy′po·thet′i·cal·ly
hys·te′ri·a
hys·ter′i·cal
hys·ter′ics
hys′ter·oid

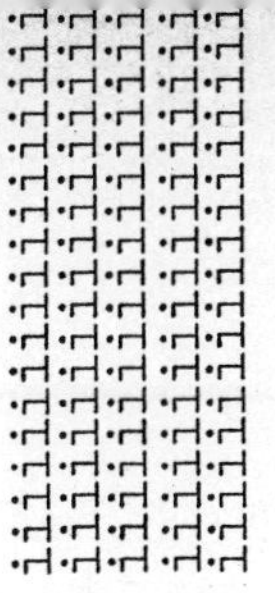

# I

i·am′bic
I·be′ri·an
i′bex
i′bis
ice
ice′berg′
ice′boat′
ice′box′
ice′break′er
ice′house′
ice′man′
ich·neu′mon
i′chor
ich′thy·ol′o·gy
i′ci·cle
i′ci·er
i′ci·est
i′ci·ly
i′ci·ness
i′con
i′cy
i·de′a
i·de′al
i·de′al·ism
i·de′al·ist
i·de′al·is′tic
i·de′al·i·za′tion
i·de′al·ize
i·de′al·ly
i′de·a′tion
i′de·a′tion·al
i·den′ti·cal
i·den′ti·fi·ca′tion
i·den′ti·fy
i·den′ti·ty
id′e·o·log′i·cal
id′e·ol′o·gy
id′i·o·cy
id′i·om
id′i·o·mat′ic
id′i·o·mat′i·cal·ly
id′i·o·syn′cra·sy
id′i·o·syn·crat′ic
id′i·ot
id′i·ot′ic
id′i·ot′i·cal·ly
i′dle
i′dled
i′dle·ness
i′dler
i′dlest
i′dly
i′dol
i·dol′a·ter
i·dol′a·trize
i·dol′a·trous
i·dol′a·try
i′dol·ize
i′dyl
i·dyl′lic
if
ig′loo
ig′ne·ous
ig·nite′
ig·nit′ed
ig·ni′tion

ig·no′ble
ig′no·min′i·ous
ig′no·min·y
ig′no·ra′mus
ig′no·rance
ig′no·rant
ig′no·rant·ly
ig·nore′
ig·nored′
i·gua′na
i′lex
Il′i·ad
ilk
ill
il·le′gal
il′le·gal′i·ty
il·leg′i·ble
il·leg′i·bly
il′le·git′i·ma·cy
il′le·git′i·mate
il·lib′er·al
il·lic′it
il·lim′it·a·ble
il·lit′er·a·cy
il·lit′er·ate
ill′ness
il·log′i·cal
il·lu′mi·nant
il·lu′mi·nate
il·lu′mi·nat′ed
il·lu′mi·na′tion
il·lu′mi·na′tor
il·lu′mine
il·lu′mined
il·lu′sion
il·lu′sive
il·lu′so·ry
il′lus·trate
il′lus·trat′ed
il′lus·tra′tion
il·lus′tra·tive
il′lus·tra′tor
il·lus′tri·ous
im′age
im′age·ry
im·ag′i·na·ble
im·ag′i·nar′y
im·ag′i·na′tion
im·ag′i·na′tive
im·ag′ine
im·ag′ined
im·ag′in·ings
i·ma′go
i·mam′
im′be·cile
im′be·cil′i·ty
im·bibe′
im·bibed′
im·bro′glio
im·bue′
im·bued′
im′i·ta·ble
im′i·tate
im′i·tat′ed
im′i·ta′tion
im′i·ta′tive
im′i·ta′tor
im·mac′u·late
im·mac′u·late·ly
im′ma·nent
im′ma·te′ri·al
im′ma·ture′
im′ma·ture′ly
im′ma·tu′ri·ty
im·meas′ur·a·ble
im·me′di·a·cy
im·me′di·ate
im·me′di·ate·ly
im·me′di·ate·ness
im′me·mo′ri·al
im·mense′
im·mense′ly
im·men′si·ty
im·merse′
im·mersed′
im·mer′sion
im′mi·grant
im′mi·grate
im′mi·grat′ed
im′mi·gra′tion
im′mi·nence
im′mi·nent
im·mo′bile
im′mo·bil′i·ty
im·mo′bi·li·za′tion
im·mo′bi·lize

im·mod'er·ate
im·mod'est
im'mo·late
im'mo·la'tion
im·mor'al
im'mo·ral'i·ty
im·mor'al·ly
im·mor'tal
im'mor·tal'i·ty
im·mor'tal·ize
im·mor'tal·ly
im'mor·telle'
im·mov'a·bil'i·ty
im·mov'a·ble
im·mov'a·ble·ness
im·mov'a·bly
im·mune'
im·mu'ni·ty
im'mu·ni·za'tion
im'mu·nize
im'mu·nol'o·gy
im·mure'
im'mu·ta·bil'i·ty
im·mu'ta·ble
imp
im'pact
im·pac'tion
im·pair'
im·paired'
im·pair'ment
im·pa'la
im·pale'
im·paled'
im·pale'ment
im·pal'pa·bil'i·ty
im·pal'pa·ble
im·pan'el
im·pan'eled
im·part'
im·part'ed
im·par'tial
im'par·ti·al'i·ty
im·par'tial·ly
im·pass'a·bil'i·ty
im·pass'a·ble
im·passe'
im·pas'sion
im·pas'sioned
im·pas'sive
im·pas'sive·ly
im'pas·siv'i·ty
im·pa'tience
im·pa'tient
im·peach'
im·peach'ment
im·pec'ca·bil'i·ty
im·pec'ca·ble
im'pe·cu'ni·os'i·ty
im'pe·cu'ni·ous
im·ped'ance
im·pede'
im·ped'ed
im·ped'i·ment
im·ped'i·men'ta
im·pel'
im·pelled'
im·pend'
im·pend'ed
im·pen'e·tra·bil'i·ty
im·pen'e·tra·ble
im·pen'i·tent
im·per'a·tive
im'per·cep'ti·ble
im'per·cep'tive
im·per'fect
im'per·fec'tion
im·per'fo·rate
im·pe'ri·al
im·pe'ri·al·ism
im·pe'ri·al·ist
im·pe'ri·al·is'tic
im·pe'ri·ous
im·per'ish·a·ble
im·per'ma·nent
im·per'me·a·ble
im'per·scrip'ti·ble
im·per'son·al
im·per'son·ate
im·per'son·at'ed
im·per'son·a'tion
im·per'ti·nence
im·per'ti·nent
im'per·turb'a·ble
im·per'vi·ous
im'pe·ti'go
im·pet'u·os'i·ty

im·pet'u·ous
im·pet'u·ous·ly
im·pet'u·ous·ness
im'pe·tus
im·pi'e·ty
im·pinge'
im·pinged'
im·pinge'ment
im'pi·ous
im'pi·ous·ly
imp'ish
im·pla'ca·bil'i·ty
im·pla'ca·ble
im·plant'
im·plant'ed
im·plau'si·bil'i·ty
im·plau'si·ble
im'ple·ment
im'ple·ment'ed
im'pli·cate
im'pli·cat'ed
im'pli·ca'tion
im·plic'it
im·plic'it·ly
im·plied'
im'plo·ra'tion
im·plore'
im·plored'
im·plor'ing·ly
im·plo'sion
im·ply'
im'po·lite'
im'po·lite'ly
im'po·lite'ness
im·pol'i·tic
im·pon'der·a·ble
im·port'
im·por'tance
im·por'tant
im'por·ta'tion
im'port'er
im·por'tu·nate
im'por·tune'
im'por·tu'ni·ty
im·pose'
im·posed'
im·pos'ing·ly
im'po·si'tion
im·pos'si·bil'i·ty
im·pos'si·ble
im'post
im·pos'tor
im·pos'ture
im'po·tence
im'po·tent
im·pound'
im·pov'er·ish
im·pov'er·ish·ment
im·pow'er
im·prac'ti·ca·ble
im·prac'ti·cal'i·ty
im'pre·cate
im'pre·ca'tion
im'pre·ca·to'ry
im·preg'na·bil'i·ty
im·preg'na·ble
im·preg'nate
im'preg·na'tion
im'pre·sa'ri·o
im'pre·scrip'ti·ble
im·press'
im·pressed'
im·pres'sion
im·pres'sion·a·ble
im·pres'sion·ism
im·pres'sive
im'pri·ma'tur
im·print'
im·print'ed
im·pris'on
im·pris'oned
im·pris'on·ment
im'prob·a·bil'i·ty
im·prob'a·ble
im·prob'a·bly
im·promp'tu
im·prop'er
im'pro·pri'e·ty
im·prov'a·ble
im·prove'
im·prove'ment
im·prov'i·dence
im·prov'i·dent
im'pro·vi·sa'tion
im'pro·vise
im'pro·vised

im·pru′dence
im·pru′dent
im·pru′dent·ly
im′pu·dence
im′pu·dent
im·pugn′
im·pugn′a·ble
im·pugned′
im·pugn′ment
im′pulse
im·pul′sion
im·pul′sive
im·pu′ni·ty
im·pure′
im·pure′ly
im·pu′ri·ty
im·put′a·ble
im′pu·ta′tion
im·put′a·tive
im·pute′
im·put′ed
in′a·bil′i·ty
in′ac·ces′si·bil′i·ty
in′ac·ces′si·ble
in·ac′cu·ra·cy
in·ac′cu·rate
in·ac′tion
in·ac′ti·vate
in·ac′tive
in′ac·tiv′i·ty
in·ad′e·qua·cy
in·ad′e·quate

in′ad·mis′si·bil′i·ty
in′ad·mis′si·ble
in′ad·vert′ence
in′ad·vert′ent
in′ad·vis′a·bil′i·ty
in′ad·vis′a·ble
in·al′ien·a·ble
in·am′o·ra′ta
in·ane′
in·an′i·mate
in′a·ni′tion
in·an′i·ty
in·ap′pli·ca·ble
in·ap′po·site
in′ap·pro′pri·ate
in·apt′
in·apt′i·tude
in′ar·tic′u·late
in′ar·tis′tic
in′as·much′
in′at·ten′tion
in′at·ten′tive
in·au′di·bil′i·ty
in·au′di·ble
in·au′di·bly
in·au′gu·ral
in·au′gu·rate
in·au′gu·rat′ed
in·au′gu·ra′tion
in′aus·pi′cious
in′board′
in′born′

in′bred′
in·cal′cu·la·ble
in′can·desce′
in′can·des′cence
in′can·des′cent
in′can·ta′tion
in′ca·pa·bil′i·ty
in·ca′pa·ble
in′ca·pac′i·tate
in′ca·pac′i·tat′ed
in′ca·pac′i·ta′tion
in′ca·pac′i·ty
in·car′cer·ate
in·car′cer·at′ed
in·car′cer·a′tion
in·car′nate
in′car·na′tion
in·cen′di·a·rism
in·cen′di·ar′y
in·cense′
in·censed′
in·cen′tive
in·cep′tion
in·cer′ti·tude
in·ces′sant
in·ces′sant·ly
in′cest
in·ces′tu·ous
inch
in·cho′ate
inch′worm′
in′ci·dence

in′ci·dent
in′ci·den′tal
in′ci·den′tal·ly
in·cin′er·ate
in·cin′er·at′ed
in·cin′er·a′tion
in·cin′er·a′tor
in·cip′i·ent
in·cise′
in·cised′
in·ci′sion
in·ci′sive
in·ci′sive·ly
in·ci′sive·ness
in·ci′sor
in′ci·ta′tion
in·cite′
in·cite′ment
in′ci·vil′i·ty
in·clem′en·cy
in·clem′ent
in′cli·na′tion
in·cline′
in·clined′
in·close′
in·closed′
in·clo′sure
in·clude′
in·clud′ed
in·clu′sive
in·clu′sive·ly
in·clu′sive·ness
in·cog′ni·to
in′co·her′ence
in′co·her′ent
in′com·bus′ti·bil′i·ty
in′com·bus′ti·ble
in′come
in′com·men′su·ra·ble
in′com·men′su·rate
in′com·mode′
in′com·mu′ni·ca′do
in·com′pa·ra·ble
in·com′pa·ra·bly
in′com·pat′i·bil′i·ty
in′com·pat′i·ble
in·com′pe·tence
in·com′pe·tent
in·com′pe·tent·ly
in′com·plete′
in′com·pre·hen′si·bil′i·ty
in′com·pre·hen′si·ble
in′com·press′i·bil′i·ty
in′com·press′i·ble
in′con·ceiv′a·bil′i·ty
in′con·ceiv′a·ble
in′con·clu′sive
in′con·clu′sive·ness
in′con·gru′i·ty
in·con′gru·ous
in·con′se·quen′tial
in′con·sid′er·a·ble
in′con·sid′er·ate
in′con·sid′er·ate·ly
in′con·sist′en·cy
in′con·sist′ent
in′con·sol′a·ble
in′con·spic′u·ous
in′con·spic′u·ous·ly
in·con′stan·cy
in·con′stant
in′con·test′a·ble
in·con′ti·nence
in·con′ti·nent
in′con·tro·vert′i·ble
in′con·ven′ience
in′con·ven′ienced
in′con·ven′ient
in′con·ven′ient·ly
in′con·ver′si·bil′i·ty
in′con·vert′i·bil′i·ty
in′con·vert′i·ble
in·cor′po·rate
in·cor′po·rat′ed
in·cor′po·ra′tion
in·cor′po·ra′tor
in′cor·rect′
in·cor′ri·gi·bil′i·ty
in·cor′ri·gi·ble
in′cor·rupt′i·bil′i·ty
in′cor·rupt′i·ble
in·crease′
in·creased′
in·creas′ing·ly
in·cred′i·bil′i·ty
in·cred′i·ble

in′cre·du′li·ty
in·cred′u·lous
in′cre·ment
in′cre·men′tal
in·cre′tion
in·crim′i·nate
in·crim′i·nat′ed
in·crim′i·na′tion
in·crim′i·na·to′ry
in′crus·ta′tion
in′cu·bate
in′cu·bat′ed
in′cu·ba′tion
in′cu·ba′tor
in′cu·bus
in·cul′cate
in·cul′cat·ed
in′cul·ca′tion
in·cul′pate
in·cul′pat·ed
in′cul·pa′tion
in·cul′pa·to′ry
in·cum′ben·cy
in·cum′bent
in′cu·nab′u·la
in·cur′
in·cur′a·ble
in·cur′a·bly
in·curred′
in·cur′sion
in·debt′ed
in·debt′ed·ness

in·de′cen·cy
in·de′cent
in·de′cent·ly
in′de·ci′sion
in′de·ci′sive
in′de·ci′sive·ly
in′de·ci′sive·ness
in·dec′o·rous
in′de·co′rum
in·deed′
in′de·fat′i·ga·bil′i·ty
in′de·fat′i·ga·ble
in′de·fea′si·ble
in′de·fen′si·ble
in′de·fin′a·ble
in·def′i·nite
in·def′i·nite·ly
in·def′i·nite·ness
in·del′i·bil′i·ty
in·del′i·ble
in·del′i·bly
in·del′i·ca·cy
in·del′i·cate
in·del′i·cate·ly
in·dem′ni·fi·ca′tion
in·dem′ni·fied
in·dem′ni·fy
in·dem′ni·ty
in·dent′
in′den·ta′tion
in·dent′ed
in·den′tion

in·den′ture
in·den′tured
in′de·pend′ence
in′de·pend′ent
in′de·scrib′a·ble
in′de·struct′i·ble
in′de·ter′mi·na·ble
in′de·ter′mi·nate
in′dex
in′dexed
in′dex·er
in′dex·es
In′di·an
in′di·cate
in′di·cat′ed
in′di·ca′tion
in·dic′a·tive
in′di·ca′tor
in′di·ca·to′ry
in′di·ces
in·di′ci·a
in·dict′
in·dict′a·ble
in·dict′ed
in·dict′ment
in·dif′fer·ence
in·dif′fer·ent
in·dif′fer·ent·ly
in′di·gence
in·dig′e·nous
in′di·gent
in′di·gest′i·bil′i·ty

in′di·gest′i·ble
in′di·ges′tion
in·dig′nant
in·dig′nant·ly
in′dig·na′tion
in·dig′ni·ty
in′di·go
in′di·rect′
in′di·rec′tion
in′di·rect′ly
in′di·rect′ness
in′dis·creet′
in′dis·creet′ly
in′dis·cre′tion
in′dis·crim′i·nate
in′dis·crim′i·nate·ly
in′dis·pen′sa·bil′i·ty
in′dis·pen′sa·ble
in′dis·pose′
in′dis·posed′
in′dis·po·si′tion
in·dis′pu·ta·ble
in·dis′so·lu·ble
in·dis′so·lu·bly
in′dis·tinct′
in′dis·tinct′ly
in·dis·tin′guish·a·ble
in·dite′
in·dit′ed
in′di·um
in′di·vid′u·al
in′di·vid′u·al·ism
in′di·vid′u·al·ist
in′di·vid′u·al′i·ty
in′di·vid′u·al·ize
in′di·vid′u·al·ly
in′di·vis′i·bil′i·ty
in′di·vis′i·ble
in·doc′tri·nate
in·doc′tri·nat′ed
in·doc′tri·na′tion
in′do·lence
in′do·lent
in′do·lent·ly
in·dom′i·ta·ble
in′doors′
in·dorse′
in·dorsed′
in·dorse′ment
in·dors′er
in·du′bi·ta·ble
in·duce′
in·duced′
in·duce′ment
in·duct′
in·duct′ance
in·duct′ed
in·duc′tion
in·duc′tive
in·duc′tor
in·due′
in·dued′
in·dulge′
in·dul′gence
in·dul′gent
in·dul′gent·ly
in′du·rate
in′du·rat′ed
in·dus′tri·al
in·dus′tri·al·ly
in·dus′tri·al·ism
in·dus′tri·al·ist
in·dus′tri·al·i·za′tion
in·dus′tri·al·ize
in·dus′tri·al·ized
in·dus′tri·ous
in·dus′tri·ous·ly
in·dus′tri·ous·ness
in′dus·try
in·e′bri·ate
in·e′bri·at′ed
in·e′bri·a′tion
in′e·bri′e·ty
in·ed′i·ble
in·ef′fa·ble
in·ef′fa·bly
in′ef·fec′tive
in′ef·fec′tu·al
in′ef·fec′tu·al·ly
in′ef·fi·ca′cious
in′ef·fi′cien·cy
in′ef·fi′cient
in′ef·fi′cient·ly
in′e·las′tic
in′e·las·tic′i·ty
in·el′e·gance

in·el'e·gant
in·el'e·gant·ly
in·el′i·gi·bil'i·ty
in·el'i·gi·ble
in′e·luc'ta·ble
in·ept'
in·ept'i·tude
in′e·qual'i·ty
in·eq′ui·ta·ble
in·eq′ui·ty
in′e·rad'i·ca·ble
in′e·rad'i·ca·bly
in·er'ran·cy
in·er'rant
in·ert'
in·er'tia
in·ert'ly
in·ert'ness
in′es·sen'tial
in·es'ti·ma·ble
in·es'ti·ma·bly
in·ev′i·ta·bil'i·ty
in·ev'i·ta·ble
in·ev'i·ta·bly
in′ex·act'
in′ex·act'i·tude
in′ex·cus'a·ble
in′ex·cus'a·bly
in′ex·haust'i·ble
in′ex·haust'i·bly
in·ex'o·ra·ble
in′ex·pe'di·ence

in′ex·pe'di·en·cy
in′ex·pe'di·ent
in′ex·pen'sive
in′ex·pe'ri·ence
in′ex·pert'
in·ex'pli·ca·ble
in·ex'pli·ca·bly
in·ex'tri·ca·ble
in·fal′li·bil'i·ty
in·fal'li·ble
in'fa·mous
in'fa·my
in'fan·cy
in'fant
in·fan'ti·cide
in'fan·tile
in·fan'ti·lism
in'fan·try
in'fan·try·man
in·farct'
in·farc'tion
in·fat'u·ate
in·fat'u·at′ed
in·fat′u·a'tion
in·fea'si·ble
in·fect'
in·fect'ed
in·fec'tion
in·fec'tious
in·fec'tious·ly
in·fec'tious·ness
in′fe·lic'i·tous

in′fe·lic'i·ty
in·fer'
in'fer·ence
in′fer·en'tial
in·fe'ri·or
in·fe′ri·or'i·ty
in·fer'nal
in·fer'nal·ly
in·fer'no
in·ferred'
in·fer'tile
in′fer·til'i·ty
in·fest'
in′fes·ta'tion
in'fi·del
in′fi·del'i·ty
in'field′
in'field′er
in·fil'trate
in·fil'trat·ed
in′fil·tra'tion
in'fi·nite
in′fin·i·tes'i·mal
in′fin·i·tes'i·mal·ly
in·fin'i·tive
in·fin'i·tude
in·fin'i·ty
in·firm'
in·fir'ma·ry
in·fir'mi·ty
in·flame'
in·flamed'

in·flam′ma·bil′i·ty
in·flam′ma·ble
in·flam′ma·bly
in′flam·ma′tion
in·flam′ma·to′ry
in·flate′
in·flat′ed
in·fla′tion
in·fla′tion·ar′y
in·fla′tion·ist
in·flect′
in·flect′ed
in·flec′tion
in·flex′i·bil′i·ty
in·flex′i·ble
in·flict′
in·flict′ed
in·flic′tion
in′flu·ence
in′flu·enced
in′flu·en′tial
in′flu·en′tial·ly
in′flu·en′za
in′flux
in·form′
in·for′mal
in′for·mal′i·ty
in·for′mal·ly
in·form′ant
in′for·ma′tion
in·form′a·tive
in·formed′
in·form′er
in·form′ing·ly
in·frac′tion
in·fran′gi·ble
in′fra·red′
in·fre′quent
in·fre′quent·ly
in·fringe′
in·fringed′
in·fringe′ment
in·fu′ri·ate
in·fu′ri·at′ed
in·fuse′
in·fused′
in·fus′es
in·fu′sion
in·gen′ious
in·gen′ious·ly
in′ge·nu′i·ty
in·gen′u·ous
in·gest′
in·gest′ed
in·ges′tion
in·ges′tive
in·glo′ri·ous
in′got
in·grain′
in·grained′
in′grate
in·gra′ti·ate
in·gra′ti·a′tion
in·gra′ti·a·to′ry
in·grat′i·tude
in·gre′di·ent
in′gress
in′grown′
in·hab′it
in·hab′it·a·ble
in·hab′it·ance
in·hab′it·ant
in·hab′i·ta′tion
in·hab′it·ed
in′ha·la′tion
in·hale′
in·haled′
in·hal′er
in′har·mo′ni·ous
in·here′
in·hered′
in·her′ence
in·her′ent
in·her′ent·ly
in·her′it
in·her′it·a·ble
in·her′it·ance
in·her′it·ed
in·her′i·tor
in·hib′it
in·hib′it·ed
in′hi·bi′tion
in·hib′i·to′ry
in·hos′pi·ta·ble
in·hos′pi·ta·bly
in·hos′pi·tal′i·ty

in·hu'man
in'hu·mane'
in'hu·man'i·ty
in'hu·ma'tion
in·hume'
in·humed'
in·im'i·cal
in·im'i·ta·ble
in·im'i·ta·bly
in·iq'ui·tous
in·iq'ui·tous·ly
in·iq'ui·ty
in·i'tial
in·i'tialed
in·i'tial·ly
in·i'ti·ate
in·i'ti·at'ed
in·i'ti·a'tion
in·i'ti·a'tive
in·i'ti·a'tor
in·i'ti·a·to'ry
in·ject'
in·ject'ed
in·jec'tion
in·jec'tor
in'ju·di'cious
in'ju·di'cious·ly
in·junc'tion
in·junc'tive
in'jure
in'jured
in·ju'ri·ous

in'ju·ry
in·jus'tice
in·jus'tic·es
ink
inked
ink'horn'
ink'ling
ink'lings
ink'stand'
ink'well'
ink'y
in·laid'
in'land
in·lay'
in·let'
in'mate
in'most
inn
in'nate
in'nate·ly
in'ner
in'ner·most
in'ning
in'nings
inn'keep'er
in'no·cence
in'no·cent
in'no·cent·ly
in·noc'u·ous
in·noc'u·ous·ly
in'no·vate
in'no·va'tion

in'no·va'tive
in'no·va'tor
in'nu·en'do
in·nu'mer·a·ble
in'ob·serv'ant
in·oc'u·late
in·oc'u·lat'ed
in·oc'u·la'tion
in'of·fen'sive
in·op'er·a·ble
in·op'er·a'tive
in·op'por·tune'
in·or'di·nate
in'or·gan'ic
in'pa'tient
in'put'
in'quest
in·qui'e·tude
in·quire'
in·quired'
in·quir'er
in·quires'
in·quir'ies
in·quir'ing·ly
in·quir'y
in'qui·si'tion
in·quis'i·tive
in·quis'i·tor
in·quis'i·to'ri·al
in·road'
in·rush'
in·sane'

in·sane′ly
in·san′i·tar′y
in·san′i·ta′tion
in·san′i·ty
in·sa′ti·a·bil′i·ty
in·sa′ti·a·ble
in·scribe′
in·scribed′
in·scrib′er
in·scrip′tion
in·scru′ta·bil′i·ty
in·scru′ta·ble
in′sect
in·sec′ti·cide
in′sec·tiv′o·rous
in′se·cure′
in′se·cu′ri·ty
in·sen′sate
in·sen′si·bil′i·ty
in·sen′si·ble
in·sen′si·tive
in·sen′si·tive·ness
in·sen′ti·ence
in·sen′ti·ent
in·sep′a·ra·ble
in·sep′a·ra·bly
in·sert′
in·sert′ed
in·ser′tion
in′set′
in′shore′
in′side′
in′sid′er
in·sides′
in·sid′i·ous
in·sid′i·ous·ly
in′sight′
in·sig′ne
in·sig′ni·a
in′sig·nif′i·cance
in′sig·nif′i·cant
in′sig·nif′i·cant·ly
in′sin·cere′
in′sin·cere′ly
in′sin·cer′i·ty
in·sin′u·ate
in·sin′u·at′ed
in·sin′u·at′ing·ly
in·sin′u·a′tion
in·sin′u·a′tive
in·sip′id
in′si·pid′i·ty
in·sip′id·ly
in·sist′
in·sist′ed
in·sist′ence
in·sist′ent
in·sist′ent·ly
in′so·bri′e·ty
in′sole′
in′so·lence
in′so·lent
in′so·lent·ly
in·sol′u·bil′i·ty
in·sol′u·ble
in·solv′a·ble
in·sol′ven·cy
in·sol′vent
in·som′ni·a
in·som′ni·ac
in′so·much′
in·sou′ci·ance
in·sou′ci·ant
in·spect′
in·spect′ed
in·spec′tion
in·spec′tor
in·spec′tor·ate
in′spi·ra′tion
in′spi·ra′tion·al
in′spi·ra′tion·al·ly
in·spir′a·to′ry
in·spire′
in·spired′
in·spir′er
in·spir′ing·ly
in·spir′it·ing·ly
in′sta·bil′i·ty
in·stall′
in′stal·la′tion
in·stalled′
in·stall′ment
in′stance
in′stant
in′stan·ta′ne·ous
in·stan′ter

in'stant·ly
in·state'
in·stat'ed
in·stead'
in'step
in'sti·gate
in'sti·gat'ed
in'sti·ga'tion
in'sti·ga'tor
in·still'
in·stilled'
in·stinct'
in·stinc'tive
in·stinc'tive·ly
in·stinc'tu·al
in'sti·tute
in'sti·tut'ed
in'sti·tu'tion
in'sti·tu'tion·al
in'sti·tu'tion·al·ize
in'sti·tu'tion·al·ly
in·struct'
in·struct'ed
in·struc'tion
in·struc'tion·al
in·struc'tive
in·struc'tor
in'stru·ment
in'stru·men'tal
in'stru·men'tal·ist
in'stru·men·tal'i·ty
in'stru·men'tal·ly
in'stru·men·ta'tion
in'sub·or'di·nate
in'sub·or'di·na'tion
in·suf'fer·a·ble
in'suf·fi'cien·cy
in'suf·fi'cient
in'su·lar
in'su·lar'i·ty
in'su·late
in'su·lat'ed
in'su·la'tion
in'su·la'tor
in'su·lin
in·sult'
in·sult'ed
in·sult'ing·ly
in·su'per·a·ble
in'sup·port'a·ble
in'sup·press'i·ble
in·sur'a·bil'i·ty
in·sur'a·ble
in·sur'ance
in·sure'
in·sured'
in·sur'er
in·sur'gen·cy
in·sur'gent
in'sur·mount'a·ble
in'sur·rec'tion
in'sur·rec'tion·ar'y
in'sur·rec'tion·ist
in·tact'
in·tagl'io
in'take'
in·tan'gi·bil'i·ty
in·tan'gi·ble
in·tar'si·a
in'te·ger
in'te·gral
in'te·gral·ly
in'te·grate
in'te·grat'ed
in'te·gra'tion
in·teg'ri·ty
in·teg'u·ment
in'tel·lect
in'tel·lec'tu·al
in'tel·lec'tu·al·ism
in'tel·lec'tu·al·ize
in'tel·lec'tu·al·ly
in·tel'li·gence
in·tel'li·gent
in·tel'li·gent'si·a
in·tel'li·gi·bil'i·ty
in·tel'li·gi·ble
in·tem'per·ance
in·tem'per·ate
in·tem'per·ate·ly
in·tend'
in·tend'ant
in·tend'ed
in·tense'
in·ten'si·fi·ca'tion
in·ten'si·fi'er

in·ten′si·fy
in·ten′si·ty
in·ten′sive
in·tent′
in·ten′tion
in·ten′tion·al
in·ten′tion·al·ly
in·tent′ly
in·tent′ness
in′ter·act′
in′ter·ac′tion
in′ter·bor′ough
in′ter·breed′
in′ter·cede′
in′ter·ced′ed
in′ter·cept′
in′ter·cept′ed
in′ter·cep′tion
in′ter·cep′tor
in′ter·ces′sion
in′ter·ces′so·ry
in′ter·change′
in′ter·change′a·bil′i·ty
in′ter·change′a·ble
in′ter·col·le′gi·ate
in′ter·com·mu′ni·cate
in′ter·con·nect′
in′ter·cos′tal
in′ter·course
in′ter·de·nom′i·na′tion·al
in′ter·de′part·men′tal
in′ter·de·pend′ence
in′ter·de·pend′ent
in′ter·dict
in′ter·dic′tion
in′ter·est
in′ter·est·ed
in′ter·est·ed·ly
in′ter·est·ing·ly
in′ter·fere′
in′ter·fered′
in′ter·fer′ence
in′ter·fer′ing·ly
in′ter·im
in·te′ri·or
in′ter·ject′
in′ter·ject′ed
in′ter·jec′tion
in′ter·lace′
in′ter·laced′
in′ter·lard′
in′ter·leaf′
in′ter·leave′
in′ter·line′
in′ter·lin′e·al
in′ter·lin′e·ar
in′ter·lin′e·a′tion
in′ter·lined′
in′ter·lock′
in′ter·locked′
in′ter·loc′u·tor
in′ter·loc′u·to′ry
in′ter·lop′er
in′ter·lude
in′ter·mar′riage
in′ter·mar′ry
in′ter·me′di·ar′y
in′ter·me′di·ate
in·ter′ment
in′ter·mez′zo
in·ter′mi·na·ble
in·ter′mi·na·bly
in′ter·min′gle
in′ter·min′gled
in′ter·mis′sion
in′ter·mit′
in′ter·mit′tence
in′ter·mit′tent
in′ter·mit′tent·ly
in′ter·mix′ture
in·tern′
in·ter′nal
in·ter′nal·ly
in′ter·na′tion·al
in′ter·na′tion·al·ize
in′ter·na′tion·al·ly
in′terne
in′ter·ne′cine
in·terned′
in·tern′ment
in′ter·pel′late
in′ter·pel·la′tion
in′ter·plan′e·tar′y
in·ter′po·late
in·ter′po·lat′ed
in·ter′po·la′tion

in′ter·pose′
in′ter·posed′
in′ter·po·si′tion
in·ter′pret
in·ter′pre·ta′tion
in·ter′pre·ta′tive
in·ter′pret·ed
in·ter′pret·er
in′ter·reg′num
in′ter·re·la′tion
in·ter′ro·gate
in·ter′ro·ga′tion
in′ter·rog′a·tive
in′ter·rog′a·to′ry
in′ter·rupt′
in′ter·rupt′ed·ly
in′ter·rup′tion
in′ter·scap′u·lar
in′ter·scho·las′tic
in′ter·sect′
in′ter·sect′ed
in′ter·sperse′
in′ter·spersed′
in′ter·state′
in′ter·stel′lar
in·ter′stice
in·ter′stic·es
in′ter·sti′tial
in′ter·sti′tial·ly
in′ter·twine′
in′ter·twined′
In′ter·type

in′ter·ur′ban
in′ter·val
in′ter·vene′
in′ter·vened′
in′ter·ven′tion
in′ter·ven′tion·ist
in′ter·ver′te·bral
in′ter·view
in′ter·viewed
in′ter·view′er
in′ter·weave′
in′ter·wo′ven
in·tes′ta·cy
in·tes′tate
in·tes′ti·nal
in·tes′tine
in′ti·ma·cy
in′ti·mate
in′ti·mat′ed
in′ti·mate·ly
in′ti·ma′tion
in·tim′i·date
in·tim′i·dat′ed
in·tim′i·da′tion
in′to
in·tol′er·a·ble
in·tol′er·ance
in·tol′er·ant
in′to·na′tion
in·tone′
in·toned′
in·tox′i·cate

in·tox′i·cat′ed
in·tox′i·cat′ing·ly
in·tox′i·ca′tion
in·trac′ta·bil′i·ty
in·trac′ta·ble
in′tra·mu′ral
in·tran′si·gence
in·tran′si·gent
in·tran′si·tive
in′tra·state′
in·trench′ment
in·trep′id
in′tre·pid′i·ty
in·trep′id·ly
in′tri·ca·cies
in′tri·ca·cy
in′tri·cate
in′tri·cate·ly
in·trigue′
in·trigued′
in·trin′sic
in·trin′si·cal
in·trin′si·cal·ly
in′tro·duce′
in′tro·duced′
in′tro·duc′tion
in′tro·duc′to·ry
in·tro′it
in′tro·jec′tion
in′tro·spect′
in′tro·spec′tion
in′tro·spec′tive

in′tro·ver′sion
in′tro·vert′
in′tro·vert′ed
in·trude′
in·trud′ed
in·trud′er
in·tru′sion
in·tru′sive
in·tru′sive·ly
in′tu·i′tion
in′tu·i′tion·al
in·tu′i·tive
in·tu′i·tive·ly
in′tu·mesce′
in′tu·mes′cence
in′tu·mes′cent
in·unc′tion
in′un·date
in′un·dat′ed
in′un·da′tion
in·ure′
in·ured′
in·ur′ed·ness
in·urn′
in·vade′
in·vad′ed
in′va·lid
in·val′i·date
in·val′i·dat′ed
in·val′i·da′tion
in′va·lid′i·ty
in·val′u·a·ble

In·var′
in·var′i·a·bil′i·ty
in·var′i·a·ble
in·var′i·a·ble·ness
in·va′sion
in·va′sive
in·vec′tive
in·veigh′
in·vei′gle
in·vei′gled
in·vent′
in·vent′ed
in·ven′tion
in·ven′tive
in·ven′tive·ly
in·ven′tive·ness
in·ven′tor
in′ven·to′ry
in·verse′
in·ver′sion
in·vert′
in·vert′ed
in·vert′i·ble
in·vest′
in·vest′ed
in·ves′ti·gate
in·ves′ti·gat′ed
in·ves′ti·ga′tion
in·ves′ti·ga′tive
in·ves′ti·ga′tor
in·ves′ti·ture
in·vest′ment

in·ves′tor
in·vet′er·ate
in·vid′i·ous
in·vid′i·ous·ly
in·vig′i·late
in·vig′or·ate
in·vig′or·at′ed
in·vig′or·at′ing·ly
in·vig′or·a′tion
in·vig′or·a′tive
in·vin′ci·bil′i·ty
in·vin′ci·ble
in·vi′o·la·bil′i·ty
in·vi′o·la·ble
in·vi′o·late
in·vis′i·bil′i·ty
in·vis′i·ble
in·vis′i·bly
in′vi·ta′tion
in′vi·ta′tion·al
in·vite′
in·vit′ed
in·vit′ing·ly
in′vo·ca′tion
in′voice
in′voiced
in′voic·es
in·voke′
in·voked′
in·vol′un·tar′i·ly
in·vol′un·tar′y
in′vo·lute

in′vo·lu′tion
in·volve′
in·volve′ment
in·vul′ner·a·bil′i·ty
in·vul′ner·a·ble
in′ward
in′ward·ly
in′ward·ness
i′o·date
i·od′ic
i′o·dide
i′o·dine
i′o·dize
i·o′do·form
i′on
I·on′ic
i′on·i·za′tion
i′on·ize
i·o′ta
ip′e·cac
I·ra′ni·an
i·ras′ci·bil′i·ty
i·ras′ci·ble
i′rate
i′rate·ly
ire
ir′i·des′cence
ir′i·des′cent
i·rid′i·um
i′ris
I′rish
I′rish·man

i·ri′tis
irk
irked
irk′some
i′ron
i′ron·bound′
i′ron·clad′
i′roned
i·ron′ic
i·ron′i·cal
i·ron′i·cal·ly
i′ron·ings
i′ron·side′
i′ron·ware′
i′ron·weed′
i′ron·wood′
i′ron·work′
i′ron·work′er
i′ro·ny
Ir′o·quois
ir·ra′di·ate
ir·ra′di·at′ed
ir·ra′di·a′tion
ir·ra′tion·al
ir·ra′tion·al′i·ty
ir·ra′tion·al·ly
ir′re·claim′a·ble
ir·rec′on·cil′a·ble
ir·rec′on·cil′i·a·bil′i·ty
ir·rec′on·cil′i·a·ble
ir′re·cov′er·a·ble
ir′re·deem′a·ble

ir′re·den′ta
ir′re·duc′i·ble
ir·ref′ra·ga·ble
ir′re·fran′gi·ble
ir·ref′u·ta·ble
ir·reg′u·lar
ir·reg′u·lar′i·ty
ir·reg′u·lar·ly
ir·rel′e·vance
ir·rel′e·vant
ir′re·li′gious
ir′re·me′di·a·ble
ir′re·mis′si·ble
ir′re·mov′a·ble
ir·rep′a·ra·ble
ir′re·place′a·ble
ir′re·press′i·ble
ir′re·proach′a·ble
ir′re·sist′i·ble
ir·res′o·lute
ir·res′o·lu′tion
ir′re·solv′a·ble
ir′re·spec′tive
ir′re·spon′si·bil′i·ty
ir′re·spon′si·ble
ir′re·spon′si·bly
ir′re·trace′a·ble
ir′re·triev′a·ble
ir·rev′er·ence
ir·rev′er·ent
ir′re·vers′i·ble
ir·rev′o·ca·ble

ir'ri·ga·ble
ir'ri·gate
ir'ri·gat'ed
ir'ri·ga'tion
ir'ri·ta·bil'i·ty
ir'ri·ta·ble
ir'ri·tant
ir'ri·tate
ir'ri·tat'ed
ir'ri·ta'tion
ir'ri·ta'tive
ir·rup'tion
ir·rup'tive
is'chi·um
i'sin·glass'
Is'lam
is'land
is'land·er
isle
is'let
i'so·bar
i'so·late
i'so·lat'ed
i·so·la'tion
i'so·la'tion·ism
i'so·la'tion·ist
i'so·mer
i'so·mer'ic
i'so·mor'phic
i·sos'ce·les
i'so·therm
i'so·tope
is'su·ance
is'sue
is'sued
is'sues
isth'mi·an
isth'mus
it
I·tal'ian
I·tal'ian·ate
i·tal'ic
i·tal'i·cize
itch
itched
itch'i·er
itch'i·est
itch'y
i'tem
i'tem·ize
i'tem·ized
it'er·ate
it'er·a'tion
it'er·a'tive
i·tin'er·a·cy
i·tin'er·an·cy
i·tin'er·ant
i·tin'er·ar'y
i·tin'er·ate
its
it·self'
i'vo·ry
i'vy

# J

jab'ber
jab'ber·ing·ly
ja'bot'
jack
jack'al
jack'a·napes'
jack'daw'
jack'et
jack'et·ed
jack'knife'
jack'stone'
jack'straw'
jack'weed'
Jac·o·be'an
jade
jad'ed
jade'ite
jagged
jag'uar
jail
jailed
jail'er

jal'ou·sie
jam
jam'bo·ree'
jammed
jan'gle
jan'i·tor
jan'i·tress
Jan'u·ar'y
Ja·pan'
Jap'a·nese'
ja·panned'
jar
jar'gon
jarred
jas'mine
jas'per
jaun'dice
jaunt
jaun'ti·er
jaun'ti·est
jaun'ti·ly
jaun'ti·ness

jaun'ty
jave'lin
jaw
jaw'bone'
jazz
jazz'y
jeal'ous
jeal'ous·y
jeer
jeered
jeer'ing·ly
Je·ho'vah
je·june'
je·ju'num
jel'lied
jel'ly
jel'ly·fish'
jen'net
jeop'ard·ize
jeop'ard·y
jer'e·mi'ad
jerk

jerked
jerk'i·ly
jer'kin
jerk'y
jer'sey
jest
jest'er
jest'ing·ly
Jes'u·it
Je'sus
jet
jet'lin·er
jet'port
jet'sam
jet'ti·son
jew'eled
jew'el·er
jew'el·ry
Jew'ish
Jew'ry
jibe
jig
jig'ger
jig'gle
jig'gled
jig'saw'
jin'gle
jin'gled
jin'go
jin'go·ism
jin·rik'i·sha
jinx

jit'ney
jit'ters
jit'ter·y
job
job'ber
jock'ey
jo·cose'
jo·cose'ly
jo·cos'i·ty
joc'u·lar
joc'u·lar'i·ty
joc'u·lar·ly
joc'und
jo·cun'di·ty
jodh'purs
jog
jogged
jog'gle
jog'gled
join
join'der
joined
join'er
join'ings
joint
joint'ed
joint'ly
join'ture
joist
joke
jok'er
jok'ing·ly

jol'li·er
jol'li·est
jol'li·fi·ca'tion
jol'li·ty
jol'ly
jolt
jolt'ed
jon'quil
jos'tle
jos'tled
jot
jot'ted
jounce
jour'nal
jour'nal·ism
jour'nal·ist
jour'nal·is'tic
jour'nal·ize
jour'nal·ized
jour'ney
jour'neyed
jour'ney·man
jo'vi·al
jo'vi·al'i·ty
jo'vi·al·ly
jowl
joy
joy'ful
joy'ful·ly
joy'ful·ness
joy'less
joy'ous

ju′bi·lance
ju′bi·lant
ju′bi·late
ju′bi·la′tion
ju′bi·lee
Ju′da·ism
judge
judged
judge′ship
judg′ment
ju′di·ca′tive
ju′di·ca·to′ry
ju′di·ca·ture
ju·di′cial
ju·di′cial·ly
ju·di′ci·ar′y
ju·di′cious
jug′gle
jug′gled
jug′gler
jug′u·lar
juice

juic′y
ju′lep
ju′li·enne′
Ju·ly′
jum′ble
jum′bled
jum′bo
jump
jumped
jump′er
junc′tion
junc′ture
June
jun′gle
jun′ior
ju′ni·per
junk
jun′ket
jun′ta
ju′rat
ju·rid′i·cal
ju′ris·con·sult′

ju′ris·dic′tion
ju′ris·pru′dence
ju′rist
ju′ror
ju′ry
ju′ry·man
just
jus′tice
jus·ti′ci·a·ble
jus′ti·fi′a·ble
jus′ti·fi·ca′tion
jus′ti·fi·ca′to·ry
jus′ti·fied
jus′ti·fy
just′ly
just′ness
jut
jute
jut′ted
ju′ve·nile
ju′ve·nil′i·ty
jux′ta·po·si′tion

kai'ser
kale
ka·lei'do·scope
ka·lei'do·scop'ic
kal'so·mine
kan'ga·roo'
ka'o·lin
ka'pok
kar'ma
kay'ak
keel
keen
keen'er
keen'est
keen'ly
keen'ness
keep
keep'er
keep'sake'
keg
kelp
ken'nel
kept
ker'a·tin
ker'chief
ker'nel
ker'o·sene'
ker'sey
ketch
ke·to'sis
ket'tle
key
key'board'
keyed
key'hole'
key'note'
key'stone'
khak'i
khe·dive'
kib'itz·er
ki'bosh
kick
kick'back'
kick'er
kick'off'
kick'shaw'
kid
kid'nap
kid'naped
kid'ney
kid'skin'
kill
killed
kill'er
kill'ings
kiln
kil'o·cy'cle
kil'o·gram
kil'o·me'ter
kilt
kilt'ed
kin
kind
kind'er
kind'est
kin'der·gar'ten

kin′dle
kin′dled
kind′li·ness
kind′ly
kind′ness
kin′dred
kine
kin′es·thet′ic
ki·net′ic
king
king′bird′
king′bolt′
king′craft
king′dom
king′fish′
king′fish′er
king′let
king′li·ness
king′ly
king′pin′
king′ship
kink
kinked
kink′y
kin′ship
kins′man
ki·osk′
kip′per
kiss
kissed
kitch′en
kitch′en·ette′
kite
kith
kit′ten
klep′to·ma′ni·a
klep′to·ma′ni·ac
knap′sack′
knave
knav′er·y
knav′ish
knead
knead′ed
knee′cap′
kneel
kneeled
knelt
knew
knick′ers
knick′knack′
knife
knifed
knight
knight′ed
knight′hood
knight′li·ness
knight′ly
knit
knit′ter
knives
knob
knock
knock′down′
knock′er
knock′out′
knoll
knot
knot′hole′
knot′ted
knot′ty
knot′work′
knout
know
know′a·ble
know′ing·ly
know′ing·ness
knowl′edge
known
knuck′le
knuck′led
knurl
knurled
knurl′y
ko′bold
ko′dak
kohl′ra′bi
ko′peck
Ko·ran′
Ko·re′an
ko′sher
kraft
krem′lin
kryp′ton
ku·lak′
ky′mo·graph
ky·pho′sis

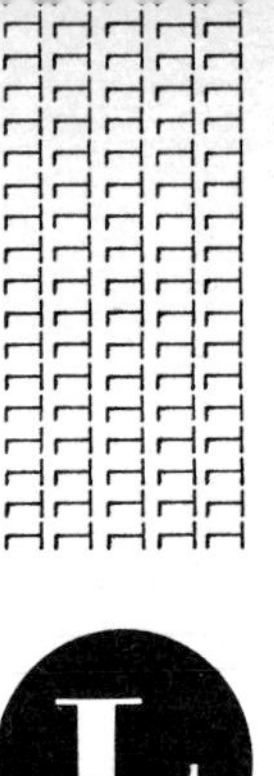

# L

la′bel
la′beled
la′bi·al
la′bor
lab′o·ra·to′ry
la′bored
la′bor·er
la·bo′ri·ous
la·bur′num
lab′y·rinth
lab′y·rin′thine
lace
laced
lac′er·ate
lac′er·at′ed
lac′er·a′tion
lac′er·a′tive
lace′wing′
lace′wood′
lace′work′
lach′es
lach′ry·mal
lach′ry·mose
lac′ings
lack
lack′a·dai′si·cal
lack′ey
lack′lus′ter
la·con′ic
lac′quer
lac′quered
la·crosse′
lac′tase
lac′tate
lac·ta′tion
lac′te·al
lac′tic
lac′tose
la·cu′na
la·cu′nae
lad′der
lad′en
la′dle
la′dled
la′dy
la′dy·like′
la′dy·ship
lag
la′ger
lag′gard
lagged
la·goon′
lair
laird
la′i·ty
lake
lamb′doid
lam′bent
lamb′kin
lamb′like′
lam′bre·quin
la′mé′
lame
lamed
lame′ly
lame′ness

la·ment′
lam′en·ta·ble
lam′en·ta′tion
la·ment′ed
lam′i·na
lam′i·nae
lam′i·nate
lam′i·nat′ed
lam′i·na′tion
lamp
lamp′black′
lam·poon′
lam·pooned′
lam′prey
lance
lanc′er
lan′cet
lan′ci·nate
lan′ci·nat′ed
lan′ci·na′tion
land
lan′dau
land′ed
land′fall′
land′hold′er
land′la′dy
land′locked′
land′lord′
land′mark′
land′own′er
land′scape
land′slide′
land′slip′
lands′man
land′ward
lan′guage
lan′guid
lan′guish
lan′guor
lan′guor·ous
lank
lank′er
lank′est
lank′y
lan′o·lin
lans′downe
lan′tern
lan′tha·num
lan′yard
lap
la·pel′
lap′ful
lap′i·dar′y
lap′i·da′tion
lapse
lapsed
lap′wing′
lar′board
lar′ce·nous
lar′ce·ny
larch
lard
lard′ed
lard′er
large
large′ly
large′ness
larg′er
lar′gess
larg′est
lar′i·at
lark
lark′spur
lar′va
lar′vae
lar′val
la·ryn′ge·al
lar′yn·gi′tis
lar′ynx
las′car
las·civ′i·ous
lash
lashed
lash′ings
lass
las′si·tude
las′so
last
last′ed
last′ing·ly
last′ly
lasts
Lat′a·ki′a
latch
latched
latch′key′

latch′string′
late
la·teen′
late′ly
la′ten·cy
late′ness
la′tent
lat′er
lat′er·al
lat′er·al·ly
lat′est
la′tex
lath
lath′er
laths
Lat′in
Lat′in·ism
La·tin′i·ty
Lat′in·i·za′tion
Lat′in·ize
lat′i·tude
lat′i·tu′di·nal
lat′i·tu′di·nar′i·an
lat′ter
lat′ter·most
lat′tice
lat′tice·work′
laud
laud′a·bil′i·ty
laud′a·ble
lau′da·num
lau·da′tion
laud′a·to′ry
laud′ed
laugh
laugh′a·ble
laugh′ing·ly
laugh′ing·stock′
laugh′ter
launch
launch′ings
laun′der
laun′dered
laun′der·ings
laun′dress
laun′dry
laun′dry·man
lau′re·ate
lau′rel
la′va
lav′a·liere′
lav′a·to′ry
lav′en·der
lav′ish
lav′ished
lav′ish·ness
law
law′break′er
law′ful
law′ful·ly
law′giv′er
law′less
law′less·ness
law′mak′er
lawn
law′suit′
law′yer
lax
lax′a·tive
lax′i·ty
lax′ly
lax′ness
lay′er
lay′man
laz′a·ret′to
la′zi·er
la′zi·est
la′zi·ly
la′zi·ness
la′zy
leach
leached
lead
lead′en
lead′er
lead′er·ship
leads′man
leaf
leaf′let
league
leagued
leak
leak′age
leak′i·ness
leak′y
lean

leaned
lean'ings
leap
leaped
learn
learned
learnt
lease
leased
lease'hold'
lease'hold'er
leash
leashed
least
leath'er
leath'ern
leath'er·oid
leath'er·y
leave
leav'en
leav'ened
leav'ing
lec'i·thin
lec'tern
lec'ture
lec'tured
lec'tur·er
ledge
ledg'er
leech
leek
leer

leered
leer'ing·ly
lee'ward
lee'way'
left
left'-hand'ed
leg
leg'a·cy
le'gal
le'gal·ism
le'gal·is'tic
le·gal'i·ty
le'gal·i·za'tion
le'gal·ize
le'gal·ly
leg'ate
leg'a·tee'
le·ga'tion
le·ga'to
leg'end
leg'end·ar'y
leg'er·de·main'
leg'gings
leg'i·bil'i·ty
leg'i·ble
le'gion
le'gion·ar'y
leg'is·late
leg'is·la'tion
leg'is·la'tive
leg'is·la'tor
leg'is·la'ture

le·git'i·ma·cy
le·git'i·mate
le·git'i·mate·ly
le·git'i·mate·ness
le·git'i·ma'tion
le·git'i·mist
le·git'i·mize
leg'ume
le·gu'mi·nous
lei'sure
lei'sure·li·ness
lei'sure·ly
lem'mings
lem'on
lem'on·ade'
lem'on·weed'
le'mur
lend
length
length'en
length'ened
length'i·er
length'i·est
length'i·ly
length'i·ness
length'ways
length'wise
length'y
le'ni·ence
le'ni·en·cy
le'ni·ent
le'ni·ent·ly

Len'in·ism
len'i·tive
len'i·ty
lens
lent
Lent'en
len·tic'u·lar
len'til
len'toid
le'o·nine
leop'ard
le'o·tard
lep'er
lep're·chaun'
lep'ro·sy
lep'rous
le'sion
less
les·see'
less'en
less'ened
less'er
les'son
les'sor
lest
let
le'thal
le·thar'gic
le·thar'gi·cal
leth'ar·gy
let's
let'ter

let'tered
let'ter·head'
let'ter·press'
let'ter·space'
let'tuce
leu'co·cyte
leu'co·cy·to'sis
leu'co·der'ma
leu·ke'mi·a
lev'ant
lev'ee
lev'el
lev'eled
lev'el·head'ed
le'ver
le'ver·age
lev'i·tate
lev'i·tat'ed
lev'i·ta'tion
lev'i·ty
lev'u·lose
lev'y
lex'i·cog'ra·pher
lex'i·cog'ra·phy
lex'i·con
li'a·bil'i·ty
li'a·ble
li'ai·son'
li'ar
li·ba'tion
li'bel
li'bel·ant

li'beled
li'bel·ous
lib'er·al
lib'er·al·ism
lib'er·al'i·ty
lib'er·al·i·za'tion
lib'er·al·ize
lib'er·al·ized
lib'er·al·ly
lib'er·ate
lib'er·at'ed
lib'er·a'tion
lib'er·a'tor
lib'er·tar'i·an
lib'er·tine
lib'er·ty
li·bi'do
li·brar'i·an
li'brar'y
li·bret'to
lice
li'cense
li'cen·see'
li·cen'ti·ate
li·cen'tious
li·cen'tious·ness
li'chen
li'chen·oid
lic'it
lick
lic'o·rice
lic'tor

lie
liege
li′en
lieu
lieu·ten′an·cy
lieu·ten′ant
life
life′guard′
life′less
life′like′
life′long′
life′time′
life′work′
lift
lift′ed
lig′a·ment
li′gate
li·ga′tion
lig′a·ture
lig′a·tured
light
light′ed
light′en
light′ened
light′er
light′er·age
light′est
light′face′
light′head′ed
light′heart′ed
light′house′
light′ly

light′ness
light′ning
light′ship′
light′weight′
lig′ne·ous
lig′ni·fy
lig′nite
lik′a·ble
like
liked
like′li·er
like′li·est
like′li·hood
like′ly
lik′en
like′ness
like′wise′
lik′ings
li′lac
lil′i·a′ceous
lilt
lilt′ing·ly
lil′y
limb
lim′ber
lim′bo
lime
lime′kiln′
lime′light′
li′men
Lim′er·ick
lime′stone′

lime′wa′ter
lim′i·nal
lim′it
lim′it·a·ble
lim′i·ta′tion
lim′it·ed
lim′it·less
limn
limned
lim·nol′o·gy
lim′ou·sine′
limp
limped
limp′er
limp′est
lim′pet
lim′pid
lim·pid′i·ty
lim′pid·ly
limp′ly
limp′ness
lin′age
lin′den
line
lin′e·age
lin′e·al
lin′e·al′i·ty
lin′e·a·ment
lin′e·ar
lined
line′man
lin′en

lin′er
lines′man
lin′ger
lin′gered
lin′ge·rie′
lin′ger·ing·ly
lin′go
lin′gual
lin′guist
lin·guis′tic
lin·guis′ti·cal·ly
lin·guis′tics
lin′i·ment
lin′ings
link
link′age
linked
Lin·nae′an
lin′net
li·no′le·um
Lin′o·type
lin′seed′
lint
lin′tel
li′on
li′on·ess
li′on·ize
lip′oid
li·po′ma
liq′ue·fa′cient
liq′ue·fac′tion
liq′ue·fac′tive
liq′ue·fi′a·ble
liq′ue·fied
liq′ue·fy
li′ques′cence
li·queur′
liq′uid
liq′ui·date
liq′ui·dat′ed
liq′ui·da′tion
liq′ui·da′tor
liq′uor
li′ra
lisp
lisped
lisp′ing·ly
lis′some
list
list′ed
lis′ten
lis′tened
lis′ten·er
list′ings
list′less
lit′a·ny
li′ter
lit′er·a·cy
lit′er·al
lit′er·al·ism
lit′er·al′i·ty
lit′er·al·ize
lit′er·al·ly
lit′er·ar′y
lit′er·ate
lit′er·a·ture
lith′arge
lithe
lithe′some
lith′i·a
lith′i·um
lith′o·graph
li·thog′ra·pher
lith′o·graph′ic
li·thog′ra·phy
li·tho′sis
li·thot′o·my
lit′i·ga·ble
lit′i·gant
lit′i·gate
lit′i·gat′ed
lit′i·ga′tion
li·ti′gious
lit′mus
lit′ter
lit′tered
lit′tle
lit′tlest
lit′to·ral
li·tur′gi·cal
lit′ur·gist
lit′ur·gy
liv′a·ble
live
live
lived

live'li·er
live'li·est
live'li·hood
live'li·ness
live'long'
live'ly
liv'er
liv'er·y
liv'er·y·man
liv'id
li·vid'i·ty
liv'ings
liz'ard
lla'ma
lla'no
load
load'ed
load'ings
loaf
loaf'er
loam
loan
loaned
loathe
loathed
loath'er
loath'ful
loath'ly
loath'some
lo'bar
lob'bied
lob'by
lob'by·ist
lob'ster
lo'cal
lo'cal·ism
lo·cal'i·ty
lo'cal·i·za'tion
lo'cal·ize
lo'cal·ized
lo'cal·ly
lo'cate
lo'cat·ed
lo·ca'tion
lo'ci
lock
lock'age
lock'er
lock'et
lock'jaw'
lock'out'
lock'smith'
lock'up'
lo'co·mo'tion
lo'co·mo'tive
lo'cus
lo'cust
lo·cu'tion
lode
lode'star'
lodge
lodged
lodg'er
lodg'ings
lodg'ment
loft
loft'i·ly
loft'i·ness
loft'y
log
lo'gan·ber'ry
log'a·rithm
log'book'
loge
log'ger·heads'
log'gia
log'ic
log'i·cal
log'i·cal·ly
lo·gi'cian
lo·gis'tics
log'or·rhe'a
log'o·type
log'wood'
loin
loi'ter
loi'tered
loi'ter·er
loll
lolled
lol'li·pop
lone
lone'li·ness
lone'ly
lone'some
lone'some·ly

lone'some·ness
long
long'boat'
longed
lon'ger
long'est
lon·gev'i·ty
long'hand'
long'horn'
long'ing·ly
long'ings
lon'gi·tude
lon'gi·tu'di·nal
long'shore'man
look
look'out'
loom
loomed
loon
loon'y
loop
loop'hole'
loose
loose'ly
loos'en
loos'ened
loose'ness
loos'er
loos'est
loot
loot'ed
lop

lop'sid'ed
lo·qua'cious
lo·qua'cious·ly
lo·quac'i·ty
lord
lord'li·ness
lord'ly
lor·do'sis
lord'ship
lore
lor'gnette'
lor'ry
los'a·ble
lose
los'er
los'es
los'ings
loss
lost
lo'tion
lot'ter·y
lo'tus
loud
loud'er
loud'est
loud'ly
loud'ness
lounge
louse
lout
lout'ish
lou'ver

lov'a·ble
love
love'less
love'li·ness
love'lorn'
love'ly
lov'er
love'sick'
lov'ing·ly
low
low'born'
low'boy'
low'bred'
low'er
low'est
low'land
low'li·er
low'li·est
low'li·ness
low'ly
low'most
loy'al
loy'al·ism
loy'al·ist
loy'al·ly
loy'al·ty
loz'enge
lu'bri·cant
lu'bri·cate
lu'bri·ca'tion
lu'bri·ca'tor
lu·bric'i·ty

lu'cent
lu'cid
lu·cid'i·ty
lu'cid·ly
lu'cid·ness
luck
luck'i·ly
luck'i·ness
luck'less
luck'y
lu'cra·tive
lu'cre
lu'cu·bra'tion
lu'di·crous
lug
lug'gage
lugged
lug'ger
lu·gu'bri·ous
luke'warm'
lull
lull'a·by'
lulled
lum·ba'go
lum'ber
lum'ber·yard'
lu'mi·nar'y
lu'mi·nes'cence
lu'mi·nes'cent
lu'mi·nif'er·ous
lu'mi·nos'i·ty
lu'mi·nous
lump
lump'i·er
lump'i·est
lump'y
lu'na·cy
lu'nar
lu'na·tic
lunch
lunch'eon
lunch'eon·ette'
lunch'room'
lu·nette'
lung
lunge
lunged
lurch
lurched
lurch'ing
lure
lured
lu'rid
lurk
lurked
lus'cious
lush
lust
lus'ter
lust'ful
lust'i·ly
lust'i·ness
lus'trous
lus'trous·ly
lus'trum
lust'y
lute
Lu'ther·an
lux·u'ri·ance
lux·u'ri·ant
lux·u'ri·ate
lux·u'ri·at'ed
lux·u'ri·ous
lux'u·ry
ly·ce'um
lydd'ite
lymph
lym·phat'ic
lymph'oid
lynx
ly'on·naise'
lyre
lyre'bird'
lyr'ic
lyr'i·cal
lyr'i·cism

ma·ca′bre
mac·ad′am
mac·ad′am·ize
macʹa·ro′ni
macʹa·roon′
ma·caw′
mac′er·ate
mac′er·atʹed
macʹer·a′tion
Mach
ma·che′te
ma·chicʹo·la′tion
mach′i·nate
machʹi·na′tion
ma·chine′
ma·chined′
ma·chin′er·y
ma·chin′ist
mack′er·el
mac′ro·cosm
mac′ro·cyte
ma′cron

mac′u·late
mad
mad′am
mad′den·ing·ly
mad′der
mad′dest
mad′houseʹ
mad′ly
mad′man
mad′ness
ma·don′na
mad′ri·gal
mael′strom
maf′fi·a
magʹa·zine′
ma·gen′ta
mag′got
Ma′gi
mag′ic
mag′i·cal
mag′i·cal·ly
ma·gi′cian

magʹis·te′ri·al
mag′is·tra·cy
mag′is·tral
mag′is·trate
mag′is·tra·ture
magʹna·nim′i·ty
mag·nan′i·mous
mag′nate
mag·ne′sia
mag·ne′si·um
mag′net
mag·net′ic
mag·net′i·cal·ly
mag′net·ism
magʹnet·i·za′tion
mag′net·ize
mag′net·ized
mag·ne′to
magʹni·fi·ca′tion
mag·nif′i·cence
mag·nif′i·cent
mag·nif′i·co

mag'ni·fi'er
mag'ni·fy
mag·nil'o·quent
mag'ni·tude
mag·no'li·a
mag'num
mag'pie
mag'uey
ma·ha'ra'ja
ma·ha'ra'ni
ma·hat'ma
ma·hog'a·ny
maid
maid'en
maid'en·hair'
maid'en·hood
maid'en·ly
maid'serv'ant
mail
mail'a·ble
mail'bag'
mail'box'
mailed
mail'er
mail'ings
maim
maimed
main
main'land'
main'ly
main'mast'
main'sail'
main'sheet'
main'spring'
main'stay'
main·tain'
main·tain'a·ble
main'te·nance
ma·jes'tic
maj'es·ty
ma·jol'i·ca
ma'jor
ma·jor'i·ty
ma·jus'cule
make
make'-be·lieve'
mak'er
make'shift'
mak'ings
mal'a·chite
mal'ad·just'ed
mal'ad·just'ment
mal'a·droit'
mal'a·dy
mal'a·pert
mal'a·prop·ism
mal'ap·ro·pos'
ma·lar'i·a
ma·lar'i·al
mal'as·sim'i·la'tion
Ma·lay'
mal'con·tent'
male
mal'e·dic'tion
mal'e·dic'to·ry
mal'e·fac'tor
ma·lef'i·cence
ma·lef'i·cent
ma·lev'o·lence
ma·lev'o·lent
mal·fea'sance
mal·fea'sor
mal'for·ma'tion
mal·formed'
mal'ice
ma·li'cious
ma·li'cious·ly
ma·li'cious·ness
ma·lign'
ma·lig'nan·cy
ma·lig'nant
ma·lig'nant·ly
ma·ligned'
ma·lig'ni·ty
ma·lign'ly
ma·lin'ger
ma·lin'ger·er
mall
mal'lard
mal'le·a·bil'i·ty
mal'le·a·ble
mal·le'o·lar
mal·le'o·lus
mal'let
mal'low
malm'sey

mal′nu·tri′tion
mal·o′dor·ous
mal′po·si′tion
mal′prac′tice
malt
malt′ase
Mal′tese′
malt′ose
mal·treat′
mal·ver·sa′tion
mam′ba
mam′mal
mam·ma′li·an
mam′ma·ry
mam′mon
mam′moth
man
man′a·cle
man′a·cled
man′age
man′age·a·ble
man′aged
man′age·ment
man′ag·er
man′a·ge′ri·al
man′a·ge′ri·al·ly
man′ag·er·ship′
man′a·tee′
man·da′mus
man′da·rin
man′date
man′dat·ed
man′da·to′ry
man′di·ble
man·dib′u·lar
man′do·lin
man′drake
man′drel
ma·neu′ver
ma·neu′vered
man′ga·nate
man′ga·nese
mange
man′ger
man′gi·ly
man′gi·ness
man′gle
man′gled
man′go
man′grove
man′gy
man′hole′
man′hood
ma′ni·a
ma′ni·ac
ma·ni′a·cal
man′i·cure
man′i·cur′ist
man′i·fest
man′i·fes·ta′tion
man′i·fest·ed
man′i·fes′to
man′i·fold
man′i·fold′ed
man′i·fold′er
man′i·kin
ma·nip′u·late
ma·nip′u·lat′ed
ma·nip′u·lates
ma·nip′u·la′tion
ma·nip′u·la′tive
ma·nip′u·la′tor
ma·nip′u·la·to′ry
man′kind′
man′like′
man′li·ness
man′ly
man′na
man′ner
man′nered
man′ner·ism
man′ner·ly
man′nish
ma·nom′e·ter
man′o·met′ric
man′or
ma·no′ri·al
man′sard
man′serv′ant
man′sion
man′slaugh′ter
man′teau
man′tel
man·til′la
man′tis
man·tis′sa

man'tle
man'u·al
man'u·al·ly
man'u·fac'to·ry
man'u·fac'ture
man'u·fac'tured
man'u·fac'tur·er
man'u·mis'sion
ma·nure'
man'u·script
Manx
man'y
Ma'o·ri
map
ma'ple
mapped
mar
mar'a·bou
mar'a·schi'no
ma·raud'
ma·raud'er
mar'ble
mar'bled
mar'ca·site
march
march'er
mar'chion·ess
mar·co'ni·gram
mare
mar'ga·rine
mar'gin
mar'gin·al
mar'gi·na'li·a
mar'gin·al·ly
mar'grave
mar'i·gold
mar'i·jua'na
ma·rim'ba
ma·ri'na
mar'i·nade'
mar'i·nate
mar'i·nat'ed
ma·rine'
mar'i·ner
mar'i·o·nette'
Mar'ist
mar'i·tal
mar'i·tal·ly
mar'i·time
mar'jo·ram
mark
marked
mark'ed·ly
mark'er
mar'ket
mar'ket·a·bil'i·ty
mar'ket·a·ble
mark'ings
marks'man
marks'man·ship
mark'weed'
marl
mar'lin
mar'ma·lade
mar'mo·set
mar'mot
ma·roon'
ma·rooned'
mar'plot'
mar·quee'
mar'qui·sette'
marred
mar'riage
mar'riage·a·ble
mar'ried
mar'row
mar'row·bone'
mar'row·fat'
mar'row·y
mar'ry
Mars
mar'shal
mar'shaled
marsh'i·ness
marsh'mal'low
marsh'y
mar·su'pi·al
mart
mar'ten
mar'tial
mar'tial·ly
Mar'ti·an
mar'ti·net'
mar'tin·gale
mar'tyr
mar'tyr·dom

mar′tyred
mar′vel
mar′veled
mar′vel·ous
mar′zi·pan
mas·car′a
mas′cot
mas′cu·line
mas′cu·lin′i·ty
mash
mashed
mash′er
mash′ie
mask
masked
mask′er
ma′son
ma·son′ic
ma′son·ry
mas′quer·ade′
mas′quer·ad′ed
mass
mas′sa·cre
mas·sage′
mas·seur′
mas′sive
mast
mas′ter
mas′tered
mas′ter·ful
mas′ter·ful·ly
mas′ter·ful·ness
mas′ter·ly
mas′ter·piece′
mas′ter·ship
mas′ter·work′
mas′ter·y
mast′head′
mas′tic
mas′ti·cate
mas′ti·cat′ed
mas′ti·ca′tion
mas′ti·ca′tor
mas′ti·ca·to′ry
mas′tiff
mas′to·don
mas′toid
mas′toid·i′tis
mat
mat′a·dor
match
matched
match′less
match′less·ly
match′mak′er
match′wood′
ma′té
ma·te′ri·al
ma·te′ri·al·ism
ma·te′ri·al·ist
ma·te′ri·al·is′tic
ma·te′ri·al′i·ty
ma·te′ri·al·i·za′tion
ma·te′ri·al·ize
ma·te′ri·al·ized
ma·te′ri·al·ly
ma·ter′nal
ma·ter′nal·ly
ma·ter′ni·ty
math′e·mat′i·cal
math′e·ma·ti′cian
math′e·mat′ics
mat′in
mat′i·nee′
ma′tri·arch
ma′tri·arch′y
ma′tri·ces
ma′tri·cide
ma·tric′u·lant
ma·tric′u·late
ma·tric′u·lat′ed
ma·tric′u·lates
ma·tric′u·la′tion
mat′ri·mo′ni·al
mat′ri·mo′ni·al·ly
mat′ri·mo′ny
ma′trix
ma′tron
ma′tron·li·ness
ma′tron·ly
matte
mat′ted
mat′ter
mat′tered
mat′tings
mat′tock

mat'tress
mat'u·rate
mat'u·rat'ed
mat'u·ra'tion
ma·tur'a·tive
ma·ture'
ma·tured'
ma·ture'ly
ma·ture'ness
ma·tu'ri·ty
ma·tu'ti·nal
maud'lin
maul
mauled
maun'der
mau'so·le'um
mauve
mav'er·ick
ma'vis
maw
mawk'ish
max'il·lar'y
max'im
max'i·mal
max'i·mize
max'i·mum
may
may'be
may'hem
may'on·naise'
may'or
may'or·al·ty
maze
ma·zur'ka
me
mead'ow
mead'ow·land'
mea'ger
meal
meal'i·er
meal'i·est
meal'time'
meal'y
meal'y·mouthed'
mean
me·an'der
mean'ing·ful
mean'ing·less
mean'ing·ly
mean'ings
mean'ly
mean'ness
mean'time'
mean'while'
mea'sles
meas'ur·a·ble
meas'ur·a·bly
meas'ure
meas'ured
meas'ure·less
meas'ure·ment
meas'ur·er
meat
meat'cut'ter
me·a'tus
me·chan'ic
me·chan'i·cal
me·chan'i·cal·ly
mech'a·ni'cian
me·chan'ics
mech'a·nism
mech'a·ni·za'tion
mech'a·nize
med'al
med'al·ist
me·dal'lion
med'dle
med'dled
med'dle·some
me'di·a
me'di·al
me'di·an
me'di·ate
me'di·at'ed
me'di·a'tion
me'di·a'tive
me'di·a'tor
med'i·cal
med'i·cal·ly
Med'i·care
med'i·cate
med'i·cat'ed
med'i·ca'tion
med'i·ca'tive
me·dic'i·nal
me·dic'i·nal·ly

med′i·cine
me′di·e′val
me′di·e′val·ist
me′di·e′val·ly
me′di·o′cre
me′di·oc′ri·ty
med′i·tate
med′i·tat′ed
med′i·ta′tion
med′i·ta′tive
me′di·um
med′lar
me·dul′la
meek
meek′er
meek′est
meek′ly
meek′ness
meer′schaum
meet
meet′ings
meet′ing·house′
meg′a·cy′cle
meg′a·phone
mei·o′sis
mei·ot′ic
mel′an·cho′li·a
mel′an·chol′ic
mel′an·chol′y
mel′a·nism
mel′a·no′sis
meld
mel′io·rate
mel′io·rat′ed
mel′io·ra′tion
mel′io·ra′tive
me·lis′ma
mel′is·mat′ic
mel·lif′lu·ous
mel′low
mel′lowed
mel′low·er
mel′low·est
me·lo′de·on
me·lod′ic
me·lo′di·on
me·lo′di·ous
me·lo′di·ous·ly
mel′o·dra′ma
mel′o·dra·mat′ic
mel′o·dy
mel′on
me′los
melt
melt′ed
melt′ing·ly
mem′ber
mem′ber·ship
mem′brane
mem′bra·nous
me·men′to
mem′oir
mem′o·ra·bil′i·a
mem′o·ra·ble
mem′o·ran′da
mem′o·ran′dum
mem′o·ran′dums
me·mo′ri·al
me·mo′ri·al·i·za′tion
me·mo′ri·al·ize
mem′o·ri·za′tion
mem′o·rize
mem′o·rized
mem′o·ry
men′ace
men′aced
me·nage′
me·nag′er·ie
mend
men·da′cious
men·dac′i·ty
mend′ed
Men·de′li·an
men′di·can·cy
men′di·cant
men′folk′
men·ha′den
me′ni·al
me′ni·al·ly
me·nin′ges
men′in·gi′tis
me·nis′cus
Men′non·ite
men′su·ra′tion
men′su·ra′tive
men′tal

men·tal′i·ty
men′tal·ly
men′thol
men′tion
men′tioned
men′tor
men′u
me·phit′ic
mer′can·tile
mer′ce·nar′y
mer′cer·ize
mer′cer·ized
mer′chan·dise
mer′chan·dis′er
mer′chant
mer′chant·man
mer′ci·ful
mer′ci·less
mer′ci·less·ly
mer·cu′ri·al
mer′cu·ry
mer′cy
mere′ly
mer′est
mer′e·tri′cious
merge
merged
merg′er
me·rid′i·an
me·ringue′
me·ri′no
mer′it
mer′it·ed
mer′i·to′ri·ous
mer′i·to′ri·ous·ly
mer′lin
mer′maid′
mer′ri·er
mer′ri·est
mer′ri·ly
mer′ri·ment
mer′ri·ness
mer′ry
mer′ry·mak′ing
me′sa
mes·cal′
mes·cal′ine
mesh
mesh′work′
mes′mer·ism
mes′on
mess
mes′sage
mes′sen·ger
Mes·si′ah
mess′man
mess′mate′
mes·ti′zo
met′a·bol′ic
me·tab′o·lism
met′a·car′pal
met′a·car′pus
met′al
me·tal′lic
me·tal′li·cal·ly
met′al·loid
met′al·lur′gic
met′al·lur′gi·cal
met′al·lur′gy
met′al·ware′
met′al·work′
met′al·work′er
met′a·mor′phose
met′a·mor′phoses
met′a·mor′pho·sis
met′a·phor
met′a·phor′ic
met′a·phor′i·cal
met′a·phor′i·cal·ly
met′a·phys′i·cal
met′a·phys′i·cal·ly
met′a·phy·si′cian
met′a·phys′ics
me·tas′ta·sis
me·tas′ta·size
met′a·tar′sal
met′a·tar′sus
mete
met′ed
me′te·or
me′te·or′ic
me′te·or·ite
me′te·or·oid′
me′te·or·ol′o·gy
me′ter
me′tered

meth′a·done
meth′ane
me·thinks′
meth′od
me·thod′i·cal
me·thod′i·cal·ly
meth′od·ist
meth′od·ol′o·gy
meth′yl
me·tic′u·lous
mé·tier′
me·ton′y·my
met′ric
met′ri·cal
Met′ro·lin·er
met′ro·nome
me·trop′o·lis
met′ro·pol′i·tan
met′tle
met′tled
met′tle·some
Mex′i·can
mez′za·nine
mi·as′ma
mi·as′mal
mi′as·mat′ic
mi′ca
mi′crobe
mi′cro·cosm
mi′cro·fiche
mi′cro·film
mi′cro·gram
mi·crom′e·ter
mi′cron
mi′cro·phone
mi′cro·scope
mi′cro·scop′ic
mi·cros′co·py
mi′cro·spore
mi′cro·struc′ture
mi′cro·tome
mi·crot′o·my
Mi′das
mid′brain′
mid′day′
mid′dle
mid′dle·man′
mid′dle·weight′
midge
midg′et
mid′i′ron
mid′land
mid′most
mid′night′
mid′riff
mid′ship′man
mid′ships′
midst
mid′stream′
mid′sum′mer
mid′way′
mid′week′
mid′wife′
mid′win′ter
mid′year′
mien
might
might′i·ly
might′i·ness
might′y
mi′graine
mi′grant
mi′grate
mi′grat·ed
mi·gra′tion
mi′gra·to′ry
mi·ka′do
milch
mild
mild′er
mild′est
mil′dew
mild′ly
mild′ness
mile
mile′age
mile′post′
mil′er
mile′stone′
mil′i·tant
mil′i·ta·rism
mil′i·ta·rist
mil′i·ta·ris′tic
mil′i·ta·rize
mil′i·tar′y
mil′i·tate

mil′i·tat′ed
mi·li′tia
milk
milk′maid′
milk′man′
milk′weed′
milk′y
mill
mill′board′
milled
mil′le·nar′y
mil·len′ni·al
mil·len′ni·um
mil′le·pede
mill′er
mil′let
mil′line′
mil′li·ner
mil′li·ner′y
mil′lion
mil′lion·aire′
mil′lion·fold′
mil′lionth
mill′pond′
mill′race′
mill′stone′
mill′work′
mill′wright′
Mil·ton′ic
mime
mim′e·o·graph′
mi·met′ic

mim′ic
mim′ic·ry
mi·mo′sa
min′a·ret′
min′a·to′ry
mince
minced
mince′meat′
minc′ing·ly
mind
mind′ed
mind′ful
mind′less
mine
min′er
min′er·al
min′er·al′o·gy
min′gle
min′gled
min′i·a·ture
min′i·a·tur·ist
min′im
min′i·mal
min′i·mi·za′tion
min′i·mize
min′i·mum
min′i·skirt
min′is·ter
min′is·tered
min′is·te′ri·al
min′is·te′ri·al·ly
min′is·tra′tion

min′is·try
min′i·ver
mink
min′now
mi′nor
mi·nor′i·ty
min′ster
min′strel
min′strel·sy
mint
mint′ed
min′u·end
min′u·et′
mi′nus
mi·nus′cule
min′ute
mi·nute′
mi·nute′ness
mi·nu′ti·a
mi·nu′ti·ae
minx
mir′a·cle
mi·rac′u·lous
mi·rage′
mire
mired
mir′ror
mir′rored
mirth
mirth′ful
mirth′ful·ly
mirth′less

mis′ad·ven**′**ture
mis′al·li**′**ance
mis**′**an·thrope
mis′an·throp**′**ic
mis′an·throp**′**i·cal
mis·an**′**thro·pism
mis·an**′**thro·pist
mis·an**′**thro·py
mis′ap·pli·ca**′**tion
mis′ap·ply**′**
mis′ap·pre·hen**′**sion
mis′ap·pro**′**pri·ate
mis′ap·pro′pri·a**′**tion
mis′ar·range**′**
mis′be·got**′**ten
mis′be·have**′**
mis′be·haved**′**
mis′be·hav**′**ior
mis′be·liev**′**er
mis·brand**′**
mis·cal**′**cu·late
mis·cal**′**cu·lat′ed
mis·call**′**
mis·car**′**riage
mis·car**′**ried
mis·car**′**ry
mis·cast**′**
mis′ce·ge·na**′**tion
mis′cel·la**′**ne·a
mis′cel·la**′**ne·ous
mis**′**cel·la′nist
mis**′**cel·la′ny
mis·chance**′**
mis**′**chief
mis**′**chie·vous
mis**′**ci·ble
mis′con·ceive**′**
mis′con·cep**′**tion
mis′con·duct**′**
mis′con·struc**′**tion
mis′con·strue**′**
mis·count**′**
mis**′**cre·ant
mis·cue**′**
mis·date**′**
mis·deal**′**
mis·deed**′**
mis′de·mean**′**or
mis′di·rect**′**
mis′di·rect**′**ed
mis′di·rec**′**tion
mis·doubt**′**
mi**′**ser
mis**′**er·a·ble
mi**′**ser·li·ness
mi**′**ser·ly
mis**′**er·y
mis·fea**′**sance
mis·fire**′**
mis·fired**′**
mis·fit**′**
mis·formed**′**
mis·for**′**tune
mis·giv**′**ings
mis·gov**′**ern
mis·gov**′**erned
mis·guide**′**
mis·guid**′**ed
mis·hap**′**
mish**′**mash′
mis′in·form**′**
mis′in·formed**′**
mis′in·ter**′**pret
mis′in·ter′pre·ta**′**tion
mis′in·ter**′**pret·ed
mis·judge**′**
mis·judged**′**
mis·laid**′**
mis·lay**′**
mis·lead**′**
mis·lead**′**ing·ly
mis·like**′**
mis·liked**′**
mis·made**′**
mis·man**′**age
mis·man**′**age·ment
mis·mate**′**
mis·mat**′**ed
mis·name**′**
mis·named**′**
mis·no**′**mer
mi·sog**′**y·nist
mis·place**′**
mis·placed**′**
mis·print**′**
mis·pri**′**sion

mis′pro·nounce′
mis·pro·nun′ci·a′tion
mis′quo·ta′tion
mis·quote′
mis·read′
mis′re·mem′ber
mis′re·mem′brance
mis′rep·re·sent′
mis′rep·re·sen·ta′tion
mis·rule′
miss
mis′sal
missed
mis·shap′en
mis′sile
mis′sion
mis′sion·ar′y
mis′sion·er
mis′sive
mis·spell′
mis·spelled′
mis·spell′ings
mis·spend′
mis·spent′
mis·state′
mis·stat′ed
mis·state′ment
mis·step′
mist
mis·take′
mis·tak′en
mis·tak′en·ly

mis·taught′
mis·teach′
mist′i·er
mist′i·est
mist′i·ly
mist′i·ness
mis′tle·toe
mis·took′
mis·treat′
mis·treat′ment
mis′tress
mis·tri′al
mis·trust′
mis·trust′ful
mist′y
mis′un·der·stand′
mis′un·der·stand′ings
mis′un·der·stood′
mis·us′age
mis·use′
mis·used′
mite
mi′ter
mi′tered
mit′i·ga·ble
mit′i·gate
mit′i·gat′ed
mit′i·ga′tion
mit′i·ga′tive
mit′i·ga·to′ry
mi·to′sis
mi·tot′ic

mi′tral
mit′ten
mit′tened
mix
mixed
mix′er
mix′ture
miz′zen·mast′
mne·mon′ic
mo′a
moan
moaned
moat
mob
mob′cap′
mo′bile
mo·bil′i·ty
mo′bi·li·za′tion
mo′bi·lize
mo′bi·lized
mob·oc′ra·cy
moc′ca·sin
Mo′cha
mock
mock′er·y
mock′ing·ly
mod′al
mo·dal′i·ty
mode
mod′el
mod′eled
mod′er·ate

mod′er·at′ed
mod′er·ate·ly
mod′er·ate·ness
mod′er·a′tion
mod′er·a′tion·ist
mod′er·a′tor
mod′ern
mod′ern·ism
mod′ern·ist
mod′ern·is′tic
mo·der′ni·ty
mod′ern·i·za′tion
mod′ern·ize
mod′ern·ized
mod′est
mod′est·ly
mod′es·ty
mod′i·cum
mod′i·fi·ca′tion
mod′i·fi·ca′tion·ist
mod′i·fied
mod′i·fi′er
mod′i·fy
mod′ish
mod′ish·ly
mod′ish·ness
mod′u·lar
mod′u·late
mod′u·lat′ed
mod′u·la′tion
mod′u·la′tive
mod′u·la′tor
mod′u·la·to′ry
mod′ule
mod′u·lus
mog′a·dore′
Mo·gul′
mo′hair′
Mo·ham′med·an
Mo′hawk
mo′ho
moi′e·ty
moil
moiled
moi·re′
moist
mois′ten
mois′tened
mois′ten·er
mois′ture
mo′lal
mo′lar
mo·lar′i·ty
mo·las′ses
mold
mold′board′
mold′ed
mold′er
mold′ings
mold′y
mole
mo·lec′u·lar
mol′e·cule
mole′hill′
mole′skin′
mo·lest′
mo′les·ta′tion
mo·lest′ed
mol′li·fi·ca′tion
mol′li·fied
mol′li·fy
mol′lusk
mol′ly·cod′dle
molt
molt′ed
mol′ten
mo′ly
mo·lyb′de·num
mo′ment
mo′men·tar′i·ly
mo′men·tar′y
mo′ment·ly
mo·men′tous
mo·men′tum
mon′ad
mo·nad′nock
mon′arch
mo·nar′chi·al
mo·nar′chi·an·ism
mo·nar′chic
mon′arch·ism
mon′arch·ist
mon′arch·is′tic
mon′arch·y
mon′as·te′ri·al
mon′as·te′ri·al·ly

mon′as·ter′y
mo·nas′tic
mo·nas′ti·cism
mon′a·tom′ic
Mon′day
mo·nel′
mon′e·tar′y
mon′e·ti·za′tion
mon′e·tize
mon′ey
mon′eyed
mon′goose
mon′grel
mon′ism
mon′i·tor
mon′i·tored
mon′i·to′ri·al
mon′i·to′ry
monk
mon′key
monk′hood
monk′ish
mon′o·bas′ic
mon′o·cle
mon′o·cled
mo·noc′u·lar
mon′o·dy
mo·nog′a·mous
mo·nog′a·my
mon′o·gram
mon′o·graph
mon′o·lith
mon′o·lith′ic
mon′o·logue
mon′o·ma′ni·a
mon′o·ma′ni·ac
mon′o·ma·ni′a·cal
mon′o·mor′phic
mon′o·plane
mon′o·ple′gi·a
mo·nop′o·lism
mo·nop′o·list
mo·nop′o·lis′tic
mo·nop′o·lis′ti·cal·ly
mo·nop′o·li·za′tion
mo·nop′o·lize
mo·nop′o·lized
mo·nop′o·ly
mon′o·rail′
mon′o·syl·lab′ic
mon′o·syl′la·ble
mon′o·the·ism
mon′o·the·is′tic
mon′o·tone
mo·not′o·nous
mo·not′o·ny
mon′o·type
mon·ox′ide
mon·si′gnor
mon·soon′
mon′ster
mon′strance
mon·stros′i·ty
mon′strous
month
month′ly
mon′u·ment
mon′u·men′tal
mon′u·men′tal·ly
mood
mood′i·ly
mood′i·ness
mood′y
moon
moon′beam′
moon′faced′
moon′fish′
moon′flow′er
moon′light′
moon′light′ed
moon′light′er
moon′light′ing
moon′rise′
moon′shine′
moon′stone′
moon′-struck
moor
moor′age
moored
moor′ings
Moor′ish
moor′land′
moose
moot
mop
mopped

mop′pet
mo·raine′
mor′al
mo·rale′
mor′al·ist
mor′al·is′tic
mo·ral′i·ty
mor′al·i·za′tion
mor′al·ize
mor′al·ized
mor′al·ly
mo·rass′
mor′a·to′ri·um
mo·ray′
mor′bid
mor·bid′i·ty
mor′bid·ly
mor′dant
more
more·o′ver
mo′res
mor′ga·nat′ic
morgue
mor′i·bund
Mor′mon
morn
morn′ing
morn′ings
mo·roc′co
mo′ron
mo·rose′
mo·rose′ly

mor′phine
mor′phin·ism
mor′phin·ize
mor·phol′o·gy
mor′ris
mor′row
mor′sel
mor′tal
mor·tal′i·ty
mor′tal·ly
mor′tar
mor′tar·board′
mort′gage
mort′gaged
mort′ga·gee′
mort′ga·gor′
mor·ti′cian
mor′ti·fi·ca′tion
mor′ti·fied
mor′ti·fy
mor′tise
mort′main
mor′tu·ar′y
mo·sa′ic
Mos′lem
mosque
mos·qui′to
moss
moss′back′
moss′i·ness
moss′y
most

most′ly
mo·tel′
mo·tet′
moth
moth′er
moth′er·hood
moth′er-in-law′
moth′er·land′
moth′er·less
moth′er·li·ness
moth′er·ly
moth′er-of-pearl′
mo·tif′
mo′tile
mo′tion
mo′tioned
mo′tion·less
mo′ti·vate
mo′ti·vat′ed
mo′ti·va′tion
mo′ti·va′tion·al
mo′tive
mot′ley
mo′tor
mo′tor·boat′
mo′tor·cy′cle
mo′tored
mo′tor·ist
mo′tor·ize
mo′tor·man
mot′tle
mot′tled

mot'to
mound
mount
moun'tain
moun'tain·eer'
moun'tain·ous
moun'tain·ous·ly
moun'te·bank
mount'ed
mount'ings
mourn
mourned
mourn'er
mourn'ful
mouse
mous'er
mouse'trap'
mousse
mouth
mouthed
mouth'ful
mouth'fuls
mouth'piece'
mov'a·bil'i·ty
mov'a·ble
mov'a·bly
move
moved
move'ment
mov'er
mov'ie
mov'ing·ly

mow
mow'er
Ms.
much
mu'ci·lage
mu'ci·lag'i·nous
muck
muck'er
muck'rak'er
muck'weed'
muck'worm'
mu'coid
mu·co'sa
mu'cous
mu'cus
mud
mud'di·er
mud'di·est
mud'di·ly
mud'di·ness
mud'dle
mud'dled
mud'dle-head'ed
mud'dy
mud'fish'
mud'weed'
muff
muf'fin
muf'fle
muf'fled
muf'fler
muf'ti

mug
mug'ging
mug'gy
mug'wump'
mu·lat'to
mul'ber'ry
mulch
mulched
mulct
mulct'ed
mule
mu'le·teer'
mu'li·eb'ri·ty
mul'ish
mull
mulled
mul'let
mul'li·ga·taw'ny
mul'ti·eth'nic
mul'ti·far'i·ous
mul'ti·fold
mul'ti·form
mul'ti·for'mi·ty
Mul'ti·graph
Mul'ti·lith'
mul'ti·mil'lion·aire'
mul'ti·na'tion·al
mul'ti·ple
mul'ti·plex
mul'ti·pli·cand'
mul'ti·pli·cate
mul'ti·pli·ca'tion

mul′ti·pli·ca′tive
mul′ti·plic′i·ty
mul′ti·plied
mul′ti·pli′er
mul′ti·ply
mul′ti·tude
mul′ti·tu′di·nous
mul′ti·va′lent
mum′ble
mum′bled
mum′mer
mum′mer·y
mum′mi·fi·ca′tion
mum′mi·fied
mum′mi·fy
mum′my
mumps
munch
munched
mun′dane
mu·nic′i·pal
mu·nic′i·pal′i·ty
mu·nic′i·pal·ly
mu·nif′i·cence
mu·nif′i·cent
mu′ni·ment
mu·ni′tion
mu′ral
mur′der
mur′dered
mur′der·er
mur′der·ous
mu′rex
mu′ri·at′ic
murk
murk′i·ly
murk′i·ness
murk′y
mur′mur
mur′mured
mur′mur·er
mur′mur·ous
mus′ca·dine
mus′cat
mus′ca·tel′
mus′cle
mus′cu·lar
mus′cu·lar′i·ty
mus′cu·lar·ly
mus′cu·la·ture
muse
mused
mu·sette′
mu·se′um
mush
mush′room
mush′roomed
mush′y
mu′sic
mu′si·cal
mu′si·cale′
mu′si·cal·ly
mu·si′cian
mu·si′cian·ly
musk
mus′keg
mus′kel·lunge
mus′ket
mus′ket·eer′
mus′ket·ry
musk′mel′on
musk′rat′
mus′lin
muss
mussed
mus′sel
muss′i·er
muss′i·est
muss′y
must
mus·tache′
mus·ta′chio
mus′tang
mus′tard
mus′ter
mus′tered
mus′ti·ness
mus′ty
mu′ta·bil′i·ty
mu′ta·ble
mu′tate
mu·ta′tion
mu′ta·tive
mute
mut′ed
mute′ness

mu'ti·late
mu'ti·lat'ed
mu'ti·la'tion
mu'ti·la'tor
mu'ti·neer'
mu'ti·nied
mu'ti·nous
mu'ti·ny
mut'ism
mut'ter
mut'tered
mut'ter·ings
mut'ton
mu'tu·al
mu'tu·al'i·ty
mu'tu·al·ly
muz'zle
muz'zled
my
my·col'o·gy
my·co'sis
my·dri'a·sis
myd'ri·at'ic
my'e·loid
My'lar
my·o'pi·a
my·op'ic
myr'i·ad
myrrh
myr'tle
my·self'
mys·te'ri·ous
mys·te'ri·ous·ly
mys'ter·y
mys'tic
mys'ti·cal
mys'ti·cal·ly
mys'ti·cism
mys'ti·fi·ca'tion
mys'ti·fied
mys'ti·fy
myth
myth'i·cal
myth'o·log'i·cal
my·thol'o·gist
my·thol'o·gy

na·celle′
na′cre
na′cre·ous
na′dir
nai′ad
nail
nailed
nail′head′
nain′sook
na·ïve′
na·ïve·té′
na′ked
na′ked·ly
na′ked·ness
nam′a·ble
name
named
name′less
name′less·ly
name′ly
name′sake′
nan·keen′

nap
na′per·y
naph′tha
naph′tha·lene
nap′kin
na·po′le·on
Na·po′le·on·a′na
Na·po′le·on′ic
napped
nar·cis′sism
nar·cis′sus
nar·co′sis
nar·cot′ic
nar·cot′i·cism
nar′co·tize
nar′co·tized
nar·rate′
nar·rat′ed
nar·ra′tion
nar′ra·tive
nar·ra′tor
nar′row

nar′rowed
nar′row·er
nar′row·est
nar′row·ly
nar′row·ness
nar′whal
na′sal
na·sal′i·ty
na′sal·ize
na′sal·ly
nas′cent
nas′ti·er
nas′ti·est
nas′ti·ly
nas′ti·ness
nas·tur′tium
nas′ty
na′tal
na·ta′tion
na′ta·to′ri·um
na′ta·to′ry
na′tion

na'tion·al
na'tion·al·ism
na'tion·al·is'tic
na'tion·al'i·ty
na'tion·al·i·za'tion
na'tion·al·ize
na'tion·al·ized
na'tion·al·ly
na'tive
na·tiv'i·ty
nat'u·ral
nat'u·ral·ism
nat'u·ral·ist
nat'u·ral·is'tic
nat'u·ral·i·za'tion
nat'u·ral·ize
nat'u·ral·ized
nat'u·ral·ly
nat'u·ral·ness
na'ture
na'tur·is'tic
naught
naugh'ti·ly
naugh'ti·ness
naugh'ty
nau'se·a
nau'se·ate
nau'se·at'ed
nau'seous
nau'ti·cal
nau'ti·lus
na'val

nave
na'vel
nav'i·ga·ble
nav'i·gate
nav'i·gat'ed
nav'i·ga'tion
nav'i·ga'tion·al
nav'i·ga'tor
na'vy
Naz'a·rene'
neap
Ne'a·pol'i·tan
near
near'by'
neared
near'er
near'est
near'ly
near'ness
near'sight'ed
neat
neat'er
neat'est
neat'herd'
neat'ly
neat'ness
neb'u·la
neb'u·lar
neb'u·los'i·ty
neb'u·lous
neb'u·lous·ly
nec'es·sar'i·ly

nec'es·sar'y
ne·ces'si·tar'i·an
ne·ces'si·tate
ne·ces'si·tat'ed
ne·ces'si·tous
ne·ces'si·ty
neck
neck'band'
neck'cloth'
neck'er·chief
neck'lace
neck'tie'
neck'wear'
nec'ro·log'i·cal
ne·crol'o·gy
nec'ro·man'cy
nec'ro·man'tic
nec'ro·pho'bi·a
ne·crop'o·lis
nec'rop·sy
ne·cro'sis
ne·crot'ic
nec'tar
nec'tar·ine'
need
need'ed
need'ful
need'ful·ly
need'i·er
need'i·est
need'i·ness
nee'dle

nee'dled
nee'dle·ful
need'less
need'less·ly
need'less·ness
nee'dle·work'
need'y
ne·far'i·ous
ne·gate'
ne·gat'ed
ne·ga'tion
neg'a·tive
neg'a·tived
neg'a·tiv·ism
neg·lect'
neg·lect'ed
neg·lect'ful
neg'li·gee'
neg'li·gence
neg'li·gent
neg'li·gi·ble
ne·go'ti·a·bil'i·ty
ne·go'ti·a·ble
ne·go'ti·ate
ne·go'ti·at'ed
ne·go'ti·a'tion
ne·go'ti·a'tor
Ne'gro
Ne'gro·phile
neigh'bor
neigh'bor·hood
neigh'bor·li·ness
neigh'bor·ly
nei'ther
nem'a·tode
Nem'e·sis
ne'o·for·ma'tion
ne'o·lith'ic
ne·ol'o·gism
ne·ol'o·gy
ne'on
ne'o·phyte
ne'o·plasm
ne·pen'the
neph'ew
ne·phrec'to·my
ne·phri'tis
nep'o·tism
nerve
nerve'less
ner'vous
nerv'ous·ly
nerv'ous·ness
nes'ci·ence
nes'ci·ent
nest
nest'ed
nes'tle
nes'tled
nest'lings
net
neth'er
neth'er·most
net'su·ke
net'ted
net'tings
net'tle
net'tled
net'work'
neu'ral
neu·ral'gia
neu'ras·the'ni·a
neu'ras·then'ic
neu·ri'tis
neu·ro'ses
neu·ro'sis
neu·rot'ic
neu'ter
neu'tral
neu'tral·ism
neu'tral·ist
neu·tral'i·ty
neu'tral·i·za'tion
neu'tral·ize
neu'tral·ized
neu'tral·iz'er
neu'tral·ly
neu'tron
nev'er
nev'er·more'
nev'er·the·less'
new
new'com'er
new'el
new'er
new'est

new′fan′gled
new′ly
new′ness
news′i·er
news′i·est
news′let′ter
news′pa′per
news′reel′
news′stand′
news′y
newt
next
nex′us
nib′ble
nib′bled
nib′lick
nice
nice′ly
nice′ness
nic′er
nic′est
ni′ce·ty
niche
nick
nicked
nick′el
nick′el·if′er·ous
nick′el·o′de·on
nick′name′
nick′named′
nic′o·tine
nic′o·tin′ic

niece
ni·el′lo
nig′gard
nig′gard·li·ness
nig′gard·ly
nig′gle
nig′gling·ly
nigh
night
night′cap′
night′fall′
night′fish′
night′gown′
night′hawk′
night′in·gale
night′ly
night′mare′
night′mar′ish
night′shade′
night′shirt′
night′time′
night′wear′
night′work′
night′work′er
ni′hil·ism
ni′hil·ist
ni′hil·is′tic
nim′ble
nim′bus
nin′com·poop
nine′pins′
nip′per

nip′ple
nip′py
nir·va′na
ni′ter
ni′trate
ni′tric
ni′tride
ni′tri·fi·ca′tion
ni′tri·fy
ni′tro·gen
ni·trog′e·nous
ni′tro·glyc′er·in
ni′trous
nit′wit′
no
no·bil′i·ty
no′ble
no′ble·man
no′bler
no′blest
no′bly
no′bod·y
noc·tur′nal
noc·tur′nal·ly
noc′turne
nod
nod′ded
node
nod′ule
no·el′
noise
noise′less

nois′i·er
nois′i·est
nois′i·ly
nois′i·ness
noi′some
nois′y
no′mad
no·mad′ic
no′men·cla′ture
nom′i·nal
nom′i·nal·ism
nom′i·nal·ly
nom′i·nate
nom′i·nat′ed
nom′i·na′tion
nom′i·na·tive
nom′i·nee′
non′a·ge·nar′i·an
non′a·gon
non′ap·pear′ance
non·call′a·ble
nonce
non′cha·lance
non′cha·lant
non′cha·lant·ly
non·com′bat·ant
non′com·mis′sioned
non′com·mit′tal
non′com·mu′ni·cant
non′con·duc′tor
non′con·form′ism
non′con·form′ist
non′con·form′i·ty
non′-co-op′er·a′tion
non′de·script
none
non·en′ti·ty
non′es·sen′tial
none′such′
non′ex·ist′ence
non·fea′sance
non·fea′sor
non·for′feit·ure
non′in·ter·ven′tion
non′met′al
non′me·tal′lic
non′pa·reil′
non′par·tic′i·pat′ing
non·par′ti·san
non·per′ma·nent
non′plus
non′plused
non·res′i·dence
non·res′i·dent
non′re·sist′ance
non′re·sist′ant
non′sense
non·sen′si·cal
non′skid′
non′stop′
non′sub·scrib′er
non′suit′
non′sup·port′
non·un′ion
noo′dle
nook
noon
noon′day′
noon′time′
noose
nor
norm
nor′mal
nor·mal′i·ty
nor′mal·ize
nor′mal·ized
nor′mal·ly
Nor′man
nor′ma·tive
Norse
north
north′east′
north′east′er
north′east′er·ly
north′east′ern
north′east′ward
north′east′ward·ly
north′er·ly
north′ern
north′ern·er
north′land
north′ward
north′west′
north′west′er·ly
north′west′ern
Nor·we′gian

nose
nose'band'
nose'bleed'
nose'gay'
nose'piece'
nos'ings
no·sol'o·gy
nos·tal'gi·a
nos·tal'gic
nos'tril
nos'trum
not
no'ta·bil'i·ty
no'ta·ble
no·tar'i·al
no·tar'i·al·ly
no'ta·ry
no·ta'tion
notch
notched
notch'weed'
note
note'book'
not'ed
note'wor'thi·ly
note'wor'thy
noth'ing
noth'ing·ness
no'tice
no'tice·a·ble
no'ticed
no'ti·fi·ca'tion
no'ti·fied
no'ti·fy
no'tion
no'to·ri'e·ty
no·to'ri·ous
no·to'ri·ous·ly
not'with·stand'ing
nou'gat
nou'ga·tine
nought
nou'me·non
noun
nour'ish
nour'ished
nour'ish·ing·ly
nour'ish·ment
nov'el
nov'el·ette'
nov'el·ist
nov'el·ize
no·vel'la
nov'el·ty
No·vem'ber
no·ve'na
nov'ice
no·vi'ti·ate
No'vo·cain'
now
now'a·days'
no'where
nox'ious
nox'ious·ness
noz'zle
nu·ance'
nu'cle·ar
nu'cle·ate
nu'cle·at'ed
nu'cle·a'tion
nu'cle·i
nu·cle'o·lus
nu'cle·us
nude
nudge
nudged
nud'ism
nud'ist
nu'di·ty
nu'ga·to'ry
nug'get
nui'sance
null
nul'li·fi·ca'tion
nul'li·fi·ca'tion·ist
nul'li·fied
nul'li·fy
nul'li·ty
numb
numbed
num'ber
num'bered
num'ber·less
numb'ness
nu'mer·al
nu'mer·ate

nu′mer·a′tion
nu′mer·a′tor
nu·mer′ic
nu·mer′i·cal
nu′mer·ous
nu′mis·mat′ics
nu·mis′ma·tist
num′skull′
nun
nun′ci·a·ture
nun′ci·o
nun′ner·y
nup′tial
nurse
nursed
nurse′maid′
nurs′er·y
nurs′er·y·maid′
nurs′er·y·man
nurs′lings
nur′ture
nur′tured
nut
nut′hatch′
nut′meg
nu′tri·a
nu′tri·ent
nu′tri·ment
nu·tri′tion
nu·tri′tion·al
nu·tri′tion·al·ly
nu·tri′tion·ist
nu·tri′tious
nu·tri′tious·ly
nu′tri·tive
nu′tri·tive·ly
nut′shell′
nuz′zle
nuz′zled
nyc′ta·lo′pi·a
ny′lon
nys·tag′mus

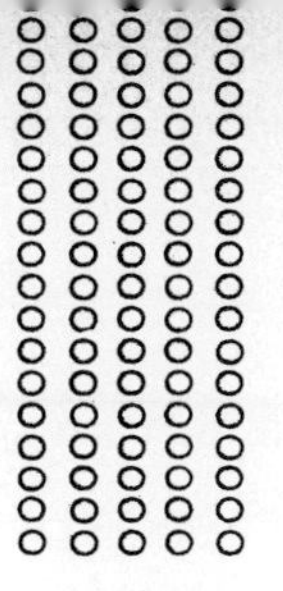

oaf
oak
oak'en
oa'kum
oar
oar'lock'
oars'man
o·a'sis
oat'en
oath
oat'meal'
ob'bli·ga'to
ob'du·ra·cy
ob'du·rate
o·be'di·ence
o·be'di·ent
o·bei'sance
ob'e·lisk
o·bese'
o·bes'i·ty
o·bey'
o·beyed'

o·bit'u·ar'y
ob·ject'
ob·ject'ed
ob·jec'tion
ob·jec'tion·a·ble
ob·jec'tive
ob·jec'tive·ly
ob·jec'tive·ness
ob'jec·tiv'i·ty
ob·jec'tor
ob'jur·gate
ob'late
ob·la'tion
ob'li·gate
ob'li·gat'ed
ob'li·ga'tion
ob·lig'a·to'ry
o·blige'
o·bliged'
o·blig'ing·ly
ob·lique'
ob·lique'ly

ob·lique'ness
ob·liq'ui·ty
ob·lit'er·ate
ob·lit'er·at'ed
ob·lit'er·a'tion
ob·liv'i·on
ob·liv'i·ous
ob·liv'i·ous·ly
ob·liv'i·ous·ness
ob'long
ob'lo·quy
ob·nox'ious
ob·nox'ious·ly
o'boe
ob·scene'
ob·scen'i·ty
ob·scure'
ob·scure'ness
ob·scu'ri·ty
ob·se'qui·ous
ob·se'qui·ous·ly
ob·se'qui·ous·ness

ob′se·quy
ob·serv′a·ble
ob·serv′ance
ob·serv′ant
ob′ser·va′tion
ob·serv′a·to′ry
ob·serve′
ob·served′
ob·serv′er
ob·serv′ing·ly
ob·sess′
ob·sessed′
ob·ses′sion
ob·ses′sion·al
ob·ses′sive
ob·sid′i·an
ob′so·les′cence
ob′so·les′cent
ob′so·lete
ob′so·lete·ly
ob′so·lete·ness
ob′sta·cle
ob·stet′ri·cal
ob′ste·tri′cian
ob·stet′rics
ob′sti·na·cy
ob′sti·nate
ob′sti·nate·ly
ob·strep′er·ous
ob·struct′
ob·struct′ed
ob·struc′tion
ob·struc′tion·ism
ob·struc′tion·ist
ob·struc′tive
ob·struc′tor
ob·tain′
ob·tain′a·ble
ob·tained′
ob·trude′
ob·trud′ed
ob·trud′er
ob·tru′sion
ob·tru′sive
ob·tuse′
ob·tuse′ly
ob·tuse′ness
ob′verse
ob′vi·ate
ob′vi·at′ed
ob′vi·a′tion
ob′vi·ous
ob′vi·ous·ly
oc′a·ri′na
oc·ca′sion
oc·ca′sion·al
oc·ca′sion·al·ly
oc·ca′sioned
oc′ci·dent
oc′ci·den′tal
oc′ci·den′tal·ly
oc·cip′i·tal
oc′ci·put
oc·clude′
oc·clud′ed
oc·clu′sion
oc·cult′
oc′cul·ta′tion
oc·cult′ism
oc·cult′ist
oc′cu·pan·cy
oc′cu·pant
oc′cu·pa′tion
oc′cu·pa′tion·al
oc′cu·pa′tion·al·ly
oc′cu·pied
oc′cu·py
oc·cur′
oc·curred′
oc·cur′rence
o′cean
o′ce·an′ic
o′ce·a·nog′ra·phy
o′ce·lot
o′cher
och·loc′ra·cy
oc′ta·gon
oc·tag′o·nal
oc·tag′o·nal·ly
oc·tam′e·ter
oc·tan′gu·lar
oc′tave
oc·ta′vo
oc·tet′
Oc·to′ber
oc′to·ge·nar′i·an

oc′to·pus
oc′u·lar
oc′u·list
odd
odd′er
odd′est
odd′i·ty
odd′ly
odd′ment
odd′ness
ode
o·de′um
o′di·ous
o′di·ous·ly
o′di·ous·ness
o′di·um
o·dom′e·ter
o′dor
o′dor·if′er·ous
o′dor·less
o′dor·ous
oe·nol′o·gy
of
off
of′fal
off′cast′
of·fend′
of·fend′ed
of·fense′
of·fen′sive
of′fer
of′fered
of′fer·ings
of′fer·to′ry
off′hand′
of′fice
of′fi·cer
of·fi′cial
of·fi′cial·ly
of·fi′ci·ate
of·fi′ci·at′ed
of·fi′ci·a′tion
of·fi′cious
of·fi′cious·ly
of·fi′cious·ness
off′ish
off′set′
off′shoot′
off′shore′
of′ten
of′ten·er
of′ten·est
of′ten·times′
o·gee′
o′give
o′gle
o′gled
o′gre
ohm
ohm′age
ohm′me′ter
oil
oiled
oil′er
oil′hole′
oil′i·er
oil′i·est
oil′i·ly
oil′i·ness
oil′man
oil′pa′per
oil′proof′
oil′seed′
oil′skin′
oil′stone′
oil′tight′
oil′y
oint′ment
o·ka′pi
o′kra
old
old′en
old′er
old′est
old′-fash′ioned
old′ish
old′ness
old′ster
o′le·ag′i·nous
o′le·an′der
o′le·ate
o·lec′ra·non
o′le·o
o′le·o·mar′ga·rine
ol·fac′to·ry
ol′i·garch′y

ol′ive
o·me′ga
om′e·let
o′men
o·men′tum
om′i·nous
o·mis′sion
o·mit′
o·mit′ted
om′ni·bus
om′nip′o·tence
om·nip′o·tent
om′ni·pres′ent
om·nis′cience
om·nis′cient
om·niv′o·rous
on
on′a·ger
once
one
one′ness
on′er·ous
one·self′
one′time′
on′ion
on′look′er
on′ly
on′o·mat′o·poe′ia
on′set′
on′slaught′
on′to
on·tog′e·ny
on·tol′o·gy
o′nus
on′ward
on′yx
o·öl′o·gy
oo′long
ooze
oozed
o·pac′i·ty
o′pal
o′pal·esce′
o′pal·es′cence
o′pal·es′cent
o·paque′
o′pen
o′pened
o′pen·er
o′pen·ings
o′pen·ly
o′pen·ness
o′pen·work′
op′er·a
op′er·a·ble
op′er·a·logue′
op′er·ate
op′er·at′ed
op′er·at′ic
op′er·at′i·cal·ly
op′er·a′tion
op′er·a′tive
op′er·a′tor
op′er·et′ta
oph′thal·mol′o·gist
oph′thal·mol′o·gy
o′pi·ate
o·pin′ion
o·pin′ion·at′ed
o·pin′ion·a′tive
o′pi·um
o·pos′sum
op·po′nent
op′por·tune′
op′por·tun′ism
op′por·tu′ni·ty
op·pos′a·ble
op·pose′
op·posed′
op·pos′er
op·pos′ing
op′po·site
op′po·si′tion
op·press′
op·pressed′
op·pres′sion
op·pres′sive
op·pres′sive·ly
op·pres′sive·ness
op·pres′sor
op·pro′bri·ous
op·pro′bri·ous·ly
op·pro′bri·ous·ness
op·pro′bri·um
opt
opt′ed

op'ta·tive
op'tic
op'ti·cal
op·ti'cian
op'tics
op'ti·mism
op'ti·mist
op'ti·mis'tic
op'ti·mis'ti·cal·ly
op'ti·mum
op'tion
op'tion·al
op'tion·al·ly
op·tom'e·trist
op·tom'e·try
op'u·lence
op'u·lent
o'pus
or
or'a·cle
o·rac'u·lar
o·rac'u·lar·ly
o'ral
o'ral·ly
or'ange
o·rang'u·tan'
o·ra'tion
or'a·tor
or'a·tor'i·cal
or'a·to'ri·o
or'a·to'ry
orb

or'bit
or'bit·al
or'bit·ed
or'chard
or'ches·tra
or·ches'tral
or'ches·trate
or'ches·trat'ed
or'ches·tra'tion
or'chid
or'chi·da'ceous
or·dain'
or·dained'
or·deal'
or'der
or'dered
or'der·li·ness
or'der·ly
or'di·nal
or'di·nance
or'di·nar'i·ly
or'di·nar'y
or'di·na'tion
ord'nance
ore
or'gan
or·gan'ic
or·gan'i·cal·ly
or'gan·ism
or'gan·ist
or'gan·i·za'tion
or'gan·i·za'tion·al

or'gan·ize
or'gan·ized
or'gy
o'ri·el
o'ri·ent
o'ri·en'tal
o'ri·en'tal·ism
o'ri·en'tal·ist
o'ri·en'tal·ly
o'ri·en·tate'
o'ri·en·ta'tion
o'ri·ent'ed
or'i·fice
or'i·gin
o·rig'i·nal
o·rig'i·nal'i·ty
o·rig'i·nal·ly
o·rig'i·nate
o·rig'i·nat'ed
o·rig'i·na'tion
o·rig'i·na'tive
o·rig'i·na'tor
o'ri·ole
O·ri'on
or'i·son
or'lop
or'mo·lu
or'na·ment
or'na·men'tal
or'na·men'tal·ly
or'na·men·ta'tion
or·nate'

or·nate'ly
or′ni·tho·log'i·cal
or′ni·thol'o·gist
or′ni·thol'o·gy
o′ro·tund
o′ro·tun'di·ty
or'phan
or'phan·age
or'phaned
or'phan·hood
or'phe·um
or'rer·y
or'tho·dox
or'tho·ëp′y
or·thog'ra·phy
or′tho·pe′dic
or·thop'tic
or'to·lan
os'cil·late
os'cil·lat′ed
os′cil·la'tion
os'cil·la′tor
os'cil·la·to′ry
os·cil'lo·scope
os'cu·late
os′cu·la'tion
os'cu·la·to′ry
o′sier
os'mi·um
os·mo'sis
os·mot'ic
os'prey
os'se·ous
os′si·fi·ca'tion
os'si·fied
os'si·fy
os·ten'si·ble
os·ten'si·bly
os′ten·ta'tion
os′ten·ta'tious
os′ten·ta'tious·ly
os'te·o·path
os′te·op'a·thy
os'tra·cism
os'tra·cize
os'tra·cized
os'trich
o·tal'gi·a
oth'er
oth'er·wise′
o'ti·ose
ot'ter
Ot'to·man
ought
ounce
our
ours
our·selves'
oust
oust'er
out
out'cast′
out·class'
out·come'
out'crop′
out'cry′
out·curve'
out·dis'tance
out·do'
out'doors'
out'er
out'er·most
out·face'
out'field′
out'fit
out'fit′ter
out·flank'
out'flow′
out·go'
out'growth′
out'ings
out·land'ish
out·land'ish·ness
out·last'
out'law′
out'law′ry
out'lay′
out'let
out'lets
out'line′
out'lined′
out·live'
out·lived'
out·look'
out'ly′ing
out'march′

out·mod'ed
out·num'ber
out'put'
out'rage
out·ra'geous
out·ra'geous·ly
out·ra'geous·ness
out·rank'
out·ranked'
out·reach'
out'rid·er
out'rig'ger
out'right'
out·run'
out'set'
out'side'
out'sid'er
out'size'
out'skirt'
out·stand'ing·ly
out·stay'
out·strip'
out·vote'
out'ward
out'ward·ly
out·wear'
out·wit'
out·work'
o'val
o'vate
o·va'tion
ov'en
ov'en·bird'
ov'en·ware'
o'ver
o'ver·age
o'ver·age'
o'ver·alls'
o'ver·awe'
o'ver·awed'
o'ver·bal'ance
o'ver·bear'
o'ver·bear'ing·ly
o'ver·bid'
o'ver·board'
o'ver·build'
o'ver·built'
o'ver·bur'den
o'ver·cap'i·tal·ize
o'ver·cast'
o'ver·charge'
o'ver·charged'
o'ver·clothes'
o'ver·coat'
o'ver·come'
o'ver·com'pen·sa'tion
o'ver·cor·rect'
o'ver·count'
o'ver·de·vel'op
o'ver·do'
o'ver·done'
o'ver·dose'
o'ver·draft'
o'ver·draw'
o'ver·drawn'
o'ver·dress'
o'ver·drew'
o'ver·drive'
o'ver·driv'en
o'ver·due'
o'ver·eat'
o'ver·es'ti·mate
o'ver·ex·pose'
o'ver·ex·po'sure
o'ver·flow'
o'ver·flow'ing·ly
o'ver·grown'
o'ver·hand'
o'ver·hang'
o'ver·haul'
o'ver·head'
o'ver·heat'
o'ver·is'sue
o'ver·land'
o'ver·lap'
o'ver·look'
o'ver·lord'
o'ver·ly
o'ver·mas'ter·ing·ly
o'ver·mod'u·la'tion
o'ver·night'
o'ver·pass'
o'ver·pay'
o'ver·pop'u·la'tion
o'ver·pow'er
o'ver·pow'ered

o'ver·pow'er·ing·ly
o'ver·pro·duc'tion
o'ver·rate'
o'ver·rat'ed
o'ver·reach'
o'ver·ride'
o'ver·ripe'
o'ver·rule'
o'ver·ruled'
o'ver·run'
o'ver·seas'
o'ver·see'
o'ver·se'er
o'ver·sell'
o'ver·shad'ow
o'ver·shad'owed
o'ver·shoe'
o'ver·side'
o'ver·sight'
o'ver·size'
o'ver·spread'
o'ver·state'
o'ver·state'ment
o'ver·stay'
o'ver·step'
o'ver·stock'
o'ver·strain'
o'ver·sub·scribe'
o'ver·sup·ply'
o'vert
o'ver·take'
o'ver·tax'
o'ver·taxed'
o'ver·threw'
o'ver·throw'
o'ver·thrown'
o'ver·time'
o'ver·tone'
o'ver·ture
o'ver·turn'
o'ver·turned'
o'ver·val'ue
o'ver·ween'ing·ly
o'ver·weight'
o'ver·whelm'
o'ver·whelmed'
o'ver·whelm'ing·ly
o'ver·wind'
o'ver·work'
o'ver·worked'
o'ver·wrought'
o'vi·duct
o·vip'a·rous
o'vi·pos'i·tor
o'vule
o'vum
owe
owed
owl
owl'et
owl'ish
own
owned
own'er
own'er·ship
ox
ox'a·late
ox·al'ic
ox'i·da'tion
ox'ide
ox'i·diz'a·ble
ox'i·dize
ox'i·dized
ox'tongue'
ox'y·gen
ox'y·gen·ate
oys'ter
oys'ter·shell'
o'zone
o'zo·nize
o'zo·nized

# P

pab'u·lum
pace
pace'mak'er
pac'er
pach'y·derm
pach'y·san'dra
pa·cif'ic
pa·cif'i·cal·ly
pa·cif'i·cate
pac'i·fi'ca'tion
pa·cif'i·ca·to'ry
pac'i·fied
pac'i·fi'er
pac'i·fism
pac'i·fist
pac'i·fy
pack
pack'age
pack'aged
pack'er
pack'et
pack'ings
pack'sack'
pack'sad'dle
pack'thread'
pact
pad
pad'ded
pad'dings
pad'dle
pad'dled
pad'dle·fish'
pad'dock
pad'lock'
pae'an
pa'gan
pa'gan·ism
pa'gan·ize
page
pag'eant
pag'eant·ry
paged
pag'i·na'tion
pa·go'da
paid
pail
pain
pained
pain'ful
pain'kill'er
pain'less
pains'tak'ing·ly
paint
paint'ed
paint'er
paint'ings
paint'pot'
pair
paired
pair'ings
pa·ja'ma
pal'ace
pal'a·din
pal'an·quin'
pal'at·a·bil'i·ty
pal'at·a·ble

pal′a·tal
pal′a·tal·ize
pal′ate
pa·la′tial
pa·la′tial·ly
pa·lat′i·nate
pal′a·tine
pa·lav′er
pale
paled
pa′le·og′ra·phy
pal′er
pal′est
pal′ette
pal′frey
pal′imp·sest
pal′in·drome
pal′ings
pal′i·node
pal′i·sade′
pall
pal·la′di·um
pall′bear′er
palled
pal′let
pal′li·ate
pal′li·at′ed
pal′li·a′tion
pal′li·a′tive
pal′lid
pal·lid′i·ty
pal′lid·ly

pal′li·um
pal′lor
palm
pal′mate
palmed
palm′er
pal·met′to
palm′ist
palm′is·try
pal′pa·bil′i·ty
pal′pa·ble
pal′pate
pal′pat·ed
pal·pa′tion
pal′pa·to′ry
pal′pi·tant
pal′pi·tate
pal′pi·tat′ed
pal′pi·tat′ing·ly
pal′pi·ta′tion
pal′sied
pal′sy
pal′ter
pal′tered
pal′try
pam′pas
pam′per
pam′pered
pam′phlet
pam′phlet·eer′
pam′phlet·ize
pan

pan′a·ce′a
pan′a·ma′
Pan′-A·mer′i·can
Pan′-A·mer′i·can·ism
pan′cake′
pan′chro·mat′ic
pan′cre·as
pan′cre·at′ic
pan′da
pan·dem′ic
pan′de·mo′ni·um
pan′der
pan′dered
pane
pan′e·gyr′ic
pan′e·gyr′i·cal
pan′e·gy·rize
pan′e·gy·rized
pan′el
pan′eled
pang
Pan′hel·len′ic
pan′ic
pan′icked
pan′ick·y
pan·jan′drum
panned
pan′nier
pan′ni·kin
pan′o·ply
pan′o·ra′ma
pan′o·ram′ic

pan′sy
pant
pan′ta·loon′
pant′ed
pan′the·ism
pan′the·ist
pan′the·is′tic
pan′the·on
pan′ther
pan′to·graph
pan′to·mime
pan′try
pan′try·man
pa′pa·cy
pa′pal
pa·pay′a
pa′per
pa′per·back′
pa′per·board′
pa′pered
pa′per·er
pap′e·terie
pa·poose′
pa·pri′ka
Pap′u·an
pap′ule
pa·py′rus
par
par′a·ble
pa·rab′o·la
par′a·bol′ic
par′a·bol′i·cal
pa·rab′o·loid
par′a·chute
pa·rade′
pa·rad′ed
par′a·digm
par′a·dise
par′a·dox
par′a·dox′i·cal
par′af·fin
par′a·gon
par′a·graph
par′a·graphed
par′a·keet
par′al·lax
par′al·lel
par′al·leled
par′al·lel·ism
par′al·lel′o·gram
pa·ral′y·sis
par′a·lyt′ic
par′a·lyt′i·cal·ly
par′a·lyze
par′a·lyzed
pa·ram′e·ter
par′a·mount
par′a·noi′a
par′a·noi′ac
par′a·noid
par′a·pet
par′a·pher·na′li·a
par′a·phrase
par′a·phrased
par′a·phras′tic
par′a·ple′gi·a
par′a·pleg′ic
par′a·site
par′a·sit′ic
par′a·sit′i·cal
par′a·sit′i·cide
par′a·sit·ism
par′a·sit·ize
par′a·sol
par′a·thy′roid
par′a·ty′phoid
par′a·vane
par′boil′
par′boiled′
par′cel
par′celed
parch
parched
parch′ment
par′don
par′don·a·ble
par′doned
pare
pared
par′e·gor′ic
pa·ren′chy·ma
par′ent
par′ent·age
pa·ren′tal
pa·ren′tal·ly
pa·ren′the·ses

pa·ren′the·sis
pa·ren′the·size
par′en·thet′i·cal
par′en·thet′i·cal·ly
par′ent·hood
pa·re′sis
par·fait′
pa·ri′ah
pa·ri′e·tal
par′ings
par′ish
pa·rish′ion·er
par′i·ty
park
par′ka
parked
park′way′
par′lance
par·lan′do
par′lay
par′ley
par′leyed
par′lia·ment
par′lia·men·tar′i·an
par′lia·men′ta·ri·ly
par′lia·men′ta·ry
par′lor
par′lous
Par′me·san′
Par·nas′sus
pa·ro′chi·al
pa·ro′chi·al·ism
pa·ro′chi·al·ly
par′o·dy
pa·role′
par′o·no·ma′si·a
pa·rot′id
par′ox·ysm
par′ox·ys′mal
par′ox·ys′mal·ly
par·quet′
par′ri·cid′al
par′ri·cid′al·ly
par′ri·cide
par′ried
par′rot
par′rot·ed
par′ry
parse
parsed
par′si·mo′ni·ous
par′si·mo′ny
pars′ley
pars′nip
par′son
par′son·age
part
par·take′
par·tak′er
part′ed
par·terre′
par′the·no·gen′e·sis
Par′the·non
Par′thi·an
par′tial
par′ti·al′i·ty
par′tial·ly
par·tic′i·pant
par·tic′i·pate
par·tic′i·pat′ed
par·tic′i·pa′tion
par·tic′i·pa′tive
par·tic′i·pa′tor
par′ti·cip′i·al
par′ti·cip′i·al·ly
par′ti·ci·ple
par′ti·cle
par·tic′u·lar
par·tic′u·lar′i·ty
par·tic′u·lar·ize
par·tic′u·lar·ized
par·tic′u·lar·ly
part′ings
par′ti·san
par′ti·san·ship′
par·ti′tion
par·ti′tioned
par′ti·tive
part′ner
part′ner·ship
par′tridge
par′ty
par′ve·nu
pas′chal
pa·sha′
pass

pass'a·ble
pas'sage
pas'sage·way'
pass'book'
passed
pas'sen·ger
pas'sion
pas'sion·ate
pas'sion·ate·ly
Pas'sion·ist
pas'sion·less
pas'sive
pas'sive·ness
pas'siv·ism
pas'siv·ist
pas·siv'i·ty
pass'key'
pass'o'ver
pass'port
pass'word'
past
paste
paste'board'
past'ed
pas·tel'
pas'tern
pas'teur·i·za'tion
pas'teur·ize
pas'teur·ized
pas·tiche'
pas·tille'
pas'time'
past'i·ness
pas'tor
pas'to·ral
pas'to·ral·ly
pas'tor·ate
pas'try
pas'try·man
pas'tur·age
pas'ture
pas'tured
past'y
pat
Pat'a·go'ni·an
patch
patched
patch'ou·li
patch'work'
patch'y
pa·tel'la
pa·tel'lar
pat'ent
pat'ent·a·ble
pat'ent·ed
pat'ent·ee'
pa'ter·fa·mil'i·as
pa·ter'nal
pa·ter'nal·ism
pa·ter'nal·is'tic
pa·ter'nal·ly
pa·ter'ni·ty
path
pa·thet'ic
pa·thet'i·cal·ly
path'less
pa·thol'o·gist
pa·thol'o·gy
pa'thos
path'way'
pa'tience
pa'tient
pat'i·na
pa'ti·o
pat'ness
pat'ois
pa'tri·arch
pa'tri·ar'chal
pa'tri·arch'ate
pa'tri·arch'y
pa·tri'cian
pat'ri·cide
pat'ri·mo'ni·al
pat'ri·mo'ny
pa'tri·ot
pa'tri·ot'ic
pa'tri·ot'i·cal·ly
pa'tri·ot·ism
pa·tris'tic
pa·trol'
pa·trolled'
pa·trol'man
pa'tron
pa'tron·age
pa'tron·ess
pa'tron·ize

pa'tron·ized
pat'ro·nym'ic
pa·troon'
pat'ted
pat'ten
pat'ter
pat'tered
pat'tern
pat'terned
pau'ci·ty
Paul'ist
paunch
paunch'i·ness
pau'per
pau'per·ism
pau'per·i·za'tion
pau'per·ize
pau'per·ized
pause
paused
pave
paved
pave'ment
pav'er
pa·vil'lion
paw
pawed
pawl
pawn
pawn'bro'ker
pawned
pawn'shop'
pay
pay'a·ble
pay'day'
pay'ee'
pay'ees'
pay'er
pay'mas'ter
pay'ment
pay'roll'
pea
peace
peace'a·ble
peace'a·bly
peace'ful
peace'mak'er
peach
pea'cock'
peak
peaked
peal
pealed
pea'nut'
pear
pearl
pearl'ite
pearl'y
peas'ant
peas'ant·ry
pea'shoot'er
peat
pea'vey
peb'ble
peb'bled
peb'ble·ware'
peb'bly
pe·can'
pec'ca·dil'lo
pec'can·cy
pec'cant
pec'ca·ry
peck
pec'tase
pec'tin
pec'to·ral
pec'u·late
pec'u·lat'ed
pec'u·la'tion
pec'u·la'tor
pe·cul'iar
pe·cu'li·ar'i·ty
pe·cul'iar·ly
pe·cu'ni·ar'y
ped'a·gog'ic
ped'a·gog'i·cal
ped'a·gog'i·cal·ly
ped'a·gogue
ped'a·go'gy
ped'al
ped'aled
ped'ant
pe·dan'tic
pe·dan'ti·cal
pe·dan'ti·cism
ped'ant·ry

| | | |
|---|---|---|
| ped'dle | pelf | pen'e·trat'ed |
| ped'dled | pel'i·can | pen'e·trat'ing·ly |
| ped'dler | pe·lisse' | pen'e·tra'tion |
| ped'es·tal | pel·la'gra | pen'e·tra'tive |
| pe·des'tri·an | pel'let | pen'guin |
| pe·des'tri·an·ism | pel·lu'cid | pen'hold'er |
| pe'di·a·tri'cian | pe·lo'ta | pen'i·cil'lin |
| pe'di·at'rics | pelt | pen·in'su·la |
| pe·dic'u·lar | pelt'ed | pen·in'su·lar |
| pe·dic'u·lo'sis | pel'try | pen'i·tence |
| ped'i·cure | pel'vic | pen'i·tent |
| ped'i·gree | pel'vis | pen'i·ten'tial |
| ped'i·greed | pem'mi·can | pen'i·ten'tial·ly |
| ped'i·ment | pen | pen'i·ten'tia·ry |
| pe·dom'e·ter | pe'nal | pen'i·tent·ly |
| peek | pe'nal·i·za'tion | pen'knife' |
| peel | pe'nal·ize | pen'man |
| peeled | pe'nal·ized | pen'man·ship |
| peel'ings | pen'al·ty | pen'nant |
| peen | pen'ance | pen'ni·less |
| peep | pen'chant' | pen'non |
| peer | pen'cil | pen'ny |
| peer'age | pen'ciled | pen'ny·roy'al |
| peered | pend'ant | pen'ny·weight' |
| peer'less | pend'en·cy | pe·nol'o·gist |
| pee'vish | pend'ing | pe·nol'o·gy |
| peg | pen'du·lous | pen'sion |
| Peg'a·sus | pen'du·lum | pen'sion·ar'y |
| pegged | pen'e·tra·bil'i·ty | pen'sioned |
| pe'jo·ra'tive | pen'e·tra·ble | pen'sion·er |
| pe'koe | pen'e·trant | pen'sive |
| pe·lag'ic | pen'e·trate | pen'stock' |

pent
pen'ta·gon
pen·tag'o·nal
pen·tam'e·ter
Pen'ta·teuch
pen·tath'lon
pen'ta·ton'ic
Pen'te·cost
pent'house'
pent·ox'ide
pe'nult
pe·nul'ti·mate
pe·num'bra
pe·nu'ri·ous
pen'u·ry
pe'on
pe'on·age
pe'o·ny
peo'ple
peo'pled
pep'lum
pep'per
pep'pered
pep'per·i·ness
pep'per·mint
pep'per·y
pep'sin
pep'tic
pep'tone
per'ad·ven'ture
per·am'bu·late
per·am'bu·la'tor
per·bo'rate
per·cale'
per·ceiv'a·ble
per·ceive'
per·ceived'
per·cent'
per·cent'age
per·cen'tile
per'cept
per·cep'ti·bil'i·ty
per·cep'ti·ble
per·cep'tion
per·cep'tive
per·cep'tu·al
per·cep'tu·al·ly
perch
per·chance'
per·cip'i·en·cy
per·cip'i·ent
per'co·late
per'co·la'tion
per'co·la'tor
per·cus'sion
per·cus'sive
per·di'tion
per·du'
per·dur'a·ble
per'e·gri·na'tion
per·emp'to·ri·ly
per·emp'to·ri·ness
per·emp'to·ry
per·en'ni·al
per·en'ni·al·ly
per'fect
per·fect'ed
per·fect'i·bil'i·ty
per·fect'i·ble
per·fec'tion
per·fec'tion·ism
per·fec'tion·ist
per'fect·ly
per·fec'to
per·fid'i·ous
per'fi·dy
per'fo·rate
per'fo·rat'ed
per'fo·ra'tion
per'fo·ra'tive
per'fo·ra'tor
per·force'
per·form'
per·form'a·ble
per·form'ance
per·formed'
per·form'er
per·fume'
per·fumed'
per·fum'er
per·fum'er·y
per·func'to·ri·ly
per·func'to·ri·ness
per·func'to·ry
per·fuse'
per·fused'

per′go·la
per·haps′
per′i·car′di·al
per′i·car·di′tis
per′i·car′di·um
per′i·gee
per′il·ous
per′il·ous·ly
per·im′e·ter
pe′ri·od
per·i′o·date
pe′ri·od′ic
pe′ri·od′i·cal
pe′ri·od′i·cal·ly
pe′ri·o·dic′i·ty
per′i·os′te·um
per′i·pa·tet′ic
pe·riph′er·al
pe·riph′er·al·ly
pe·riph′er·y
per′i·phras′tic
per′i·scope
per′i·scop′ic
per′ish
per′ish·a·ble
per′ished
per′i·stal′sis
per′i·stal′tic
per′i·stal′ti·cal·ly
per′i·style
per′i·to·ne′um
per′i·to·ni′tis

per′i·win′kle
per′jure
per′jured
per′jur·er
per·ju′ri·ous·ly
per′ju·ry
perk′y
perm′al·loy′
per′ma·nence
per′ma·nent
per′ma·nent·ly
per·man′ga·nate
per′me·a·bil′i·ty
per′me·a·ble
per′me·ate
per′me·at′ed
per′me·a′tion
per·mis′si·bil′i·ty
per·mis′si·ble
per·mis′sion
per·mis′sive·ness
per·mit′
per·mit′ted
per′mu·ta′tion
per·mute′
per·mut′ed
per·ni′cious
per′o·ra′tion
per·ox′ide
per′pen·dic′u·lar
per′pen·dic′u·lar′i·ty
per′pe·trate

per′pe·trat′ed
per′pe·tra′tion
per′pe·tra′tor
per·pet′u·al
per·pet′u·al·ly
per·pet′u·ate
per·pet′u·at′ed
per·pet′u·a′tion
per·pet′u·a′tor
per′pe·tu′i·ty
per·plex′
per·plexed′
per·plex′ed·ly
per·plex′ing·ly
per·plex′i·ty
per′qui·site
per′qui·si′tion
per′se·cute
per′se·cut′ed
per′se·cu′tion
per′se·cu′tor
per′se·ver′ance
per·sev′er·a′tion
per′se·vere′
per′se·vered′
per′si·flage
per·sim′mon
per·sist′
per·sist′ence
per·sist′en·cy
per·sist′ent
per·sist′ing·ly

per'son
per'son·a·ble
per'son·age
per'son·al
per′son·al'i·ty
per'son·al·ize
per'son·al·ly
per'son·al·ty
per·son′i·fi·ca'tion
per·son'i·fied
per·son'i·fy
per′son·nel'
per·spec'tive
per′spi·ca'cious
per′spi·cac'i·ty
per·spic'u·ous
per′spi·ra'tion
per·spir'a·to′ry
per·spire'
per·spired'
per·suade'
per·suad'ed
per·suad'er
per·sua'sion
per·sua'sive
per·sua'sive·ness
per·sul'phate
pert
per·tain'
per·tained'
per′ti·na'cious
per′ti·nac'i·ty
per'ti·nence
per'ti·nent
per·turb'
per·turb'a·ble
per′tur·ba'tion
per·turbed'
pe·rus'al
pe·ruse'
pe·rused'
Pe·ru'vi·an
per·vade'
per·vad'ed
per·vad'ing·ly
per·va'sion
per·va'sive
per·verse'
per·ver'sion
per·ver'si·ty
per·ver'sive
per·vert'
per·vert'ed
per'vi·ous
pes'si·mism
pes'si·mist
pes′si·mis'tic
pes′si·mis'ti·cal·ly
pest
pes'ter
pes'tered
pest'hole′
pest'house′
pes·tif'er·ous
pes'ti·lence
pes'ti·lent
pes′ti·len'tial
pes′ti·len'tial·ly
pes'tle
pet
pet'al
pe·tard'
pe·tite'
pe·ti'tion
pe·ti'tioned
pe·ti'tion·er
pet'rel
pet′ri·fac'tion
pet′ri·fac'tive
pet'ri·fy
pet'rol
pet′ro·la'tum
pe·tro'le·um
pe·trol'o·gy
pet'ted
pet'ti·coat
pet'ti·er
pet'ti·est
pet'ti·fog′ger
pet'ti·ly
pet'ti·ness
pet'tish
pet'ty
pet'u·lance
pet'u·lant
pe·tu'ni·a

pew
pew′ter
pha′e·ton
phag′o·cyte
phal′ange
phal′an·ster′y
pha′lanx
phan′tasm
phan·tas′ma·go′ri·a
phan′tom
Phar′aoh
phar′ma·ceu′tic
phar′ma·ceu′ti·cal
phar′ma·ceu′tics
phar′ma·cist
phar′ma·col′o·gy
phar′ma·co·poe′ia
phar′ma·cy
phar′yn·gi′tis
phar′ynx
phase
phased
pheas′ant
phe′nol
phe·nom′e·na
phe·nom′e·nal
phe·nom′e·nol′o·gy
phe·nom′e·non
phi′al
phi·lan′der
phi·lan′der·er
phil′an·throp′ic
phil′an·throp′i·cal
phi·lan′thro·pist
phi·lan′thro·py
phil′a·tel′ic
phi·lat′e·list
phi·lat′e·ly
phil′har·mon′ic
phi·lip′pic
Phil′ip·pine
Phil·is′tine
phi·lol′o·gist
phi·lol′o·gy
phi·los′o·pher
phil′o·soph′ic
phil′o·soph′i·cal
phi·los′o·phize
phi·los′o·phy
phil′ter
phle·bi′tis
phle·bot′o·my
phlegm
phleg·mat′ic
phleg·mat′i·cal·ly
phlo′em
phlox
pho′bi·a
phoe′nix
phone
pho·net′ic
pho·net′i·cal·ly
pho′ne·ti′cian
pho·net′ics
phon′ic
pho′no·graph
phos′phate
phos′phide
phos′phite
phos′pho·resce′
phos′pho·res′cence
phos·phor′ic
phos′pho·rous
phos′pho·rus
pho′to·cop′i·er
pho′to·e·lec′tric
pho′to·en·grav′ing
pho′to·gen′ic
pho′to·graph
pho′to·graphed
pho·tog′ra·pher
pho′to·graph′ic
pho·tog′ra·phy
pho′to·gra·vure′
pho′to·lith′o·graph
pho′to·mi′cro·graph
pho′ton
pho′to·play′
pho′to·sen′si·tize
Pho′to·stat
pho′to·syn′the·sis
phrase
phrased
phra′se·ol′o·gy
phre·net′ic
phren′ic

phre·nol′o·gist
phre·nol′o·gy
phthi′sis
phy·lac′ter·y
phys′ic
phys′i·cal
phys′i·cal·ly
phy·si′cian
phys′i·cist
phys′ics
phys′i·og′no·my
phys′i·o·log′i·cal
phys′i·o·log′i·cal·ly
phys′i·ol′o·gy
phy·sique′
pi′a·nis′si·mo
pi·an′ist
pi·a′no
pi·an′o·for′te
pi·az′za
pi′ca
pic′a·resque′
pic′co·lo
pick
pick′ax
picked
pick′er
pick′er·el
pick′et
pick′et·ed
pick′ings
pick′le
pick′led
pick′lock′
pick′pock′et
pick′up′
pic′nic
pic′nick·er
pic′ric
pic′to·graph
pic·to′ri·al
pic·to′ri·al·ly
pic′ture
Pic′ture·phone
pic′tur·esque′
pie
pie′bald′
piece
piece′meal′
piece′work′
pie′crust′
pied
pie′plant′
pier
pierce
pierced
pi′e·ty
pig
pi′geon
pi′geon·hole′
pig′fish′
pig′ger·y
pig′gish
pig′head′ed
pig′let
pig′ment
pig′men·tar′y
pig′men·ta′tion
pig′ment·ed
pig′nut′
pig′pen′
pig′skin′
pig′stick′er
pig′sty′
pig′tail′
pig′weed′
pike
pik′er
pike′staff′
pi·las′ter
pil′chard
pile
piled
pile′work′
pile′worm′
pil′fer
pil′fer·age
pil′fered
pil′fer·ings
pil′grim
pil′grim·age
pill
pil′lage
pil′laged
pil′lar
pil′lion

pil′lo·ry
pil′low
pil′low·case′
pil′lowed
pi′lot
pi′lot·ed
pi·men′to
pim′per·nel
pim′ple
pin
pin′a·fore′
pin′cers
pinch
pinched
pin′cush′ion
pine
pine′ap′ple
pined
pin′feath′er
pin′fish′
ping′-pong′
pin′guid
pin′hole′
pin′ion
pink
pink′ish
pink′weed′
pink′wood′
pin′nace
pin′na·cle
pinned
pi′noch′le

pin′prick′
pint
pin′to
pin′weed′
pin′worm′
pi′o·neer′
pi′o·neered′
pi′ous
pi′ous·ly
pip
pip′age
pipe
piped
pipe′line′
pip′er
pipe′stem′
pipe′stone′
pi·pette′
pipe′wood′
pip′ing·ly
pip′ings
pip′it
pip′kin
pip·sis′se·wa
pi′quan·cy
pi′quant
pique
pi·qué′
piqued
pi′ra·cy
pi′rate
pi′rat·ed

pi·rat′ic
pi·rat′i·cal
pi·rogue′
pir′ou·ette′
pir·ou·et′ted
pis′ca·tol′o·gy
pis′ca·to′ri·al
pis′ca·to′ri·al·ly
pis·tach′i·o
pis′tol
pis·tole′
pis′ton
pit
pitch
pitched
pitch′er
pitch′fork′
pit′e·ous
pit′e·ous·ness
pit′fall′
pith
pith′i·ly
pith′i·ness
pith′y
pit′i·a·ble
pit′i·ful
pit′i·less
pit′i·less·ly
pit′i·less·ness
pit′tance
pit′ted
pi·tu′i·tar′y

pit′y
pit′y·ing·ly
piv′ot
piv′ot·al
piv′ot·ed
pla′ca·bil′i·ty
pla′ca·ble
plac′ard
pla′cate
pla′cat·ed
pla′ca·tive·ly
pla′ca·to′ry
place
pla·ce′bo
place′man
place′ment
pla·cen′ta
plac′er
plac′id
pla·cid′i·ty
plac′id·ly
plack′et
pla′gi·a·rism
pla′gi·a·rist
pla′gi·a·rize
pla′gi·a·ry
plague
plagued
plaid
plain
plain′er
plain′est
plain′ly
plain′ness
plaint
plain′tiff
plain′tive
plait
plait′ed
plait′ings
plan
plan·chette′
plane
plan′et
plan′e·tar′i·an
plan′e·tar′i·um
plan′e·tar′y
plan′et·oid
plan′gent
plan′i·sphere
plank
planked
plank′ton
plan′less
planned
pla′no·graph′ic
plant
plan′tain
plan′tar
plan·ta′tion
plant′ed
plant′er
plant′ings
plaque
plas′ma
plas′ter
plas′tered
plas′ter·er
plas′ter·work′
plas′tic
plas·tic′i·ty
plas′tron
plate
pla·teau′
plat′ed
plate′hold′er
plate′let
plat′en
plat′er
plat′form′
plat′i·na
plat′i·nate
plat′ings
pla·tin′ic
plat′i·nize
plat′i·noid
plat′i·num
plat′i·tude
plat′i·tu′di·nize
plat′i·tu′di·nous
pla·toon′
plat′ter
plat′y·pus
plau′dit
plau′si·bil′i·ty
plau′si·ble

play
play'back'
play'bill'
play'boy'
played
play'er
play'ful
play'ful·ness
play'ground'
play'ings
play'mate'
play'read'er
play'room'
play'script'
play'thing'
play'time'
play'wright'
pla'za
plea
plead
plead'ed
plead'er
plead'ing·ly
plead'ings
pleas'ant
pleas'ant·ly
pleas'ant·ness
pleas'ant·ry
please
pleased
pleas'ur·a·ble
pleas'ure

pleat
ple·be'ian
pleb'i·scite
pledge
pledged
pledg'ee'
pledge'or'
pledg'er
pledg'et
ple'na·ri·ly
ple'na·ry
plen'i·po·ten'ti·ar'y
plen'i·tude
plen'te·ous
plen'ti·ful
plen'ty
ple'num
ple'o·nasm
ple'o·nas'tic
pleth'o·ra
ple·thor'ic
pleu'ra
pleu'ral
pleu'ri·sy
plex'us
pli'a·bil'i·ty
pli'a·ble
pli'an·cy
pli'ant
pli'ers
plight
plight'ed

plinth
plod
plod'ded
plod'der
plod'ding·ly
plot
plot'ted
plot'ter
plough
plov'er
plow
plow'boy
plow'ings
plow'man
plow'share'
pluck
plucked
pluck'i·er
pluck'i·est
pluck'i·ly
pluck'i·ness
pluck'y
plug
plugged
plum
plum'age
plumb
plum·ba'go
plum'bate
plumbed
plumb'er
plum'bic

plum'bous
plume
plumed
plum'met
plum'met·ed
plump
plump'er
plump'est
plump'ly
plump'ness
plun'der
plun'dered
plun'der·er
plunge
plunged
plung'er
plunk
plunked
plu'ral
plu'ral·ism
plu'ral·ist
plu·ral·is'tic
plu·ral'i·ty
plu'ral·ize
plu'ral·ized
plus
plush
plu·toc'ra·cy
plu'to·crat
plu'to·crat'ic
plu'to·crat'i·cal·ly
plu·ton'ic
plu·to'ni·um
ply
pneu·mat'ic
pneu·mat'i·cal·ly
pneu·mat'ics
pneu·mo'ni·a
poach
poach'er
pock'et
pock'et·book'
pock'et·knife'
pock'mark'
pod
po·dag'ra
po·di'a·try
po'di·um
po'em
po'e·sy
po'et
po'et·as'ter
po·et'ic
po·et'i·cal
po'et·ry
po'i
poign'an·cy
poign'ant
poin'ci·an'a
poin·set'ti·a
point
point'ed
point'ed·ly
point'er
point'less
point'less·ly
poise
poised
poi'son
poi'soned
poi'son·er
poi'son·ous
poke
poked
pok'er
poke'weed'
po'lar
po·lar'i·ty
po'lar·i·za'tion
po'lar·ize
po'lar·ized
po'lar·iz'er
pole
pole'cat'
po·lem'ic
po·lem'i·cal
po·lem'i·cist
po·lem'ics
pole'star'
po·lice'
po·liced'
po·lice'man
pol'i·cy
pol'ish
pol'ished
pol'ish·er

po·lite′
po·lite′ly
po·lite′ness
pol′i·tic
po·lit′i·cal
po·lit′i·cal·ly
pol′i·ti′cian
pol′i·tics
pol′ka
poll
pol′lard
pol′lard·ed
polled
pol′len
pol′li·nate
pol′li·na′tion
poll′ster
pol·lute′
pol·lut′ed
pol·lu′tion
po′lo
pol′o·naise′
po·lo′ni·um
pol·troon′
pol′y·an′drous
pol′y·an′dry
pol′y·chrome
pol′y·clin′ic
po·lyg′a·mist
po·lyg′a·mous
po·lyg′a·my
pol′y·glot
pol′y·gon
po·lyg′o·nal
pol′y·mer′ic
po·lym′er·ism
pol′y·mer·i·za′tion
pol′y·mer·ize
pol′y·no′mi·al
pol′yp
po·lyph′o·ny
pol′y·syl·lab′ic
pol′y·tech′nic
po·made′
po′man·der
po·ma′tum
pome′gran′ate
Pom′er·a′ni·an
pom′mel
pom′meled
po·mol′o·gy
pomp
pom′pa·dour
pom′pa·no
Pom·pe′ian
pom′pon
pom·pos′i·ty
pomp′ous
pon′cho
pond
pon′der
pon′der·a·ble
pon′dered
pon′der·o′sa
pon′der·os′i·ty
pon′der·ous
pond′fish′
pond′weed′
pon·gee′
pon′iard
pon′tiff
pon·tif′i·cal
pon·tif′i·cal·ly
pon·tif′i·cate
pon·toon′
po′ny
poo′dle
pool
pooled
pool′room′
poor
poor′er
poor′est
poor′house′
poor′ly
poor′ness
pop
pop′corn′
pop′gun′
pop′in·jay
pop′lar
pop′lin
pop′o′ver
popped
pop′pet
pop′py

pop'u·lace
pop'u·lar
pop'u·lar'i·ty
pop'u·lar·i·za'tion
pop'u·lar·ize
pop'u·lar·ized
pop'u·late
pop'u·lat'ed
pop'u·la'tion
pop'u·lous
por'ce·lain
porch
por'cu·pine
pore
pored
por'gy
pork
por·nog'ra·phy
po·ros'i·ty
po'rous
por'phy·ry
por'poise
por'ridge
por'rin·ger
port
port'a·ble
por'tage
por'tal
port·cul'lis
por·tend'
por·tend'ed
por'tent

por·ten'tous
por'ter
por'ter·house'
port·fo'li·o
port'hole'
por'ti·co
por·tiere'
por'tion
por'tioned
port·man'teau
por'trait
por'trait·ist
por'trai·ture
por·tray'
por·tray'al
por·trayed'
Por'tu·guese
por'tu·la'ca
pose
posed
po·si'tion
pos'i·tive
pos'i·tiv·ism
pos'i·tiv·is'tic
pos'i·tron
pos'se
pos·sess'
pos·sessed'
pos·ses'sion
pos·ses'sive
pos·ses'sor
pos·ses'sor·ship

pos'si·bil'i·ty
pos'si·ble
pos'si·bly
pos'sum
post
post'age
post'al
post'box'
post'date'
post'dat'ed
post'ed
post'er
pos·te'ri·or
pos·ter'i·ty
pos'tern
post·grad'u·ate
post'haste'
post'hole'
post'hu·mous
pos·til'ion
post'im·pres'sion·ism
post'ings
post'lude
post'man
post·mar'i·tal
post'mark'
post'mas'ter
post'me·rid'i·an
post'mis'tress
post'-mor'tem
post·nup'tial
post'op'er·a·tive

post'paid'
post·pone'
post·poned'
post·pone'ment
post·pran'di·al
post'script
pos'tu·lant
pos'tu·late
pos'tu·lat'ed
pos'tu·la'tion
pos'ture
pos'tured
pos'tur·ings
po'sy
pot
po'ta·bil'i·ty
po'ta·ble
pot'ash'
po·tas'si·um
po·ta'tion
po·ta'to
pot'boil'er
po'ten·cy
po'tent
po'ten·tate
po·ten'tial
po·ten'ti·al'i·ty
po·ten'tial·ly
po·ten'ti·om'e·ter
pot'herb'
pot'hole'
pot'hook'
pot'house'
po'tion
pot'latch'
pot'luck'
pot'pie'
pot'pour'ri'
pot'sherd'
pot'tage
pot'ter
pot'ter·y
pouch
poult
poul'ter·er
poul'tice
poul'ticed
poul'try
pounce
pounced
pound
pound'age
pound'cake'
pound'ed
pound'ings
pour
poured
pout
pout'ed
pov'er·ty
pow'der
pow'dered
pow'der·y
pow'er
pow'ered
pow'er·ful
pow'er·ful·ly
pow'er·less
pow'er·less·ly
pow'er·less·ness
pow'wow'
prac'ti·ca·bil'i·ty
prac'ti·ca·ble
prac'ti·ca·bly
prac'ti·cal
prac'ti·cal'i·ty
prac'ti·cal·ly
prac'tice
prac'ticed
prac'ti·cum
prac·ti'tion·er
prag·mat'ic
prag·mat'i·cal
prag·mat'i·cal·ly
prag'ma·tism
prag'ma·tist
prai'rie
praise
praised
praise'wor·thy
pra'line
prance
pranced
pranc'ing·ly
prank
prank'ster

prate
prat′ed
prat′ings
pra·tique′
prat′tle
prat′tling·ly
prawn
pray
prayed
prayer
prayer′ful
prayer′ful·ly
preach
preached
preach′er
preach′ment
preach′y
pre′ad·o·les′cent
pre′am′ble
pre′ar·range′
pre′ar·range′ment
preb′en·dar′y
pre·can′celed
pre·car′i·ous
pre·cau′tion
pre·cau′tion·ar′y
pre·cede′
pre·ced′ed
pre·ced′ence
prec′e·dent
pre′cept
pre·cep′tor
pre·cep′tress
pre·ces′sion
pre·chill′
pre′cinct
pre′ci·os′i·ty
pre′cious
pre′cious·ly
prec′i·pice
pre·cip′i·tan·cy
pre·cip′i·tant
pre·cip′i·tate
pre·cip′i·tat′ed
pre·cip′i·tate·ly
pre·cip′i·ta′tion
pre·cip′i·tous
pré·cis′
pre·cise′
pré·cised′
pre·cise′ly
pre·cise′ness
pre·ci′sion
pre·ci′sion·ist
pre·clin′i·cal
pre·clude′
pre·clud′ed
pre·clu′sion
pre·co′cious
pre·co′cious·ly
pre·coc′i·ty
pre·con·ceived′
pre′con·cep′tion
pre·cook′
pre·cool′
pre·cur′sor
pre·cur′so·ry
pre·da′ceous
pre·dac′i·ty
pre·date′
pre·da′tion
pred′a·tive
pred′a·tor
pred′a·to′ry
pre′de·cease′
pred′e·ces′sor
pre′de·cide′
pre·des′ig·nat′ed
pre′des·ig·na′tion
pre·des′ti·nar′i·an
pre·des′ti·nar·i·an·ism
pre·des′ti·na′tion
pre·des′tine
pre·des′tined
pre′de·ter′mi·nant
pre′de·ter′mi·nate
pre′de·ter′mi·na·tion
pre′de·ter′mine
pre′de·ter′mined
pre′di·as·tol′ic
pre·dic′a·ment
pred′i·cate
pred′i·cat′ed
pred′i·ca′tion
pred′i·ca′tive
pre·dict′

pre·dict′a·ble
pre·dict′ed
pre·dic′tion
pre·dic′tion·al
pre·dic′tive
pre′di·gest′
pre′di·gest′ed
pre′di·ges′tion
pre′di·lec′tion
pre′dis·clo′sure
pre′dis·pose′
pre′dis·posed′
pre′dis·po·si′tion
pre·dom′i·nance
pre·dom′i·nant
pre·dom′i·nate
pre·dom′i·nat′ed
pre·dom′i·nate·ly
pre·dom′i·nat′ing·ly
pre·draft′
pre·dry′
pre-em′i·nence
pre-em′i·nent
pre-empt′
pre-empt′ed
pre-emp′tion
pre-emp′tive
preen
preened
pre-es′ti·mate
pre′-ex·ist′
pre′-ex·ist′ent

pref′ace
pref′aced
pre·fash′ion
pref′a·to′ry
pre′fect
pre′fec·ture
pre·fer′
pref′er·a·ble
pref′er·a·bly
pref′er·ence
pref′er·en′tial
pref′er·en′tial·ly
pre·fer′ment
pre·ferred′
pre·fig′ure
pre·fig′ured
pre′fix
pre′fix·al
pre·fixed′
pre·form′
pre·formed′
pre·gath′er
preg′nan·cy
preg′nant
pre·har′vest
pre·hen′sile
pre′hen·sil′i·ty
pre′his·tor′ic
pre′im·ag′ine
pre′in·au′gu·ral
pre′in·cline′
pre′in·clined′

pre·in′ven·to′ry
pre·judge′
pre·judged′
prej′u·diced
prej′u·di′cial
prej′u·di′cial·ly
prel′a·cy
prel′ate
pre·lim′i·nar′y
pre·lit′er·ate
prel′ude
pre′ma·ter′ni·ty
pre′ma·ture′
pre·med′i·cal
pre·med′i·tate
pre·med′i-tat′ed
pre′med·i·ta′tion
pre′mi·er
prem′ise
prem′is·es
pre′mi·um
pre′mo·ni′tion
pre·mon′i·to′ry
pre·na′tal
pre·na′tal·ly
pre·oc′cu·pa′tion
pre·oc′cu·pied
pre·oc′cu·py
pre·op′er·a′tive
pre′or·dain′
pre′or·dained′
pre·paid′

prep′a·ra′tion
pre·par′a·tive
pre·par′a·to′ry
pre·pare′
pre·pared′
pre·par′ed·ness
pre·pay′
pre·pay′ment
pre·pense′
pre·pon′der·ance
pre·pon′der·ant
pre·pon′der·ate
pre·pon′der·at′ingly
prep′o·si′tion
prep′o·si′tion·al
pre′pos·sess′
pre′pos·ses′sion
pre·pos′ter·ous
pre·print′
pre′re·lease′
pre·req′ui·site
pre·rog′a·tive
pre·sage′
pre·saged′
pres′by·ter
Pres′by·te′ri·an
pres′by·ter′y
pre′sci·ence
pre′sci·ent
pre·scribe′
pre·scribed′
pre·scrip′tion
pre·scrip′tive
pres′ence
pres′ent
pre·sent′a·bil′i·ty
pre·sent′a·ble
pres′en·ta′tion
pre·sent′ed
pre·sen′ti·ment
pres′ent·ly
pre·sent′ment
pres′er·va′tion
pre·serv′a·tive
pre·serve′
pre·serv′er
pre·side′
pre·sid′ed
pres′i·den·cy
pres′i·dent
pres′i·den′tial
press
press′board′
pressed
pres′sings
press′man
press′room′
pres′sure
press′work′
pres′ti·dig′i·ta′tor
pres·tige′
pres·tig′i·ous
pres′to
pre·sum′a·ble
pre·sume′
pre·sumed′
pre·sum′ed·ly
pre·sump′tion
pre·sump′tive
pre·sump′tu·ous
pre′sup·pose′
pre′sys·tol′ic
pre·tend′
pre·tend′ed
pre·tend′er
pre·tense′
pre·ten′sion
pre·ten′tious
pre·ten′tious·ly
pre·ten′tious·ness
pret′er·it
pre′ter·mit′
pre′ter·mit′ted
pre′ter·nat′u·ral
pre′text
pret′ti·er
pret′ti·est
pret′ti·ly
pret′ti·ness
pret′ty
pret′zel
pre·vail′
pre·vailed′
pre·vail′ing·ly
prev′a·lence
prev′a·lent

prev′a·lent·ly
pre·var′i·cate
pre·var′i·cat′ed
pre·var′i·ca′tion
pre·var′i·ca′tor
pre·vent′
pre·vent′a·bil′i·ty
pre·vent′a·ble
pre·vent′ed
pre·ven′tion
pre·ven′tive
pre′view′
pre′vi·ous
pre·vi′sion
pre′vo·ca′tion·al
prey
price
priced
price′less
prick
pricked
prick′le
prick′led
prick′li·ness
prick′ly
pride
pride′ful
priest
priest′ess
priest′hood
priest′ly
prig′gish
prim
pri′ma·cy
pri′mal
pri′ma·ri·ly
pri′ma·ry
pri′mate
pri′mate·ship
prime
primed
prim′er
pri·me′val
prim′i·tive
prim′i·tiv·ism
prim′ly
prim′ness
pri′mo·gen′i·ture
pri·mor′di·al
prim′rose′
prince
prince′li·ness
prince′ling
prince′ly
prin′ces
prin′cess
prin′ci·pal
prin′ci·pal′i·ty
prin′ci·pal·ly
prin′ci·ple
prin′ci·pled
print
print′a·ble
print′ed
print′er
print′ings
print′out
pri′or
pri·or′i·ty
pri′o·ry
prism
pris·mat′ic
pris′on
pris′on·er
pris′tine
pri′va·cy
pri′vate
pri′va·teer′
pri′vate·ly
pri′vate·ness
pri·va′tion
priv′et
priv′i·lege
priv′i·ly
priv′i·ty
priv′y
prize
prized
prob′a·bil′i·ty
prob′a·ble
prob′a·bly
pro′bate
pro·ba′tion
pro·ba′tion·ar′y
probe
prob′i·ty

prob'lem
prob'lem·at'ic
pro·bos'cis
pro·ce'dur·al
pro·ce'dure
pro·ceed'
pro·ceed'ed
pro·ceed'ings
proc'ess
proc'essed
proc'ess·es
pro·ces'sion
proc'ess·or
pro·claim'
pro·claimed'
proc'la·ma'tion
pro·cliv'i·ty
pro·con'sul
pro·cras'ti·nate
pro·cras'ti·nat'ed
pro·cras'ti·na'tion
pro·cras'ti·na'tor
pro'cre·a'tion
pro'cre·a'tive
proc'tor
pro·cur'a·ble
proc'u·ra'tion
proc'u·ra'tor
pro·cure'
pro·cured'
pro·cure'ment
prod
prod'ded
prod'i·gal
prod'i·gal'i·ty
prod'i·gal·ly
pro·di'gious
pro·di'gious·ly
prod'i·gy
pro·duce'
pro·duced'
pro·duc'er
prod'uct
pro·duc'tion
pro·duc'tive
pro'duc·tiv'i·ty
pro'em
prof'a·na'tion
pro·fan'a·to'ry
pro·fane'
pro·faned'
pro·fan'i·ty
pro·fess'
pro·fessed'
pro·fess'ed·ly
pro·fes'sion
pro·fes'sion·al
pro·fes'sion·al·ism
pro·fes'sion·al·ize
pro·fes'sion·al·ly
pro·fes'sor
pro'fes·so'ri·al
pro·fes'sor·ship
prof'fer
prof'fered
pro·fi'cien·cy
pro·fi'cient
pro·fi'cient·ly
pro'file
prof'it
prof'it·a·ble
prof'it·a·bly
prof'it·ed
prof'it·eer'
prof'it·less
prof'li·ga·cy
prof'li·gate
pro·found'
pro·found'ness
pro·fun'di·ty
pro·fuse'
pro·fuse'ly
pro·fuse'ness
pro·fu'sion
pro·gen'i·tor
prog'e·ny
prog·no'sis
prog·nos'tic
prog·nos'ti·cate
prog·nos'ti·cat'ed
pro'gram
pro'gramed
pro'gram·er
pro·gress'
pro·gressed'
pro·gres'sion

pro·gres′sive
pro·hib′it
pro·hib′it·ed
pro′hi·bi′tion
pro′hi·bi′tion·ist
pro·hib′i·tive
pro·hib′i·to′ry
pro·ject′
pro·ject′ed
pro·jec′tile
pro·jec′tion
pro·jec′tive
pro·jec′tor
pro′le·tar′i·an
pro′le·tar′i·at
pro·lif′er·ate
pro·lif′er·a′tion
pro·lif′ic
pro·lif′i·ca′tion
pro·lix′
pro·lix′i·ty
pro′logue
pro·long′
pro·lon′gate
pro′lon·ga′tion
pro·longed′
prom′e·nade′
prom′e·nad′ed
prom′i·nence
prom′i·nent
prom′is·cu′i·ty
pro·mis′cu·ous
pro·mis′cu·ous·ly
pro·mis′cu·ous·ness
prom′ise
prom′ised
prom′is·ing·ly
prom′is·so′ry
prom′on·to′ry
pro·mote′
pro·mot′ed
pro·mot′er
pro·mo′tion
pro·mo′tion·al
prompt
prompt′ed
prompt′er
prompt′est
promp′ti·tude
prompt′ly
prompt′ness
pro·mul′gate
pro·mul′gat·ed
pro′mul·ga′tion
pro′nate
pro·na′tion
prone
prong
prong′horn′
pro·nom′i·nal
pro′noun
pro·nounce′
pro·nounce′a·ble
pro·nounced′
pro·nounce′ment
pro·nun′ci·a′tion
proof
proofed
prop
prop′a·gan′da
prop′a·gan′dist
prop′a·gate
prop′a·gat′ed
prop′a·ga′tion
pro·pel′
pro·pel′lant
pro·pelled′
pro·pel′ler
pro·pen′si·ty
prop′er
prop′er·ly
prop′er·ty
proph′e·cy
proph′e·sied
proph′e·sy
proph′et
pro·phet′ic
pro·phet′i·cal·ly
pro′phy·lac′tic
pro′phy·lax′is
pro·pin′qui·ty
pro·pi′ti·ate
pro·pi′ti·at′ed
pro·pi′ti·a′tion
pro·pi′ti·a·to′ry
pro·pi′tious

pro·po′nent
pro·por′tion
pro·por′tion·a·ble
pro·por′tion·al
pro·por′tion·al·ly
pro·por′tion·ate
pro·por′tion·ate·ly
pro·por′tioned
pro·pos′al
pro·pose′
pro·posed′
prop′o·si′tion
pro·pound′
pro·pound′ed
pro·pri′e·tar′y
pro·pri′e·tor
pro·pri′e·to′ri·al
pro·pri′e·to′ri·al·ly
pro·pri′e·tor·ship′
pro·pri′e·to′ry
pro·pri′e·ty
pro·pul′sion
pro·pul′sive
pro′rate′
pro′rat′ed
pro·ra′tion
pro′ro·ga′tion
pro·rogue′
pro·rogued′
pro·sa′ic
pro·sa′i·cal·ly
pro·sce′ni·um
pro·scribe′
pro·scribed′
pro·scrip′tion
prose
pros′e·cute
pros′e·cut·ed
pros′e·cu′tion
pros′e·cu′tor
pros′e·lyte
pros′e·lyt′ed
pros′e·lyt·ize
pros′e·lyt·iz′er
pros′i·er
pros′i·est
pros′i·fy
pros′i·ly
pros′i·ness
pros′o·dy
pros′pect
pros′pect·ed
pro·spec′tive
pros′pec·tor
pro·spec′tus
pros′per
pros′pered
pros·per′i·ty
pros′per·ous
pros′per·ous·ly
pros′the·sis
pros·thet′ic
pros′trate
pros′trat·ed
pros·tra′tion
pros′y
pro·tag′o·nist
pro′te·an
pro·tect′
pro·tect′ed
pro·tect′ing·ly
pro·tec′tion
pro·tec′tion·ism
pro·tec′tion·ist
pro·tec′tive
pro·tec′tive·ly
pro·tec′tive·ness
pro·tec′tor
pro·tec′tor·ate
pro′té·gé
pro′te·in
pro·test′
prot′es·tant
prot′es·ta′tion
pro·test′ed
pro·test′ers
pro·thon′o·tar′y
pro′to·col
pro′ton
pro′to·plasm
pro′to·type
pro·tox′ide
Pro′to·zo′a
pro·tract′
pro·tract′ed
pro·trac′tile

pro·trac′tion
pro·trac′tive
pro·trac′tor
pro·trude′
pro·trud′ed
pro·tru′sion
pro·tru′sive
pro·tu′ber·ance
pro·tu′ber·ant
proud
proud′er
proud′est
proud′ly
prov′a·ble
prove
proved
prov′en
prov′e·nance
Prov′en·çal′
prov′en·der
prov′erb
pro·ver′bi·al
pro·ver′bi·al·ly
pro·vide′
pro·vid′ed
prov′i·dence
prov′i·dent
prov′i·den′tial
prov′i·den′tial·ly
pro·vid′er
prov′ince
pro·vin′cial
pro·vin′cial·ism
pro·vin′ci·al′i·ty
pro·vin′cial·ly
pro·vi′sion
pro·vi′sion·al
pro·vi′sion·al·ly
pro·vi′so
pro·vi′so·ry
prov′o·ca′tion
pro·voc′a·tive
pro·voke′
pro·voked′
pro·vok′ing·ly
prov′ost
prow
prow′ess
prowl
prowled
prowl′er
prox′i·mal
prox′i·mal·ly
prox′i·mate
prox·im′i·ty
prox′i·mo
prox′y
prude
pru′dence
pru′dent
pru·den′tial
pru·den′tial·ly
pru′dent·ly
prud′er·y
prud′ish
prune
pruned
pru′ri·ence
pru′ri·ent
pru·ri′tus
Prus′sian
pry
pry′ing·ly
psalm
psalm′book′
psalm′ist
psal′mo·dist
psal′mo·dy
psal′ter
pseu′do·nym
pso·ri′a·sis
psy′chi·at′ric
psy′chi·at′ri·cal·ly
psy·chi′a·trist
psy·chi′a·try
psy′chic
psy′chi·cal
psy′chi·cal·ly
psy′cho·a·nal′y·sis
psy′cho·bi·ol′o·gy
psy′cho·dy·nam′ics
psy′cho·gen′e·sis
psy′cho·ge·net′ic
psy′cho·log′i·cal
psy·chol′o·gist
psy·chol′o·gy

psy′cho·path′ic
psy′cho·pa·thol′o·gy
psy·chop′a·thy
psy·cho′sis
psy·chot′ic
Ptol′e·ma′ic
pto′maine
pub′lic
pub′li·ca′tion
pub′li·cist
pub·lic′i·ty
pub′lic·ly
pub′lish
pub′lished
pub′lish·er
puce
puck
puck′er
puck′ered
pud′dings
pud′dle
pud′dled
pud′dler
pu′den·cy
pudg′i·ness
pudg′y
pueb′lo
pu′er·ile
pu′er·il′i·ty
puff
puf′fin
puff′i·ness
puff′y
pug
pu′gil·ism
pu′gil·ist
pu′gil·is′tic
pug·na′cious·ly
pug·nac′i·ty
pu′is·sance
pu′is·sant
pul′chri·tude
pul′chri·tu′di·nous
pul′ing
pul′ing·ly
pull
pulled
pul′let
pul′ley
Pull′man
pul′lu·late
pul′mo·nar′y
Pul′mo′tor
pulp
pulp′i·er
pulp′i·est
pulp′i·ness
pul′pit
pul′pit·eer′
pulp′y
pul′sate
pul′sat·ed
pul·sa′tion
pul·sa′tor
pul′sa·to′ry
pulse
pul′ver·i·za′tion
pul′ver·ize
pul′ver·iz′er
pum′ice
pump
pum′per·nick′el
pump′kin
pun
punch
punched
pun′cheon
punch′ings
punc·til′i·o
punc·til′i·ous
punc·til′i·ous·ly
punc·til′i·ous·ness
punc′tu·al
punc′tu·al′i·ty
punc′tu·al·ly
punc′tu·ate
punc′tu·at′ed
punc′tu·a′tion
punc′ture
punc′tured
pun′dit
pung
pun′gen·cy
pun′gent
pu′ni·ness
pun′ish

pun′ish·a·ble
pun′ished
pun′ish·ment
pu′ni·tive
punk
punt
pu′ny
pup
pu′pa
pu′pae
pu′pil
pup′pet
pup′pet·eer′
pup′pet·ry
pup′py
pur′blind′
pur′chase
pur′chased
pur′chas·er
pure
pure′ly
pur′er
pur′est
pur′ga·tive
pur′ga·to′ry
purge
purged
pu′ri·fi·ca′tion
pu′ri·fied
pu′ri·fi′er
pu′ri·fy
pur′ism
pur′ist
Pu′ri·tan
pu′ri·tan′ic
pu′ri·tan′i·cal
Pu′ri·tan·ism
pu′ri·ty
purl
pur′lieu
pur·loin′
pur′ple
pur′plish
pur·port′
pur·port′ed
pur′pose
pur′pose·ful
pur′pose·ful·ly
pur′pose·ful·ness
pur′pose·less
pur′pose·ly
pur′pos·ive
purr
purred
purse
pursed
purs′er
purs′lane
pur·su′ance
pur·su′ant
pur·sue′
pur·sued′
pur·suit′
pur′sui·vant
pur′sy
pu′ru·lence
pu′ru·len·cy
pu′ru·lent
pur·vey′
pur·vey′ance
pur·vey′or
pur′view
pus
push
push′cart′
push′er
pu′sil·la·nim′i·ty
pu′sil·lan′i·mous
puss′y·foot′
pus′tu·lant
pus′tu·lar
pus′tu·late
pus′tu·la′tion
pus′tule
put
pu′ta·tive
pu′tre·fac′tion
pu′tre·fac′tive
pu′tre·fied
pu′tre·fy
pu·tres′cence
pu·tres′cent
pu′trid
putt
put′tee
putt′er

put'ty
puz'zle
puz'zled
puz'zler
puz'zles
py·e'mi·a
pyg'my
py·ja'ma

py'lon
py·lo'rus
py'or·rhe'a
pyr'a·mid
py·ram'i·dal
pyre
py'rex
py·rex'i·a

py·ri'tes
py·rog'ra·phy
py'ro·ma'ni·a
py·rom'e·ter
py'ro·tech'nics
py·rox'y·lin
Pyr'rhic
py'thon

quack
quack′er·y
quad
quad′ran′gle
quad·ran′gu·lar
quad′rant
quad′rat
quad·rat′ic
quad·rat′ics
quad′ra·ture
quad·ren′ni·al
quad·ren′ni·al·ly
quad·ren′ni·um
quad′ri·lat′er·al
qua·drille′
quad′ri·par′tite
quad′ru·ped
quad·ru′ple
quad′ru·plet
quad′ru·plex
quad·ru′pli·cate
quaff
quag′mire′
qua′hog
quail
quailed
quaint
quaint′ly
quaint′ness
quake
quaked
quak′er
quak′ing·ly
qual′i·fi·ca′tion
qual′i·fied
qual′i·fi′er
qual′i·fy
qual′i·ta′tive
qual′i·ties
qual′i·ty
qualm
quan′da·ry
quan′ti·ta′tive
quan′ti·ties
quan′ti·ty
quan′tum
quar′an·tine
quar′an·tined
quar′rel
quar′reled
quar′rel·some
quar′ri·er
quar′ry
quar′ry·man
quart
quar′tan
quar′ter
quar′ter·back′
quar′tered
quar′ter·ings
quar′ter·ly
quar′ter·mas′ter
quar′ter·saw′
quar·tet′
quar′tile
quar′to

quartz
quash
qua′si
qua·ter′na·ry
quat′rain
quat′re·foil′
qua′ver
qua′vered
qua′ver·ing·ly
quay
quay′age
quea′sy
queen
queen′ly
queer
queer′er
queer′est
quell
quelled
quench
quenched
quench′less
que′ried
quer′u·lous
que′ry
quest
quest′ing·ly
ques′tion
ques′tion·a·ble
ques′tion·er
ques′tion·ing·ly
ques′tion·naire′

queue
quib′ble
quick
quick′en
quick′ened
quick′er
quick′est
quick′lime′
quick′ly
quick′ness
quick′sand′
quick′sil′ver
quick′step′
quid′di·ty
qui·es′cence
qui′et
qui′et·ed
qui′et·ly
qui′et·ness
qui′e·tude
qui·e′tus
quill
quilled
quill′work′
quilt
quilt′ed
quince
qui′nine
quin·quen′ni·al
quin′tal
quint·es′sence
quin′tes·sen′tial

quin·tet′
quin′tu·plet
quip
qui′pu
quire
quirk
quirt
quit
quit′claim′
quite
quit′rent′
quit′tance
quit′ter
quiv′er
quiv′ered
quiv′er·ing·ly
quix·ot′ic
quiz
quiz′zi·cal
quoin
quoit
quon′dam
quo′rum
quo′ta
quot′a·ble
quo·ta′tion
quote
quot′ed
quoth
quo·tid′i·an
quo′tient
quot′ing

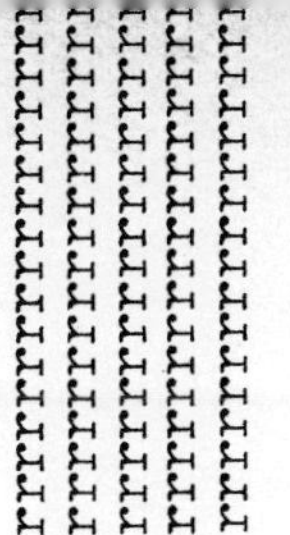

# R

rab'bet
rab·bin'i·cal
rab'bit
rab'bit·ry
rab'ble
rab'id
rab'id·ly
ra'bi·es
rac·coon'
race
raced
rac'er
race'way'
ra·chit'ic
ra·chi'tis
ra'cial
ra'cial·ly
rac'i·ly
rac'i·ness
rac'ism
rac'ist
rack'et
rac'y
ra'di·al
ra'di·al·ly
ra'di·ance
ra'di·ant
ra'di·ant·ly
ra'di·ate
ra'di·at'ed
ra'di·a'tion
ra'di·a'tor
rad'i·cal
rad'i·cal·ism
rad'i·cal·ly
ra·dic'u·lar
ra'di·i
ra'di·o
ra'di·o·ac'tive
ra'di·o·ac·tiv'i·ty
ra'di·o·gram'
ra'di·o·graph'
ra'di·om'e·ter
ra'di·o·phone'
ra'di·o·pho'to·graph
ra'di·o·scope'
ra'di·o·sen'si·tive
ra'di·o·tel'e·gram
rad'ish
ra'di·um
ra'di·us
ra'di·us·es
ra'dix
ra'don
raf'fi·a
raf'fle
raf'fled
raft
raft'er
rafts'man
rag
rag'a·muf'fin
rage
raged
rag'ged
rag'lan

ra·gout′
rag′pick′er
rag′time′
rag′weed′
raid
rail
rail′bird′
railed
rail′head′
rail′ing·ly
rail′ings
rail′ler·y
rail′road′
rail′road′er
rail′way′
rai′ment
rain
rain′bow′
rain′coat′
rained
rain′fall′
rain′spout′
rain′storm′
rain′y
raise
raised
rai′sin
ra′ja
rake
rak′ish
ral′lied
ral′ly

ram
ram′ble
ram′bled
ram′bler
ram·bunc′tious
ram′e·kin
ram′i·fi·ca′tion
ram′i·fied
ram′i·fy
rammed
ram′mer
ramp
ram′page
ramp′ant
ram′part
ram′rod′
ram′shack′le
ranch
ranch′er
ran·che′ro
ranch′man
ran′cho
ran′cid
ran·cid′i·ty
ran′cid·ly
ran′cor
ran′cor·ous
ran′dom
range
ranged
rang′er
rank

ranked
ran′kle
ran′kled
rank′ling·ly
ran′sack
ran′som
ran′somed
rant
rant′ed
rant′ing·ly
ra·pa′cious
ra·pac′i·ty
rap′id
ra·pid′i·ty
rap′id·ly
ra′pi·er
rap′ine
rap·port′
rap·scal′lion
rapt
rap·to′ri·al
rap′ture
rap′tur·ous
rap′tur·ous·ly
rap′tur·ous·ness
rare
rar′e·fac′tion
rar′e·fy
rare′ly
rare′ness
rar′er
rar′est

rar′i·ty
ras′cal
ras·cal′i·ty
ras′cal·ly
rash
rash′er
rash′est
rash′ly
rash′ness
rasp
rasp′ber′ry
rasped
rasp′ing·ly
rat
rat′a·ble
ratch′et
rate
rat′ed
rath′er
raths′kel′ler
rat′i·fi·ca′tion
rat′i·fied
rat′i·fy
rat′ings
ra′tio
ra′ti·oc′i·na′tion
ra′ti·oc′i·na′tive
ra′tion
ra′tion·al
ra′tion·al·ism
ra′tion·al·ist
ra′tion·al·is′tic
ra′tion·al·i·za′tion
ra′tion·al·ize
ra′tion·al·ized
ra′tion·al·ly
ra′tioned
rat′line
rat·tan′
rat′ter
rat′tle
rat′tle·brain′
rat′tle·brained′
rat′tled
rat′tle·head′ed
rat′tler
rat′tle·snake′
rat′tlings
rat′tly
rau′cous
rav′age
rav′aged
rave
raved
rav′el
rav′eled
ra′ven
rav′en·ous
rav′en·ous·ly
rav′en·ous·ness
ra′vi′gote′
ra·vine′
rav′ings
ra·vi·o′li
rav′ish
rav′ished
rav′ish·er
rav′ish·ing·ly
rav′ish·ment
raw
raw′boned′
raw′er
raw′est
raw′hide′
raw′ness
ray
ray′less
ray′on
raze
razed
ra′zor
ra′zor·back′
ra′zor·edge′
reach
reached
reach′ings
re·act′
re·act′ance
re·ac′tion
re·ac′tion·ar′y
re·ac′ti·vate
re′ac·ti·va′tion
read
read′a·bil′i·ty
read′a·ble
read′er

read′i·ly
read′i·ness
read′ings
re′ad·just′
re′ad·just′a·ble
re′ad·just′ment
re′ad·mis′sion
re′ad·mit′
read′y
re′af·firm′
re′af·fir·ma′tion
re·a′gent
re′al
re′a·lign′
re′al·ism
re′al·ist
re′al·is′tic
re′al·is′ti·cal·ly
re·al′i·ty
re′al·iz′a·ble
re′al·i·za′tion
re′al·ize
re′al·ized
re′al·ly
realm
re′al·tor
re′al·ty
ream
reamed
ream′er
re·an′i·mate
reap
reap′er
re′ap·pear′
re′ap·pear′ance
re′ap·point′
re′ap·point′ment
rear
reared
re·ar′gue
re·arm′
re·ar′ma·ment
re·armed′
rear′most
re′ar·range′
re′ar·range′ment
rear′ward
rea′son
rea′son·a·ble
rea′son·a·ble·ness
rea′son·a·bly
rea′soned
re′as·sem′ble
re′as·sert′
re′as·sert′ed
re′as·sign′
re′as·sume′
re′as·sur′ance
re′as·sure′
re′as·sured′
re′bate
re′bat·ed
re·bel′
re·belled′
re·bel′lion
re·bel′lious
re·bind′
re·birth′
re·born′
re·bound′
re·buff′
re·buffed′
re·build′
re·built′
re·buke′
re·buked′
re·buk′ing·ly
re′bus
re·but′
re·but′tal
re·but′ted
re·but′ter
re·cal′ci·trance
re·cal′ci·trant
re·call′
re·called′
re·cant′
re′can·ta′tion
re·cant′ed
re·cap′i·tal·ize
re′ca·pit′u·late
re′ca·pit′u·lat′ed
re′ca·pit′u·la′tion
re′ca·pit′u·la·to′ry
re·cap′ture
re·cast′

re·cede′
re·ced′ed
re·ceipt′
re·ceipt′ed
re·ceiv′a·ble
re·ceiv′a·bles
re·ceive′
re·ceived′
re·ceiv′er
re·ceiv′er·ship
re′cent
re′cent·ly
re·cep′ta·cle
re·cep′tion
re·cep′tion·ist
re·cep′tive
re·cep′tive·ly
re·cep′tive·ness
re′cep·tiv′i·ty
re·cep′tor
re·cess′
re·cessed′
re·cess′es
re·ces′sion
re·ces′sion·al
re·ces′sive
re·charge′
re·charged′
re·cher′ché′
re·cid′i·vism
re·cid′i·vist
rec′i·pe
re·cip′i·ent
re·cip′ro·cal
re·cip′ro·cal·ly
re·cip′ro·cate
re·cip′ro·cat′ed
re·cip′ro·ca′tion
re·cip′ro·ca′tive
re·cip′ro·ca′tor
rec′i·proc′i·ty
re·cit′al
re·cit′al·ist
rec′i·ta′tion
rec′i·ta·tive′
re·cite′
re·cit′ed
reck
reck′less
reck′less·ly
reck′less·ness
reck′on
reck′oned
reck′on·er
reck′on·ings
re·claim′
re·claim′a·ble
re·claimed′
rec′la·ma′tion
re·cline′
re·clined′
re·cluse′
rec′og·ni′tion
rec′og·niz′a·ble
re·cog′ni·zance
rec′og·nize
rec′og·nized
re·coil′
re·coiled′
rec′ol·lect′
rec′ol·lect′ed
rec′ol·lec′tion
re′com·mence′
rec′om·mend′
rec′om·men·da′tion
rec′om·mend′a·to′ry
rec′om·mend′ed
re′com·mit′
rec′om·pen′sa·ble
rec′om·pense
rec′om·pensed
rec′on·cil′a·ble
rec′on·cile
rec′on·ciled
rec′on·cile′ment
rec′on·cil′i·a′tion
rec′on·cil′i·a·to′ry
rec′on·dite
re·con′nais·sance
rec′on·noi′ter
rec′on·noi′tered
re·con′quer
re′con·sid′er
re·con′sti·tute
re′con·struct′
re′con·struct′ed

re′con·struc′tion
re′con·struc′tive
re·con′vert
re′con·vey′
re·cord′
re·cord′ed
re·cord′er
re·cord′ings
re·count′
re·count′ed
re·coup′
re·couped′
re·coup′ment
re·course′
re·cov′er
re·cov′er·a·ble
re·cov′er·y
rec′re·ant
re′-cre·ate′
rec′re·a′tion
rec′re·a′tion·al
re·crim′i·nate
re·crim′i·na′tion
re·crim′i·na′tive
re·crim′i·na·to′ry
re′cru·des′cence
re′cru·des′cent
re·cruit′
re·cruit′ed
re·cruit′ment
re′crys·tal·li·za′tion
re·crys′tal·lize

rec′tan′gle
rec·tan′gu·lar
rec·tan′gu·lar′i·ty
rec′ti·fi′a·ble
rec′ti·fi·ca′tion
rec′ti·fied
rec′ti·fi′er
rec′ti·fy
rec′ti·lin′e·ar
rec′ti·tude
rec′tor
rec′tor·ate
rec·to′ri·al
rec′to·ry
re·cum′ben·cy
re·cum′bent
re·cu′per·ate
re·cu′per·at′ed
re·cu′per·a′tion
re·cu′per·a′tive
re·cu′per·a·to′ry
re·cur′
re·curred′
re·cur′rence
re·cur′rent
re·cur′rent·ly
re·cy′cle
red
red′bird′
red′breast′
red′bud′
red′den

red′dened
red′der
red′dest
red′dish
re·deal′
re·deem′
re·deem′a·bil′i·ty
re·deem′a·ble
re·deemed′
re·deem′er
re·demp′tion
Re·demp′tor·ist
re·demp′to·ry
re′de·ter′mine
re′de·vel′op
re′di·rect′
re′di·rect′ed
re·dis′count
re′dis·cov′er
re′dis·trib′ute
re′dis·tri·bu′tion
re·dis′trict
red′ness
red′o·lence
red′o·lent
re·dou′ble
re·doubt′
re·doubt′a·ble
re·dound′
re·draft′
re·dress′
re·dressed′

re·duce′
re·duced′
re·duc′er
re·duc′i·ble
re·duc′tion
re·dun′dance
re·dun′dan·cy
re·dun′dant
re·dun′dant·ly
re·du′pli·cate
re·du′pli·cat′ed
re·du·pli·ca′tion
red′wood′
re-ech′o
re-ech′oed
reed
reed′bird′
reed′i·ness
re-ed′it
re-ed′u·cate
re′-ed·u·ca′tion
reed′y
reef
reef′er
reek
reek′ing·ly
reel
re′-e·lect′
re′-em·bark′
re′-em·bar·ka′tion
re′-em·ploy′
re′-en·act′
re′-en·force′
re′-en·force′ment
re′-en·gage′
re′-en·grave′
re′-en·list′
re-en′ter
re-en′trance
re-en′try
re′-es·tab′lish
re′-ex·am′i·na′tion
re′-ex·am′ine
re′-ex·port′
re′-ex·por·ta′tion
re·fec′to·ry
re·fer′
ref′er·a·ble
ref′er·ee′
ref′er·ence
ref′er·en′dum
re·ferred′
re·fig′ure
re′fill
re′fi·nance′
re·fine′
re·fined′
re·fine′ment
re·fin′er
re·fin′er·y
re·fit′
re·flect′
re·flect′ed
re·flect′ing·ly
re·flec′tion
re·flec′tive
re·flec′tor
re′flex
re·flex′ive
re′flux
re′for·est·a′tion
re·form′
ref′or·ma′tion
re·form′a·tive
re·form′a·to′ry
re·formed′
re·form′er
re·fract′
re·fract′ed
re·frac′tion
re·frac′tion·ist
re·frac′tive
re′frac·tiv′i·ty
re·frac′tor
re·frac′to·ry
re·frain′
re·frained′
re·fresh′
re·freshed′
re·fresh′er
re·fresh′ing·ly
re·fresh′ment
re·frig′er·ant
re·frig′er·ate
re·frig′er·at′ed
re·frig′er·a′tion

re·frig′er·a′tive
re·frig′er·a′tor
ref′uge
ref′u·gee′
re·ful′gence
re·ful′gent
re·fund′
re·fund′ed
re·fur′nish
re·fus′al
re·fuse′
re·fused′
ref′u·ta′tion
re·fute′
re·fut′ed
re·gain′
re·gained′
re′gal
re·gale′
re·galed′
re·gale′ment
re·ga′li·a
re·gal′i·ty
re′gal·ly
re·gard′
re·gard′ed
re·gard′ful
re·gard′less
re·gat′ta
re′ge·la′tion
re′gen·cy
re·gen′er·a·cy
re·gen′er·ate
re·gen′er·at′ed
re·gen′er·a′tion
re·gen′er·a′tive
re·gen′er·a′tor
re′gent
reg′i·cid′al
reg′i·cide
re·gime′
reg′i·men
reg′i·ment
reg′i·men′tal
reg′i·men′tals
reg′i·men·ta′tion
reg′i·ment′ed
re′gion
re′gion·al
re′gion·al·ism
re′gion·al·ize
re′gion·al·ly
reg′is·ter
reg′is·tered
reg′is·trar
reg′is·tra′tion
reg′is·try
re′gress
re·gres′sion
re·gres′sive
re·gret′
re·gret′ful
re·gret′ful·ly
re·gret′ful·ness
re·gret′ta·ble
re·gret′ted
reg′u·lar
reg′u·lar′i·ty
reg′u·lar·i·za′tion
reg′u·lar·ize
reg′u·late
reg′u·lat′ed
reg′u·lates
reg′u·la′tion
reg′u·la′tor
re·gur′gi·tate
re·gur′gi·tat′ed
re·gur′gi·ta′tion
re′ha·bil′i·tate
re′ha·bil′i·tat′ed
re′ha·bil′i·ta′tion
re·hash′
re·hears′al
re·hearse′
re·hearsed′
re·heat′
reign
reigned
re′im·burse′
re′im·bursed′
re′im·port′
re′im·por·ta′tion
rein
re′in·car′nate
re′in·car·na′tion
rein′deer′

reined
re′in·force′
re′in·forced′
re′in·sert′
re′in·stall′
re′in·state′
re′in·stat′ed
re′in·state′ment
re′in·sur′ance
re′in·sure′
re·in′te·grate
re′in·tro·duce′
re′in·vest′
re′in·vig′o·rate
re·is′sue
re·it′er·ate
re·it′er·at′ed
re·it′er·a′tion
re·it′er·a′tive
re·ject′
re·ject′ed
re·jec′tion
re·joice′
re·joiced′
re·joic′es
re·joic′ing·ly
re·join′
re·join′der
re·ju′ve·nate
re·ju′ve·nat′ed
re·ju′ve·na′tion
re·ju′ve·na′tive
re·ju′ve·nes′cence
re·ju′ve·nes′cent
re·kin′dle
re·lapse′
re·lapsed′
re·late′
re·lat′ed
re·la′tion
re·la′tion·al
re·la′tion·ship
rel′a·tive
rel′a·tive·ly
rel′a·tiv·ism
rel′a·tiv′i·ty
re·la′tor
re·lax′
re′lax·a′tion
re·laxed′
re·lax′es
re·lay′
re·layed′
re·lease′
re·leased′
rel′e·gate
rel′e·gat′ed
rel′e·ga′tion
re·lent′
re·lent′ed
re·lent′ing·ly
re·lent′less
rel′e·vance
rel′e·van·cy
rel′e·vant
re·li′a·bil′i·ty
re·li′a·ble
re·li′ant
rel′ic
re·lief′
re·lieve′
re·lieved′
re·li′gion
re·li′gious
re·li′gious·ly
re·lin′quish
re·lin′quished
re·lin′quish·ment
rel′i·quar′y
rel′ish
rel′ished
re·live′
re·load′
re·lo′cate
re·lo′cat·ed
re′lo·ca′tion
re·lo′ca·tor
re·lu′cent
re·luc′tance
re·luc′tant
re·luc′tant·ly
re·ly′
re·main′
re·main′der
re·mained′
re·make′

re·mand′
re·mand′ed
re·mark′
re·mark′a·ble
re·marʹried
re·mar′ry
re·me′di·a·ble
re·me′di·al
rem′e·died
rem′e·dy
re·mem′ber
re·mem′bered
re·mem′brance
re·mind′
re·mind′ed
re·mind′er
re·mind′ful
re·mind′ing·ly
remʹi·nis′cence
remʹi·nis′cent
re·miss′
re·mis′sion
re·mit′
re·mit′tal
re·mit′tance
re·mit′ted
re·mit′tent
re·mit′ter
rem′nant
re·mod′el
re·monʹe·ti·za′tion
re·mon′e·tize
re·mon′strance
re·mon′strant
re·mon′strate
re·mon′strat·ed
re·mon′strat·ing·ly
reʹmon·straʹtion
reʹmon′stra·tive
re·morse′
re·morse′ful
re·morse′ful·ly
re·morse′less
re·mote′
re·mote′ness
re·mot′er
re·mot′est
re·mount′
re·movʹa·bil′i·ty
re·mov′a·ble
re·mov′al
re·move′
re·moved′
re·moves′
re·mu′ner·ate
re·muʹner·at′ed
re·muʹner·a′tion
re·mu′ner·a′tive
renʹais·sance′
re′nal
re·nas′cent
rend
ren′der
ren′dered
ren′der·ings
ren′dez·vous
ren·di′tion
ren′e·gade
re·nege′
reʹne·go′ti·ate
re·new′
re·newʹa·ble
re·new′al
re·newed′
ren′net
re·nom′i·nate
re·nomʹi·na′tion
re·nounce′
re·nounced′
ren′o·vate
ren′o·vatʹed
renʹo·va′tion
re·nown′
re·nowned′
rent
rent′al
rent′ed
re·num′ber
re·nunʹci·a′tion
re·nun′ci·aʹtive
re·nun′ci·a·toʹry
re·oʹpen
re·orʹder
reʹor·gan·i·za′tion
re·or′gan·ize
re·oʹri·ent

re·paid′
re·paint′
re·pair′
re·paired′
re·pair′er
rep′a·ra·ble
rep′a·ra′tion
re·par′a·tive
rep′ar·tee′
re·past′
re·pa′tri·ate
re·pay′
re·pay′ment
re·peal′
re·pealed′
re·peal′er
re·peat′
re·peat′ed·ly
re·peat′er
re·pel′
re·pelled′
re·pel′lence
re·pel′len·cy
re·pel′lent
re·pel′ling·ly
re·pent′
re·pent′ance
re·pent′ed
re′per·cus′sion
re′per·cus′sive
rep′er·toire
rep′er·to′ry

rep′e·tend
rep′e·ti′tion
rep′e·ti′tious
re·pet′i·tive
re·phrase′
re·pine′
re·pined′
re·place′
re·placed′
re·place′ment
re·plant′
re·plen′ish
re·plen′ished
re·plen′ish·ment
re·plete′
re·ple′tion
re·plev′in
rep′li·ca
rep′li·ca′tion
re·plied′
re·ply′
re·port′
re·port′ed
re·port′er
re·pose′
re·posed′
re·pose′ful
re·pos′i·to′ry
re′pos·sess′
re′pos·sessed′
rep′re·hend′
rep′re·hen′si·ble

rep′re·hen′sion
rep′re·hen′sive
rep′re·sent′
rep′re·sen·ta′tion
rep′re·sent′a·tive
rep′re·sent′ed
re·press′
re·pres′sion
re·pres′sive
re·prieve′
re·prieved′
rep′ri·mand
rep′ri·mand′ed
rep′ri·mand′ing·ly
re′print′
re·print′ed
re·pris′al
re·prise′
re·proach′
re·proached′
re·proach′ful
re·proach′ful·ly
re·proach′ful·ness
rep′ro·bate
rep′ro·ba′tion
re′pro·duce′
re′pro·duc′er
re′pro·duc′tion
re′pro·duc′tive
re·proof′
re·prove′
re·proved′

re·prov′ing·ly
rep′tile
rep·til′i·an
re·pub′lic
re·pub′li·can
re·pub′li·can·ism
re·pub′li·can·ize
re·pub′lish
re·pu′di·ate
re·pu′di·a′tion
re·pug′nance
re·pug′nant
re·pulse′
re·pulsed′
re·pul′sion
re·pul′sive
re·pul′sive·ness
re·pur′chase
rep′u·ta·ble
rep′u·ta′tion
re·pute′
re·put′ed
re·put′ed·ly
re·quest′
re′qui·em
re·quire′
re·quired′
re·quire′ment
req′ui·site
req′ui·si′tion
re·quit′al
re·quite′
re·quit′ed
rere′dos
re·run′
re·sale′
re·scind′
re·scind′ed
re·scis′sion
re·score′
res′cue
res′cued
re·search′
re·search′er
re·sec′tion
re·sem′blance
re·sem′ble
re·sem′bled
re·sent′
re·sent′ed
re·sent′ful
re·sent′ful·ness
re·sent′ment
res′er·va′tion
res′er·va′tion·ist
re·serve′
re·served′
re·serv′ist
res′er·voir
re·set′
re·set′tle
re·set′tle·ment
re·ship′
re·ship′ment
re·side′
re·sid′ed
res′i·dence
res′i·den·cy
res′i·dent
res′i·den′tial
re·sid′u·al
re·sid′u·ar′y
res′i·due
re·sid′u·um
re·sign′
res′ig·na′tion
re·signed′
re·sign′ed·ly
re·sil′i·en·cy
re·sil′i·ent
res′in
res′in·ous
re·sist′
re·sist′ance
re·sist′ant
re·sist′i·ble
re·sis′tive
re′sis·tiv′i·ty
re·sist′less
re·sol′u·ble
res′o·lute
res′o·lute·ness
res′o·lu′tion
re·solv′a·ble
re·solve′
re·solved′

re·sol′vent
res′o·nance
res′o·nant
res′o·nate
res′o·na′tor
re·sort′
re·sort′ed
re·sound′
re·sound′ed
re·sound′ing·ly
re·source′
re·source′ful
re·source′ful·ness
re·spect′
re·spect′a·bil′i·ty
re·spect′a·ble
re·spect′ed
re·spect′er
re·spect′ful
re·spec′tive
re·spec′tive·ly
re·spell′
re·spir′a·ble
res′pi·ra′tion
res′pi·ra′tor
re·spir′a·to′ry
re·spire′
re·spired′
res′pite
re·splend′ence
re·splend′en·cy
re·splend′ent

re·spond′
re·spond′ed
re·spond′ent
re·sponse′
re·spon′si·bil′i·ties
re·spon′si·bil′i·ty
re·spon′si·ble
re·spon′sive
re·spon′sive·ness
rest
re·state′
re·state′ment
res′tau·rant
res′tau·ra·teur′
rest′ed
rest′ful
rest′ful·ly
rest′ful·ness
res′ti·tu′tion
res′tive
res′tive·ly
res′tive·ness
rest′less
rest′less·ness
re·stock′
res′to·ra′tion
re·stor′a·tive
re·store′
re·stored′
re·strain′
re·strained′
re·strain′ed·ly

re·strain′ing·ly
re·straint′
re·strict′
re·strict′ed
re·stric′tion
re·stric′tive
re·sult′
re·sult′ant
re·sum′a·ble
re·sume′
re·sumed′
re·sump′tion
re·sur′gence
re·sur′gent
res′ur·rect′
res′ur·rect′ed
res′ur·rec′tion
re·sus′ci·tate
re·sus′ci·tat′ed
re·sus′ci·ta′tion
re·sus′ci·ta′tive
re·sus′ci·ta′tor
re′tail
re′tailed
re′tail·er
re·tain′
re·tained′
re·tain′er
re·take′
re·tal′i·ate
re·tal′i·at′ed
re·tal′i·a′tion

re·tal'i·a'tion·ist
re·tal'i·a'tive
re·tal'i·a·to'ry
re·tard'
re'tar·da'tion
re·tard'ed
re·tard'er
retch
retched
re·tell'
re·tell'ings
re·ten'tion
re·ten'tive
re'ten·tiv'i·ty
ret'i·cence
ret'i·cent
ret'i·cent·ly
ret'i·cle
re·tic'u·lar
re·tic'u·late
re·tic'u·lat'ed
re·tic'u·la'tion
ret'i·cule
ret'i·na
ret'i·nal
ret'i·ni'tis
ret'i·nue
re·tire'
re·tired'
re·tire'ment
re·tir'ing·ly
re·told'
re·tort'
re·tort'ed
re·touch'
re·touch'er
re·trace'
re·trace'a·ble
re·tract'
re·tract'ed
re·trac'tile
re·trac'tion
re·trac'tive
re·trac'tor
re-tread'
re·treat'
re·treat'ed
re·trench'
re·trenched'
re·trench'ment
re·tri'al
ret'ri·bu'tion
re·trib'u·tive
re·triev'al
re·trieve'
re·trieved'
re·triev'er
ret'ro·ac'tive
ret'ro·ac·tiv'i·ty
ret'ro·cede'
ret'ro·ces'sion
ret·ro·ces'sive
ret'ro·flex
ret'ro·flex'ion
ret'ro·grade
ret'ro·grad'ed
ret'ro·gress
ret'ro·gres'sion
ret'ro·gres'sive
ret'ro·spect
ret'ro·spec'tion
ret'ro·spec'tive
ret'ro·ver'sion
re·turn'
re·turn'a·ble
re·turned'
re·un'ion
re'u·nite'
re-use'
re-used'
re·vac'ci·nate
re·val'i·date
re·val'or·ize
re'val·u·a'tion
re·val'ue
re·vamp'
re·veal'
re·vealed'
re·veal'ing·ly
re·veal'ment
rev'eil·le
rev'el
rev'e·la'tion
rev'e·la·to'ry
rev'eled
rev'el·er

rev′el·ry
re·venge′
re·venged′
re·venge′ful
rev′e·nue
re·ver′ber·ant
re·ver′ber·ate
re·ver′ber·at′ed
re·ver′ber·a′tion
re·ver′ber·a′tive
re·ver′ber·a′tor
re·ver′ber·a·to′ry
re·vere′
re·vered′
rev′er·ence
rev′er·end
rev′er·ent
rev′er·en′tial
rev′er·ie
re·ver′sal
re·verse′
re·versed′
re·vers′i·bil′i·ty
re·vers′i·ble
re·ver′sion
re·ver′sion·ar′y
re·vert′
re·vert′ed
re·vert′i·ble
re·vest′
re·vet′
re·vet′ment
re·vict′ual
re·view′
re·viewed′
re·view′er
re·vile′
re·viled′
re·vile′ment
re·vil′ing·ly
re·vin′di·cate
re·vise′
re·vised′
re·vis′er
re·vi′sion
re·vi′sion·ism
re·vi′sion·ist
re·vis′it
re·viv′al
re·viv′al·ism
re·viv′al·ist
re·vive′
re·vived′
re·viv′i·fi·ca′tion
re·viv′i·fi′er
re·viv′i·fy
rev′o·ca′tion
re·vok′a·ble
re·voke′
re·voked′
re·volt′
re·volt′ed
re·volt′ing·ly
rev′o·lu′tion
rev′o·lu′tion·ar′y
rev′o·lu′tion·ist
rev′o·lu′tion·ize
rev′o·lu′tion·ized
re·volve′
re·volved′
re·volv′er
re·vue′
re·vul′sion
re·vul′sive
re·ward′
re·ward′ed
re·ward′ing·ly
re·wind′
re·wire′
re·word′
re·worked′
re·write′
re·writ′ten
rhap·sod′ic
rhap′so·dist
rhap′so·dize
rhap′so·dized
rhap′so·dy
rhe′ni·um
rhe′o·stat
rhe′sus
rhet′o·ric
rhe·tor′i·cal
rhet′o·ri′cian
rheum
rheu·mat′ic

rheu'ma·tism
rheu'ma·toid
rheum'y
rhine'stone'
rhi·ni'tis
rhi·noc'er·os
rhi·nol'o·gy
rhi'no·scope
rhi·nos'co·py
rhi'zome
rho'di·um
rhom'boid
rhom'bus
rhu'barb
rhyme
rhymed
rhythm
rhyth'mic
rhyth'mi·cal
Ri·al'to
ri'ant
rib
rib'ald
rib'ald·ry
ribbed
rib'bon
rice
rich
rich'er
rich'es
rich'est
rich'ly
rich'ness
rich'weed'
rick'ets
ric'o·chet'
rid'dance
rid'den
rid'dle
ride
rid'er
rid'er·less
ridge
ridged
rid'i·cule
rid'i·culed
ri·dic'u·lous
ri·dic'u·lous·ly
ri·dot'to
rife
rif'fle
rif'fled
riff'raff'
ri'fle
ri'fled
ri'fle·man
ri'flings
rift
rig
rig'a·doon'
rigged
rig'ger
right
right'ed
right'eous
right'eous·ly
right'eous·ness
right'ful
right'ful·ly
right'ly
right'ness
rig'id
ri·gid'i·ty
rig'id·ly
rig'id·ness
rig'or
rig'or·ous
rig'or·ous·ly
rile
riled
rill
rim
rime
rind
ring
ring'bolt'
ring'bone'
ringed
ring'er
ring'ing·ly
ring'lead'er
ring'let
ring'let·ed
ring'mas'ter
ring'side'
ring'worm'

rink
rinse
rinsed
ri'ot
ri'ot·ed
ri'ot·er
ri'ot·ous
ri'ot·ous·ly
ri'ot·ous·ness
rip
ri·par'i·an
ripe
ripe'ly
rip'en
rip'ened
rip'er
rip'est
ri·poste'
rip'ple
rip'pled
rip'pling·ly
rip'ply
rip'rap'
rise
ris'en
ris'er
ris'i·bil'i·ty
ris'i·ble
ris'ings
risk
risked
risk'y

rite
rit'u·al
rit'u·al·ism
rit'u·al·ist
rit'u·al·is'tic
rit'u·al·ly
ri'val
ri'valed
ri'val·ry
rive
riv'er
riv'er·side'
riv'et
riv'et·ed
riv'et·er
riv'u·let
roach
road
road'a·bil'i·ty
road'bed'
road'house'
road'man
road'side'
road'stead
road'ster
road'way'
road'weed'
roam
roamed
roam'er
roam'ings
roar

roared
roar'ings
roast
roast'ed
roast'er
rob
robbed
rob'ber
rob'ber·y
robe
robed
rob'in
ro'bot
ro·bust'
ro·bust'ly
ro·bust'ness
rock
rock'er
rock'et
rock'fish'
rock'weed'
rock'work'
rock'y
ro·co'co
rod
ro'dent
ro'de·o
rod'man
roe
roent'gen
rogue
ro'guer·y

ro′guish
ro′guish·ly
ro′guish·ness
roil
roiled
roist′er
roll
rolled
roll′er
roll′mop'
ro·maine′
Ro′man
ro·mance′
Ro'man·esque′
ro·man′tic
ro·man′ti·cal·ly
ro·man′ti·cism
ro·man′ti·cist
ro·man′ti·cize
romp
romp′ers
ron′deau
ron′do
roof
roof′er
roof′less
roof′tree'
rook′er·y
room
roomed
room′er
room′ful
room′i·ness
room′mate'
room′y
roost
roost′er
root
root′ed
root′er
root′let
root′worm'
rope
rope′danc'er
rope′mak'er
rope′work'
ro·quet′
ro·sa′ceous
ro′sa·ry
rose
ro′se·ate
rose′mar'y
ro·sette′
rose′wood'
ros′i·ly
ros′in
ros′i·ness
ros′ter
ros′trum
ros′y
rot
Ro·tar′i·an
ro′ta·ry
ro′tate
ro′tat·ed
ro·ta′tion
ro·ta′tion·al
ro′ta·tive
ro′ta·tor
ro′ta·to'ry
rote
ro′te·none
ro'to·gra·vure′
ro′tor
rot′ten
rot′ten·ness
rot′ter
ro·tund′
ro·tun′da
ro·tun′di·ty
rouge
rouged
rough
rough′age
rough′cast'
rough'dry′
rough′en
rough′ened
rough′er
rough′est
rough'hew′
rough′hewn′
rough′house'
rough′ish
rough′ly
rough′neck'

rough′ness
rough′rid′er
rou·lade′
rou·leau′
rou·lette′
round
round′a·bout′
round′ed
roun′de·lay
round′er
round′est
round′fish′
round′house′
round′ish
round′ly
round′ness
rounds′man
round′worm′
rouse
roused
rous′ing·ly
roust′a·bout′
rout
route
rout′ed
rout′ed
rou·tine′
rou·tin′i·za′tion
rou·tin′ize
rov′er
rov′ing·ly
rov′ings

row
row
row′boat
row′dy
rowed
row′el
row′eled
row′en
row′er
row′lock
roy′al
roy′al·ism
roy′al·ist
roy′al·ly
roy′al·ty
rub
rubbed
rub′ber
rub′ber·ize
rub′ber·ized
rub′ber·y
rub′bings
rub′bish
rub′ble
rub′down′
ru′be·fa′cient
ru′be·fac′tion
ru·be′o·la
ru′bi·cund
ru·bid′i·um
ru′ble
ru′bric

ru′bri·ca′tor
ru′by
ruch′ing
ruck′sack′
ruck′us
rud′der
rud′der·post′
rud′di·er
rud′di·est
rud′di·ly
rud′di·ness
rud′dy
rude
rude′ly
rude′ness
rud′er
rud′est
ru′di·ment
ru′di·men′tal
ru′di·men′ta·ry
rue
rued
rue′ful
ruff
ruf′fi·an
ruf′fi·an·ism
ruf′fle
ruf′fled
Rug′by
rug′ged
rug′ged·ness
ru′gose

ru·gos'i·ty
ru'in
ru'in·a'tion
ru'ined
ru'in·ous
rule
ruled
rul'er
rul'ings
rum
rum'ble
rum'bled
rum'bling·ly
rum'blings
ru'mi·nant
ru'mi·nate
ru'mi·nat'ed
ru'mi·nat'ing·ly
ru'mi·na'tion
ru'mi·na'tive
rum'mage
rum'maged
rum'my
ru'mor
ru'mored
rump
rum'ple
rum'pled
rum'pus
run
run'a·bout'
run'a·gate
rune
rung
ru'nic
run'ner
run'off'
runt
run'way'
ru·pee'
rup'ture
rup'tured
ru'ral
ru'ral·ism
ru'ral·i·za'tion
ru'ral·ize
ru'ral·ly
ruse
rush
rush'ing·ly
rush'light'
rusk
rus'set
Rus'sian
rust
rust'ed
rus'tic
rus'ti·cate
rus'ti·cat'ed
rus'ti·ca'tion
rus'ti·cism
rus·tic'i·ty
rus'tic·ly
rust'i·er
rust'i·est
rus'tle
rus'tled
rus'tler
rus'tling·ly
rus'tlings
rust'proof'
rust'y
rut
ru'ta·ba'ga
ruth
ru·the'ni·um
ruth'less
rye

SSSSSSSSSSSSSSSSSSSSSSSSSSSSSSSSSSSSSSSSSSSSSSSSSSSSSSSSSSSSSSSSSSSSSSSSSSSSSSSSSSSS

# S

Sab'ba·tar'i·an
Sab'bath
sab·bat'i·cal
sab'ba·tine
sa'ber
sa'ble
sab'o·tage'
sac'cha·rine
sac'er·do'tal
sa'chem
sa·chet'
sack'but
sack'cloth'
sacked
sack'ful
sa'cral
sac'ra·ment
sac'ra·men'tal
sac'ra·men'tal·ism
sac'ra·men'tal·ist
sac'ra·men'tal·ly
sac'ra·men·tar'i·an

sa'cred
sa'cred·ly
sa'cred·ness
sac'ri·fice
sac'ri·ficed
sac'ri·fi'cial
sac'ri·lege
sac'ri·le'gious
sac'ris·tan
sac'ris·ty
sac'ro·sanct
sa'crum
sad
sad'der
sad'dest
sad'dle
sad'dle·back'
sad'dle·bag'
sad'dled
sad'dler
sad'dler·y
sad'i'ron

sad'ly
sad'ness
sa·fa'ri
safe
safe'guard'
safe'keep'ing
safe'ly
safe'ness
saf'er
saf'est
safe'ty
saf'fron
sag
sa'ga
sa·ga'cious
sa·ga'cious·ly
sa·gac'i·ty
sag'a·more
sage
sagged
sag'it·tal
sa'go

sa′hib
said
sail
sail′boat′
sailed
sail′fish′
sail′ings
sail′or
saint
saint′ed
saint′hood
saint′li·ness
saint′ly
sake
sa′ker
sa·laam′
sal′a·bil′i·ty
sal′a·ble
sa·la′cious
sa·la′cious·ly
sa·la′cious·ness
sal′ad
sal′a·man′der
sal′a·ried
sal′a·ry
sale
sal′e·ra′tus
sales′man
sales′man·ship
sales′peo′ple
sales′per′son
sales′room′
sales′wom′an
sal′i·cyl′ic
sa′li·ence
sa′li·ent
sa·lif′er·ous
sa′line
sa·li′va
sal′i·vant
sal′i·vate
sal′i·va′tion
sal′low
sal′low·er
sal′low·est
sal′ly
salm′on
sa·loon′
sal′si·fy
salt
sal′ta·to′ry
salt′cel′lar
salt′ed
salt′i·er
salt′i·est
salt′pe′ter
salt′y
sa·lu′bri·ous
sa·lu′bri·ty
sal′u·tar′y
sal′u·ta′tion
sa·lu′ta·to′ri·an
sa·lu′ta·to′ry
sa·lute′
sa·lut′ed
sal′vage
sal′vaged
sal·va′tion
salve
salved
sal′ver
sal′vo
Sa·mar′i·tan
sa·ma′ri·um
same
same′ness
sam′ite
Sa·mo′an
sam′o·var
sam′pan
sam′ple
sam′pled
sam′pler
sam′plings
sam′u·rai
san′a·tive
san′a·to′ri·um
san′a·to′ry
sanc′ti·fi·ca′tion
sanc′ti·fied
sanc′ti·fy
sanc′ti·mo′ni·ous
sanc′ti·mo′ni·ous·ly
sanc′ti·mo′ni·ous·ness
sanc′tion
sanc′tioned

sanc'ti·tude
sanc'ti·ty
sanc'tu·ar'y
sanc'tum
sand
san'dal
san'dal·wood'
sand'bag'
sand'bank'
sand'blast'
sand'box'
sand'bur'
sand'ed
sand'er
sand'fish'
sand'flow'er
sand'i·ness
sand'man'
sand'pa'per
sand'pip'er
sand'stone'
sand'storm'
sand'wich
sand'wiched
sand'worm'
sand'y
sane
sane'ly
san'er
san'est
sang
san'gui·nar'y
san'guine
san'i·tar'i·um
san'i·tar'y
san'i·ta'tion
san'i·ty
sank
San'skrit
sap
sa'pi·ence
sa'pi·ent
sap'lings
sa·pon'i·fi·ca'tion
sa·pon'i·fy
sap'per
sap'phire
sap'pi·er
sap'pi·est
sap'py
sap'wood'
sar'a·band
Sar'a·cen
sar'casm
sar·cas'tic
sar·cas'ti·cal·ly
sar·co'ma
sar·co'ma·ta
sar'co·phag'ic
sar·coph'a·gus
sar·dine'
Sar·din'i·an
sar·don'ic
sar·don'i·cal·ly
sar'do·nyx
sar·gas'so
sa'ri
sa·rong'
sar'sa·pa·ril'la
sar·to'ri·al
sash
sas'sa·fras
sat
Sa'tan
sa·tan'ic
satch'el
sate
sat'ed
sa·teen'
sat'el·lite
sa'ti·ate
sa'ti·at'ed
sa'ti·a'tion
sa·ti'e·ty
sat'in
sat'i·nette'
sat'ire
sa·tir'ic
sa·tir'i·cal
sa·tir'i·cal·ly
sat'i·rist
sat'i·rize
sat'i·rized
sat'is·fac'tion
sat'is·fac'to·ri·ly
sat'is·fac'to·ry

sat'is·fied
sat'is·fy
sat'is·fy'ing·ly
sa'trap
sat'u·rate
sat'u·rat'ed
sat'u·ra'tion
Sat'ur·day
Sat'urn
sat'ur·nine
sat'yr
sat'yr·esque'
sauce
sauce'boat'
sauce'dish'
sauce'pan'
sau'cer
sau'cer·like'
sau'ci·er
sau'ci·est
sau'ci·ly
sau'cy
saun'ter
saun'tered
saun'ter·er
saun'ter·ing·ly
saun'ter·ings
sau'ri·an
sau'sage
sau·té'
sau·téed'
sau·terne'

sav'a·ble
sav'age
sav'age·ly
sav'age·ry
sa·van'na
sa·vant'
save
saved
sav'ings
sav'ior
sa'vor
sa'vor·less
sa'vor·y
saw
saw'dust'
sawed
saw'fish'
saw'fly'
saw'horse'
saw'mill'
saw'yer
Sax'on
say
say'ings
says
scab
scab'bard
scab'by
sca'bi·es
sca'bi·ous
sca'brous
scaf'fold

sca'lar
scald
scald'ed
scale
scaled
sca·lene'
scal'er
scal'lion
scal'lop
scalp
scalped
scal'pel
scalp'er
scal'y
scamp
scamped
scam'per
scam'pered
scan
scan'dal
scan'dal·i·za'tion
scan'dal·ize
scan'dal·ized
scan'dal·ous
scan'dal·ous·ly
Scan'di·na'vi·a
scan'di·um
scanned
scan'ner
scan'sion
scan·so'ri·al
scant

scant′ed
scant′i·ly
scant′i·ness
scant′lings
scant′y
scape′goat′
scape′grace′
scap′u·la
scap′u·lar
scar
scar′ab
scarce
scarce′ly
scarc′er
scarc′est
scar′ci·ty
scare
scared
scarf
scar′i·fi·ca′tion
scar′i·fied
scar′i·fi′er
scar′i·fy
scar′la·ti′na
scar′let
scarred
scathed
scathe′less
scath′ing
scath′ing·ly
scat′ter
scat′ter·brain′

scat′tered
scat′ter·ing·ly
scat′ter·ings
scav′en·ger
sce·na′ri·o
scen′er·y
scene′shift′er
sce′nic
sce′ni·cal
scent
scent′ed
scent′less
scent′wood′
scep′ter
scep′tered
sched′ule
sched′uled
sche·mat′ic
sche·mat′i·cal·ly
sche′ma·tize
sche′ma·tized
scheme
schemed
schem′er
schem′ing·ly
scher·zan′do
scher′zo
schism
schis·mat′ic
schis·mat′i·cal
schist
schiz′oid

schiz′o·phre′ni·a
schiz′o·phren′ic
schnapps
schnau′zer
schnit′zel
schol′ar
schol′ar·ly
schol′ar·ship
scho·las′tic
scho·las′ti·cal
scho·las′ti·cal·ly
scho·las′ti·cism
scho′li·ast
scho′li·um
school
school′book′
schooled
school′house′
school′man
school′mas′ter
schoon′er
schot′tische
sci·at′ic
sci·at′i·ca
sci′ence
sci′en·tif′ic
sci′en·tif′i·cal·ly
sci′en·tist
scim′i·tar
scin·til′la
scin′til·lant
scin′til·late

scin'til·lat'ed
scin'til·lat'ing·ly
scin'til·la'tion
sci'on
scis'sors
scle·ri'tis
scle·ro'sis
scle·rot'ic
scle'ro·ti'tis
scle·rot'o·my
scoff
scoffed
scoff'er
scoff'ing·ly
scoff'law'
scold
scold'ed
scold'ing·ly
scold'ings
sco'li·o'sis
sconce
scone
scoop
scooped
scoop'ing·ly
scoot
scoot'er
scope
scorch
scorched
scorch'er
scorch'ing·ly
score
scored
scor'er
scor'ings
scorn
scorned
scorn'er
scorn'ful
scorn'ful·ly
scor'pi·on
Scot
Scotch
Scotch'man
Scots'man
Scot'tish
scoun'drel
scoun'drel·ly
scour
scoured
scour'er
scourge
scourged
scourg'ing·ly
scour'ings
scout
scout'ed
scow
scowl
scowled
scowl'ing·ly
scrab'ble
scrab'bled
scrab'blings
scrag'gy
scram'ble
scram'bled
scram'blings
scrap
scrap'book'
scrape
scraped
scrap'er
scrap'ing·ly
scrap'ings
scrap'man
scrap'pi·er
scrap'pi·est
scrap'ple
scrap'py
scratch
scratched
scratch'i·ness
scratch'ings
scratch'y
scrawl
scrawled
scrawl'ings
scraw'ni·ly
scraw'ni·ness
scraw'ny
scream
screamed
scream'ing·ly
screech

screeched
screech′i·er
screech′i·est
screech′y
screed
screen
screened
screen′ings
screen′play′
screw
screw′driv′er
screwed
scrib′ble
scrib′bled
scrib′bler
scrib′bling·ly
scrib′blings
scribe
scrib′er
scrim
scrim′mage
scrimp
scrimped
scrimp′i·ly
scrimp′i·ness
scrimp′ing·ly
scrim′shaw′
scrip
script
scrip′tur·al
scrip′tur·al·ism
scrip′tur·al·ist
scrip′ture
scrive′ner
scrod
scrof′u·la
scrof′u·lous
scroll
scrolled
scroll′work′
scroug′er
scrounge
scrub
scrub′bed
scrub′bi·er
scrub′bi·est
scrub′bings
scrub′by
scrub′land′
scruff
scrum′mage
scrump′tious
scrunch
scrunched
scru′ple
scru′pled
scru′pu·los′i·ty
scru′pu·lous
scru′pu·lous·ly
scru′pu·lous·ness
scru′ti·ni·za′tion
scru′ti·nize
scru′ti·nized
scru′ti·niz′ing·ly
scru′ti·ny
scud
scud′ded
scuff
scuffed
scuf′fle
scuf′fled
scuf′fling·ly
scuf′flings
scull
sculled
scull′er
scul′ler·y
scul′lion
scul′pin
sculp′tor
sculp′tur·al
sculp′ture
sculp′tur·esque′
scum
scum′my
scup′per
scup′per·nong
scurf
scur·ril′i·ty
scur′ril·ous
scur′ril·ous·ly
scur′ril·ous·ness
scur′ry
scur′vy
scut′tle
scut′tled

scut′tle·ful
scu′tum
scythe
sea
sea′board′
sea′coast′
sea′far′er
sea′fowl′
sea′go′ing
seal
sealed
seal′er
seal′skin′
seam
sea′man
sea′man·like′
sea′man·ship
seamed
seam′stress
seam′y
sea′plane′
sea′port′
sear
search
searched
search′er
search′ing·ly
search′light′
seared
sea′scape
sea′shore′
sea′sick′
sea′sick′ness
sea′side′
sea′son
sea′son·a·ble
sea′son·al
sea′son·al·ly
sea′soned
sea′son·ings
seat
seat′ed
sea′ward
sea′wor′thi·ness
sea′wor′thy
se·ba′ceous
se′cant
se·cede′
se·ced′ed
se·ces′sion
se·ces′sion·ism
se·ces′sion·ist
se·clude′
se·clud′ed
se·clu′sion
sec′ond
sec′ond·ar′i·ly
sec′ond·ar′y
sec′ond·ed
sec′ond·er
sec′ond·hand′
sec′ond·ly
se′cre·cy
se′cret
sec′re·tar′i·al
sec′re·tar′i·at
sec′re·tar′y
se·crete′
se·cret′ed
se·cre′tion
se·cre′tive
se·cre′tive·ly
se·cre′tive·ness
se′cret·ly
se·cre′to·ry
sect
sec·tar′i·an
sec·tar′i·an·ism
sec′ta·ry
sec′tion
sec′tion·al
sec′tion·al·ism
sec′tion·al·ize
sec′tion·al·ized
sec′tion·al·ly
sec′tor
sec′u·lar
sec′u·lar·ism
sec′u·lar·ist
sec′u·lar′i·ty
sec′u·lar·i·za′tion
sec′u·lar·ize
sec′u·lar·ized
sec′u·lar·iz′er
se·cure′
se·cured′

se·cure′ly
se·cu′ri·ty
se·dan′
se·date′
se·date′ly
se·date′ness
se·da′tion
sed′a·tive
sed′en·tar′y
sedge
sed′i·ment
sed′i·men′tal
sed′i·men′ta·ry
sed′i·men·ta′tion
se·di′tion
se·di′tious
se·di′tious·ly
se·di′tious·ness
se·duce′
se·duced′
se·duc′er
se·duc′i·ble
se·duc′tion
se·duc′tive
se·duc′tive·ly
se·duc′tive·ness
sed′u·lous
sed′u·lous·ly
sed′u·lous·ness
se′dum
see
seed
seed′ed
seed′i·er
seed′i·est
seed′i·ness
seed′less
seed′less·ness
seed′lings
seed′y
seek
seek′er
seem
seemed
seem′ing·ly
seem′ly
seen
seep
seep′age
seep′weed′
se′er
seer′ess
seer′suck′er
see′saw′
seethe
seethed
seg′ment
seg·men′tal
seg′men·tar′y
seg′men·ta′tion
seg′re·gate
seg′re·gat′ed
seg′re·ga′tion
seg′re·ga′tion·ist
se′gui·dil′la
seine
seis′mic
seis′mo·graph
seis·mol′o·gy
seiz′a·ble
seize
seized
sei′zure
sel′dom
se·lect′
se·lect′ed
se·lec′tion
se·lec′tive
se·lec′tiv′i·ty
se·lect′man
se·lect′men
se·lec′tor
sel′e·nate
se·le′nic
sel′e·nide
sel′e·nite
se·le′ni·um
self
self′-as·ser′tion
self′-as·ser′tive
self′-as·sured′
self′-cen′tered
self′-col′ored
self′-com·mand′
self′-com·pla′cent
self′-com·posed′

self′-con·ceit′
self′-con·cern′
self′-con′fi·dence
self′-con′scious
self′-con′scious·ness
self′-con·tained′
self′-con′tra·dic′tion
self′-con·trol′
self′-cov′ered
self′-de·ceit′
self′-de·fense′
self′-de·ni′al
self′-de·struc′tion
self′-de·ter′mi·na′tion
self′-de·ter′mined
self′-dis′ci·pline
self′-dis·trust′
self′-ed′u·cat′ed
self′-ef·face′ment
self′-ef·fac′ing·ly
self′-es·teem′
self′-ev′i·dent
self′-ex·am′i·na′tion
self′-ex′e·cut′ing
self′-ex·plain′ing
self′-ex·plan′a·to′ry
self′-ex·pres′sion
self′-for·get′ful
self′-gov′erned
self′-gov′ern·ment
self′-help′
self′-im·por′tance
self′-im·prove′ment
self′-in·duced′
self′-in·duc′tance
self′-in·dul′gent
self′-in′ter·est
self′ish
self′ish·ly
self′ish·ness
self′-knowl′edge
self′less
self′-lim′it·ed
self′-liq′ui·dat′ing
self′-love′
self′-made′
self′-mas′ter·y
self′-o·pin′ion·at′ed
self′-pos·sessed′
self′-pos·ses′sion
self′-pres′er·va′tion
self′-pro·pel′ling
self′-rat′ing
self′-read′ing
self′-re′al·i·za′tion
self′-re·gard′
self′-reg′is·ter·ing
self′-re·li′ance
self′-re·li′ant
self′-re·nun′ci·a′tion
self′-re·proach′
self′-re·proach′ful
self′-re·proach′ing·ly
self′-re·spect′
self′-re·straint′
self′-right′eous
self′-right′eous·ness
self′-sac′ri·fice
self′-sac′ri·fic′ing·ly
self′same′
self′-sat′is·fied
self′-seek′er
self′-serv′ice
self′-start′er
self′-stud′y
self′-styled′
self′-suf·fi′cien·cy
self′-suf·fi′cient
self′-sup·port′
self′-sur·ren′der
self′-sus·tain′ing
self′-un′der·stand′ing
self′-will′
self′-willed′
self′-wind′ing
sell
sell′er
sell′out′
Selt′zer
sel′vage
se·man′tic
sem′a·phore
sem′blance
se·mes′ter
sem′i·an′nu·al
sem′i·cir′cle

sem′i·civ′i·lized
sem′i·co′lon
sem′i·con′scious
sem′i·de·tached′
sem′i·fi′nal
sem′i·fi′nal·ist
sem′i·fin′ished
sem′i·month′ly
sem′i·nar′
sem′i·nar′i·an
sem′i·nar′y
Sem′i·nole
sem′i·per′me·a·ble
sem′i·pre′cious
sem′i·se′ri·ous
sem′i·skilled′
Sem′ite
Se·mit′ic
Sem′i·tism
sem′i·tone′
sem′i·week′ly
sem′o·li′na
sem′pi·ter′nal
sen′ate
sen′a·tor
sen′a·to′ri·al
sen′a·to′ri·al·ly
sen′a·tor·ship′
send
send′er
Sen′e·ca
se·nes′cence

se·nes′cent
sen′es·chal
se′nile
se·nil′i·ty
sen′ior
sen·ior′i·ty
sen′na
sen′nit
sen′sate
sen·sa′tion
sen·sa′tion·al
sen·sa′tion·al·ism
sen·sa′tion·al·ly
sense
sense′less
sense′less·ly
sense′less·ness
sen′si·bil′i·ty
sen′si·ble
sen′si·tive
sen′si·tive·ly
sen′si·tive·ness
sen′si·tiv′i·ty
sen′si·ti·za′tion
sen′si·tize
sen′si·tized
sen′si·tiz′er
sen′si·tom′e·ter
sen·so′ri·um
sen′so·ry
sen′su·al
sen′su·al·ism

sen′su·al·ist
sen′su·al·is′tic
sen′su·al′i·ty
sen′su·al·i·za′tion
sen′su·al·ize
sen′su·al·ized
sen′su·al·ly
sen′su·ous
sen′su·ous·ly
sen′su·ous·ness
sen′tence
sen′tenced
sen·ten′tious
sen·ten′tious·ly
sen·ten′tious·ness
sen′ti·ence
sen′ti·en·cy
sen′ti·ment
sen′ti·men′tal
sen′ti·men′tal·ism
sen′ti·men′tal·ist
sen′ti·men·tal′i·ty
sen′ti·men′tal·ize
sen′ti·men′tal·ized
sen′ti·nel
sen′try
sep′a·ra·bil′i·ty
sep′a·ra·ble
sep′a·rate
sep′a·rat′ed
sep′a·rate·ly
sep′a·ra′tion

sep′a·ra′tion·ist
sep′a·ra·tism
sep′a·ra′tist
sep′a·ra′tive
sep′a·ra′tor
sep′a·ra·to′ry
se′pi·a
se′poy
sep′sis
Sep·tem′ber
sep·ten′ni·al
sep·tet′
sep′tic
sep′ti·ce′mi·a
Sep′tu·a·gint
sep′tum
sep′ul·cher
se·pul′chral
se·pul′tur·al
sep′ul·ture
se′quel
se·que′la
se′quence
se′quenc·er
se·quen′tial
se·quen′tial·ly
se·ques′ter
se·ques′tered
se·ques′trate
se·ques′trat·ed
se′ques·tra′tion
se′quin

Se·quoi′a
se·ragl′io
se·ra′pe
ser′aph
se·raph′ic
se·raph′i·cal
ser′a·phim
Ser′bi·an
sere
ser′e·nade′
ser′e·nad′ed
ser′e·nad′er
ser′e·na′ta
ser′en·dip′i·ty
se·rene′
se·rene′ly
se·rene′ness
se·ren′i·ty
serf
serf′dom
serge
ser′geant
se′ri·al
se′ri·al·i·za′tion
se′ri·al·ize
se′ri·al·ly
se′ri·a′tim
ser′i·cul′ture
se′ries
ser′if
se′ri·ous
se′ri·ous·ly

se′ri·ous·ness
ser′mon
ser′mon·ize
ser′mon·ized
se′rous
ser′pent
ser′pen·tine
ser·pig′i·nous
ser′rate
ser·ra′tion
ser′ried
se′rum
serv′ant
serve
served
serv′er
serv′ice
serv′ice·a·bil′i·ty
serv′ice·a·ble
serv′ice·a·bly
serv′iced
Serv′i·dor
ser′vile
ser·vil′i·ty
serv′ings
ser′vi·tor
ser′vi·tude
ser′vo·mech′a·nism
ser′vo·mo′tor
ses′a·me
ses′qui·sul′phide
ses′sion

ses'terce
ses·tet'
set
set'back'
set'off'
set·tee'
set'ter
set'tings
set'tle
set'tled
set'tle·ment
set'tler
sev'er
sev'er·a·ble
sev'er·al
sev'er·al·ly
sev'er·al·ty
sev'er·ance
sev'er·a'tion
se·vere'
sev'ered
se·vere'ly
se·ver'er
se·ver'est
se·ver'i·ty
sew
sew'age
sewed
sew'er
sew'er·age
sewn
sex'tant

sex·tet'
sex'ton
sex'tu·ple
sex·tu'pli·cate
shab'bi·ly
shab'bi·ness
shab'by
shack
shack'le
shack'led
shade
shad'ed
shad'i·er
shad'i·est
shad'i·ly
shad'i·ness
shad'ings
shad'ow
shad'owed
shad'ow·less
shad'ow·y
shad'y
shaft
shag
shag'bark'
shag'gi·er
shag'gi·est
shag'gi·ly
shag'gy
sha·green'
shake
shake'down'

shak'en
shak'er
Shake·spear'e·an
shake'-up'
shak'i·er
shak'i·est
shak'i·ly
shak'i·ness
shak'o
shak'y
shale
shall
shal'lop
shal·lot'
shal'low
shal'lowed
shal'low·er
shal'low·est
shal'low·ly
shal'low·ness
sham
sha'man
sham'ble
sham'bled
sham'bling·ly
shame
shamed
shame'faced'
shame·fac'ed·ly
shame'ful
shame'ful·ly
shame'ful·ness

shame'less·ly
shame'less·ness
shammed
sham'mer
sham·poo'
sham·pooed'
sham'rock
shan'dy·gaff
shang·hai'
shang·haied'
shank
shan't
shan'ty
shape
shaped
shape'less
shape'less·ly
shape'less·ness
shape'li·ness
shape'ly
shard
share
shared
share'hold'er
shark
sharp
sharp'en
sharp'ened
sharp'en·er
sharp'er
sharp'est
sharp'ly

sharp'ness
sharp'shoot'er
sharp'-wit'ted
shas'tra
shat'ter
shat'tered
shat'ter·ing·ly
shat'ter·proof'
shave
shaved
shav'er
shave'tail'
shav'ings
shaw
shawl
she
sheaf
shear
sheared
shear'ings
shears
sheathe
sheathed
sheaves
shed
sheen
sheep
sheep'herd'er
sheep'ish
sheep'ish·ly
sheep'ish·ness
sheep'man

sheep'skin'
sheer
sheer'er
sheer'est
sheer'ly
sheet
sheet'ed
sheet'ings
sheet'ways'
sheet'wise'
sheet'work'
shek'el
shel'drake'
shelf
shell
shel·lac'
shell'back'
shell'burst'
shelled
shell'fish'
shell'proof'
shell'work'
shel'ter
shel'tered
shel'ter·ing·ly
shel'ter·less
shelve
shelved
shelves
shep'herd
shep'herd·ed
shep'herd·ess

Sher'a·ton
sher'bet
sher'iff
Sher'pa
sher'ry
Shet'land
shew'bread'
shib'bo·leth
shied
shield
shield'ed
shift
shift'ed
shift'i·er
shift'i·est
shift'i·ly
shift'i·ness
shift'less
shift'y
shil·le'lagh
shil'lings
shim
shimmed
shim'mer
shim'mered
shim'mer·ing·ly
shim'mer·y
shin
shin'bone'
shine
shin'er
shin'gle
shin'gled
shin'i·ly
shin'i·ness
shin'ing·ly
shin'ny
shin'plas'ter
Shin'to'
Shin'to·ism
Shin'to·ist
Shin'to·is'tic
shin'y
ship
ship'board'
ship'build'er
ship'load'
ship'mas'ter
ship'mate'
ship'ment
ship'own'er
ship'per
ship'shape'
ship'worm'
ship'wreck'
ship'wright'
ship'yard'
shire
shirk
shirked
shirk'er
shirr
shirred
shirt
shirt'ings
shirt'less
shiv'er
shiv'ered
shiv'er·ing·ly
shiv'er·ings
shoal
shoal'ness
shock
shocked
shock'ing·ly
shod
shod'di·er
shod'di·est
shod'dy
shoe
shoe'horn'
shoe'lace'
shoe'less
shoe'mak'er
shoe'man
shoes
shoe'string'
sho'gun'
shook
shoot
shoot'er
shoot'ings
shop
shop'keep'er
shop'lift'er
shop'man

shop'per
shop'work'
shop'worn'
shore
shored
shorn
short
short'age
short'bread'
short'cake'
short'change'
short'com'ings
short'en
short'ened
short'en·ing
short'er
short'est
short'fall'
short'hand'
short'hand'ed
short'horn'
short'ish
short'leaf'
short'-lived'
short'ly
short'ness
short'-range'
short'sight'ed
short'-time'
shot
shot'gun'
shot'ted
should
shoul'der
shoul'dered
shout
shout'ed
shove
shoved
shov'el
shov'eled
shov'el·head'
show
show'boat'
show'down'
showed
show'er
show'ered
show'i·er
show'i·est
show'i·ly
show'i·ness
show'ings
show'man
show'man·ship
shown
show'room'
show'y
shrank
shrap'nel
shred
shred'ded
shred'der
shrew
shrewd
shrewd'er
shrewd'est
shrewd'ly
shrewd'ness
shriek
shrieked
shrift
shrike
shrill
shrilled
shrill'er
shrill'est
shrill'ness
shrill'y
shrimp
shrimp'er
shrine
Shrin'er
shrink
shrink'age
shrink'er
shrink'ing·ly
shrive
shriv'el
shriv'eled
shriv'en
shroud
shroud'ed
shrub
shrub'ber·y
shrub'wood'

shrug
shrugged
shrunk
shrunk'en
shuck
shucked
shud'der
shud'dered
shud'der·ing·ly
shud'der·ings
shuf'fle
shuf'fled
shuf'fling·ly
shuf'flings
shun
shunt
shunt'ed
shut
shut'off'
shut'ter
shut'tered
shut'tle
shut'tled
shy
shy'ly
shy'ness
shy'ster
Si'a·mese'
sib'i·lance
sib'i·lant
sib'i·late
sib'ling
sib'yl
sib'yl·line
Si·cil'i·an
sick
sick'bed'
sick'en
sick'ened
sick'en·ing·ly
sick'er
sick'est
sick'le
sick'li·er
sick'li·est
sick'li·ness
sick'ly
sick'ness
sick'room'
side
side'board'
side'car'
sid'ed
side'long'
side'piece'
si·de're·al
sid'er·ite
side'split'ting
side'walk'
side'ways'
side'wise'
sid'ings
si'dle
si'dled
siege
si·en'na
si·er'ra
si·es'ta
sieve
sift
sift'age
sift'ed
sift'ings
sigh
sighed
sigh'ing·ly
sigh'ings
sight
sight'ed
sight'ings
sight'less
sight'li·ness
sight'ly
sig'ma
sign
sig'nal
sig'naled
sig'nal·ize
sig'nal·ized
sig'nal·ly
sig'na·to'ry
sig'na·ture
sign'board'
signed
sign'er
sig'net

sig·nif′i·cance
sig·nif′i·cant
sig·nif′i·cant·ly
sig′ni·fi·ca′tion
sig′ni·fied
sig′ni·fy
sign′post′
sign′writ′er
si′lage
si′lence
si′lenced
si′lenc·er
si′lent
si′lent·ly
si′lent·ness
si′lex
sil′hou·ette′
sil′i·ca
sil′i·cate
sil′i·con
sil′i·co′sis
silk
silk′en
silk′i·er
silk′i·est
silk′i·ly
silk′i·ness
silk′weed′
silk′worm′
silk′y
sil′la·bub
sil′li·er
sil′li·est
sil′li·ness
sil′ly
si′lo
silt
sil·ta′tion
silt′ed
sil′van
sil′ver
sil′vered
sil′ver·smith′
sil′ver·ware′
sil′ver·y
sim′i·an
sim′i·lar
sim′i·lar′i·ty
sim′i·lar·ly
sim′i·le
si·mil′i·tude
sim′mer
sim′mered
sim′mer·ing·ly
sim′o·ny
si·moon′
sim′per
sim′pered
sim′per·ing·ly
sim′ple
sim′pler
sim′plest
sim′ple·ton
sim′plex
sim·plic′i·ty
sim′pli·fi·ca′tion
sim′pli·fied
sim′pli·fy
sim′ply
sim′u·la′crum
sim′u·late
sim′u·la′tion
sim′u·la′tor
si′mul·ta′ne·ous
sin
since
sin·cere′
sin·cere′ly
sin·cere′ness
sin·cer′er
sin·cer′est
sin·cer′i·ty
sine
si′ne·cure
sin′ew
sin′ew·y
sin′ful
sin′ful·ly
sin′ful·ness
sing
sing′a·ble
singe
singed
sing′er
sin′gle
sin′gled

sin'gle·ness
sin'gle·ton
sin'gly
sin'gu·lar
sin'gu·lar'i·ty
sin'gu·lar·ly
sin'is·ter
sin'is·tral
sink
sink'age
sink'er
sink'hole'
sink'ings
sink'less
sin'less
sin'less·ly
sin'less·ness
sinned
sin'ner
Sin'o·log'i·cal
Si·nol'o·gist
Sin'o·logue
Sin'o·phile
sin'ter
sin'u·os'i·ty
sin'u·ous
si'nus·i'tis
Sioux
sip
si'phon
si'phoned
sipped
sip'per
sir
sir·dar'
sire
sired
si'ren
sir'loin'
si·roc'co
sir'up
sir'up·y
si'sal
sis'kin
sis'si·fied
sis'sy
sis'ter
sis'ter·hood
sis'ter-in-law'
sis'ter·ly
Sis'tine
sis'trum
sit
site
sit'ter
sit'tings
sit'u·ate
sit'u·at'ed
sit'u·a'tion
sixth
siz'a·ble
size
sized
siz'er
siz'es
siz'ings
siz'zle
siz'zled
siz'zling·ly
skate
skat'ed
skat'er
skein
skel'e·tal
skel'e·ton
skel'e·ton·ize
skel'e·ton·ized
skep'tic
skep'ti·cal
skep'ti·cal·ly
skep'ti·cism
sketch
sketched
sketch'i·ly
sketch'i·ness
sketch'y
skew
skewed
skew'er
skew'ered
skew'ings
ski
ski'a·gram
ski'a·graph
ski·am'e·try
skid

skid′ded
skied
skiff
ski·jor′ing
skill
skilled
skil′let
skill′ful
skill′ful·ly
skill′ful·ness
skim
skimmed
skim′mer
skim′ming·ly
skimp
skimped
skimp′i·ness
skimp′y
skin
skin′flint′
skink′er
skinned
skin′ner
skin′ni·er
skin′ni·est
skin′ny
skin′worm′
skip
skipped
skip′per
skip′ping·ly
skir′mish
skir′mished
skir′mish·er
skir′mish·ing·ly
skirt
skirt′ed
skirt′ings
skit
skit′ter
skit′tish
skit′tish·ly
skit′tish·ness
skit′tles
skive
skived
skiv′er
skiv′ings
skoal
skulk
skulked
skull
skunk
skunk′weed′
sky
sky′jack′er
sky′larked′
sky′light′
sky′rock′et
sky′scape
sky′scrap′er
sky′shine′
sky′ward
sky′writ′er
sky′writ′ing
slab
slack
slacked
slack′en
slack′ened
slack′er
slack′est
slack′ness
slag
slain
slake
slaked
slam
slammed
slan′der
slan′dered
slan′der·er
slan′der·ing·ly
slan′der·ous
slan′der·ous·ly
slan′der·ous·ness
slang
slang′y
slank
slant
slant′ed
slant′ing·ly
slant′ways′
slant′wise′
slap
slap′dash′

slap'stick'
slash
slashed
slash'er
slash'ing·ly
slash'ings
slate
slat'er
slat'ted
slat'tern
slat'tern·ly
slaugh'ter
slaugh'tered
slaugh'ter·er
slaugh'ter·house'
slave
slaved
slav'er
slav'er·y
slav'ish
slav'ish·ly
slav'ish·ness
slaw
slay
slay'er
slay'ings
sleave
slea'zi·ness
slea'zy
sled
sledge
sleek

sleek'er
sleek'est
sleek'ly
sleek'ness
sleep
sleep'er
sleep'i·er
sleep'i·est
sleep'i·ly
sleep'i·ness
sleep'less
sleep'less·ness
sleep'y
sleet
sleeve
sleigh
sleight
slen'der
slen'der·er
slen'der·est
slen'der·ness
slept
sleuth
sleuthed
sleuth'hound'
slew
slewed
slice
sliced
slic'er
slick
slick'er

slick'est
slid
slide
sli'er
sli'est
slight
slight'ed
slight'er
slight'est
slight'ing·ly
slight'ly
slight'ness
slim
slime
slim'i·er
slim'i·est
slim'i·ly
slim'i·ness
slim'mer
slim'mest
slim'ness
slim'y
sling
slink
slink'i·er
slink'i·est
slink'y
slip
slip'case'
slip'knot'
slip'page
slipped

slip′per
slip′per·i·ness
slip′per·y
slip′shod′
slit
slith′er
slith′ered
slit′ter
sliv′er
sliv′ered
sliv′er·y
slob
slob′ber
sloe
sloe′ber′ry
slog
slo′gan
slo′gan·eer′
slogged
sloop
slop
slope
sloped
slop′ing·ly
slopped
slop′py
slosh
sloshed
slot
sloth
sloth′ful
sloth′ful·ly
sloth′ful·ness
slot′ted
slouch
slouched
slouch′i·ly
slouch′i·ness
slouch′ing·ly
slough
slough
sloughed
slov′en
slov′en·li·ness
slov′en·ly
slow
slowed
slow′er
slow′est
slow′go′ing
slow′ly
slow′poke′
sloyd
slub
slubbed
sludge
slug
slug′gard
slug′gard·ly
slugged
slug′ger
slug′gish
slug′gish·ly
slug′gish·ness
sluice
sluiced
sluice′way′
sluic′ings
slum
slum′ber
slum′bered
slum′ber·er
slum′ber·ing·ly
slum′ber·land′
slum′ber·ous
slump
slumped
slung
slur
slurred
slur′ring·ly
slur′ry
slush
slush′i·ly
slush′i·ness
slush′y
slut′tish
sly
sly′boots′
sly′ly
sly′ness
smack
smacked
smack′ing·ly
small
small′er

small′est
small′ness
small′pox′
smart
smart′ed
smart′en
smart′ened
smart′er
smart′est
smart′ing·ly
smart′ly
smart′ness
smash
smash′up′
smat′ter
smat′ter·ings
smear
smeared
smear′i·er
smear′i·est
smear′i·ness
smear′y
smell
smelled
smelt
smelt′ed
smelt′er
smelt′er·y
smidg′en
smi′lax
smile
smiled
smil′ing·ly
smirch
smirched
smirk
smirked
smirk′ing·ly
smirk′ish
smite
smith
Smith·so′ni·an
smith′y
smit′ten
smock
smoke
smoked
smoke′house′
smoke′less
smoke′proof′
smok′er
smoke′stack′
smoke′wood′
smok′i·er
smok′i·est
smok′i·ness
smok′y
smol′der
smol′dered
smooth
smooth′bore′
smoothed
smooth′er
smooth′est
smooth′ing·ly
smooth′ly
smooth′ness
smote
smoth′er
smoth′ered
smoth′er·ing·ly
smudge
smudged
smudg′i·ly
smudg′i·ness
smudg′y
smug
smug′gle
smug′gled
smug′gler
smug′ly
smug′ness
smut
smut′ted
smut′ti·er
smut′ti·est
smut′ti·ly
smut′ti·ness
smut′ty
snack
snaf′fle
sna·fu′
snag
snag′ged
snag′gled
snail

snake
snake'bird'
snaked
snake'like'
snake'stone'
snake'weed'
snake'wood'
snak'i·er
snak'i·est
snak'i·ly
snak'i·ness
snak'y
snap
snap'drag'on
snapped
snap'per
snap'pi·er
snap'pi·est
snap'ping·ly
snap'pish
snap'py
snap'shot'
snap'weed'
snare
snared
snarl
snarled
snarl'ing·ly
snarl'y
snatch
snatched
snatch'ing·ly
snatch'y
snath
sneak
sneaked
sneak'er
sneak'i·er
sneak'i·est
sneak'ing·ly
sneak'y
sneer
sneered
sneer'ing·ly
sneeze
sneezed
sneeze'weed'
snick'er
snick'ered
snick'er·ing·ly
snick'er·ings
sniff
sniffed
sniff'i·ly
sniff'i·ness
sniff'ing·ly
sniff'ings
snif'fle
snif'fled
sniff'y
snig'ger·ing·ly
snip
snipe
snipped
snip'pet
snip'pi·er
snip'pi·est
snip'pi·ness
snip'py
sniv'el
sniv'eled
sniv'el·er
sniv'el·ings
snob
snob'ber·y
snob'bish
snob'bish·ly
snob'bish·ness
snood
snook'er
snoop
snoop'er
snoot
snooze
snore
snored
snor'ing·ly
snor'ings
snor'kel
snort
snort'ing·ly
snort'ings
snout
snow
snow'ball'
snow'bell'

snow'ber'ry
snow'bird'
snow'bound'
snow'bush'
snow'cap'
snow'drift'
snow'drop'
snowed
snow'fall'
snow'flake'
snow'flow'er
snow'i·er
snow'i·est
snow'plow'
snow'shed'
snow'shoe'
snow'slide
snow'slip
snow'storm
snow'worm'
snow'y
snub
snubbed
snub'ber
snub'bing·ly
snub'bings
snuff
snuffed
snuff'er
snuf'fle
snuf'fled
snuf'fling·ly
snuf'flings
snug
snug'ger
snug'ger·y
snug'gest
snug'gle
snug'gled
snug'ly
snug'ness
so
soak
soaked
soap
soap'box'
soaped
soap'i·ness
soap'root'
soap'stone'
soap'suds'
soap'y
soar
soared
soar'ing·ly
sob
sobbed
sob'bing·ly
so·be'it
so'ber
so'bered
so'ber·er
so'ber·est
so'ber·ing·ly
so'ber·ly
so'ber·sides'
so·bri'e·ty
so'bri·quet
soc'age
soc'cer
so'cia·bil'i·ty
so'cia·ble
so'cia·bly
so'cial
so'cial·ism
so'cial·ist
so'cial·is'tic
so'cial·i·za'tion
so'cial·ize
so'cial·ized
so'cial·iz'er
so·ci'e·tal
so·ci'e·tar'i·an
so·ci'e·tar'i·an·ism
so·ci'e·ty
so'ci·o·log'i·cal
so'ci·o·log'i·cal·ly
so'ci·ol'o·gist
so'ci·ol'o·gy
sock
sock'et
sock'et·ed
So·crat'ic
sod
so'da
so·dal'i·ty

sod′den
so′di·um
so′fa
soft
sof′ten
sof′tened
sof′ten·er
soft′er
soft′est
soft′ly
soft′ware
soft′wood′
sog′gi·ly
sog′gi·ness
sog′gy
soil
soiled
so·journ′
so·journed′
so·journ′er
sol′ace
sol′aced
so′lar
so·lar′i·um
sold
sol′der
sol′dered
sol′dier
sol′diered
sol′dier·ly
sol′dier·y
sole
sol′e·cism
soled
sole′ly
sol′emn
so·lem′ni·ty
sol′em·ni·za′tion
sol′em·nize
sol′em·nized
sol′emn·ly
so′le·noid
so′le·noi′dal
sole′print′
sol′fe·ri′no
so·lic′it
so·lic′i·ta′tion
so·lic′it·ed
so·lic′i·tor
so·lic′it·ous
so·lic′i·tude
sol′id
sol′i·dar′i·ty
so·lid′i·fi′a·ble·ness
so·lid′i·fi·ca′tion
so·lid′i·fy
so·lid′i·ty
sol′id·ly
so·lil′o·quize
so·lil′o·quized
so·lil′o·quy
sol′i·taire′
sol′i·tar′i·ly
sol′i·tar′y
sol′i·tude
so′lo
so′loed
so′lo·ist
sol′stice
sol′u·bil′i·ty
sol′u·ble
sol′ute
so·lu′tion
solv′a·ble
sol′vate
sol·va′tion
solve
solved
sol′ven·cy
sol′vent
so·mat′ic
so′ma·tol′o·gy
som′ber
som·bre′ro
some
some′bod′y
some′how
some′one′
som′er·sault
some′thing
some′time′
some′what′
some′where′
som·nam′bu·lism
som·nam′bu·list
som′no·lent

son
so'nant
so·na'ta
so'na·ti'na
song
song'bird'
song'book'
song'ful
song'ful·ness
song'ster
son'ic
son'-in-law'
son'net
son'net·eer'
so·nor'i·ty
so·no'rous
soon
soon'er
soon'est
soot
soot'ed
soothe
soothed
sooth'ing·ly
sooth'say'er
soot'i·er
soot'i·est
soot'i·ly
soot'y
sop
soph'ism
soph'ist
so·phis'tic
so·phis'ti·cal
so·phis'ti·cate
so·phis'ti·cat'ed
so·phis'ti·ca'tion
soph'ist·ry
soph'o·more
soph'o·mor'ic
soph'o·mor'i·cal
so'po·rif'ic
so'pra·ni'no
so·pra'no
sor'cer·er
sor'cer·ess
sor'cer·y
sor'did
sor'did·ness
sore
sore'head'
sore'ly
sore'ness
sor'ghum
so·ror'i·ty
so·ro'sis
sor'rel
sor'ri·er
sor'ri·est
sor'row
sor'rowed
sor'row·ful
sor'row·ful·ly
sor'ry
sort
sort'ed
sort'er
sor'tie
sor'ti·lege
sos'te·nu'to
sot
sot'tish
sot'tish·ness
sou·brette'
souf'flé'
sought
soul
soul'ful
soul'ful·ly
soul'ful·ness
soul'less
soul'less·ly
soul'less·ness
sound
sound'ed
sound'er
sound'est
sound'ing·ly
sound'ings
sound'less
sound'less·ly
sound'less·ness
sound'ly
sound'ness
sound'proof'
soup

soup'bone'
sour
source
soured
sour'er
sour'est
souse
soused
sou·tane'
south
south'east'
south'east'er
south'east'er·ly
south'east'ern
south'er·ly
south'ern
south'ern·er
south'ern·most
south'ward
south'west'
south'west'er
south'west'er·ly
sou've·nir'
sov'er·eign
sov'er·eign·ty
so'vi·et'
so'vi·et'ism
so'vi·et'i·za'tion
so'vi·et'ize
so'vi·et·ol'o·gist
sow
sow

sowed
sow'er
sow'ings
soy
soy'bean'
spa
space
space'craft
space'man
spa'cious
spa'cious·ly
spa'cious·ness
spade
spad'ed
spade'fish'
spade'work'
spa·ghet'ti
spal·peen'
span
span'drel
span'gle
span'gled
Span'iard
span'iel
Span'ish
spank
spanked
spank'ing·ly
spank'ings
span'ner
spare
spared

spare'rib'
spar'ing·ly
spark
spark'ed
spar'kle
spar'kled
spar'kler
spar'kling·ly
sparred
spar'ring·ly
spar'row
sparse
sparse'ly
sparse'ness
spars'er
spars'est
spar'si·ty
Spar'tan
spasm
spas·mod'ic
spas·mod'i·cal
spas·mod'i·cal·ly
spas'tic
spas'ti·cal·ly
spas·tic'i·ty
spat
spat'ter
spat'tered
spat'ter·ing·ly
spat'ter·ings
spat'ter·proof'
spat'ter·work'

spat'u·la
spat'u·late
spav'ined
spawn
spawned
speak
speak'er
spear
speared
spear'fish'
spear'head'
spear'mint'
spear'wood'
spe'cial
spe'cial·ist
spe'cial·i·za'tion
spe'cial·ize
spe'cial·ized
spe'cial·ly
spe'cial·ty
spe'cie
spe'cies
spe·cif'ic
spe·cif'i·cal·ly
spec'i·fi·ca'tion
spec'i·fied
spec'i·fy
spec'i·men
spe'cious
spe'cious·ly
spe'cious·ness
speck
specked
speck'le
speck'led
spec'ta·cle
spec'ta·cles
spec·tac'u·lar
spec·tac'u·lar·ly
spec·ta'tor
spec'ter
spec'tral
spec·trom'e·ter
spec'tro·scope
spec'trum
spec'u·late
spec'u·lat'ed
spec'u·la'tion
spec'u·la'tive
spec'u·la'tive·ly
spec'u·la'tive·ness
spec'u·la'tor
spec'u·la·to'ry
spec'u·lum
speech
speech'less
speech'less·ly
speech'less·ness
speed
speed'boat'
speed'ed
speed'er
speed'i·er
speed'i·est
speed'i·ly
speed'i·ness
speed'ing·ly
speed·om'e·ter
speed'way'
speed'y
spe'le·ol'o·gist
spe'le·ol'o·gy
spell
spell'bind'er
spell'bound'
spelled
spell'er
spell'ings
spel'ter
Spen·ce'ri·an
spend
spend'er
spend'ings
spend'thrift'
spent
sper'ma·ce'ti
spew
spewed
sphag'num
sphere
spher'i·cal
spher'i·cal·ly
sphe·ric'i·ty
sphe'roid
sphinx
spice

spiced
spic'i·ly
spic'i·ness
spic'y
spi'der
spi'der·y
spied
spig'ot
spike
spiked
spik'y
spile
spiled
spill
spilled
spill'way'
spin
spin'ach
spi'nal
spin'dle
spine
spine'less
spin'et
spin'i·er
spin'i·est
spin'na·ker
spin'ner
spin'ner·et
spin'ney
spin'ning·ly
spin'ster
spin'ster·hood

spin'y
spi'ral
spi'raled
spi'ral·ly
spire
spired
spir'it
spir'it·ed
spir'it·ed·ly
spir'it·u·al
spir'it·u·al·ism
spir'it·u·al·ist
spir'it·u·al·is'tic
spir'it·u·al'i·ty
spir'it·u·al·ize
spir'it·u·al·ized
spir'it·u·al·ly
spir'it·u·ous
spi'ro·chete
spit
spit'ball'
spite
spite'ful
spite'ful·ly
spite'ful·ness
spit'fire'
spit·toon'
splash
splash'down
splash'i·er
splash'i·est
splash'ing·ly

splash'ings
splash'y
splat'ter
splat'ter·work'
splayed
splay'foot'
spleen
splen'did
splen'did·ly
splen'dor
splen'dor·ous
sple·net'ic
splen'i·tive
splice
spliced
splic'er
splic'ings
splint
splint'ed
splin'ter
splin'tered
splin'ter·proof'
split
split'tings
split'worm'
splotch
splotched
splotch'y
splurge
splurged
splut'ter
splut'tered

spoil
spoil'age
spoiled
spoils'man
spoil'sport'
spoke
spo'ken
spoke'shave'
spokes'man
spo'li·a'tion
spo'li·a'tive
spo'li·a·to'ry
spon'dee
sponge
sponge'cake'
sponged
spong'er
spon'gi·er
spon'gi·est
spong'ings
spon'gy
spon'sor
spon'sor·ship
spon'ta·ne'i·ty
spon·ta'ne·ous
spon·ta'ne·ous·ly
spon·ta'ne·ous·ness
spoof
spook
spook'i·ness
spook'y
spool

spooled
spoon
spoon'bill'
spooned
spoon'er·ism
spoon'ful
spoon'fuls
spoor
spo·rad'ic
spore
sport
sport'ed
spor'tive
spor'tive·ly
sports'cast'er
sports'man
sports'man·ship
sports'wear'
sport'y
spot
spot'less
spot'less·ly
spot'less·ness
spot'light'
spot'ted
spot'ter
spot'ti·er
spot'ti·est
spot'ty
spouse
spout
spout'ed

spout'ings
sprain
sprained
sprang
sprat
sprawl
sprawled
sprawl'ing·ly
spray
sprayed
spray'er
spread
spread'er
spread'ing·ly
spree
sprig
spright'li·er
spright'li·est
spright'li·ness
spright'ly
spring
spring'board'
spring'bok'
spring'fish'
spring'i·ly
spring'i·ness
spring'ing·ly
spring'time'
spring'wood'
spring'y
sprin'kle
sprin'kled

sprin'kler
sprin'kling·ly
sprin'klings
sprint
sprint'er
sprite
sprit'sail'
sprock'et
sprout
sprout'ed
sprout'ling
spruce
spruc'er
spruc'est
sprung
spry
spud
spume
spumed
spu·mo'ne
spun
spunk
spunk'i·er
spunk'i·est
spunk'y
spur
spu'ri·ous
spu'ri·ous·ly
spurn
spurned
spurred
spurt
spurt'ed
sput'nik
sput'ter
sput'tered
sput'ter·ing·ly
sput'ter·ings
spu'tum
spy
spy'glass'
squab
squab'ble
squab'bled
squab'bling·ly
squab'blings
squad
squad'ron
squal'id
squa·lid'i·ty
squal'id·ly
squall
squalled
squall'ings
squall'y
squal'or
squan'der
squan'dered
square
squared
square'head'
square'ly
square'ness
squash
squashed
squat
squat'ted
squat'ter
squaw
squaw'fish'
squawk
squeak
squeal
squealed
squeam'ish
squee'gee
squeeze
squeezed
squelch
squelched
squelch'ing·ly
squib
squid
squig'gle
squig'gly
squint
squint'ed
squint'ing·ly
squire
squirm
squirmed
squirm'ing·ly
squirm'ings
squir'rel
squir'rel·fish'
squir'rel·proof'

squirt
stab
stabbed
stab′bing·ly
stab′bings
sta·bil′i·ty
sta′bi·li·za′tion
sta′bi·lize
sta′bi·lized
sta′bi·liz′er
sta′ble
stac·ca′to
stack
sta′di·a
sta′di·um
staff
stag
stage
stage′coach′
stage′craft′
staged
stage′hand′
stag′er
stage′wor′thy
stag′ger
stag′gered
stag′ger·ing·ly
stag′horn′
stag′hound′
stag′hunt′
stag′nant
stag′nate
stag′nat·ed
stag·na′tion
staid
stain
stained
stain′less
stair
stair′case′
stair′way′
stake
staked
sta·lac′tite
sta·lag′mite
stale
stale′mate′
stal′er
stal′est
stalk
stalked
stalk′er
stalk′ing·ly
stall
stalled
stal′lion
stal′wart
sta′men
stam′i·na
stam′mer
stam′mered
stam′mer·er
stam′mer·ing·ly
stamp
stamped
stam·pede′
stam·ped′ed
stamp′er
stamp′ings
stance
stanch
stan′chion
stand
stand′ard
stand′ard·i·za′tion
stand′ard·ize
stand′ings
stand′off′
stand′pipe′
stand′point′
stand′still′
stank
stan′nate
stan′nic
stan′nous
stan′za
sta′ple
sta′pled
sta′pler
star
star′board
starch
starched
starch′y
stare
stared

star'fish'
star'gaz'er
star'ing·ly
stark
star'less
star'let
star'light'
star'like'
star'lings
starred
star'ri·er
star'ri·est
star'ry
start
start'ed
start'er
star'tle
star'tled
star'tling·ly
star·va'tion
starve
starved
starve'ling
state
stat'ed
state'hood
State'house'
state'li·ness
state'ly
state'ment
state'room'
states'man

states'man·like'
stat'ic
sta'tion
sta'tion·ar'y
sta'tioned
sta'tion·er
sta'tion·er'y
stat'ism
stat'ist
sta·tis'ti·cal
sta·tis'ti·cal·ly
stat'is·ti'cian
sta·tis'tics
stat'u·ar'y
stat'ue
stat'u·esque'
stat'u·ette'
stat'ure
sta'tus
stat'ute
stat'u·to'ry
stave
stay
stayed
stead
stead'fast
stead'fast·ly
stead'fast·ness
stead'i·er
stead'i·est
stead'i·ly
stead'y

steak
steal
stealth
stealth'i·er
stealth'i·est
stealth'i·ly
steam
steam'boat'
steamed
steam'er
steam'i·er
steam'i·est
steam'i·ness
steam'ship'
steam'y
ste'a·tite
steel
steel'head'
steel'work'
steel'yard
steep
steep'er
steep'est
stee'ple
stee'ple·chase'
steer
steer'age
steered
steer'ing
steers'man
stein
stel'lar

stem
stemmed
stench
sten′cil
sten′ciled
ste·nog′ra·pher
sten′o·graph′ic
ste·nog′ra·phy
ste·no′sis
sten·to′ri·an
step
step′child′
step′daugh′ter
step′lad′der
step′moth′er
steppe
stepped
step′sis′ter
step′son′
ster′e·o
ster′e·o·phon′ic
ster′e·op′ti·con
ster′e·o·scope′
ster′e·o·scop′ic
ster′ile
ste·ril′i·ty
ster′i·li·za′tion
ster′i·lize
ster′i·lized
ster′i·liz′er
ster′ling
stern
stern′er
stern′est
stern′ly
stern′ness
stern′post′
ster′num
ster′nu·ta′tion
ster′to·rous
stet
steth′o·scope
ste′ve·dore′
stew
stew′ard
stew′ard·ess
stewed
stick
stick′er
stick′ful
stick′i·er
stick′i·est
stick′i·ly
stick′i·ness
stick′le·back′
stick′ler
stick′pin′
stick′weed′
stick′y
stiff
stiff′en
stiff′ened
stiff′en·er
stiff′er
stiff′est
stiff′ness
sti′fle
sti′fled
sti′fling·ly
stig′ma
stig·mat′a
stig·mat′ic
stig′ma·tism
stig′ma·ti·za′tion
stig′ma·tize
stig′ma·tized
stile
sti·let′to
still
still′born′
stilled
still′er
still′est
still′ness
still′room′
still′y
stilt
stilt′ed
stim′u·lant
stim′u·late
stim′u·lat′ed
stim′u·lat′ing
stim′u·la′tion
stim′u·lus
sting
sting′er

sting'fish'
stin'gi·er
stin'gi·est
sting'ing·ly
stin'gy
stink
stink'bug'
stink'er
stink'ing·ly
stink'pot'
stink'weed'
stink'wood'
stint
stint'ed
stint'ing·ly
stipe
sti'pend
sti·pen'di·ar'y
sti·pen'di·um
stip'ple
stip'pled
stip'plings
stip'u·late
stip'u·lat'ed
stip'u·lates
stip'u·la'tion
stip'u·la·to'ry
stir
stir'pes
stirps
stirred
stir'ring·ly
stir'rings
stir'rup
stitch
stitched
stitch'er
stitch'ings
stitch'work'
sti'ver
sto'a
stoat
stock
stock·ade'
stock·ad'ed
stock'breed'er
stock'bro'ker
stocked
stock'fish'
stock'hold'er
stock'house'
stock'i·ness
stock'i·net'
stock'ings
stock'job'ber
stock'keep'er
stock'mak'er
stock'man
stock'own'er
stock'pile'
stock'pot'
stock'tak'er
stock'y
stock'yard'
stodg'i·er
stodg'i·est
stodg'y
sto'gy
sto'ic
sto'i·cal
sto'i·cal·ly
sto'i·cism
stoke
stoked
stoke'hold'
stok'er
stole
sto'len
stol'id
sto·lid'i·ty
stol'id·ly
stom'ach
stom'ach·ful
sto·mach'ic
stone
stone'boat'
stoned
stone'fish'
stone'ma'son
stone'ware'
stone'weed'
stone'wood'
stone'work'
stone'yard'
ston'i·er
ston'i·est

ston'i·ly
ston'y
stood
stool
stoop
stooped
stoop'ing·ly
stop
stop'cock'
stope
stop'gap'
stop'o'ver
stop'page
stopped
stop'per
stop'pered
stop'ple
stor'age
store
stored
store'house'
store'keep'er
store'room'
sto'ried
stork
storm
storm'bound'
stormed
storm'i·er
storm'i·est
storm'ing·ly
storm'y
sto'ry
sto'ry·tell'er
stoup
stout
stout'er
stout'est
stout'heart'ed
stout'ly
stout'ness
stove
stow
stow'age
stra·bis'mus
strad'dle
strad'dled
strad'dling·ly
strafe
strag'gle
strag'gled
strag'gler
strag'gling·ly
straight
straight'edge'
straight'en
straight'ened
straight'er
straight'est
straight'for'ward
straight'for'ward·ly
straight'for'ward·ness
straight'way'
straight'ways'
strain
strained
strain'er
strain'ing·ly
strain'ings
strait
strait'en
strait'ened
strait'er
strait'est
strake
strand
strand'ed
strange
strange'lings
strange'ly
strange'ness
stran'ger
strang'est
stran'gle
stran'gled
stran'gler
stran'gles
stran'gling·ly
stran'glings
stran'gu·late
stran'gu·lat'ed
stran'gu·la'tion
strap
strap'less
strap·pa'do
strapped

strap'pings
stra'ta
strat'a·gem
stra·te'gic
stra·te'gi·cal
strat'e·gist
strat'e·gy
strat'i·fi·ca'tion
strat'i·fied
strat'i·fy
strat'o·sphere
stra'tum
straw
straw'ber'ry
straw'flow'er
stray
strayed
streak
streaked
streak'i·er
streak'i·est
streak'y
stream
streamed
stream'er
stream'ing·ly
stream'line'
stream'way'
street
strength
strength'en
strength'ened
strength'en·er
stren'u·ous
stren'u·ous·ly
stren'u·ous·ness
stress
stressed
stress'ful
stretch
stretched
stretch'er
stretch'er·man
stretch'-out'
strew
strewed
strewn
stri'ate
stri'at·ed
stri·a'tion
strick'en
strict
strict'ly
strict'ness
stric'ture
stride
stri'dent
stri'dent·ly
strid'ing·ly
strid'u·lous
strife
strig'il
strike
strike'break'er
strik'er
strik'ing·ly
string
stringed
strin'gen·cy
strin'gent
strin'gent·ly
string'er
string'i·er
string'i·est
string'piece'
string'y
strip
stripe
striped
strip'lings
strip'per
strip'pings
strive
striv'en
strob'o·scope
strode
stroke
stroked
strok'ings
stroll
strolled
stroll'er
strong
strong'box'
strong'er
strong'est

strong'hold'
strong'ly
stron'ti·um
strop
stro'phe
stroph'ic
strove
struck
struc'tur·al
struc'tur·al·ly
struc'ture
struc'tured
stru'del
strug'gle
strug'gled
strug'gler
strug'gling·ly
strug'glings
strum
strummed
strung
strut
strut'ted
strut'ter
strut'ting·ly
strut'tings
strych'nine
stub
stubbed
stub'bi·ness
stub'ble
stub'bly
stub'born
stub'by
stuc'co
stuck
stud
stud'book'
stud'ded
stu'dent
stud'fish'
stud'horse'
stud'ied
stu'di·o
stu'di·ous
stu'di·ous·ly
stu'di·ous·ness
stud'work'
stud'y
stuff
stuffed
stuff'er
stuff'ings
stuff'i·er
stuff'i·est
stuff'i·ly
stuff'i·ness
stuff'y
stul'ti·fi·ca'tion
stul'ti·fied
stul'ti·fy
stum'ble
stum'bled
stum'bling·ly
stump
stump'age
stumped
stump'i·er
stump'i·est
stump'y
stun
stung
stunk
stunned
stun'ner
stun'ning·ly
stunt
stunt'ed
stu'pe·fa'cient
stu'pe·fac'tion
stu'pe·fied
stu'pe·fy
stu·pen'dous
stu'pid
stu·pid'i·ty
stu'pid·ly
stu'por
stu'por·ous
stur'di·ly
stur'di·ness
stur'dy
stur'geon
stut'ter
stut'tered
stut'ter·er
stut'ter·ing·ly

sty
Styg'i·an
style
style'book'
styled
styl'ings
styl'ish
styl'ish·ness
styl'ist
sty·lis'tic
sty·lis'ti·cal·ly
styl'ize
styl'ized
sty'lo·graph
sty'lo·graph'ic
sty'lus
sty'mie
styp'tic
Styx
su'a·bil'i·ty
su'a·ble
sua'sion
suave
suave'ly
suave'ness
suav'i·ty
sub'a·cute'
sub'a·dult'
sub·a'gent
sub·al'tern
sub'a·quat'ic
sub·a'que·ous
sub·arc'tic
sub'a·tom'ic
sub·cal'i·ber
sub'cap'tion
sub'cel'lar
sub'class'
sub'com·mit'tee
sub·con'scious
sub·con'scious·ly
sub·con'scious·ness
sub'con·stel·la'tion
sub·con'ti·nent
sub·con'tract
sub'con·tract'ed
sub'con·trac'tor
sub'cu·ta'ne·ous
sub·dea'con
sub'di·vide'
sub'di·vid'ed
sub'di·vi'sion
sub·due'
sub·dued'
sub·du'ing·ly
sub·ed'i·tor
sub·fam'i·ly
sub'foun·da'tion
sub'grade'
sub'group'
sub'head'
sub·head'ings
sub·hu'man
sub'ject
sub·ject'ed
sub·jec'tion
sub·jec'tive
sub·jec'tive·ly
sub·jec'tive·ness
sub·jec'tiv·ism
sub'jec·tiv'i·ty
sub·join'
sub·join'der
sub·joined'
sub'ju·gate
sub'ju·gat'ed
sub'ju·ga'tion
sub·junc'tive
sub·king'dom
sub'lap·sar'i·an
sub'lease'
sub'les·see'
sub·les'sor
sub·let'
sub'li·mate
sub'li·mat'ed
sub'li·ma'tion
sub·lime'
sub·limed'
sub·lim'er
sub·lim'est
sub·lim'i·nal
sub·lim'i·ty
sub'lu·nar'y
sub'lux·a'tion
sub·mar'gin·al

sub′ma·rine′
sub′ma·rin′er
sub·merge′
sub·merged′
sub·mer′gence
sub·mers′i·ble
sub·mer′sion
sub·me′ter·ing
sub·mis′sion
sub·mis′sive
sub·mis′sive·ly
sub·mis′sive·ness
sub·mit′
sub·mit′tal
sub·mit′ted
sub·mit′ting·ly
sub·nor′mal
sub′nor·mal′i·ty
sub′o·ce·an′ic
sub·or′der
sub·or′di·nate
sub·or′di·nat′ed
sub·or′di·nat′ing·ly
sub·or′di·na′tion
sub·or′di·na′tive
sub·orn′
sub′or·na′tion
sub·orned′
sub·orn′er
sub·phy′lum
sub′plinth′
sub′plot′

sub·poe′na
sub·poe′naed
sub·ro·ga′tion
sub·scribe′
sub·scribed′
sub·scrib′er
sub′script
sub·scrip′tion
sub′se·quent
sub′se·quent·ly
sub·serve′
sub·served′
sub·ser′vi·ence
sub·ser′vi·en·cy
sub·ser′vi·ent
sub·side′
sub·sid′ed
sub·sid′ence
sub·sid′i·ar′y
sub′si·dize
sub′si·dized
sub′si·dy
sub·sist′
sub·sist′ed
sub·sist′ence
sub′soil′
sub′spe′cies
sub′stance
sub·stand′ard
sub·stan′tial
sub·stan′tial·ly
sub·stan′ti·ate

sub·stan′ti·at′ed
sub·stan′ti·a′tion
sub′stan·tive
sub′sta′tion
sub′sti·tute
sub′sti·tut′ed
sub′sti·tu′tion
sub·stra′tum
sub·struc′ture
sub·sur′face
sub·tan′gent
sub·ten′ant
sub·tend′
sub·tend′ed
sub′ter·fuge
sub′ter·ra′ne·an
sub′ter·ra′ne·ous
sub′ti′tle
sub′tle
sub′tler
sub′tlest
sub′tle·ty
sub′tly
sub·tract′
sub·tract′ed
sub·trac′tion
sub′tra·hend′
sub·treas′ur·y
sub·trop′i·cal
sub′urb
sub·ur′ban
sub·ur′ban·ite

sub·ven'tion
sub·ver'sion
sub·ver'sive
sub·vert'
sub·vert'ed
sub'way'
suc·ceed'
suc·ceed'ed
suc·ceed'ing·ly
suc·cess'
suc·cess'ful
suc·cess'ful·ly
suc·ces'sion
suc·ces'sive
suc·ces'sor
suc·cinct'
suc·cinct'ly
suc'cor
suc'cored
suc'co·tash
suc'cu·lence
suc'cu·lent
suc'cu·lent·ly
suc·cumb'
suc·cumbed'
such
suck
sucked
suck'er
suck'le
suck'led
suck'lings
suc'tion
sud'den
sud'den·ly
sud'den·ness
su'dor·if'er·ous
su'dor·if'ic
suds
sue
sued
suède
su'et
suf'fer
suf'fer·a·ble
suf'fer·ance
suf'fered
suf'fer·er
suf'fer·ing·ly
suf'fer·ings
suf·fice'
suf·ficed'
suf·fi'cien·cy
suf·fi'cient
suf'fix
suf'fo·cate
suf'fo·cat'ed
suf'fo·cat'ing·ly
suf'fo·ca'tion
suf'fo·ca'tive
suf'fra·gan
suf'frage
suf'fra·gist
suf·fuse'
suf·fused'
suf·fu'sion
sug'ar
sug'ared
sug'ar·plum'
sug'ar·y
sug·gest'
sug·gest'ed
sug·gest'i·bil'i·ty
sug·gest'i·ble
sug·ges'tion
sug·ges'tive
sug·ges'tive·ness
su'i·cid'al
su'i·cid'al·ly
su'i·cide
suit
suit'a·bil'i·ty
suit'a·ble
suit'case'
suite
suit'ed
suit'ing·ly
suit'ings
suit'or
sulk
sulked
sulk'i·er
sulk'i·est
sulk'i·ly
sulk'i·ness
sulk'y

sul'len
sul'len·ly
sul'len·ness
sul'lied
sul'ly
sul'phate
sul'phide
sul'phite
sul'phur
sul·phu'ric
sul'phu·rous
sul'tan
sul·tan'a
sul'tan·ate
sul'tri·er
sul'tri·est
sul'try
sum
su'mac
sum'ma·ri·ly
sum'ma·ri·ness
sum'ma·rize
sum'ma·rized
sum'ma·ry
sum·ma'tion
summed
sum'mer
sum'mered
sum'mer·y
sum'mit
sum'mon
sum'moned
sump
sump'ter
sump'tu·ar'y
sump'tu·ous
sump'tu·ous·ly
sump'tu·ous·ness
sun
sun'beam'
sun'bon'net
sun'burn'
sun'burned
sun'burst'
sun'dae
Sun'day
sun'der
sun'der·ance
sun'dered
sun'di'al
sun'dry
sun'fish'
sun'flow'er
sun'glass'
sun'glow'
sunk
sunk'en
sun'less
sun'light'
sun'lit'
sunned
sun'ni·ness
sun'ny
sun'proof'
sun'rise'
sun'room'
sun'set'
sun'shade'
sun'shine'
sun'shin'y
sun'spot'
sun'stone'
sun'stroke'
sun'ward
sup
su'per·a·ble
su'per·a·bun'dance
su'per·a·bun'dant
su'per·an'nu·ate
su'per·an'nu·at'ed
su'per·an'nu·a'tion
su·perb'
su'per·bowl
su'per·cal'en·dered
su'per·car'go
su'per·charg'er
su'per·cil'i·ous
su'per·cil'i·ous·ly
su'per·cil'i·ous·ness
su'per·con·duc·tance
su'per·con'duc·tiv'i·ty
su'per·con·duc·tor
su'per·cool'
su'per·dread·nought'
su'per·em'i·nence
su'per·em'i·nent

su′per·er′o·ga′tion
su′per·fam′i·ly
su′per·fi′cial
su′per·fi′ci·al′i·ty
su′per·fi′cial·ly
su′per·fine′
su′per·flu′i·ty
su·per′flu·ous
su·per′flu·ous·ly
su·per′flu·ous·ness
su′per·heat′
su′per·heat′ed
su′per·het′er·o·dyne′
su′per·hu′man
su′per·hu′man·ly
su′per·im·pose′
su′per·im·posed′
su′per·im′po·si′tion
su′per·im·po′sure
su′per·in·duce′
su′per·in·duced′
su′per·in·tend′
su′per·in·tend′ed
su′per·in·tend′ence
su′per·in·tend′en·cy
su′per·in·tend′ent
su·pe′ri·or
su·pe′ri·or′i·ty
su′per·jet
su·per′la·tive
su′per·man′
su·per′nal
su·per′nal·ly
su′per·nat′u·ral
su′per·nat′u·ral·ly
su′per·nat′u·ral·ism
su′per·nat′u·ral·ist
su′per·nor′mal
su′per·nu′mer·ar′y
su′per·po·si′tion
su′per·sat′u·rate
su′per·sat′u·rat′ed
su′per·sat′u·ra′tion
su′per·scribe′
su′per·scribed′
su′per·scrip′tion
su′per·sede′
su′per·sed′ed
su′per·ses′sion
su′per·son′ic
su′per·sti′tion
su′per·sti′tious
su′per·sti′tious·ly
su′per·stra′tum
su′per·struc′ture
su′per·tax′
su′per·vene′
su′per·vened′
su′per·vise′
su′per·vised′
su′per·vi′sion
su′per·vi′sor
su′per·vi′so·ry
su·pine′
su·pine′ness
sup′per
sup·plant′
sup·plant′ed
sup′ple
sup′ple·ment
sup′ple·men′tal
sup′ple·men′ta·ry
sup′ple·men·ta′tion
sup′ple·ment′ed
sup′pli·ant
sup′pli·cant
sup′pli·cate
sup′pli·cat′ed
sup′pli·cat′ing·ly
sup′pli·ca′tion
sup′pli·ca·to′ry
sup·plied′
sup·pli′er
sup·ply′
sup·port′
sup·port′ed
sup·port′er
sup·pose′
sup·posed′
sup·pos′ed·ly
sup′po·si′tion
sup·pos′i·ti′tious
sup·pos′i·ti′tious·ly
sup·press′
sup·pressed′
sup·pres′sion

sup·pres′sive
sup′pu·rate
sup′pu·rat′ed
sup′pu·ra′tion
sup′pu·ra′tive
su·prem′a·cy
su·preme′
su·preme′ly
sur′base′
sur·cease′
sur·charge′
sur·charged′
sur′cin′gle
surd
sure
sure′ly
sure′ness
sure′ty
sure′ty·ship
surf
sur′face
sur′faced
sur′fac·ings
sur′feit
sur′feit·ed
surge
surged
sur′geon
sur′ger·y
sur′gi·cal
sur′li·er
sur′li·est
sur′li·ness
sur′ly
sur·mise′
sur·mised′
sur·mount′
sur·mount′ed
sur′name′
sur′named′
sur·pass′
sur·passed′
sur·pass′ing·ly
sur′plice
sur′pliced
sur′plus
sur′plus·age
sur·prise′
sur·prised′
sur·pris′ed·ly
sur·pris′ing·ly
sur′re·but′tal
sur′re·but′ter
sur′re·join′der
sur·ren′der
sur·ren′dered
sur′rep·ti′tious
sur′rep·ti′tious·ly
sur′rep·ti′tious·ness
sur′rey
sur′ro·gate
sur′ro·ga′tion
sur·round′
sur·round′ed
sur·round′ings
sur′tax′
sur·tout′
sur·veil′lance
sur·vey′
sur·veyed′
sur·vey′or
sur·viv′al
sur·viv′al·ism
sur·vive′
sur·vived′
sur·vi′vor
sur·vi′vor·ship
sus·cep′ti·bil′i·ty
sus·cep′ti·ble
sus·cep′ti·bly
sus·pect′
sus·pect′ed
sus·pend′
sus·pend′ed
sus·pend′ers
sus·pense′
sus·pense′ful
sus·pen′sion
sus·pen′sive
sus·pen′sive·ly
sus·pen′sive·ness
sus·pi′cion
sus·pi′cious
sus·pi′cious·ly
sus·pi′cious·ness
sus·pire′

sus·tain′
sus·tained′
sus·tain′ed·ly
sus·tain′ing·ly
sus′te·nance
sus′ten·tac′u·lar
sus′ten·ta′tion
su′sur·ra′tion
sut′ler
sut·tee′
su′ture
su′tured
su′ze·rain
su′ze·rain·ty
svelte
swab
swabbed
swad′dle
swad′dled
swad′dling
swad′dlings
swag
swage
swaged
swag′ger
swag′gered
swag′ger·ing·ly
Swa·hi′li
swain
swal′low
swal′lowed
swal′low·er
swal′low-tailed′
swa′mi
swamp
swamped
swan
swan′herd′
swank
swank′i·er
swank′i·est
swank′y
swans′down′
swap
swapped
sward
swarm
swarmed
swart
swarth′y
swash
swas′ti·ka
swat
swatch
swath
swathe
swat′ter
sway
swayed
sway′ing·ly
swear
swear′ing·ly
sweat
sweat′band′
sweat′box′
sweat′er
sweat′i·er
sweat′i·est
sweat′i·ly
sweat′i·ness
sweat′shop
sweat′y
Swed′ish
sweep
sweep′er
sweep′ing·ly
sweep′ings
sweep′stake′
sweet
sweet′bread′
sweet′bri′er
sweet′en
sweet′ened
sweet′en·er
sweet′en·ings
sweet′heart′
sweet′ish
sweet′ish·ly
sweet′ly
sweet′meat′
sweet′ness
sweet′root′
sweet′shop′
sweet′wa′ter
sweet′weed′
sweet′wood′

swell
swelled
swell'er
swell'fish'
swell'ings
swel'ter
swel'tered
swel'ter·ing·ly
swept
swerve
swerved
swift
swift'er
swift'est
swift'ly
swift'ness
swig
swigged
swill
swilled
swim
swim'mer
swim'ming·ly
swin'dle
swin'dled
swin'dler
swine
swine'herd'
swing
swing'ing·ly
swin'ish
swink

swipe
swiped
swirl
swirled
swirl'ing·ly
swish
swished
Swiss
switch
switch'blade'
switch'board'
switch'gear'
switch'keep'er
switch'man
switch'tail'
switch'yard'
swiv'el
swiv'eled
swol'len
swoon
swooned
swoon'ing·ly
swoop
swooped
sword
sword'bill'
sword'fish'
sword'play'
swords'man
sword'stick'
sword'tail'
swore

sworn
swung
swum
syb'a·rite
syc'a·more
syc'o·phan·cy
syc'o·phant
syc'o·phan'tic
syl'la·bi
syl·lab'ic
syl·lab'i·cate
syl·lab'i·cat'ed
syl·lab'i·ca'tion
syl·lab'i·fi·ca'tion
syl·lab'i·fy
syl'la·ble
syl'la·bus
syl'la·bus·es
syl'lo·gism
syl'lo·gis'tic
syl'lo·gize
sylph
syl'van
sym'bi·o'sis
sym'bi·ot'ic
sym'bol
sym·bol'ic
sym·bol'i·cal
sym·bol'i·cal·ly
sym'bol·ism
sym'bol·ist
sym'bol·i·za'tion

sym'bol·ize
sym'bol·ized
sym·met'ri·cal
sym'me·try
sym'pa·thec'to·my
sym'pa·thet'ic
sym'pa·thet'i·cal·ly
sym'pa·thize
sym'pa·thized
sym'pa·thiz'er
sym'pa·thiz'ing·ly
sym'pa·thy
sym·phon'ic
sym'pho·ny
sym'phy·sis
sym·po'si·um
symp'tom
symp'to·mat'ic
symp'tom·a·tol'o·gy
syn'a·gogue
syn·apse'
syn·ap'sis
syn'chro·nism
syn'chro·ni·za'tion
syn'chro·nize
syn'chro·nized
syn'chro·nous
syn'co·pate
syn'co·pat'ed
syn'co·pa'tion
syn'co·pe
syn'cre·tism
syn'dic
syn'di·cal
syn'di·cal·ism
syn'di·cal·ize
syn'di·cate
syn'di·cat'ed
syn'di·ca'tion
syn'dro·me
syn'er·gis'tic
syn'od
syn'od·ist
syn'o·nym
syn·on'y·mous
syn·op'ses
syn·op'sis
syn·op'tic
syn·o'vi·al
syn'o·vi'tis
syn·tac'ti·cal
syn'tax
syn'the·ses
syn'the·sis
syn'the·size
syn'the·sized
syn·thet'ic
syn·thet'i·cal·ly
syr'inge
syr'up
sys'tem
sys'tem·at'ic
sys'tem·a·ti·za'tion
sys'tem·a·tize
sys'tem·a·tized
sys'tem·a·tiz'er
sys'tem·a·tol'o·gy
sys·tem'ic
sys·tem'i·cal·ly
sys'to·le
sys·tol'ic
syz'y·gy

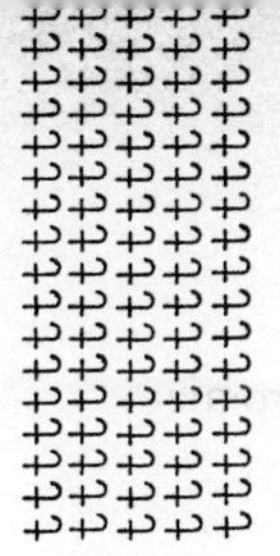

tab
tab'ard
ta·bas'co
tab'er·nac'le
tab'er·nac'led
ta'bes
tab'la·ture
ta'ble
tab'leau
ta'ble·cloth'
ta'bled
ta'ble·maid'
ta'ble·man
ta'ble·spoon'
tab'let
ta'ble·ware'
tab'loid
ta·boo'
ta'bor
tab'o·ret
ta·bu'
tab'u·lar
tab'u·late
tab'u·lat'ed
tab'u·la'tion
tab'u·la'tor
ta·chis'to·scope
ta·chom'e·ter
ta·chyg'ra·pher
ta·chyg'ra·phy
tac'it
tac'it·ly
tac'i·turn
tac'i·tur'ni·ty
tack
tacked
tack'le
tack'led
tack'ler
tack'y
tact
tact'ful
tact'ful·ly
tact'ful·ness
tac'ti·cal
tac·ti'cian
tac'tics
tac'tile
tact'less
tact'less·ly
tact'less·ness
tad'pole'
taf'fe·ta
taff'rail
taf'fy
tag
tag'board'
tagged
Ta·hi'ti·an
tail
tail'board'
tailed
tail'first'
tail'ings
tail'less
tai'lor

tai'lored
tail'piece'
tail'race'
tail'stock'
taint
taint'ed
take
take'down'
tak'en
tak'er
tak'ing·ly
tak'ing·ness
tak'ings
talc
tal'cum
tale
tale'bear'er
tal'ent
tal'ent·ed
tal'i·pes
tal'is·man
tal'is·man'ic
talk
talk'a·tive
talked
talk'er
tall
tall'er
tall'est
tall'ish
tall'ness
tal'low
tal'lowed
tal'low·i·ness
tal'low·root'
tal'low·wood'
tal'low·y
tal'ly
tal'ly·ho'
tal'ly·man
Tal'mud
Tal·mud'ic
tal'on
tal'oned
tam'a·rack
tam'a·rind
tam'bour
tam'bou·rine'
tame
tamed
tame'ness
tam'er
tam'est
Tam'il
Tam'ma·ny
tamp'er
tam'pered
tam'per·proof'
tam'pon
tan
tan'a·ger
tan'bark'
tan'dem
tang
tan'gent
tan·gen'tial
tan·gen'ti·al'i·ty
tan'ge·rine'
tan'gi·ble
tan'gi·bly
tan'gle
tan'gled
tan'gle·root'
tan'gling·ly
tan'go
tang'y
tank
tank'age
tank'ard
tanked
tank'er
tan'nage
tanned
tan'ner
tan'ner·y
tan'nic
tan'nin
tan'nings
tan'sy
tan'ta·li·za'tion
tan'ta·lize
tan'ta·lized
tan'ta·lum
tan'ta·lus
tan'ta·mount'
tan'trum

tan·vat
tan'wood'
tap
tape
taped
tape'line'
tape'man
ta'per
ta'pered
ta'per·ing·ly
tap'es·try
tape'worm'
tap'hole'
tap'house'
tap'i·o'ca
ta'pir
tap'per
tap'pet
tap'pings
tap'room'
tap'root'
tap'ster
tar
tar'an·tel'la
ta·ran'tu·la
tar'board'
tar·boosh'
tar'brush'
tar'bush'
tar'di·er
tar'di·est
tar'di·ly

tar'di·ness
tar'dy
tare
tar'flow'er
targe
tar'get
tar'iff
tar'la·tan
tar'nish
tar'nished
tar'ot
tar·pau'lin
tar'pon
tar'ra·gon
tarred
tar'ried
tar'ry
tar'ry·ing·ly
tart
tar'tan
tar'tar
tart'let
tart'ness
tar'trate
tar'weed'
task
task'mas'ter
task'mis'tress
task'work'
Tas·ma'ni·an
tas'sel
tas'seled

taste
tast'ed
taste'ful
taste'ful·ly
taste'ful·ness
taste'less
taste'less·ly
taste'less·ness
tast'er
tast'i·er
tast'i·est
tast'i·ly
tast'ing·ly
tast'ings
tast'y
Ta'tar
tat'ter
tat'tered
tat'ting
tat'tle
tat'tled
tat'tler
tat·too'
tat·tooed'
tat·too'er
taught
taunt
taunt'ed
taunt'ing·ly
taupe
tau'rine
taut

taut′en
taut′ened
tau′to·log′i·cal
tau·tol′o·gy
tav′ern
taw′dri·er
taw′dri·est
taw′dri·ly
taw′dri·ness
taw′dry
taw′ny
tax
tax′a·ble
tax·a′tion
taxed
tax′es
tax′i
tax′i·cab′
tax′i·der′mist
tax′i·der′my
tax′i·me′ter
tax′ing·ly
tax·on′o·my
tax′paid′
tax′pay′er
tea
tea′ber′ry
tea′cart′
teach
teach′a·bil′i·ty
teach′a·ble
teach′er
teach′er·age
teach′ing·ly
teach′ings
tea′cup′
teak
tea′ket′tle
teal
team
teamed
team′mate′
team′ster
team′work′
tea′pot′
tear
tear
tear′ful
tear′ful·ly
tear′ful·ness
tear′less
tear′less·ly
tea′room′
tear′stain′
tear′y
tease
teased
teas′er
teas′ing·ly
tea′spoon′
tea′spoon·ful
tea′tast′er
tech′ni·cal
tech′ni·cal′i·ty
tech′ni·cal·ly
tech·ni′cian
tech·nique′
tech·noc′ra·cy
tech′no·crat
tech′no·log′i·cal
tech·nol′o·gy
te′di·ous
te′di·ous·ly
te′di·ous·ness
te′di·um
tee
teed
teem
teemed
teem′ing·ly
tee′ter
tee′ter·board′
tee′tered
teeth
tee·to′tal
tee·to′tal·er
tee·to′tal·ly
tel·au′to·graph
tel′e·cast
tel′e·com·mu′ni·ca′tion
tel′e·gram
tel′e·graph
te·leg′ra·pher
tel′e·graph′ic
te·leg′ra·phy
tel′e·ol′o·gy

tel′e·path′ic
te·lep′a·thy
tel′e·phone
tel′e·phon′ic
tel′e·pho′to
Tel′e-Promp-Ter
tel′e·scope
tel′e·scop′ic
tel′e·type
tel′e·type′set′ter
tel′e·type′writ′er
tel′e·vise
tel′e·vised
tel′e·vi′sion
tel′ford
tell
tell′er
tell′ing·ly
tell′ings
tell′tale′
tel·lu′ri·um
tel′pher
Tel′star
te·mer′i·ty
tem′per
tem′per·a·ment
tem′per·a·men′tal
tem′per·a·men′tal·ly
tem′per·ance
tem′per·ate
tem′per·ate·ly
tem′per·a·ture

tem′pered
tem′pest
tem·pes′tu·ous
tem·pes′tu·ous·ly
tem·pes′tu·ous·ness
tem′plate
tem′ple
tem′pled
tem′po
tem′po·ral
tem′po·ral·ty
tem′po·rar′i·ly
tem′po·rar′y
tem′po·ri·za′tion
tem′po·rize
tem′po·rized
tem′po·riz′er
tem′po·riz′ing·ly
tempt
temp·ta′tion
tempt′ed
tempt′er
tempt′ing·ly
tempt′ing·ness
tempt′ress
ten′a·bil′i·ty
ten′a·ble
te·na′cious
te·na′cious·ly
te·na′cious·ness
te·nac′i·ty
ten′an·cy

ten′ant
ten′ant·a·ble
ten′ant·ed
ten′ant·less
ten′ant·ry
tend
tend′ed
tend′en·cy
tend′er
ten′dered
ten′der·er
ten′der·est
ten′der·foot′
ten′der·loin′
ten′der·ly
ten′der·ness
ten′don
ten′dril
Ten′e·brae
ten′e·brous
ten′e·ment
ten′et
ten′nis
ten′on
ten′or
ten′pins′
tense
tense′ly
tense′ness
tens′er
tens′est
ten′sile

ten'sion
ten'sor
tent
ten'ta·cle
ten'ta·tive
ten'ter·er
ten'ter·hooks'
ten·u'i·ty
ten'u·ous
ten'u·ous·ly
ten'ure
te'pee
tep'id
te·pid'i·ty
tep'id·ly
ter'a·tol'o·gy
ter·cen'te·nar'y
te·re'do
ter'gi·ver·sate'
term
ter'ma·gant
termed
ter'mi·na·ble
ter'mi·nal
ter'mi·nate
ter'mi·nat'ed
ter'mi·na'tion
ter'mi·na'tive
ter'mi·no·log'i·cal
ter'mi·no·log'i·cal·ly
ter'mi·nol'o·gy
ter'mi·nus

ter'mite
term'less
tern
ter'na·ry
ter'race
ter'raced
ter·rain'
ter'ra·pin
ter·raz'zo
ter·res'tri·al
ter'ri·ble
ter'ri·bly
ter'ri·er
ter·rif'ic
ter·rif'i·cal·ly
ter'ri·fied
ter'ri·fy
ter'ri·fy'ing·ly
ter·rine'
ter'ri·to'ri·al
ter'ri·to'ri·al'i·ty
ter'ri·to'ry
ter'ror
ter'ror·ism
ter'ror·ist
ter'ror·is'tic
ter'ror·i·za'tion
ter'ror·ize
ter'ror·ized
terse
terse'ness
ters'er

ters'est
ter'tian
ter'ti·ar'y
tes'sel·late
tes'sel·lat'ed
tes'sel·la'tion
test
tes'ta·ment
tes'ta·men'ta·ry
tes·ta'tor
test'ed
tes'ter
tes'ti·fied
tes'ti·fy
tes'ti·mo'ni·al
tes'ti·mo'ny
test'ing·ly
test'ings
tes'ty
tet'a·nus
teth'er
teth'ered
tet'ra·gon
te·trag'o·nal
te·tral'o·gy
te·tram'e·ter
te'trarch
te·trig'id
Tex'an
tex'as
text
text'book'

tex'tile
tex'tu·al
tex'tu·al·ism
tex'tu·al·ist
tex'tu·al·ly
tex'tur·al
tex'tur·al·ly
tex'ture
tex'tured
tha·las'sic
thal'li·um
than
than'a·top'sis
thane
thank
thanked
thank'ful
thank'ful·ly
thank'ful·ness
thank'less
thanks
thanks·giv'ing
that
thatch
thatched
thau'ma·tur'gist
thau'ma·tur'gy
thaw
the'a·ter
the·at'ri·cal
the·at'ri·cal·ism
the·at'ri·cal'i·ty
the·at'ri·cal·ly
the·at'ri·cals
thee
theft
their
theirs
the'ism
the'ist
the·is'tic
them
the·mat'ic
the·mat'i·cal
theme
them·selves'
then
thence
thence'forth'
thence'for'ward
the·oc'ra·cy
the·od'o·lite
the'o·lo'gi·an
the'o·log'i·cal
the'o·log'i·cal·ly
the·ol'o·gy
the'o·rem
the'o·ret'ic
the'o·ret'i·cal
the'o·ret'i·cal·ly
the'o·rist
the'o·rize
the'o·rized
the'o·riz'er
the'o·ry
the'o·soph'ic
the'o·soph'i·cal
the'o·soph'i·cal·ly
the·os'o·phism
the·os'o·phist
the·os'o·phy
ther'a·peu'tic
ther'a·peu'ti·cal
ther'a·peu'ti·cal·ly
ther'a·py
there
there'a·bouts'
there'a·bove'
there·aft'er
there·at'
there·by'
there'fore
there·from'
there·in'
there'in·aft'er
there·in'be·fore'
there·of'
there·on'
there·to'
there'to·fore'
there·un'der
there'un·to'
there'up·on'
there·with'
ther'mal
therm'i'on

therm′i·on′ic
ther′mite
ther′mo·e·lec′tric
ther·mom′e·ter
ther′mo·met′ric
ther′mo·met′ri·cal
ther′mo·met′ri·cal·ly
ther′mo·stat
the·sau′rus
these
the′ses
the′sis
thew
they
thick
thick′en
thick′ened
thick′en·er
thick′er
thick′est
thick′et
thick′et·ed
thick′head′ed
thick′ly
thick′ness
thick′set′
thick′-skinned′
thick′-wit′ted
thief
thiev′er·y
thiev′ing·ly
thiev′ish

thigh
thill
thim′ble
thim′ble·ful
thim′ble·rig′ger
thin
thing
things
think
think′a·ble
think′er
think′ing·ly
thinks
thin′ly
thin′ner
thin′ness
thin′nest
third
thirst
thirst′ed
thirst′i·ly
thirst′i·ness
thirst′ing·ly
thirst′y
this
this′tle
thith′er
thole
thong
tho·rac′ic
tho′rax
Thor

thorn
thorn′bush′
thorned
thorn′i·er
thorn′i·est
thorn′y
thor′ough
thor′ough·bred′
thor′ough·fare′
thor′ough·go′ing
thor′ough·ly
thor′ough·ness
those
thou
though
thought
thought′ful
thought′ful·ly
thought′ful·ness
thought′less
thought′less·ly
thought′less·ness
thou′sand
thou′sand·fold′
thou′sandth
thrall
thrall′dom
thrash
thrashed
thrash′er
thrash′ings
thra·son′i·cal

thread
thread′bare′
thread′ed
thread′weed′
thread′worm′
thread′y
threat
threat′en
threat′ened
threat′en·ing·ly
three
three′some
thren′o·dy
thre′nos
thresh
threshed
thresh′er
thresh′old
threw
thrice
thrift
thrift′i·er
thrift′i·est
thrift′i·ly
thrift′i·ness
thrift′less
thrift′less·ly
thrift′less·ness
thrift′y
thrill
thrilled
thrill′ing·ly

thrips
thrive
thriv′ing·ly
throat
throat′ed
throat′i·er
throat′i·est
throat′i·ly
throat′i·ness
throat′root′
throat′wort′
throat′y
throb
throbbed
throb′bing·ly
throes
throm·bo′sis
throm′bus
throne
throne′less
throne′like′
throng
thronged
throng′ing·ly
throt′tle
throt′tled
throt′tling·ly
through
through·out′
throw
throw′back′
throw′er

thrown
throw′off′
thrum
thrummed
thrush
thrust
thud
thud′ded
thud′ding·ly
thug
thug′ger·y
thu′li·um
thumb
thumbed
thumb′mark′
thumb′nail′
thumb′piece′
thumb′print′
thump
thumped
thump′ing·ly
thump′ings
thun′der
thun′der·bird′
thun′der·bolt′
thun′dered
thun′der·fish′
thun′der·head′
thun′der·ing
thun′der·ing·ly
thun′der·ings
thun′der·ous

thun′der·show′er
thun′der·struck′
thun′der·y
thun′drous
thu′ri·ble
Thurs′day
thus
thwack
thwacked
thwack′ing·ly
thwart
thwart′ed
thwart′ing·ly
thy
thyme
thy′mus
thy′roid
thy·self′
ti·ar′a
tib′i·a
tick
ticked
tick′er
tick′et
tick′et·ed
tick′ings
tick′le
tick′led
tick′ler
tick′ling·ly
tick′lish
tick′lish·ly
tick′lish·ness
tid′al
tid′bit′
tide
tid′ed
tide′race′
tide′wa′ter
tide′way′
ti′died
ti′di·er
ti′di·est
ti′di·ly
ti′di·ness
ti′dings
ti′dy
tie
tie′back′
tied
tier
tiered
tiff
tif′fa·ny
tiffed
tif′fin
ti′ger
ti′ger·ish
ti′ger·like′
ti′ger·wood′
tight
tight′en
tight′ened
tight′en·er
tight′en·ing
tight′er
tight′est
tight′fist′ed
tight′ly
tight′rope′
tight′wad′
til′bu·ry
til′de
tile
tiled
tile′fish′
til′er
tile′root′
till
till′a·ble
till′age
tilled
till′er
tilt
tilt′ed
tilth
tilt′yard′
tim′bale
tim′ber
tim′bered
tim′ber·land′
tim′ber·wood′
tim′ber·work′
time
timed
time′keep′er

time′less
time′less·ly
time′less·ness
time′li·ness
time′ly
time′piece′
tim′er
time′serv′ing
time′ta′ble
tim′id
ti·mid′i·ty
tim′id·ly
tim′ings
tim′or·ous
tim′or·ous·ly
tin
tinct
tinct′ed
tinc′ture
tinc′tured
tin′der
tin′der·box′
tine
tined
tine′weed′
tinge
tinged
tin′gle
tin′gled
tin′gling·ly
tin′glings
tin′horn′

tink′er
tink′ered
tin′kle
tin′kled
tin′kling·ly
tin′klings
tinned
tin′ni·er
tin′ni·est
tin′ni·ly
tin′ni·ness
tin·ni′tus
tin′ny
tin′sel
tin′seled
tin′smith′
tint
tint′ed
tin′tin·nab′u·la′tion
tin′type′
tin′ware′
tin′work′
ti′ny
tip
tipped
tip′pet
tip′ple
tip′pled
tip′pler
tip′si·er
tip′si·est
tip′ster

tip′sy
tip′toe′
tip′toed′
tip′toe′ing·ly
tip′top′
ti′rade
tire
tired
tire′less
tire′less·ly
tire′less·ness
tire′some
tire′some·ly
tire′some·ness
tir′ing·ly
tis′sue
tis′sued
tis′sues
Ti′tan
ti·tan′ic
ti′tan·if′er·ous
ti·ta′ni·um
tit′bit′
tith′a·ble
tithe
tithed
tith′ings
ti′tian
tit′il·late
tit′il·lat′ed
tit′il·lat′ing·ly
tit′il·la′tion

tit'il·la'tive
tit'i·vate
tit'i·vat'ed
tit'i·va'tion
ti'tle
ti'tled
ti'tle·hold'er
tit'mouse'
ti'trate
ti'trat·ed
ti·tra'tion
tit'ter
tit'tered
tit'ter·ingly
tit'ter·ings
tit'tle
tit'tup
tit'u·lar
tit'u·lar·ly
tit'u·lar'y
to
toad
toad'fish'
toad'root'
toad'stone'
toad'stool'
toad'y
toast
toast'ed
toast'er
to·bac'co
to·bog'gan
to·bog'ganed
toc·ca'ta
toc'sin
to·day'
tod'dle
tod'dled
tod'dler
tod'dy
toe
toe'cap'
toed
toe'nail'
toe'plate'
tof'fee
to'ga
to·geth'er
to·geth'er·ness
tog'gle
tog'gled
toil
toiled
toil'er
toi'let
toi'let·ry
toi'let·ware'
toil'ing·ly
To·kay'
to'ken
to'kened
told
tol'er·a·ble
tol'er·a·bly
tol'er·ance
tol'er·ant
tol'er·ate
tol'er·at'ed
tol'er·a'tion
tol'er·a'tion·ism
tol'er·a'tive
toll
tolled
toll'gate'
toll'house'
tom'a·hawk
to·ma'to
tomb
tombed
tom'bo·la
tom'boy'
tomb'stone'
tom'cat'
tom'cod'
tome
tom'fool'
tom'fool'er·y
tom'fool'ish·ness
to·mor'row
ton
ton'al
ton'al·ist
to·nal'i·ty
tone
toned
tone'less

tongs
tongue
tongued
ton'ic
ton'i·cal·ly
to·nic'i·ty
to·night'
ton'ka
ton'nage
ton·neau'
ton'sil
ton'sil·li'tis
ton·so'ri·al
ton'sure
ton'tine
too
took
tool
tool'box'
tooled
tool'ings
tool'mak'er
tool'room'
tool'smith'
toot
toot'ed
tooth
tooth'ache'
tooth'brush'
toothed
tooth'less
tooth'less·ly
tooth'less·ness
tooth'pick'
tooth'some
too'tle
too'tled
top
to'paz
top'coat'
top'er
to'pi·a·rist
to'pi·ar'y
top'ic
top'i·cal
top'knot'
top'less
top'loft'y
top'man
top'mast'
top'most
to·pog'ra·pher
top'o·graph'ic
top'o·graph'i·cal
top'o·graph'i·cal·ly
to·pog'ra·phy
topped
top'per
top'piece'
top'ping·ly
top'pings
top'ple
top'pled
top'sail'
top'side'
top'stone'
toque
torch
torch'light'
torch'weed'
torch'wood'
tore
tor'e·a·dor'
tor·ment'
tor·ment'ed
tor·ment'ing·ly
tor·men'tor
tor·na'do
tor·pe'do
tor·pe'doed
tor'pid
tor·pid'i·ty
tor'pid·ly
tor'por
torque
tor'rent
tor·ren'tial
tor·ren'tial·ly
tor'rid
tor·rid'i·ty
tor'rid·ly
tor'sion
tor'sion·al
tor'so
tort
tor'toise

tor′tu·os′i·ty
tor′tu·ous
tor′tu·ous·ly
tor′tu·ous·ness
tor′ture
tor′tured
tor′tur·er
tor′tur·ing·ly
tor′tur·ous
tor′tur·ous·ly
To′ry
toss
tossed
toss′ing·ly
toss′ings
toss′up′
to′tal
to′taled
to·tal′i·tar′i·an
to·tal′i·tar′i·an·ism
to·tal′i·ty
to′tal·i·za′tion
to′tal·i·za′tor
to′tal·ize
to′tal·ized
to′tal·iz′er
to′tal·ly
tote
tot′ed
to′tem
toth′er
tot′ter
tot′tered
tot′ter·ing·ly
tot′ter·ings
tot′ter·y
tou·can′
touch
touch′a·ble
touch′down′
touched
touch′hole′
touch′i·er
touch′i·est
touch′i·ly
touch′i·ness
touch′ing·ly
touch′stone′
touch′wood′
touch′y
tough
tough′en
tough′ened
tough′er
tough′est
tou·pee′
tour
toured
tour′ism
tour′ist
tour′ma·line
tour′na·ment
tour′ney
tour′ni·quet
tou′sle
tou′sled
tout
tout′ed
to·va′rish
tow
tow′age
to′ward
to′wards
tow′boat′
towed
tow′el
tow′el·ings
tow′er
tow′ered
tow′er·ing·ly
tow′er·man
tow′head′
tow′line′
town
town′folk′
town′ship
towns′man
town′wear′
tow′path′
tow′rope′
tox·e′mi·a
tox′ic
tox·ic′i·ty
tox′i·co·log′i·cal
tox′i·col′o·gist
tox′i·col′o·gy

tox'i·co'sis
tox'oid
toy
toyed
toy'ing·ly
toy'man
toy'shop'
trace
trace'a·ble
traced
trac'er
trac'er·y
tra'che·a
tra'che·al
tra·cho'ma
trac'ings
track
track'age
tracked
track'er
track'lay'er
track'less
track'man
track'mas'ter
tract
trac'ta·bil'i·ty
trac'ta·ble
trac'ta·bly
trac·tar'i·an
trac'tate
trac'tile
trac'tion
trac'tive
trac'tor
trac'tor·ize
trade
trad'ed
trad'er
trades'man
tra·di'tion
tra·di'tion·al
tra·di'tion·al·ism
tra·di'tion·al·ly
tra·duce'
tra·duced'
tra·duc'er
tra·duc'ing·ly
traf'fic
traf'ficked
trag'a·canth
tra·ge'di·an
tra·ge'di·enne'
trag'e·dy
trag'ic
trag'i·cal
trag'i·cal·ly
trag'i·com'e·dy
tra'gus
trail
trailed
trail'er
trail'ing·ly
train
train'band'
trained
train'er
train'ful
train'load'
train'man
trait
trai'tor
trai'tor·ous
trai'tor·ous·ly
tra·jec'to·ry
tram
tram'car'
tram'mel
tram'meled
tram'mel·ing·ly
tra·mon'tane
tramp
tramped
tram'ple
tram'pled
tram'po·lin
tram'road'
tram'way'
trance
trance'like'
tran'quil
tran'quil·i·za'tion
tran'quil·ize
tran'quil·ized
tran'quil·iz'er
tran'quil·iz'ing·ly
tran·quil'li·ty

tran′quil·ly
trans·act′
trans·act′ed
trans·ac′tion
trans·al′pine
trans′at·lan′tic
tran·scend′
tran·scend′ed
tran·scend′ence
tran·scend′en·cy
tran·scend′ent
tran′scen·den′tal
tran′scen·den′tal·ism
tran′scen·den′tal·ist
trans′con·ti·nen′tal
tran·scribe′
tran·scribed′
tran·scrib′er
tran′script
tran·scrip′tion
trans·duc′er
trans·duc′tion
tran′sept
trans·fer′
trans·fer′a·bil′i·ty
trans·fer′a·ble
trans·fer′al
trans·fer′ence
trans′ferred′
trans·fer′rer
trans·fig′u·ra′tion
trans·fig′ure
trans·fig′ured
trans·fig′ure·ment
trans·fix′
trans·fixed′
trans·form′
trans′for·ma′tion
trans·formed′
trans·form′er
trans·form′ing·ly
trans·fuse′
trans·fused′
trans·fu′sion
trans·fu′sions
trans·gress′
trans·gressed′
trans·gress′ing·ly
trans·gres′sion
trans·gres′sor
tran′sient
tran·sis′tor
tran·sis′tor·ize
trans′it
tran·si′tion
tran·si′tion·al
tran·si′tion·al·ly
tran′si·tive
tran′si·tive·ly
tran′si·tive·ness
tran′si·to′ry
trans·lat′a·ble
trans·late′
trans·lat′ed
trans·la′tion
trans·la′tor
trans·la′to·ry
trans·lit′er·ate
trans·lu′cence
trans·lu′cen·cy
trans·lu′cent
trans·lu′cent·ly
trans′ma·rine′
trans·mi′grant
trans′mi·gra′tion
trans·mis′si·ble
trans·mis′sion
trans·mit′
trans·mit′tal
trans·mit′ted
trans·mit′ter
trans·mog′ri·fi·ca′tion
trans·mog′ri·fied
trans·mog′ri·fy
trans·mut′a·ble
trans′mu·ta′tion
trans·mute′
trans·mut′ed
tran′som
trans′pa·cif′ic
trans·par′en·cy
trans·par′ent
tran′spi·ra′tion
tran·spir′a·to′ry
tran·spire′
tran·spired′

trans·plant'
trans'plan·ta'tion
trans·plant'ed
trans·port'
trans'por·ta'tion
trans·port'ed
trans·port'ing·ly
trans·pos'al
trans·pose'
trans·posed'
trans'po·si'tion
trans·ship'
trans·ship'ment
tran'sub·stan'ti·a'tion
trans·ver'sal
trans·verse'
trap
trap door
tra·peze'
tra·pe'zi·um
trap'e·zoid
trapped
trap'per
trap'pings
Trap'pist
trap'rock'
trap'shoot'ing
trash
trash'i·er
trash'i·est
trash'y
trau'ma

trau'ma·ta
trau·mat'ic
trau·mat'i·cal·ly
trau'ma·tism
trau'ma·tize
trav'ail
trav'el
trav'eled
trav'el·er
trav'e·logue
trav'ers·a·ble
trav'ers·al
trav'erse
trav'ersed
trav'er·tine
trav'es·ty
trawl
trawl'er
tray
treach'er·ous
treach'er·ous·ly
treach'er·ous·ness
treach'er·y
trea'cle
tread
trea'dle
tread'mill'
trea'son
trea'son·a·ble
treas'ure
treas'ured
treas'ur·er

treas'ur·y
treat
treat'ed
trea'tise
treat'ment
trea'ty
tre'ble
tre'bled
tree
treed
tree'nail'
trek
trekked
trel'lis
trel'lised
trem'ble
trem'bled
trem'bling·ly
trem'blings
tre·men'dous
tre·men'dous·ly
tre'mo·lan'do
trem'o·lo
trem'or
trem'u·lous
trem'u·lous·ly
trem'u·lous·ness
trench
trench'an·cy
trench'ant
trench'ant·ly
trench'er

trench'er·man
trend
trend'ed
tre·pan'
tre·phine'
tre·phined'
trep'i·da'tion
tres'pass
tres'passed
tres'pass·er
tress
tres'tle
tres'tle·work'
tri'ad
tri·ad'ic
tri'al
tri'an'gle
tri·an'gu·lar
tri·an'gu·lar'i·ty
tri·an'gu·late
tri·an'gu·lat'ed
tri·an'gu·la'tion
trib'al
trib'al·ism
tri·bas'ic
tribe
tribes'man
trib'u·la'tion
tri·bu'nal
trib'une
trib'u·tar'y
trib'ute

trice
tri'ceps
tri·chi'na
trich'i·no'sis
tri·chot'o·my
trick
tricked
trick'er·y
trick'i·er
trick'i·est
trick'i·ly
trick'i·ness
trick'le
trick'led
trick'ling·ly
trick'lings
trick'ster
trick'sy
trick'y
tri'col'or
tri'corn
tri'cot
tri'cy·cle
tri'dent
tried
tri·en'ni·al
tri·en'ni·al·ly
tri'fle
tri'fled
tri'fler
tri'fling·ly
tri'flings

trig
trig'ger
trig'gered
trig'ger·fish'
tri'glyph
trig'o·no·met'ric
trig'o·no·met'ri·cal
trig'o·nom'e·try
tri·lem'ma
tri·lin'gual
trill
trilled
tril'lion
Tril'li·um
tri'lo·bite
tril'o·gy
tri·mes'ter
trimmed
trim'mer
trim'mings
trim'ness
tri·month'ly
trin'i·ty
trin'ket
tri·no'mi·al
tri'o
tri'ode
tri'o·let
trip
tri·par'tite
tripe
triph'thong

tri'ple
tri'pled
tri'plet
tri'plex
trip'li·cate
trip'li·cat'ed
trip'li·ca'tion
tri'ply
tri'pod
tripped
trip'per
trip'ping·ly
trip'tych
tri'reme
tri'sect'
tri'sect'ed
tri·sec'tion
tri·sec'tor
tris·kel'i·on
tris'yl·lab'ic
trite
trite'ly
trite'ness
Tri'ton
tri'tone'
trit'u·rate
trit'u·rat'ed
trit'u·ra'tion
tri'umph
tri·um'phal
tri·um'phant
tri'umphed
tri'umph·ing·ly
tri·um'vir
tri·um'vi·rate
tri'une
tri·va'lent
triv'et
triv'i·a
triv'i·al
triv'i·al'i·ty
triv'i·al·ly
tro·cha'ic
tro'che
troi'ka
troll
trolled
trol'ley
trom'bone
troop
trooped
troop'er
troop'ship'
trope
tro'phy
trop'ic
trop'i·cal
trop'i·cal·ly
tro'pism
trop'ist
tro·pol'o·gy
trop'o·pause
trop'o·sphere
trot
troth
trot'line'
trot'ted
trot'ter
trou'ba·dour
trou'ble
trou'bled
trou'ble·some
trou'ble·some·ly
trou'ble·some·ness
trou'bling·ly
trou'blous
trough
trough'like'
trounce
trounced
trounc'ings
troupe
troup'er
trou'sers
trous'seau'
trout
trout'let
trout'ling
trow'el
trow'eled
troy
tru'an·cy
tru'ant
tru'ant·ism
truce
tru'cial

truck
truck'age
trucked
truck'er
truck'le
truck'led
truck'ling·ly
truck'man
truc'u·lence
truc'u·lent
trudge
trudged
trudg'en
true
trued
true'love'
true'ness
truf'fle
truf'fled
tru'ism
tru'ly
trump
trumped
trump'er·y
trum'pet
trum'pet·ed
trum'pet·er
trum'pet·ings
trum'pet·like'
trum'pet·weed'
trum'pet·wood'
trun'cate
trun'cat·ed
trun·ca'tion
trun'cheon
trun'dle
trun'dled
trunk
trun'nion
truss
trussed
truss'ings
trust
trus·tee'
trus·tee'ship
trust'ful
trust'ful·ly
trust'ful·ness
trust'i·er
trust'i·est
trust'ing·ly
trust'wor'thi·ness
trust'wor'thy
trust'y
truth
truth'ful
truth'ful·ly
truth'ful·ness
try
try'ing·ly
try'sail'
tryst
tryst'ed
tset'se
tub
tu'ba
tubbed
tub'bi·er
tub'bi·est
tub'bings
tub'by
tube
tu'ber
tu'ber·cle
tu·ber'cu·lar
tu·ber'cu·lin
tu·ber'cu·lo'sis
tu·ber'cu·lous
tu'ber·os'i·ty
tu'ber·ous
tub'ings
tu'bu·lar
tu'bu·la'tion
tuck
tucked
Tu'dor
Tues'day
tuft
tuft'ed
tuft'ings
tug
tug'boat'
tugged
tug'ging·ly
tug'gings
tu·i'tion

tu'la·re'mi·a
tu'lip
tu'lip·wood'
tulle
tum'ble
tum'bled
tum'bler
tum'ble·weed'
tum'bling·ly
tum'brel
tu'me·fac'tion
tu'me·fied
tu'me·fy
tu'mid
tu·mid'i·ty
tu'mor
tu'mor·ous
tu'mult
tu·mul'tu·ous
tu·mul'tu·ous·ly
tu·mul'tu·ous·ness
tu'mu·lus
tun
tu'na
tun'dra
tune
tuned
tune'ful
tune'less
tune'less·ly
tune'less·ness
tun'er
tung'sten
tu'nic
tun'ings
Tu·ni'sian
tun'nel
tun'neled
tun'ny
tu'pe·lo
tur'ban
tur'bid
tur·bid'i·ty
tur'bid·ly
tur'bi·nate
tur'bine
tur'bot
tur'bu·lence
tur'bu·lent
tur'bu·lent·ly
tu·reen'
turf
turfed
turf'man
tur'gid
tur·gid'i·ty
tur'gid·ly
Turk
tur'key
Turk'ish
tur'mer·ic
tur'moil
turn
turn'buck'le
turn'coat'
turn'cock'
turned
turn'er
turn'ings
tur'nip
turn'key'
turn'off'
turn'out'
turn'o'ver
turn'pike'
turn'spit'
turn'stile'
tur'pen·tine
tur'pi·tude
tur'quoise
tur'ret
tur'ret·ed
tur'tle
Tus'can
tusk
tusked
tus'sle
tus'sled
tus'sock
tu'te·lage
tu'te·lar'y
tu'tor
tu'tored
tu·to'ri·al
tux·e'do
twad'dle

twad'dled
twain
twang
twanged
tweak
tweaked
tweed
tweez'ers
twice
twid'dle
twid'dled
twig
twi'light'
twill
twilled
twin
twin'born'
twine
twined
twinge
twinged
twin'kle
twin'kled
twin'kling·ly

twin'klings
twirl
twirled
twist
twist'ed
twist'er
twist'ings
twit
twitch
twitched
twit'ted
twit'ter
twit'tered
twit'ter·ing·ly
twit'ter·ings
two
two'fold'
two'some
ty·coon'
type
typed
type'set'ter
type'writ'er
type'writ·ten

ty'phoid
ty·phoi'dal
ty·phoon'
ty'phous
ty'phus
typ'i·cal
typ'i·cal·ly
typ'i·fi·ca'tion
typ'i·fy
typ'ings
typ'ist
ty·pog'ra·pher
ty'po·graph'ic
ty·pog'ra·phy
ty·poth'e·tae
ty·ran'ni·cal
ty·ran'ni·cide
tyr'an·nize
tyr'an·nized
ty'ran·niz'ing·ly
tyr'an·nous
tyr'an·ny
ty'rant
ty'ro

# U

u·biq'ui·tous
u·biq'ui·tous·ly
u·biq'ui·ty
ud'der
ug'li·er
ug'li·est
ug'li·ness
ug'ly
uh'lan
u·kase'
u'ku·le'le
ul'cer
ul'cer·ate
ul'cer·at'ed
ul'cer·a'tion
ul'cer·a'tive
ul'cer·ous
ul'cer·ous·ly
ul'na
ul'nar
ul'ster
ul·te'ri·or

ul'ti·mate
ul'ti·mate·ly
ul'ti·ma'tum
ul'ti·mo
ul'tra·ism
ul'tra·le·gal'i·ty
ul'tra·ma·rine'
ul'tra·mi'cro·scope
ul'tra·mod'ern
ul'tra·mon'tane
ul'tra·na'tion·al·ism
ul'tra·na'tion·al·ist
ul'tra·red'
ul'tra·son'ic
ul'tra·vi'o·let
ul'u·late
ul'u·lat'ed
ul'u·la'tion
um'ber
um'bra
um'brage
um·bra'geous

um·brel'la
um'laut
um'pire
um'pired
un·a'ble
un'a·bridged'
un'ac·cent'ed
un'ac·cept'a·ble
un'ac·com'mo·dat'ing
un'ac·com'pa·nied
un'ac·count'a·ble
un'ac·cus'tomed
un'ac·quaint'ed
un'a·dorned'
un'a·dul'ter·at'ed
un'af·fect'ed
un'al·loyed'
un·al'ter·a·ble
un'al'tered
un'-A·mer'i·can
un·a'mi·a·ble
u·nan'i·mous

un·an′swer·a·ble
un′ap·peas′a·ble
un′ap·proach′a·ble
un′ap·pro′pri·at′ed
un′ap·prov′ing·ly
un·armed′
un′a·shamed′
un·asked′
un′as·sail′a·ble
un′as·signed′
un′as·sim′i·lat′ed
un′as·sist′ed
un′as·sum′ing·ly
un′at·tached′
un′at·tain′a·ble
un′at·tempt′ed
un′at·trac′tive·ly
un·au′thor·ized
un′a·vail′a·ble
un′a·vail′ing·ly
un′a·void′a·ble
un′a·ware′
un·bal′anced
un·bal′last·ed
un·bar′
un·barred′
un·bear′a·bly
un·beat′a·ble
un′be·com′ing·ly
un′be·fit′ting·ly
un′be·known′
un′be·knownst′

unbe·lief′
un′be·liev′a·ble
un′be·liev′er
un′be·liev′ing·ly
un′be·liev′ing·ness
un·bend′
un·bend′ing·ly
un·bi′ased
un·bid′den
un·bind′
un·blem′ished
un·blessed′
un·blocked′
un·blush′ing·ly
un·bolt′
un·bolt′ed
un·born′
un·bos′om
un·bos′omed
un·bound′
un·bound′ed
un·bowed′
un·break′a·ble
un·bri′dled
un·bro′ken
un·buck′le
un·bur′den
un·bur′dened
un·burned′
un·busi′ness·like′
un·but′ton
un·but′toned

un·cage′
un·can′ny
un·cap′ti·vat′ed
un·car′pet·ed
un·cat′a·logued
un·ceas′ing·ly
un′cer·e·mo′ni·ous
un·cer′tain
un·cer′tain·ly
un·cer′tain·ness
un·cer′tain·ty
un·chal′lenged
un·change′a·ble
un·change′a·bly
un·chang′ing·ly
un·char′i·ta·ble
un·chid′ing·ly
un·chris′tened
un·chris′tian
un′ci·al
un·civ′il
un·civ′i·lized
un·clad′
un·claimed′
un·clasp′
un′cle
un·clean′
un·clean′ly
un·closed′
un·clothe′
un·coil′
un′col·lect′ed

un·colt′
un·com′fort·a·ble
un·com′fort·a·ble·ness
un·com′mon
un′com·mu′ni·ca′tive
un·com′pa·nied
un·com′pro·mis′ing
un′con·cerned′
un′con·di′tion·al
un′con·di′tion·al′i·ty
un′con·fined′
un′con·firmed′
un′con·form′i·ty
un′con·gen′ial
un·con′quer·a·ble
un·con′quered
un·con′scion·a·ble
un·con′scious
un·con′scious·ly
un·con′scious·ness
un·con′se·crat′ed
un·con′se·quen′tial
un′con·se·quen′tial·ly
un′con·sid′er·ate·ly
un′con·sid′ered
un′con·sti·tu′tion·al
un′con·sti·tu′tion·al·ly
un′con·strained′
un′con·strain′ed·ly
un′con·tam′i·nat′ed
un′con·tra·dic′to·ry
un′con·trol′la·ble
un′con·trolled′
un′con·ven′tion·al
un′con·ven′tion·al·ly
un′con·vert′ed
un′con·vinced′
un′con·vinc′ing·ly
un′co-op′er·a′tive
un·cork′
un·corked′
un′cor·rect′ed
un′cor·rupt′ed
un·count′a·ble
un·count′ed
un·cou′ple
un·cou′pled
un·couth′
un·couth′ness
un·cov′er
un·cov′ered
un·cowed′
un·creased′
un·crit′i·cal
un·crit′i·ciz′ing·ly
un·crowd′ed
un·crowned′
unc′tion
unc′tu·ous
un·cul′ti·vat′ed
un·cul′tured
un·curbed′
un·curl′
un·cut′
un·dam′aged
un·damped′
un·dashed′
un·dat′ed
un·daunt′ed
un′de·ceive′
un′de·ceived′
un′de·cid′ed
un′de·ci′pher·a·ble
un′de·ci′phered
un·dec′o·rous
un′de·feat′ed
un′de·fend′ed
un′de·filed′
un′de·fin′a·ble
un′de·liv′er·a·ble
un′dem·o-crat′ic
un′de·mon′stra-tive
un′de·ni′a·ble
un′de·pend′a·ble
un′de·pos′it·ed
un′der
un′der·a·chiev′er
un′der·arm′
un′der·bid′
un′der·bod′y
un′der·brush′
un′der·buy′
un′der·cap′i·tal·i·za′tion
un′der·cap′i·tal·ize
un′der·car′riage
un′der·charge′

un′der·charged′
un′der·class′man
un′der·clothes′
un′der·coat′
un′der·con·sump′tion
un′der·cov′er
un′der·cur′rent
un′der·cut′
un′der·done′
un′der·dose′
un′der·es′ti·mate
un′der·ex·pose′
un′der·feed′
un′der·foot′
un′der·gar′ment
un′der·glaze′
un′der·go′
un′der·grad′u·ate
un′der·ground′
un′der·growth′
un′der·hand′ed
un′der·hand′ed·ly
un′der·hand′ed·ness
un′der·hung′
un′der·laid′
un′der·lay′
un′der·lie′
un′der·line′
un′der·lined′
un′der·lings
un′der·manned′
un′der·mine′
un′der·mined′
un′der·neath′
un′der·nour′ish
un′der·nour′ished
un′der·nour′ish·ment
un′der·pass′
un′der·pin′nings
un′der·priv′i·leged
un′der·pro·duc′tion
un′der·quote′
un′der·rate′
un′der·rat′ed
un′der·score′
un′der·scored′
un′der·sec′re·tar′y
un′der·sell′
un′der·shirt′
un′der·shot′
un′der·signed′
un′der·sized′
un′der·skirt′
un′der·slung′
un′der·sparred′
un′der·stand′
un′der·stand′ing·ly
un′der·stand′ings
un′der·state′
un′der·state′ment
un′der·stood′
un′der·stud′y
un′der·take′
un′der·tak′en
un′der·tak′er
un′der·tak′ings
un′der·things′
un′der·tone′
un′der·took′
un′der·tow′
un′der·turn′
un′der·val′ue
un′der·wa′ter
un′der·wear′
un′der·weight′
un′der·world′
un′der·write′
un′der·writ′er
un′de·scrib′a·ble
un′de·served′
un′de·sir′a·ble
un′de′sired′
un′de·stroyed′
un′de·tect′ed
un′de·ter′mined
un′de·vel′oped
un′di·ag·nosed′
un·di′a·pered
un′di·gest′ed
un·dig′ni·fied
un′di·lut′ed
un′di·min′ished
un·dimmed′
un′di·rect′ed
un·dis′ci·plined
un′dis·closed′

un'dis·cov'ered
un'dis·crim'i·nat'ing·ly
un'dis·guised'
un'dis·tin'guished
un'dis·trib'ut·ed
un'di·vid'ed
un·do'
un'do·mes'ti·cat'ed
un·done'
un·doubt'ed
un·doubt'ed·ly
un'dra·mat'i·cal·ly
un·draped'
un·drawn'
un·dress'
un·dressed'
un·drink'a·ble
un·due'
un'du·lant
un'du·late
un'du·lat'ed
un'du·la'tion
un·du'ly
un·du'ti·ful
un·dy'ing·ly
un·earned'
un·earth'
un·earthed'
un·earth'ly
un·eas'i·er
un·eas'i·est
un·eas'i·ly
un·eas'i·ness
un·eas'y
un·eat'a·ble
un·ed'u·ca·ble
un·ed'u·cat'ed
un'em·bar'rassed
un'em·bit'tered
un'em·broi'dered
un'e·mo'tion·al
un'em·ploy'a·ble
un'em·ploy'a·ble·ness
un'em·ployed'
un'em·ploy'ment
un'en·cum'bered
un'en·dan'gered
un·end'ing
un'en·dorsed'
un'en·dur'a·ble
un'en·force'a·ble
un'en·gaged'
un'en·graved'
un'en·grossed'
un'en·larged'
un'en·light'ened
un'en·slaved'
un·en'tered
un·en'ter·pris'ing
un'en·ter·tain'ing
un'en·thu'si·as'tic
un'en·thu'si·as'ti·cal·ly
un·en'vi·a·ble
un·en'vi·a·bly
un·en'vied
un·e'qual
un·e'qual·a·ble
un·e'qualed
un·e'qual·ize
un·e'qual·ized
un·e'qual·ly
un'e·quipped'
un'e·quiv'o·cal
un'e·rad'i·cat'ed
un'e·ras'a·ble
un'e·rased'
un'err'ing
un·err'ing·ly
un'es·sen'tial
un·es'ti·mat'ed
un·eth'i·cal
un·eth'i·cal·ly
un·e'ven
un·e'ven·ly
un'e·vent'ful
un'e·vent'ful·ly
un'ex·am'pled
un'ex·celled'
un'ex·cep'tion·a·ble
un'ex·cep'tion·al
un'ex·cit'a·ble
un'ex·cit'ing
un'ex·cused'
un·ex'e·cut'ed
un'ex·haust'ed
un'ex·pect'ed

un′ex·pect′ed·ly
un′ex·pect′ed·ness
un′ex·plain′a·ble
un′ex·plained′
un′ex·ploit′ed
un′ex·posed′
un′ex·pressed′
un′ex·press′i·ble
un·ex′pur·gat′ed
un′ex·tin′guished
un·ex′tri·cat′ed
un·fad′ed
un·fad′ing·ly
un·fail′ing·ly
un·fair′
un·fair′ly
un·fair′ness
un·faith′ful
un·faith′ful·ly
un·faith′ful·ness
un·fal′ter·ing
un′fa·mil′iar
un·farmed′
un·fash′ion·a·ble
un·fash′ion·a·bly
un·fas′ten
un·fas′tened
un·fa′ther·ly
un·fath′om·a·ble
un·fath′omed
un′fa·tigue′a·ble
un′fa·tigued′
un·fa′vor·able
un·fa′vor·a·bly
un·fear′ing·ly
un·fea′si·ble
un·fea′si·bly
un·fed′
un·feel′ing·ly
un·feigned′
un·felt′
un·fem′i·nine
un·fenced′
un′fe·nes′trat·ed
un′fer·ment′ed
un·fer′ti·lized
un·fet′ter
un·fet′tered
un·filed′
un·fil′i·al
un·fil′i·al·ly
un·fill′a·ble
un·fil′tered
un·fin′ished
un·fit′
un·fit′ting·ly
un·flag′ging·ly
un·flat′ter·ing·ly
un·flick′er·ing·ly
un·flinch′ing·ly
un·flinch′ing·ness
un·flood′ed
un·flur′ried
un·flus′tered
un·fo′cused
un·fold′
un·fold′ed
un·forced′
un′fore·see′a·ble
un′fore·seen′
un′fore·tell′a·ble
un·for′feit·ed
un′for·get′ta·ble
un′for·get′ting·ly
un′for·giv′a·ble
un′for·giv′en
un′for·giv′ing·ly
un′for·giv′ing·ness
un′for·got′ten
un·for′mal·ized
un·formed′
un·for′ti·fied
un·for′tu·nate
un·for′tu·nate·ly
un·found′ed
un·frayed′
un′fre·quent′ed
un·friend′ed
un·friend′li·ness
un·friend′ly
un·frock′
un·frocked′
un·fru′gal
un·fruit′ful
un·fu′eled
un′ful·filled′

un·fund′ed
un·fun′ny
un·fur′bished
un·furl′
un·furled′
un·fur′nished
un·gain′li·ness
un·gain′ly
un·gal′lant
un·gar′land·ed
un·gar′nished
un·gen′er·ous
un·gen′tle
un·gen′tle·man·ly
un·ger′mi·nat′ed
un·gift′ed
un·girt′
un·glazed′
un·glo′ri·ous
un·gloved′
un·god′li·ness
un·god′ly
un·gov′ern·a·ble
un·gov′ern·a·bly
un·gra′cious
un·gra′cious·ly
un·grad′ed
un′gram·mat′i·cal
un·grate′ful
un·grate′ful·ly
un·grate′ful·ness
un·ground′ed
un·grudg′ing·ly
un·guard′ed
un·guard′ed·ly
un′guent
un·guid′ed
un·gummed′
un·hack′neyed
un·hal′lowed
un·ham′pered
un·hand′i·ness
un·hand′some
un·hand′y
un·hanged′
un·hap′pi·er
un·hap′pi·est
un·hap′pi·ly
un·hap′pi·ness
un·hap′py
un·hard′ened
un·harmed′
un·har′ness
un·har′nessed
un·har′vest·ed
un·hatched′
un·healed′
un·health′ful
un·health′ful·ness
un·health′y
un·heard′
un·heat′ed
un·heed′ed
un·heed′ful·ly
un·heed′ing·ly
un·help′ful
un·her′ald·ed
un′he·ro′ic
un·hes′i·tat′ing
un·hes′i·tat′ing·ly
un·hin′dered
un·hinge′
un·hinged′
un·hitch′
un·hitched′
un·ho′li·ness
un·ho′ly
un·home′like′
un·hon′ored
un·hook′
un·hooked′
un·hoped′
un·horse′
un·hum′bled
un·hu′mor·ous
un·hurt′
un′hy·gi·en′ic
un·hy′phen·at′ed
u′ni·corn
u′ni·cy′cle
un′i·den′ti·fi′a·ble
un′i·den′ti·fied
u′ni·fi·ca′tion
u′ni·fied
u′ni·form
u′ni·formed

u′ni·form′i·ty
u′ni·fy
u′ni·lat′er·al
u′ni·lat′er·al·ly
un′il·lu′mi·nat′ing
un′im·ag′i·na·ble
un′im·ag′i·na′tive
un′im·paired′
un′im·peach′a·ble
un′im·ped′ed
un′im·por′tant
un′im·por′tant·ly
un′im·pos′ing
un′im·pressed′
un′im·pres′sion·a·ble
un′im·pres′sive
un′im·proved′
un′in·cor′po·rat′ed
un′in·dem′ni·fied
un·in′dexed
un′in·dict′ed
un·in′flu·enced
un′in·formed′
un′in·hab′it·a·ble
un′in·hab′it·ed
un′in·hib′it·ed
un·in′jured
un·inked′
un′in·scribed′
un′in·spired′
un′in·spir′ing·ly
un′in·struct′ed
un′in·struc′tive
un·in′su·lat′ed
un′in·sur′a·ble
un′in·sured′
un·in′te·grat′ed
un′in·tel′li·gent
un′in·tel′li·gi·ble
un′in·tend′ed
un′in·ten′tion·al
un′in·ten′tion·al·ly
un·in′ter·est·ed
un·in′ter·est·ed·ly
un·in′ter·est·ing·ly
un′in·ter·mit′ting·ly
un′in·ter·rupt′ed·ly
un·in′ti·mat′ed
un′in·tim′i·dat′ed
un′in·tox′i·cat′ed
un′in·vad′ed
un′in·ven′tive
un′in·vig′o·rat′ed
un′in·vit′ing·ly
un′ion
un′ion·ism
un′ion·ist
un′ion·i·za′tion
un′ion·ize
un′ion·ized
u·nique′
u·nique′ly
u·nique′ness
un′ir·ra′di·at′ed
u′ni·son
un·is′sued
u′nit
U′ni·tar′i·an
U′ni·tar′i·an·ism
u′ni·tar′y
u·nite′
u·nit′ed
u·nit′ed·ly
u′ni·ty
u′ni·ver′sal
U′ni·ver′sal·ist
u′ni·ver·sal′i·ty
u′ni·ver′sal·ly
u′ni·verse
u′ni·ver′si·ty
un·jok′ing·ly
un·just′
un·jus′ti·fi′a·ble
un·jus′ti·fi′a·bly
un·jus′ti·fied
un·just′ly
un·kempt′
un·killed′
un·kind′
un·kind′li·ness
un·kind′ly
un·know′a·ble
un·know′ing·ly
un·known′
un·la′beled
un·lace′

un·laced'
un·la'dy·like'
un'la·ment'ed
un·lashed'
un·latch'
un·law'ful
un·law'ful·ly
un·law'ful·ness
un·lead'ed
un·learn'
un·leash'
un·leashed'
un·leav'ened
un·less'
un·let'tered
un·lib'er·at'ed
un·li'censed
un·light'ed
un·lik'a·ble
un·like'
un·like'li·hood
un·like'ly
un·lim'ber
un·lim'bered
un·lim'it·ed
un·lined'
un·list'ed
un·load'
un·load'ed
un·lo'cal·ized
un·lock'
un·locked'
un·looked'
un·loos'en
un·loved'
un·lov'ing·ly
un·luck'i·ly
un·luck'y
un·made'
un·mag'ni·fied
un·maid'en·ly
un·mail'a·ble
un·make'
un·man'
un·man'age·a·ble
un·man'li·ness
un·man'ly
un·manned'
un·man'ner·li·ness
un·man'ner·ly
un·marked'
un·mar'riage·a·ble
un·mar'ried
un·mask'
un·masked'
un·matched'
un·meas'ur·a·ble
un·meas'ured
un·men'tion·a·ble
un·men'tioned
un·mer'ci·ful
un·mer'ci·ful·ly
un·mer'it·ed
un·me'tered
un·mind'ful
un'mis·tak'a·ble
un·mit'i·gat'ed
un·mixed'
un'mo·lest'ed
un·moored'
un·mort'gaged
un·mo'ti·vat'ed
un·mount'ed
un·moved'
un·mov'ing·ly
un·named'
un·nat'u·ral
un·nat'u·ral·ly
un·nav'i·ga·ble
un·nec'es·sar'i·ly
un·nec'es·sar'y
un·need'ed
un·neigh'bor·ly
un·nerve'
un·no'tice·a·ble
un·no'ticed
un·num'bered
un'ob·serv'ant
un'ob·served'
un'ob·tain'a·ble
un·oc'cu·pied
un'of·fi'cial
un·o'pened
un'o·pin'ion·at'ed
un'op·posed'
un·or'ches·trat'ed

un·or′gan·ized
un·or′tho·dox
un′os·ten·ta′tious
un·pac′i·fied
un·pack′
un·paged′
un·paid′
un·paint′ed
un·pal′at·a·ble
un·par′al·leled
un·par′don·a·ble
un·par′doned
un′par·lia·men′ta·ry
un·pas′teur·ized
un·pat′ent·a·ble
un·pat′ent·ed
un′pa·tri·ot′ic
un′pa·tri·ot′i·cal·ly
un′pa·trolled′
un·paved′
un′per·ceived′
un·per′fo·rat′ed
un′per·formed′
un′per·turbed′
un·pit′y·ing
un·pit′y·ing·ly
un·planned′
un·plas′tered
un·play′a·ble
un·pleas′a·ble
un·pleas′ant
un·pleas′ant·ly
un·pleas′ant·ness
un·pleas′ing·ly
un·pledged′
un·plowed′
un·plugged′
un·plumbed′
un′po·et′ic
un′po·liced′
un·pol′ished
un′pol·lut′ed
un′pop′u·lar
un·pop′u·lat′ed
un·pop′u·lous
un·prac′ticed
un·prec′e·dent′ed
un·prec′e·dent′ed·ly
un′pre·dict′a·ble
un·prej′u·diced
un′pre·med′i·tat′ed
un′pre·pared′
un′pre·par′ed·ness
un′pre·pos·sess′ing
un′pre·sent′a·ble
un′pre·tend′ing·ly
un′pre·ten′tious
un′pre·ten′tious·ly
un′pre·ten′tious·ness
un·prin′ci·pled
un·print′a·ble
un·print′ed
un′pro·duced′
un′pro·duc′tive
un′pro·fes′sion·al
un·prof′it·a·ble
un′pro·gres′sive
un·prom′is·ing
un·prompt′ed
un′pro·nounce′a·ble
un′pro·pi′tious
un′pro·tect′ed
un·prov′a·ble
un·proved′
un′pro·vid′ed
un′pro·voked′
un·pub′lished
un·punc′tu·al
un′punc·tu·al′i·ty
un·punc′tu·al·ly
un·pun′ished
un·qual′i·fied
un·quelled′
un·quench′a·bly
un·ques′tion·a·ble
un·ques′tion·a·bly
un·ques′tioned
un·ques′tion·ing·ly
un·ran′somed
un·rav′el
un·rav′eled
un·reach′a·ble
un·read′
un·read′a·ble
un·re′al
un′re·al·is′tic

un′re·al′i·ty
un·re′al·ized
un·rea′son·a·ble
un·rea′son·a·bly
un·rea′soned
un·rea′son·ing·ly
un′re·buked′
un′re·ceipt′ed
un′re·cep′tive
un′re·claim′a·ble
un·rec′og·niz′a·ble
un·rec′og·nized
un·rec′og·niz′ing·ly
un·rec′on·cil′a·ble
un′re·cord′ed
un′re·deem′a·ble
un′re·deemed′
un·re·fill′a·ble
un′re·fined′
un′re·frig′er·at′ed
un′re·fut′ed
un′re·gen′er·ate
un·reg′u·lat′ed
un′re·hearsed′
un′re·lat′ed
un′re·lent′ing·ly
un′re·li′a·bil′i·ty
un′re·li′a·ble
un′re·mit′ting
un′re·mu′ner·a′tive
un′re·mu′ner·a′tive·ly
un·rent′a·ble

un·rent′ed
un′re·pent′ed
un′re·port′a·ble
un′re·port′ed
un′rep·re·sent′a·tive
un′re·proach′ing·ly
un′re·proved′
un′re·quit′ed
un′re·served′
un′re·serv′ed·ly
un′re·sist′ing·ly
un′re·solved′
un′re·source′ful
un′re·spon′sive
un·rest′
un·rest′ed
un′re·strained′
un′re·strict′ed
un′re·veal′ing·ly
un′re·ward′ed
un·rhymed′
un·right′eous
un·right′eous·ly
un·right′ful·ly
un·ripe′
un·ri′pened
un·ri′valed
un·roll′
un·rolled′
un·ruf′fle
un·ruf′fled
un·ruled′

un·rul′y
un·sad′dened
un·sad′dle
un·sad′dled
un·safe′
un·said′
un·sal′a·ble
un·sal′a·ried
un·sanc′ti·fied
un·sa′ti·at′ed
un′sat·is·fac′to·ri·ly
un′sat·is·fac′to·ry
un·sat′is·fied
un·sat′is·fy′ing·ly
un·sat′u·rat′ed
un·sa′vor·i·ly
un·sa′vor·y
un·scathed′
un·scent′ed
un·schooled′
un′sci·en·tif′ic
un·scram′ble
un·screw′
un·screwed′
un·scru′pu·lous
un·scru′pu·lous·ly
un·seal′
un·sealed′
un·sea′son·a·ble
un·sea′soned
un·seat′ed
un·sea′wor′thy

un·sec′ond·ed
un′se·cured′
un·see′ing·ly
un·seem′ing·ly
un·seem′ly
un·seen′
un′se·lect′ed
un·self′ish
un·self′ish·ly
un·sen′si·tized
un′sen·ti·men′tal
un·sep′a·rat′ed
un·serv′ice·a·ble
un·set′tle
un·set′tled
un·shack′le
un·shack′led
un·shad′ed
un·shak′a·ble
un·shak′en
un·sharp′ened
un·shav′en
un·sheathe′
un·shed′
un·shel′tered
un·shield′ed
un·ship′
un·shipped′
un·shrink′a·ble
un·shuf′fled
un·sight′ed
un·sight′ly
un·signed′
un·sing′a·ble
un·sink′a·ble
un·sis′ter·ly
un·sized′
un·skilled′
un·skill′ful
un·skimmed′
un·smil′ing·ly
un·smirched′
un·smoked′
un·smudged′
un·snarl′
un·so′cia·ble
un·soft′ened
un·soil′
un·soiled′
un·sold′
un·sol′dier·ly
un′so·lic′it·ed
un′so·phis′ti·cat′ed
un·sought′
un·sound′
un·sound′ly
un·speak′a·ble
un·spe′cial·ized
un·spec′i·fied
un·spoiled′
un·spo′ken
un·sports′man·like′
un·spot′ted
un·sprin′kled
un·sta′ble
un·stained′
un·stamped′
un·stead′i·ly
un·stead′y
un·ster′i·lized
un·stint′ed
un·stint′ing·ly
un·strained′
un·stressed′
un·strung′
un′sub·stan′tial
un′sub·stan′ti·at′ed
un′suc·cess′ful
un·suf′fer·a·ble
un·suit′a·ble
un·sul′lied
un·sum′moned
un·sung′
un′su·per·vised′
un·sure′
un′sur·pass′a·ble
un′sur·passed′
un′sus·pect′ed
un′sus·pect′ing
un′sus·pect′ing·ly
un·swayed′
un·sweet′ened
un·swerv′ing·ly
un·sworn′
un′sym·pa·thet′ic
un·sym′pa·thiz′ing·ly

un'sys·tem·at'ic
un·sys'tem·a·tized
un·taint'ed
un·tal'ent·ed
un·tamed'
un·tan'gle
un·tanned'
un·tast'ed
un·taught'
un·tax'a·ble
un·taxed'
un·teach'a·ble
un·tech'ni·cal
un·tempt'ed
un·ten'ant·a·ble
un·ten'ant·ed
un·tend'ed
un·ter'ri·fied
un·thick'ened
un·think'a·ble
un·think'ing
un·think'ing·ly
un·ti'di·ly
un·ti'dy
un·tie'
un·tied'
un·til'
un·time'ly
un·tint'ed
un·tir'ing·ly
un·ti'tled
un'to
un·told'
un·touch'a·ble
un·touched'
un·to'ward
un·trace'a·ble
un·trad'ed
un·trained'
un·tram'meled
un'trans·lat'a·ble
un·trav'eled
un·tried'
un·trimmed'
un·trod'den
un·trou'bled
un·true'
un·trussed'
un·trust'wor'thy
un·truth'
un·truth'ful
un·tuned'
un·turned'
un·tu'tored
un·twine'
un·twist'
un'un·der·stand'a·ble
un'up·braid'ing·ly
un·us'a·ble
un·used'
un·u'su·al
un·u'su·al·ly
un·ut'ter·a·ble
un·ut'ter·a·bly
un·ut'tered
un·val'i·dat'ed
un·val'ued
un·van'quished
un·var'ied
un·var'nished
un·var'y·ing·ly
un·vaunt'ing·ly
un·veil'
un·veiled'
un·ver'bal·ized
un·ver'i·fied
un·versed'
un·vis'it·ed
un·voiced'
un·walled'
un·war'i·ly
un·warned'
un·war'rant·a·ble
un·war'rant·ed
un·war'y
un·washed'
un·wa'tered
un·wa'ver·ing·ly
un·wea'ried
un·wea'ry·ing·ly
un·wed'
un·wed'ded
un·wel'come
un·well'
un·wept'
un·whole'some

un·whole′some·ly
un·wield′i·ness
un·wield′y
un·will′ing
un·will′ing·ly
un·will′ing·ness
un·winc′ing·ly
un·wind′
un·wind′ing·ly
un·wink′ing·ly
un·wise′
un·wit′nessed
un·wit′ting·ly
un·wom′an·ly
un·wont′ed
un·work′a·ble
un·work′man·like′
un·world′li·ness
un·world′ly
un·worn′
un·wor′ried
un·wor′thi·ly
un·wor′thi·ness
un·wor′thy
un·wound′
un·wound′ed
un·wrap′
un·wrapped′
un·wreathe′
un·wrin′kled
un·writ′ten
un·yield′ing·ly
un·yoked′
up
u′pas
up′beat′
up·braid′
up·braid′ed
up·braid′ing·ly
up·bring′ing
up′coun′try
up′draft′
up′grade′
up′growth′
up·heav′al
up·held′
up′hill′
up·hold′
up·hold′er
up·hol′ster
up·hol′stered
up·hol′ster·er
up·hol′ster·y
up′keep′
up′land′
up·lift′
up·lift′ed
up·lift′ing·ly
up′most
up·on′
up′per
up′per·most
up′pers
up·raise′
up·raised′
up′right′
up′right′ly
up′right′ness
up·ris′ings
up′roar′
up·roar′i·ous
up·roar′i·ous·ness
up·root′
up·root′ed
up·set′
up·set′ting·ly
up′shot′
up′side′
up′stairs′
up′start′
up′state′
up′stream′
up′stroke′
up′take′
up′-to-date′
up′town′
up·turn′
up·turned′
up′ward
up′wind′
u·ra′ni·um
ur′ban
ur·bane′
ur·bane′ly
ur′ban·ite
ur·ban′i·ty

ur′ban·i·za′tion
ur′ban·ize
ur′ban·ized
ur′chin
urge
urged
ur′gen·cy
ur′gent
ur′gent·ly
urg′ings
urn
us
us′a·bil′i·ty
us′a·ble
us′age
use
used
use′ful
use′ful·ly
use′ful·ness
use′less
use′less·ly
use′less·ness
us′er
us′es
ush′er
ush′ered
u′su·al
u′su·al·ly
u′su·fruct
u′su·rer
u·su′ri·ous
u·surp′
u′sur·pa′tion
u·surp′er
u′su·ry
u·ten′sil
u·til′i·tar′i·an
u·til′i·tar′i·an·ism
u·til′i·ties
u·til′i·ty
u′ti·liz′a·ble
u′ti·li·za′tion
u′ti·lize
u′ti·lized
ut′most
u·to′pi·a
u·to′pi·an
u·to′pi·an·ism
ut′ter
ut′ter·ance
ut′tered
ut′ter·ly
ut′ter·most
u′vu·la
u′vu·lar

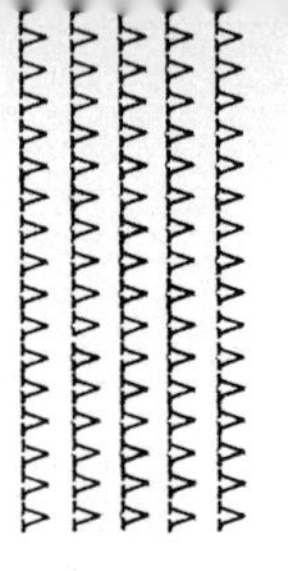

va′can·cy
va′cant
va′cate
va′cat·ed
va·ca′tion
va·ca′tioned
va·ca′tion·ist
vac′ci·nate
vac′ci·nat′ed
vac′ci·na′tion
vac′ci·na′tor
vac′cine
vac′il·late
vac′il·lat′ed
vac′il·la′tion
vac′il·lat′ing·ly
vac′il·la·to′ry
va·cu′i·ty
vac′u·ous
vac′u·um
vag′a·bond
vag′a·bond′age

vag′a·bon′di·a
vag′a·bond·ism
vag′a·bond·ize
va·gar′y
va′gran·cy
va′grant
vague
va′guer
va′guest
va′gus
vain
vain′glo′ri·ous
vain′glo′ry
vain′ly
vain′ness
val′ance
vale
val′e·dic′tion
val′e·dic·to′ri·an
val′e·dic′to·ry
va′lence
val′en·tine

va·le′ri·an
val′et
val′e·tu′di·nar′i·an
Val·hal′la
val′iant
val′id
val′i·date
val′i·dat′ed
val′i·da′tion
va·lid′i·ty
val′id·ly
va·lise′
val′ley
val′or
val′or·i·za′tion
val′or·ize
val′or·ous
val′u·a·ble
val′u·a′tion
val′ue
val′ued
val′ue·less

valve
val'vu·lar
vamp
vam'pire
va·na'di·um
van'dal
van'dal·ism
van'dal·ize
vane
van'guard'
va·nil'la
van'il·lin
van'ish
van'ished
van'ish·ing·ly
van'i·ty
van'quish
van'quished
van'tage
vap'id
vap'id·ly
va'por
va'por·ings
va'por·i·za'tion
va'por·ize
va'por·ized
va'por·iz'er
va'por·ous
var'i·a·bil'i·ty
var'i·a·ble
var'i·ance
var'i·ant
var'i·a'tion
var'i·col'ored
var'i·cose
var'i·cos'i·ty
var'ied
var'i·e·gate
var'i·e·gat'ed
var'i·e·ga'tion
va·ri'e·tal
va·ri'e·ty
va·ri'o·la
var'i·o'rum
var'i·ous
var'i·ous·ly
var'let
var'nish
var'nished
var'nish·ings
var'y
var'y·ing·ly
vas'cu·lar
vase
Vas'e·line
vas'sal
vas'sal·age
vast
vast'er
vast'est
vast'ly
vat
Vat'i·can
vaude'ville
vault
vault'ed
vaunt
vaunt'ed
vaunt'ing·ly
veal
vec'tor
ve·dette'
veer
veered
veg'e·ta·ble
veg'e·tar'i·an
veg'e·tar'i·an·ism
veg'e·tate
veg'e·tat'ed
veg'e·ta'tion
veg'e·ta'tive
ve'he·mence
ve'he·ment
ve'he·ment·ly
ve'hi·cle
ve'hi·cles
ve·hic'u·lar
veil
veiled
vein
veined
vein'ings
vein'let
vel'lum
ve·loc'i·pede
ve·loc'i·ty

ve′lo·drome
ve·lours′
vel′vet
vel′vet·een′
vel′vet·y
ve′nal
ve·nal′i·ty
ve′nal·i·za′tion
ve′nal·ize
ve·na′tion
vend
vend′ed
vend·ee′
ven·det′ta
vend′i·ble
ven′dor
ve·neer′
ve·neered′
ven′er·a·ble
ven′er·ate
ven′er·at′ed
ven′er·a′tion
ven′er·a′tive
Ve·ne′tian
venge′ance
venge′ful
venge′ful·ness
ve′ni·al
ve′ni·al′i·ty
ve′ni·al·ly
ven′i·son
ven′om
ven′om·ous
ven′om·ous·ly
vent
vent′ed
vent′hole′
ven′ti·late
ven′ti·lat′ed
ven′ti·la′tion
ven′ti·la′tor
ven′tral
ven′tri·cle
ven·tric′u·lar
ven·tril′o·quism
ven·tril′o·quist
ven′ture
ven′tured
ven′ture·some
ven′ue
ve·ra′cious
ve·ra′cious·ly
ve·rac′i·ty
ve·ran′da
ver′bal
ver′bal·ism
ver′bal·ist
ver′bal·i·za′tion
ver′bal·ize
ver′bal·ized
ver′bal·ly
ver·ba′tim
ver·be′na
ver′bi·age
ver·bose′
ver·bos′i·ty
ver′dant
ver′dict
ver′di·gris
ver′dure
verge
verged
ver′ger
ver′i·est
ver′i·fi′a·ble
ver′i·fi·ca′tion
ver′i·fied
ver′i·fy
ver′i·ly
ver′i·si·mil′i·tude
ver′ism
ver′i·ta·ble
ver′i·ta·bly
ver′i·ties
ver′i·ty
ver′meil
ver′mi·cel′li
ver′mi·cide
ver·mic′u·late
ver·mic′u·la′tion
ver·mic′u·lite
ver′mi·form
ver′mi·fuge
ver·mil′ion
ver′min
ver′min·ous

ver·nac′u·lar
ver′nal
ver′ni·er
ver′sa·tile
ver′sa·til′i·ty
verse
ver′si·cle
ver′si·fi·ca′tion
ver′si·fied
ver′si·fi′er
ver′si·fy
ver′sion
ver′so
ver′sus
ver′te·bra
ver′te·brae
ver′te·brate
ver′tex
ver′ti·cal
ver′ti·cal·ly
ver·tig′i·nous
ver′ti·go
ver′vain
verve
ver′y
ves′i·cle
ves′per
ves′sel
vest
ves′tal
vest′ed
ves·tib′u·lar
ves′ti·bule
ves′tige
ves·tig′i·al
vest′ment
ves′try
ves′ture
vetch
vet′er·an
vet′er·i·nar′i·an
vet′er·i·nar′y
ve′to
ve′toed
vex
vex·a′tion
vex·a′tious
vexed
vi′a
vi·a·bil′i·ty
vi′a·ble
vi′a·duct
vi′al
vi′and
vi·at′i·cum
vi′bran·cy
vi′brant
vi′brate
vi′brat·ed
vi′brat·ing·ly
vi·bra′tion
vi·bra′tion·less
vi·bra′to
vi′bra·tor
vi′bra·to′ry
vic′ar
vic′ar·age
vi·car′i·ate
vi·car′i·ous
vi·car′i·ous·ly
vice
vice′ge′ral
vice′ge′rent
vice′reine
vice′roy
vic′i·nage
vi·cin′i·ties
vi·cin′i·ty
vi′cious
vi′cious·ly
vi′cious·ness
vi·cis′si·tude
vic′tim
vic′tim·ize
vic′tim·ized
vic′tor
Vic·to′ri·an
vic·to′ri·ous
vic·to′ri·ous·ly
vic′to·ry
Vic·tro′la
vict′ual
vi·cu′ña
vid′e·o
vid′e·o·tape
vie

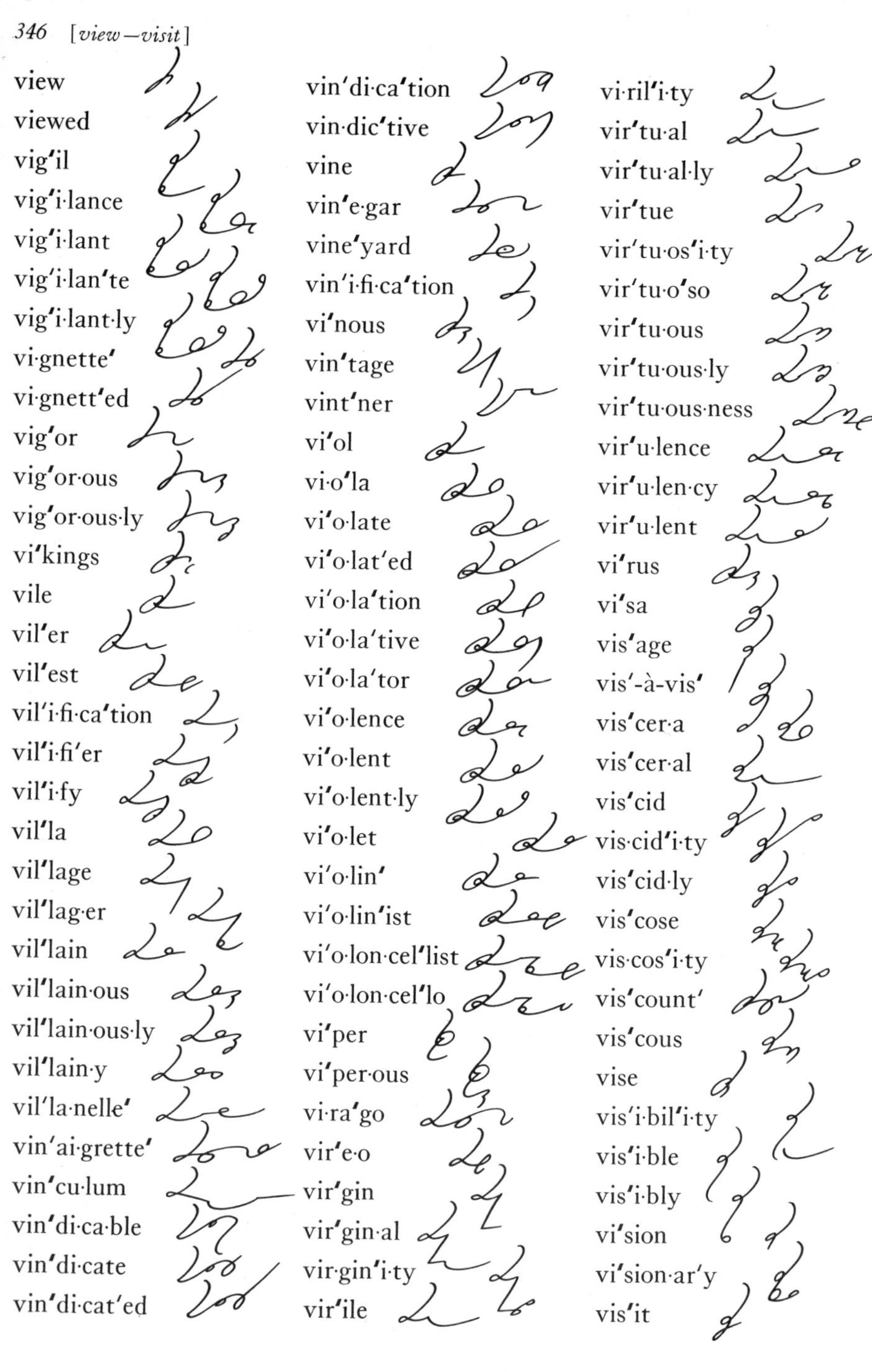
view
viewed
vig'il
vig'i·lance
vig'i·lant
vig'i·lan'te
vig'i·lant·ly
vi·gnette'
vi·gnett'ed
vig'or
vig'or·ous
vig'or·ous·ly
vi'kings
vile
vil'er
vil'est
vil'i·fi·ca'tion
vil'i·fi'er
vil'i·fy
vil'la
vil'lage
vil'lag·er
vil'lain
vil'lain·ous
vil'lain·ous·ly
vil'lain·y
vil'la·nelle'
vin'ai·grette'
vin'cu·lum
vin'di·ca·ble
vin'di·cate
vin'di·cat'ed
vin'di·ca'tion
vin·dic'tive
vine
vin'e·gar
vine'yard
vin'i·fi·ca'tion
vi'nous
vin'tage
vint'ner
vi'ol
vi·o'la
vi'o·late
vi'o·lat'ed
vi'o·la'tion
vi'o·la'tive
vi'o·la'tor
vi'o·lence
vi'o·lent
vi'o·lent·ly
vi'o·let
vi'o·lin'
vi'o·lin'ist
vi'o·lon·cel'list
vi'o·lon·cel'lo
vi'per
vi'per·ous
vi·ra'go
vir'e·o
vir'gin
vir'gin·al
vir·gin'i·ty
vir'ile
vi·ril'i·ty
vir'tu·al
vir'tu·al·ly
vir'tue
vir'tu·os'i·ty
vir'tu·o'so
vir'tu·ous
vir'tu·ous·ly
vir'tu·ous·ness
vir'u·lence
vir'u·len·cy
vir'u·lent
vi'rus
vi'sa
vis'age
vis'-à-vis'
vis'cer·a
vis'cer·al
vis'cid
vis·cid'i·ty
vis'cid·ly
vis'cose
vis·cos'i·ty
vis'count'
vis'cous
vise
vis'i·bil'i·ty
vis'i·ble
vis'i·bly
vi'sion
vi'sion·ar'y
vis'it

vis′it·a′tion
vis′it·ed
vis′i·tor
vis′ta
vis′u·al
vis′u·al·i·za′tion
vis′u·al·ize
vis′u·al·ized
vis′u·al·ly
vi′tal
vi·tal′i·ty
vi′tal·ize
vi′tal·ized
vi′tal·ly
vi′ta·min
vi′ti·ate
vi′ti·at′ed
vi′ti·a′tion
vit′re·ous
vit′ri·fac′tion
vit′ri·fi·ca′tion
vit′ri·fied
vit′ri·fy
vit′ri·ol
vit′ri·ol′ic
vi·tu′per·ate
vi·tu′per·at′ed
vi·tu′per·a′tion
vi·tu′per·a′tive
vi·tu′per·a′tive·ly
vi·va′cious
vi·va′cious·ly
vi·vac′i·ty
vi·var′i·um
viv′id
viv′id·ly
viv′i·fy
vi·vip′a·rous
viv′i·sect
viv′i·sec′tion
viv′i·sec′tion·ist
vix′en
vix′en·ish
viz′ard
vi·zier′
vo′ca·ble
vo·cab′u·lar′y
vo′cal
vo′cal·ism
vo′cal·ist
vo′cal·i·za′tion
vo′cal·ize
vo′cal·ized
vo′cal·ly
vo·ca′tion
vo·ca′tion·al
vo·ca′tion·al·ly
voc′a·tive
vo·cif′er·ate
vo·cif′er·at′ed
vo·cif′er·a′tion
vo·cif′er·ous
vod′ka
vogue
voice
voiced
voice′less
voice′less·ly
voice′less·ness
void
void′a·ble
void′ed
vol′a·tile
vol′a·til′i·ty
vol′a·til·i·za′tion
vol′a·til·ize
vol′a·til·ized
vol·can′ic
vol·ca′no
vol′can·ol′o·gy
vo·li′tion
vo·li′tion·al
vo·li′tion·al·ly
vol′ley
vol′ley·ball′
vol′leyed
volt
volt′age
vol·ta′ic
vol·tam′e·ter
volt′am′me·ter
volt′me′ter
vol′u·bil′i·ty
vol′u·ble
vol′u·bly
vol′ume

vol′u·met′ric
vo·lu′mi·nous
vo·lu′mi·nous·ly
vo·lu′mi·nous·ness
vol′un·tar′i·ly
vol′un·tar′y
vol′un·teer′
vol′un·teered′
vo·lup′tu·ar′y
vo·lup′tu·ous
vo·lup′tu·ous·ly
vo·lup′tu·ous·ness
vo·lute′
vol′vu·lus
vom′it
vom′it·ed
vom′i·to′ry
voo′doo
voo′doo·ism
vo·ra′cious
vo·rac′i·ty
vor′tex
vor′ti·cal
vor′ti·cal·ly
vo′ta·ry
vote
vot′ed
vot′er
vo′tive
vouch
vouched
vouch′er
vouch·safe′
vouch·safed′
vow
vowed
vow′el
vow′el·i·za′tion
vow′el·ize
voy′age
voy′aged
voy′ag·er
vul′can·i·za′tion
vul′can·ize
vul′can·ized
vul′can·iz′er
vul′gar
vul·gar′i·an
vul′gar·ism
vul·gar′i·ty
vul′gar·i·za′tion
vul′gar·ize
vul′gar·ized
vul′gar·iz′er
vul′gar·ly
vul′gate
vul′ner·a·bil′i·ty
vul′ner·a·ble
vul′ner·a·bly
vul′ture

wad
wad′ded
wad′dings
wad′dle
wad′dling·ly
wade
wad′ed
wad′er
wa′fer
waf′fle
waft
wag
wage
waged
wa′ger
wa′gered
wa′ger·ings
wag′es
wagged
wag′gish
wag′gle
wag′gled
wag′gling·ly
Wag·ne′ri·an
wag′on
wag′tail′
waif
wail
wailed
wail′ing·ly
wail′ings
wain
wain′scot
waist
waist′band′
waist′coat′
waist′line′
wait
wait′ed
wait′er
wait′ress
waive
waived
waiv′er
wake
waked
wake′ful
wake′ful·ly
wake′ful·ness
wak′en
wak′ened
wak′ing·ly
wale
waled
walk
walked
walk′er
walk′o′ver
walk′-up′
walk′way′
wall
wall′board′
walled
wal′let
wall′eyed′
walk′out

Wal·loon′
wal′lop
wal′low
wal′lowed
wall′pa′per
wal′nut
wal′rus
waltz
waltzed
wam′pum
wan
wand
wan′der
wan′dered
wan′der·er
wan′der·ing·ly
wan′der·ings
wane
waned
wan′gle
wan′gled
want
want′ed
want′ing·ly
wan′ton
war
war′ble
war′bled
war′bler
war′bling·ly
war′blings
ward

ward′ed
ward′en
ward′er
ward′robe′
ward′room′
ware′house′
ware′house′man
ware′room′
wares
war′fare′
war′i·ly
war′i·ness
war′like′
war′lock
warm
warmed
warm′er
warm′est
warm′heart′ed
warm′ly
warm′ness
war′mon′ger
warmth
warn
warned
warn′ing·ly
warn′ings
warp
warp′age
war′path′
warped
war′plane′

war′rant
war′rant·a·ble
war′rant·ed
war′ran·tor
war′ran·ty
warred
war′ren
war′ship′
wart
war′time′
wart′less
war′y
was
wash
wash′a·ble
wash′board′
wash′bowl′
wash′cloth′
washed
wash′er
wash′house′
wash′ings
wash′out′
wash′room′
wash′stand′
wash′-up′
wash′wom′an
wasp
wasp′ish
was′sail
wast′age
waste

waste'bas'ket
wast'ed
waste'ful
waste'ful·ly
waste'ful·ness
waste'land'
waste'pa'per
wast'er
wast'ing·ly
wast'rel
watch
watch'case'
watch'dog'
watched
watch'er
watch'ful
watch'ful·ly
watch'ful·ness
watch'house'
watch'keep'er
watch'mak'er
watch'man
watch'tow'er
watch'word'
wa'ter
wa'tered
wa'ter·fall'
wa'ter·find'er
wa'ter·fowl'
wa'ter·i·ness
wa'ter·ings
wa'ter·line'

wa'ter·log'
wa'ter·logged'
Wa'ter·loo'
wa'ter·man
wa'ter·mark'
wa'ter·mel'on
wa'ter·proof'
wa'ter·proofed'
wa'ter·shed'
wa'ter·side'
wa'ter·spout'
wa'ter·way'
wa'ter·weed'
wa'ter·works'
wa'ter·y
watt
watt'age
wat'tle
wat'tled
watt'me'ter
wave
waved
wave'me'ter
wa'ver
wa'vered
wa'ver·ing·ly
wa'ver·ings
wav'i·ness
wav'y
wax
waxed
wax'en

wax'i·ness
wax'ing·ly
wax'wing'
wax'work'
wax'y
way
way'bill'
way'far'er
way'fel'low
way'laid'
way'lay'
way'side'
way'ward
we
weak
weak'en
weak'ened
weak'er
weak'est
weak'ling
weak'ly
weak'ness
weal
wealth
wealth'i·er
wealth'i·est
wealth'y
wean
weaned
weap'on
weap'on·less
wear

wear'a·bil'i·ty
wear'a·ble
wear'er
wea'ried
wea'ri·er
wea'ri·est
wea'ri·ly
wea'ri·ness
wear'ings
wea'ri·some
wea'ri·some·ness
wea'ry
wea'sel
weath'er
weath'er·board'
weath'er·cock'
weath'ered
weath'er·proof'
weath'er·proofed'
weave
weav'er
web
webbed
web'bings
wed
wed'ded
wed'dings
wedge
wedged
wed'lock
Wednes'day
weed
weed'ed
weed'i·er
weed'i·est
weed'y
week
week'day'
week'end'
week'lies
week'ly
weep
weep'ing·ly
wee'vil
weft
weigh
weighed
weigh'mas'ter
weight
weight'ed
weight'i·er
weight'i·est
weight'ings
weight'less·ness
weight'y
weir
weird
weird'ly
weird'ness
wel'come
wel'comed
wel'com·ing·ly
weld
weld'ed
wel'fare'
wel'kin
well
well'born'
welled
well'head'
well'hole'
well'spring'
welt
welt'ed
wel'ter
wel'tered
wen
wench
wend
wend'ed
went
wept
were
were'wolf'
west
west'er·ly
west'ern
west'ern·er
west'ward
wet
wet'ness
wet'ta·bil'i·ty
wet'ta·ble
wet'ted
wet'ter
wet'test

wet'tings
we've
whack
whacked
whale
whale'back'
whale'bone'
whale'man
whal'er
wharf
wharf'age
wharf'in·ger
what
what·ev'er
what'not'
what'so·ev'er
wheat
wheat'en
wheat'worm'
whee'dle
whee'dled
whee'dling·ly
wheel
wheel'bar'row
wheeled
wheel'house'
wheel'wright'
wheeze
wheezed
wheez'i·er
wheez'i·est
wheez'i·ly

wheez'ing·ly
wheez'y
whelk
whelp
whelped
when
whence
whence'forth'
when·ev'er
when'so·ev'er
where
where'a·bouts'
where·aft'er
where·as'
where·at'
where·by'
where'fore
where·from'
where·in'
where·of'
where·on'
where'so·ev'er
where'up·on'
wher·ev'er
where·with'
where'with·al'
wher'ry
whet
wheth'er
whet'ted
whet'stone'
whey

which
which·ev'er
which'so·ev'er
whiff
whiffed
whif'fle
whif'fled
Whig
while
whiled
whi'lom
whim
whim'per
whim'pered
whim'per·ing·ly
whim'per·ings
whim'sey
whim'si·cal
whine
whined
whin'ing·ly
whin'ings
whin'nied
whin'ny
whip
whip'cord'
whipped
whip'per·snap'per
whip'pet
whip'ping·ly
whip'pings
whip'poor·will'

whip'saw'
whip'stitch'
whip'stock'
whip'worm'
whir
whirl
whirled
whirl'i·gig'
whirl'ing·ly
whirl'pool'
whirl'wind'
whirred
whisk
whisked
whisk'er
whisk'ered
whis'ky
whis'per
whis'pered
whis'per·er
whis'per·ing·ly
whis'per·ings
whist
whis'tle
whis'tled
whis'tling·ly
whis'tlings
whit
white
white'cap'
whit'ed
white'fish'
whit'en
whit'ened
white'ness
white'wash'
white'washed'
white'wing'
white'wood'
whith'er
whit'ings
whit'ish
whit'low
whit'tle
whit'tled
whit'tlings
who
who·ev'er
whole
whole'heart'ed
whole'heart'ed·ly
whole'sale'
whole'sal'er
whole'some
whole'some·ly
whol'ly
whom
whom·ev'er
whom'so·ev'er
whoop
whooped
whoop'ing·ly
whose
who'so·ev'er
why
wick
wick'ed
wick'ed·ly
wick'ed·ness
wick'er
wick'er·work'
wick'et
wide
wide'ly
wid'en
wid'ened
wide'ness
wid'er
wide'spread'
wid'est
wid'ow
wid'owed
wid'ow·er
wid'ow·hood
width
wield
wield'ed
wife
wife'hood
wife'less
wife'ly
wig
wig'gle
wig'gled
wig'gler
wig'glings

wight
wig'mak'er
wig'wag'
wig'wam'
wild
wild'er
wil'der·ness
wild'est
wild'fire'
wild'ness
wile
wil'i·er
wil'i·est
will
willed
will'ful
will'ful·ly
will'ful·ness
will'ing·ly
will'ing·ness
wil'low
wilt
wilt'ed
wil'y
win
wince
winced
winc'ing·ly
wind
wind
wind'age
wind'bag'
wind'break'
wind'ed
wind'er
wind'fall'
wind'i·ly
wind'i·ness
wind'ing·ly
wind'ings
wind'jam'mer
wind'lass
wind'mill'
win'dow
win'dowed
win'dow·pane'
wind'pipe'
wind'row'
wind'rowed'
wind'shield'
wind'storm'
wind'ward
wind'ward ly
wind'way'
wind'y
wine
wine'ber'ry
wined
wine'glass'
wine'skin'
wing
winged
wing'fish'
wing'less
wing'spread'
wink
winked
wink'ing·ly
win'kle
win'ner
win'ning·ly
win'nings
win'now
win'nowed
win'some
win'ter
win'tered
win'ter·ize
wipe
wiped
wip'er
wire
wired
wire'less
wire'pull'er
wire'pull'ing
wire'way'
wire'work'
wire'work'er
wire'worm'
wir'y
wis'dom
wise
wise'a'cre
wise'crack'
wise'crack'er

wise'ly
wise'ness
wis'er
wis'est
wish
wish'bone'
wished
wish'ful
wish'ful·ly
wish'ful·ness
wish'ing·ly
wisp
wisp'i·er
wisp'i·est
wisp'y
wis·te'ri·a
wist'ful
wist'ful·ly
wist'ful·ness
wit
witch
witch'craft'
witch'er·y
witch'ing·ly
witch'weed'
with
with·al'
with·draw'
with·draw'al
with·drawn'
with·drew'
with'er
with'ered
with'er·ing·ly
with·held'
with·hold'
with·hold'ings
with·in'
with·out'
with·stand'
with·stood'
wit'less
wit'less·ly
wit'less·ness
wit'ness
wit'nessed
wit'ti·cism
wit'ti·er
wit'ti·est
wit'ting·ly
wit'ty
wived
wives
wiz'ard
wiz'ard·ly
wiz'ard·ry
wiz'ened
woad
wob'ble
wob'bled
wob'bli·ness
wob'bling·ly
wob'bly
woe
woe'be·gone'
woe'ful
woe'ful·ly
woe'ful·ness
wolf
wolfed
wolf'hound'
wolf'ish
wol'ver·ine'
wolves
wom'an
wom'an·hood
wom'an·ish
wom'an·kind'
wom'an·like'
wom'an·li·ness
wom'an·ly
wom'en
won
won'der
won'dered
won'der·ful
won'der·ful·ly
won'der·ing·ly
won'der·land'
won'der·ment
won'der·work'
won'drous
won'drous·ly
won't
wont
woo

wood
wood'bin'
wood'bine'
wood'chuck'
wood'craft'
wood'cut'
wood'ed
wood'en
wood'en·head'
wood'fish'
wood'land
wood'man
wood'peck'er
wood'pile'
wood'shop'
woods'man
wood'work'
wood'work'er
wood'worm'
wooed
woo'er
woof
wool
wool'en
wool'li·er
wool'li·est
wool'li·ness
wool'ly
wool'work'
wool'work'er
wooz'y
word

word'age
word'build'ing
word'ed
word'i·er
word'i·est
word'i·ly
word'i·ness
word'less
word'play'
word'y
wore
work
work'a·bil'i·ty
work'a·ble
work'bag'
work'bas'ket
work'bench'
work'book'
work'box'
work'day'
worked
work'er
work'house'
work'ing·man'
work'ings
work'less
work'man
work'man·like'
work'man·ship
work'men
work'out'
work'pan'

work'peo'ple
work'place'
work'room'
work'shop'
work'ta'ble
work'wom'an
work'wom'en
world
world'li·ness
world'ly
worm
wormed
worm'hole'
worm'i·er
worm'i·est
worm'like'
worm'proof'
worm'wood'
worm'y
worn
wor'ried
wor'ried·ly
wor'ri·er
wor'ri·ment
wor'ri·some
wor'ri·some·ness
wor'ry
worse
wors'en
wors'ened
wor'ship
wor'shiped

wor'ship·er
wor'ship·ful
wor'ship·ful·ly
worst
worst'ed
wor'sted
worth
wor'thi·er
wor'thi·est
wor'thi·ly
wor'thi·ness
worth'while'
wor'thy
would
wound
wound
wound'ed
wound'ing·ly
wound'less
wove
wo'ven
wrack
wraith
wraith'like'
wran'gle
wran'gled
wrap
wrapped
wrap'per
wrap'pings
wrath
wrath'ful
wrath'ful·ly
wrath'ful·ness
wreak
wreaked
wreath
wreathed
wreck
wreck'age
wrecked
wreck'er
wren
wrench
wrenched
wrest
wrest'ed
wres'tle
wres'tled
wres'tler
wretch
wretch'ed
wretch'ed·ly
wretch'ed·ness
wrig'gle
wrig'gled
wrig'gling·ly
wrig'gly
wring
wring'er
wrin'kle
wrin'kled
wrin'kli·er
wrin'kli·est
wrin'kly
wrist
wrist'band'
wrist'bone'
wrist'let
wrist'lock'
writ
writ'a·ble
write
writ'er
writhe
writhed
writh'ing·ly
writ'ings
writ'ten
wrong
wrong'do'er
wronged
wrong'ful
wrong'ful·ly
wrong'head'ed
wrong'ly
wrong'ness
wrote
wroth
wrought
wrung
wry
wry'neck'

xe′non
xen′o·phile
xen'o·pho′bi·a
xe'ro·der′ma
xe·rog′ra·phy
xe·ro'sis
Xer′ox
X ray
xy′lo·phone

yacht
yachts′man
yak
Yale
yam
yam′mer
yank
Yan′kee
yard
yard′age
yard′arm'
yard′man
yard′mas'ter
yard′stick'
yarn
yar′row
yat′a·ghan
yaw
yawl
yawn
yawned
yawn′ing·ly
ye
yea
year
year′book'
year′ling
year′ly
yearn
yearned
yearn′ing·ly
yearn′ings
yeast
yeast′y
yell
yelled
yel′low
yel′lowed
yel′low·er
yel′low·est
yel′low·ish
yel′low·ish·ness
yelp
yelped
yeo′man
yeo′man·ry
yes
yes′ter·day
yet
yew
Yid′dish
yield
yield′ed
yield′ing·ly
yield′ing·ness
yo'del

yo'deled
yo'del·er
yo'ga
yo'ghurt
yoke
yoked
yoke'fel'low
yo'kel
yo'kel·ry
yolk
yon
yon'der
yore
you
young
young'er
young'est
young'ish
young'ster
your
yours
your·self'
your·selves'
youth
youth'ful
youth'ful·ly
youth'ful·ness
youths
yt·ter'bi·um
yt'tri·um
Yuc'ca
yule
yule'tide'

za'ny
zeal
zeal'ot
zeal'ot·ry
zeal'ous
zeal'ous·ly
zeal'ous·ness
ze'bra
ze'broid
ze'bu
ze'nith
ze'o·lite
zeph'yr
Zep'pe·lin
ze'ro
zest
zest'ful
zig'zag'
zinc
Zi'on
Zi'on·ism
ZIP
zip'per
zir'con
zir·co'ni·um
zith'er
zo'di·ac
zone
zoned
zoo
zo'o·log'i·cal
zo·ol'o·gist
zo·ol'o·gy
zoom
zoomed
Zu'lu
zy'mase
zy·mol'o·gy

# PART TWO

Part Two consists of 1,314 entries of personal and geographical names divided as follows:

835 Geographical Names. The largest group consists of the names of American cities and towns that are likely to be encountered in business dictation. The names of the American states are given. A relatively small group of foreign geographical names is given—the foreign countries and cities that are most likely to occur in American business dictation. The lists are not intended to be complete or exhaustive. The attempt has been made, however, to include the geographical names that occur most frequently in ordinary business dictation.

243 Surnames. This group represents the commonest American surnames that are likely to be used in business dictation.

113 First Names of Women. This list contains the most frequently used feminine first names.

123 First Names of Men. This list contains the more frequently used masculine first names.

The four groups of names listed above are combined in one alphabetical list in Part Two.

With the exception of the states and of a few of the largest cities, the geographical names are written very fully. This is done with the understanding that the writer will use these full outlines for the names that occur only occasionally in the dictation. When some name occurs more frequently in the dictation, an abbreviated form would be used.

The shorthand writer in Oregon would ordinarily have little occasion to use the outline for *Corpus Christi*. The shorthand writer in Texas might use it so frequently that he would abbreviate it to *kk*.

The names of most cities that are composed of nouns or adjectives that appear in Part One have been omitted, names such as *Grove Hill, Egg Harbor, Spring Valley, Key West.* The shorthand outlines for such cities and towns are not likely to cause the writer any stenographic difficulty.

The writing and transcribing of proper names can present many traps for the shorthand writer. When he writes in shorthand the name *Pittsburgh,* he will not know whether to transcribe it *Pittsburg* or *Pittsburgh* until he knows whether the dictator had in mind *Pittsburg,* Kansas, or *Pittsburgh,* Pennsylvania. He can be tricked similarly by such a pair as *Worcester,* Massachusetts, and *Wooster,* Ohio.

The writer may confidently write *b-r-o-w-n* in his shorthand notes without realizing that the dictator may not be referring to his familiar correspondent, Mr. *Brown,* but to some strange *Browne* or *Braun.*

Unless the writer is absolutely sure of the identity of the proper names used by the dictator, he should always check them with the greatest possible care. Almost everyone is annoyed when his name or the name of his city or town is spelled incorrectly.

# PERSONAL AND GEOGRAPHICAL NAMES

Aaron
Aberdeen
Abilene
Abington
Abraham
Adams
Adelbert
Adolph
Agatha
Aiken
Aileen
Ainsworth
Akron
Alabama
Alameda
Alaska
Albany
Albert
Albuquerque
Alexander
Alfred
Algeria

Algernon
Allentown
Allison
Alphonsine
Alphonso
Alton
Altoona
Alvin
Amanda
Amarillo
Amelia
Amesbury
Amherst
Amityville
Amsterdam
Anderson
Andover
Angela
Angelica
Angora
Annabel
Annapolis

Anniston
Anthony
Antioch
Antoinette
Antwerp
Appleton
Arabia
Archibald
Argentina
Arizona
Arkansas
Arlington
Arnold
Arthur
Asheboro
Asheville
Ashley
Astoria
Atchison
Atkinson
Atlanta
Atlantic

Augusta
Augustin
Aurelia
Aurora
Austin
Australia
Austria
Avery
Baird
Bakersfield
Baldwin
Ballard
Baltimore
Bangkok
Bangladesh
Barberton
Barcelona
Barlow
Barnard
Barnesville
Barrington
Bartholomew
Bartlett
Bartow
Basil
Batavia
Batesville
Baton Rouge
Bauer
Bayonne
Beatrice
Beckley

Bedford
Belfast
Belgium
Belinda
Bellefontaine
Belleville
Bellevue
Bellingham
Belmont
Beloit
Belvedere
Bemidji
Benedict
Benjamin
Bennett
Bennington
Bentley
Bergenfield
Berkeley
Bernard
Bernstein
Bertha
Berwick
Bethlehem
Beulah
Beverly
Biloxi
Binghamton
Birmingham
Bismarck
Blackstone
Blackwell

Blairsville
Blakely
Blanchard
Bloomington
Bloomsburg
Bluffton
Bogota
Boise
Bolivia
Bonham
Boniface
Boonville
Bordeaux
Boston
Bosworth
Boulder
Bowen
Bowman
Boyd
Boyle
Braddock
Bradenton
Bradford
Bradley
Brattleboro
Brazil
Bremen
Bremerton
Brenham
Brentwood
Brian
Bridgeport

Bridgeton
Brigham
Brisbane
Bristow
Brockton
Bronxville
Brookfield
Brownsville
Brunswick
Bryan
Bryant
Bucharest
Budapest
Buenos Aires
Buffalo
Bulgaria
Burbank
Burke
Burlington
Burma
Burns
Burroughs
Burton
Butte
Byron
Cadillac
Caesar
Calcutta
Calhoun
California
Callahan
Calumet City

Camden
Camilla
Campbell
Canada
Canfield
Cannon
Canonsburg
Canton
Caracas
Carbondale
Carlisle
Carlotta
Carlsbad
Carlson
Carlstadt
Carlton
Carmel
Carnegie
Carol
Carpenter
Carrollton
Carson
Carter
Cartersville
Carthage
Casper
Catharine
Catskill
Cecelia
Cedarhurst
Cedartown
Celia

Centralia
Chalmers
Chambersburg
Chandler
Chanute
Chapman
Charleston
Charlottesville
Chattanooga
Cheboygan
Chelsea
Cherbourg
Cherokee
Cheyenne
Chicago
Chicopee
Childress
Chillicothe
Chippewa Falls
Chisholm
Christabel
Christchurch
Christina
Christine
Christopher
Cicely
Cicero
Cincinnati
Claremont
Clarinda
Clarksburg
Clarksville

Claudia
Clearfield
Clearwater
Cleburne
Clement
Cleveland
Clifford
Coaldale
Coatesville
Coeur d'Alene
Coffeyville
Cohen
Coldwater
Coleman
Collier
Collingdale
Collingswood
Collinsville
Cologne
Colorado
Colton
Columbia
Columbus
Comstock
Concord
Concordia
Condon
Conklin
Conley
Connecticut
Connersville
Connolly

Connor
Conrad
Constance
Conway
Cooley
Coolidge
Copenhagen
Corbin
Cork
Cornelia
Corning
Corona
Corpus Christi
Cortland
Corvallis
Corwin
Costa Rica
Covington
Crafton
Crandall
Cranford
Crawford
Creston
Cromwell
Crowley
Cuba
Cudahy
Culbertson
Cullman
Cumberland
Cummings
Cummins

Curtis
Cuthbert
Cynthia
Dagmar
Dalton
Daly
Daniel
Danville
Daphne
Darby
Davenport
Davidson
Dawson
Dearborn
Deborah
Dedham
Deerfield
Defiance
Delaware
Delhi
Delia
Denise
Denison
Denmark
Denver
Des Moines
Detroit
Dewey
Dexter
Diana
Dickinson
Dillon

District of Columbia
Dolores
Dominic
Donald
Donora
Donovan
Dormont
Dorothy
Dougherty
Doyle
Dresden
Dublin
Dubuque
Dudley
Duluth
Dunbar
Duncan
Dunkirk
Dunmore
Dunn
Duquesne
Durham
Dwight
Easthampton
Eastman
Easton
Eau Claire
Ecuador
Edgar
Edinburgh
Edmonton
Edward

Edwardsville
Edwin
Effingham
Egan
Egbert
Egypt
Eileen
Elbert
Eleanor
Electra
Elgin
Elizabeth
Elizabethton
Elkhart
Elkins
Ellensburg
Elliott
Ellsworth
Elmhurst
Elmira
El Paso
Elvira
Elwood
Ely
Elyria
Emil
Emily
Emmanuel
Emporia
Endicott
England
Englewood

Enrico
Enright
Ernest
Ernestine
Erwin
Esther
Esthonia
Ethel
Ethiopia
Euclid
Europe
Evangeline
Evanston
Evansville
Evelina
Everard
Everett
Exeter
Fairbanks
Fairbury
Fairfield
Fairmont
Fargo
Farrell
Fayetteville
Feldman
Ferdinand
Ferguson
Ferndale
Findlay
Finley
Fisher

Fitchburg
Fitzgerald
Flagstaff
Fleming
Florence
Florida
Floyd
Fond du Lac
Ford
Fort Atkinson
Fort Lauderdale
Fort Madison
Fort Myers
Fort Wayne
Fort Worth
Foster
Fostoria
Framingham
Frances
Francis
Frankfort
Franklin
Frederic
Fredonia
Freehold
Freeport
Fullerton
Fulton
Gabriel
Gaffney
Gainesville
Galesburg

Galion
Gallagher
Gallup
Galveston
Gardner
Garfield
Gasper
Gastonia
Geneva
Genevieve
Genoa
George
Georgia
Gerald
Germany
Gertrude
Gettysburg
Gibson
Gifford
Gilbert
Girard
Glasgow
Gleason
Gloria
Gloversville
Goddard
Godfrey
Goodwin
Gordon
Gould
Grafton
Great Britain

Greeley
Greensboro
Greensburg
Greenville
Greenwood
Gregory
Gretchen
Griffiths
Grinnell
Guam
Guatemala
Gutenberg
Guthrie
Hackensack
Haggerty
Halifax
Hamburg
Hamilton
Hammond
Hampton
Hancock
Hanford
Hanoi
Hanover
Hanson
Harding
Harold
Harriet
Harriman
Harrington
Harrisburg
Harrison

Hartford
Hartman
Hattiesburg
Haverford
Haverstraw
Hawaii
Hawthorne
Hayward
Healy
Hedwig
Heloise
Hempstead
Henderson
Henrietta
Herbert
Herkimer
Herman
Higgins
Hilda
Hillsboro
Hinsdale
Hinton
Hobart
Hoboken
Hoffman
Holdenville
Hollywood
Holt
Holyoke
Homewood
Honduras
Hong Kong

Honolulu
Hopewell
Hopkinsville
Horatio
Hornel
Hortense
Houston
Howard
Howell
Hubert
Hudson
Humboldt
Humphrey
Hungary
Huntington
Huron
Hutchinson
Hyattsville
Iceland
Idaho
Illinois
India
Indiana
Indianapolis
Inglewood
Iowa
Ironton
Ironwood
Irvington
Irwin
Isaac
Isidore

Isolde
Israel
Istanbul
Ithaca
Ivan
Jacksonville
Jacobs
Jacqueline
Jamaica
Jamestown
Janesville
Janet
Japan
Jason
Jasper
Jeannette
Jeffersonville
Jeffrey
Jemima
Jennifer
Jeremiah
Jersey City
Jerusalem
Jessamine
Jessica
Jocelin
Johnson
Johnston
Johnstown
Jonathan
Jonesboro
Joplin

Joseph
Judith
Julian
Juliet
Julius
Justin
Kalamazoo
Kalispell
Kankakee
Kansas
Kansas City
Karl
Katharine
Kathleen
Kearny
Keith
Kennedy
Kenneth
Kenosha
Kenton
Kentucky
Kerrville
Keyser
Kilgore
Kingsford
Kingston
Kirkwood
Knoxville
Kokomo
Korea
Kuwait
Lackawanna

La Crosse
Lafayette
Lakeland
Lakewood
Lambert
Lancaster
Lancelot
Lansdale
Lansford
Lansing
La Paz
La Porte
Larchmont
Laredo
Larksville
Larson
La Salle
Las Vegas
Latrobe
Laughlin
Laura
Laurel
Laurens
Lavinia
Lawrence
Lawrenceville
Lazarus
Leah
Leavenworth
Lebanon
Lehighton
Lehman

Leipsig
Leningrad
Lenoir
Leominster
Leon
Leonard
Leonia
Leopold
Leroy
Leslie
Lettice
Lewiston
Lexington
Lillian
Lima
Lincoln
Lindstrom
Lionel
Lisbon
Litchfield
Lithuania
Liverpool
Livingston
Llewellyn
Lloyd
Lockhart
Lockport
Lodi
Logansport
Lois
Lombard
London

Longview
Lorain
Lorenzo
Los Angeles
Louis
Louise
Louisiana
Louisville
Lowell
Lubbock
Lucretia
Ludington
Luella
Lufkin
Lumberton
Luther
Luxembourg
Lydia
Lynbrook
Lynchburg
Lyndhurst
Lynwood
Lyons
Madisonville
Magdalene
Maguire
Mahanoy City
Mahoney
Malden
Malvern
Manchester
Manhattan

Manila
Manistique
Manitoba
Mannheim
Manuel
Maplewood
Marblehead
Marcella
Marcia
Marcus
Margaret
Marian
Marianna
Marion
Marlboro
Marquette
Marseilles
Marshall
Martin
Martinsburg
Martinsville
Mason
Massachusetts
Massillon
Mathilda
Matthew
Maxwell
Maynard
Maysville
Mayville
Maywood
McAdoo

McCarthy
McCook
McCormack
McDonald
McGregor
McKenzie
McKinney
McMillan
Meadville
Medford
Melbourne
Melissa
Menasha
Mercedes
Meriden
Merrill
Methuen
Mexico
Meyer
Miami
Michigan
Middleboro
Midland
Mildred
Milford
Millburn
Millbury
Milledgeville
Milton
Milwaukee
Minersville
Minneapolis

Minnesota
Mississippi
Missouri
Mitchell
Mobile
Monica
Monmouth
Monroe
Montana
Montebello
Montevideo
Montpelier
Montreal
Mooresville
Moorhead
Morocco
Morris
Morse
Mortimer
Moscow
Moultrie
Moundsville
Muncie
Munhall
Munich
Murdock
Muriel
Murray
Muscatine
Muskegon
Myers
Myrtle

Naomi
Naperville
Napoleon
Nashua
Nashville
Natalie
Natchez
Natchitoches
Nathaniel
Natick
Naugatuck
Nazareth
Nebraska
Needham
Nelson
Neptune
Netherlands
Nevada
Newark
Newberry
New Britain
New Brunswick
Newburgh
New Hampshire
New Haven
New Jersey
New London
New Mexico
New Orleans
New Rochelle
Newton
New York

New Zealand
Niagara Falls
Nicaragua
Norfolk
Norma
Norman
Northampton
North Carolina
North Dakota
Norwalk
Norway
Norwich
Norwood
Nova Scotia
Nyack
Oakwood
O'Brien
Ocala
O'Connor
Odessa
O'Donnell
Oelwein
Ogdensburg
Ohio
Oklahoma
Olean
Olney
Olson
Olympia
Omaha
Oneida
O'Neil

Ontario
Ophelia
Oregon
Orlando
Oscar
Oshkosh
Oslo
Ossining
Oswald
Oswego
Ottawa
Owego
Owensboro
Packard
Paducah
Pakistan
Palestine
Pamela
Panama
Paraguay
Parkersburg
Parsons
Pasadena
Passaic
Patchogue
Paterson
Patrick
Pawtucket
Peabody
Pearson
Peekskill
Pekin

Pelham
Pendleton
Pennsylvania
Pensacola
Peoria
Percival
Perth Amboy
Petaluma
Petersburg
Petersen
Peterson
Philadelphia
Philander
Philippine Islands
Phillipsburg
Phoenixville
Piedmont
Pittsburgh
Pittsfield
Pius
Plainfield
Plattsburg
Pleasantville
Plymouth
Ponca City
Pontiac
Portage
Port Arthur
Port Chester
Porterville
Port Huron
Portland

Portsmouth
Portugal
Potter
Pottsville
Poughkeepsie
Powell
Presque Isle
Prichard
Princeton
Priscilla
Providence
Provo
Pueblo
Puerto Rico
Putnam
Quebec
Quinn
Rachel
Racine
Radford
Rahway
Randall
Randolph
Rankin
Raton
Ravenna
Raymond
Rebecca
Redwood City
Regina
Reginald
Reinhardt

Rensselaer
Reuben
Revere
Reynolds
Rhea
Rhinelander
Rhode Island
Richard
Richfield
Richmond
Richwood
Ridgeway
Rio de Janeiro
Roanoke
Robbinsdale
Robert
Robinson
Rochester
Rockford
Rockland
Rockville
Roderick
Romania
Roosevelt
Rosalind
Rosemary
Roseville
Rossville
Roswell
Rotterdam
Rowena
Ruby

Rudolph
Rupert
Rushville
Russia
Rutherford
Ryan
Ryerson
Sacramento
Saigon
St. Albans
St. Augustine
St. Joseph
St. Louis
St. Petersburg
Salisbury
Salt Lake City
Sampson
Samuel
San Angelo
San Antonio
San Diego
Sandusky
San Fernando
Sanford
San Francisco
San Jose
San Luis Obispo
San Mateo
San Rafael
Santa Barbara
Santiago
Sarasota

Sault Ste. Marie
Savannah
Sawyer
Sayreville
Schenectady
Schneider
Schroeder
Schultz
Schuyler
Schwartz
Scotland
Seattle
Sedalia
Seminole
Serena
Seville
Seward
Sewickley
Sexton
Seymour
Shanghai
Sharon
Sharpsburg
Sheboygan
Sheffield
Shelbyville
Sheldon
Shenandoah
Sheridan
Sherman
Sherwood
Shippensburg

Shirley
Shorewood
Shreveport
Siam
Sicily
Silvester
Silvia
Simmons
Simpson
Sinclair
Singapore
Sioux Falls
Solomon
Somerset
Somerville
Sorensen
South America
Southampton
South Carolina
South Dakota
Southington
Sparks
Spartanburg
Spokane
Springfield
Stafford
Stamford
Stanford
Stanley
Statesboro
Staunton
Sterling

Steubenville
Stewart
Stillwater
Stockholm
Stoneham
Stoughton
Stratford
Straus
Stroudsburg
Struthers
Stuart
Sturgis
Stuttgart
Suffolk
Sullivan
Sumner
Sumter
Sunbury
Susan
Sweetwater
Switzerland
Sybil
Sydney
Sylvester
Syracuse
Tacoma
Tallahassee
Tampa
Tampico
Tarrytown
Taunton
Taylorville

Teaneck
Tenafly
Tennessee
Terre Haute
Texas
Thaddeus
The Hague
Theodore
Thomasville
Tifton
Timothy
Tipton
Titusville
Tokyo
Toledo
Topeka
Toronto
Torrington
Trenton
Trinidad
Truman
Tucson
Tulsa
Turkey
Tuscaloosa
Tyrone
Ukraine
Underhill
Union
United Kingdom
United States
Upton

Uruguay
Utah
Utica
Valentine
Valeria
Vanderlip
Van Horn
Venezuela
Vera Cruz
Vermont
Vernon
Vicksburg
Victoria
Vienna
Viet Nam
Vincent
Viola
Virgil
Virginia
Vivian
Wabash
Waddington
Wadsworth
Wakefield
Walker
Wallace
Wallington
Walpole
Walsh
Walter
Waltham
Warrensburg
Warsaw
Washington
Waterbury
Waterville
Watsonville
Waverly
Waynesboro
Weatherford
Webster
Welch
Wellesley
Wellington
Wellsburg
Westbrook
West Chester
Westfield
Weston
West Virginia
Westwood
Weymouth
Wheaton
Wheeling
Whitman
Whittier
Wichita
Wilbur
Wilfred
Wilkes-Barre
Wilkinsburg
Willard
Williamsport
Williston
Willmar
Wilmette
Wilmington
Wilson
Winfield
Winifred
Winnipeg
Winona
Winslow
Winston-Salem
Winthrop
Wisconsin
Woburn
Woodbury
Woodward
Woonsocket
Wooster
Worcester
Worthington
Wyoming
Xenia
Yakima
Yates
Yokohama
Yonkers
York
Youngstown
Ypsilanti
Yugoslavia
Yuma
Zanesville
Zion

# PART THREE

Part Three consists of a compilation of 1,368 useful business phrases presented in alphabetic order.

These phrases were selected from a study of the phrasing content of 1,500 business letters representing 50 types of businesses. In all, these letters contained 250,143 running words.

Phrases for common expressions are very helpful to the writer seeking to gain shorthand speed. However, they can be a handicap to him if he cannot write them without the slightest hesitation. If the writer must pause for even the smallest fraction of a second in composing or thinking of a phrase, that phrase becomes a speed handicap rather than a help.

If the writer cannot immediately think of the phrase for a combination of words, he will be well advised to write the words separately.

# FREQUENTLY USED GREGG SHORTHAND PHRASES

able to say
about it
about my
about that
about that time
about the
about the matter
about the time
about them
about this
about this time
about those
about which
about your
after that
after that time
after the
after these
after this
along this
among the
among these

and are
and have
and his
and hope
and I will
and I will be
and is
and let us
and let us know
and our
and see
and that
and the
and they
any one
any one of our
any one of the
any one of them
any other
any time
any way
are not

are sure
are you
as a result
as if
as it has been
as it is
as it will
as it will be
as many
as much
as soon as
as soon as possible
as soon as the
as soon as you can
as that
as that is not
as the
as there was
as there will be
as these
as they
as they are
as they can
as they can be
as they cannot
as they did
as they have
as they will
as this
as this is
as this may
as this may be
as those
as though
as to
as to that
as to the
as to these
as to this
as we
as we are
as we are not
as we can
as we cannot
as well
as yet
as you
as you are
as you can
as you cannot
as you did
as you do
as you do not
as you have
as you know
as you may
as you may be
as you may have
as you might
as you might be
as you might have
as you must
as you must be
as you must have

as you will
as you will be
as you will find
as you will have
as you will not
as you will not be
as you will see
as you would
as you would be
as you would be able
as you would have
as you would not
as your
ask the
ask you
at a loss
at a time
at last
at least
at length
at such a time
at that
at that time
at the
at the time
at these
at this
at this time
at which time
be able
be done
be glad

be glad to know
be glad to see
be sure
been able
before it is
before many
before that
before that time
before the
before they
before us
before you
before you are
before you can
before your
being able
being sure
between the
between them
between these
between us
business world
by it
by mail
by means
by Mr.
by myself
by that
by that time
by the
by the time
by the way

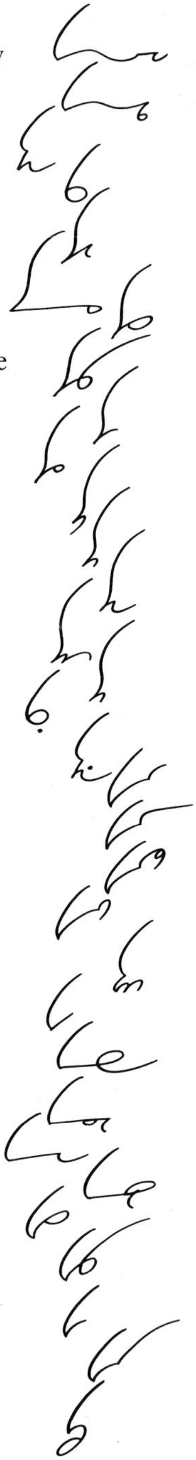

by them
by themselves
by these
by this
by this time
by those
by us
by which
by which it is
by which time
by which you can
by which you may
by you
can be
can be done
can be sure
can have
can say
can see
can you
can you give
can you give us
cannot be
cannot be done
cannot be sure
cannot have
cannot pay
cannot say
cannot see
can't be
centuries ago
check up

Cordially yours
could be
could be done
could be sure
could have
could have been
could not
could not be
could not say
could not see
could say
could see
day or two
day or two ago
days ago
Dear Madam
Dear Miss
Dear Mr.
Dear Mrs.
Dear Sir
Dear Sirs
did not
do it
do not
do not have
do not pay
do not say
do not see
do so
do that
do the
do this

do you
do you know
do you mean
do you think
do you want
does not
does not have
doing so
during the last
during the past
during the year
during which time
each case
each day
each month
each morning
each one
each other
each time
ever since
every minute
every month
every one
every one of the
every one of them
every one of these
every one of those
every other
face to face
few days
few days ago
few minutes

few minutes ago
few moments
few moments ago
few months
few months ago
few times
for a few days
for a few minutes
for a few months
for a long time
for his
for it
for me
for Mr.
for Mrs.
for my
for myself
for next month
for next year
for one
for one thing
for our
for so long a time
for some years
for that
for the
for the last
for the present
for the purpose
for the time
for them
for these

for this
for those
for us
for which
for whom
for you
for your convenience
for your information
for yourself
from him
from his
from it
from our
from that
from that time
from the
from them
from these
from this
from time
from us
from which
from you
gave me
gave us
gave you
give me
give us
give you
glad to have
glad to hear
glad to know
glad to say
glad to see
glad to send
good deal
good many
good many of the
good many of them
good many of these
good time
great many
great many of the
great many of them
had been
had not
had not been
has been
has been able
has been done
has come
has done
has given
has made
has not
has not been
has not been able
has not yet
has not yet been
has that
has the
has this
has to
has written

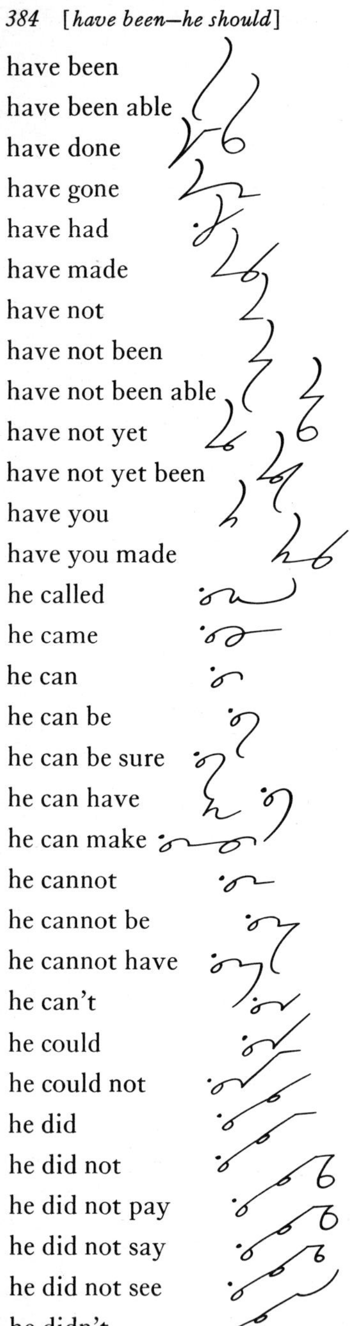

have been
have been able
have done
have gone
have had
have made
have not
have not been
have not been able
have not yet
have not yet been
have you
have you made
he called
he came
he can
he can be
he can be sure
he can have
he can make
he cannot
he cannot be
he cannot have
he can't
he could
he could not
he did
he did not
he did not pay
he did not say
he did not see
he didn't

he does
he does not
he felt
he found
he gave
he gives
he is
he is not
he knew
he knows
he lost
he made
he may
he may be
he may be able
he may be sure
he may have
he mentioned
he might be
he might have
he might have been
he might not
he must
he must be
he must have
he needed
he needs
he said
he saw
he says
he seemed
he should

he should be
he should be able
he should have
he should not
he told
he took
he wanted
he wants
he was
he will
he will be
he will be able
he will be glad
he will find
he will have
he will not
he will not be able
he will see
he wished
he would
he would be
he would be able
he would be glad
he would have
he would not
he would not be
hear from him
hear from you
help us
help you
here are
here is

here is the
hope that
hope you will
hours ago
how many
how many of the
how many of them
how many of these
how many times
how much
I am
I am glad
I am of the opinion
I am sure
I came
I can
I can be
I can have
I can say
I can see
I cannot
I cannot be
I cannot be sure
I cannot have
I can't
I could
I could be
I could have
I could not
I desire
I did
I did not

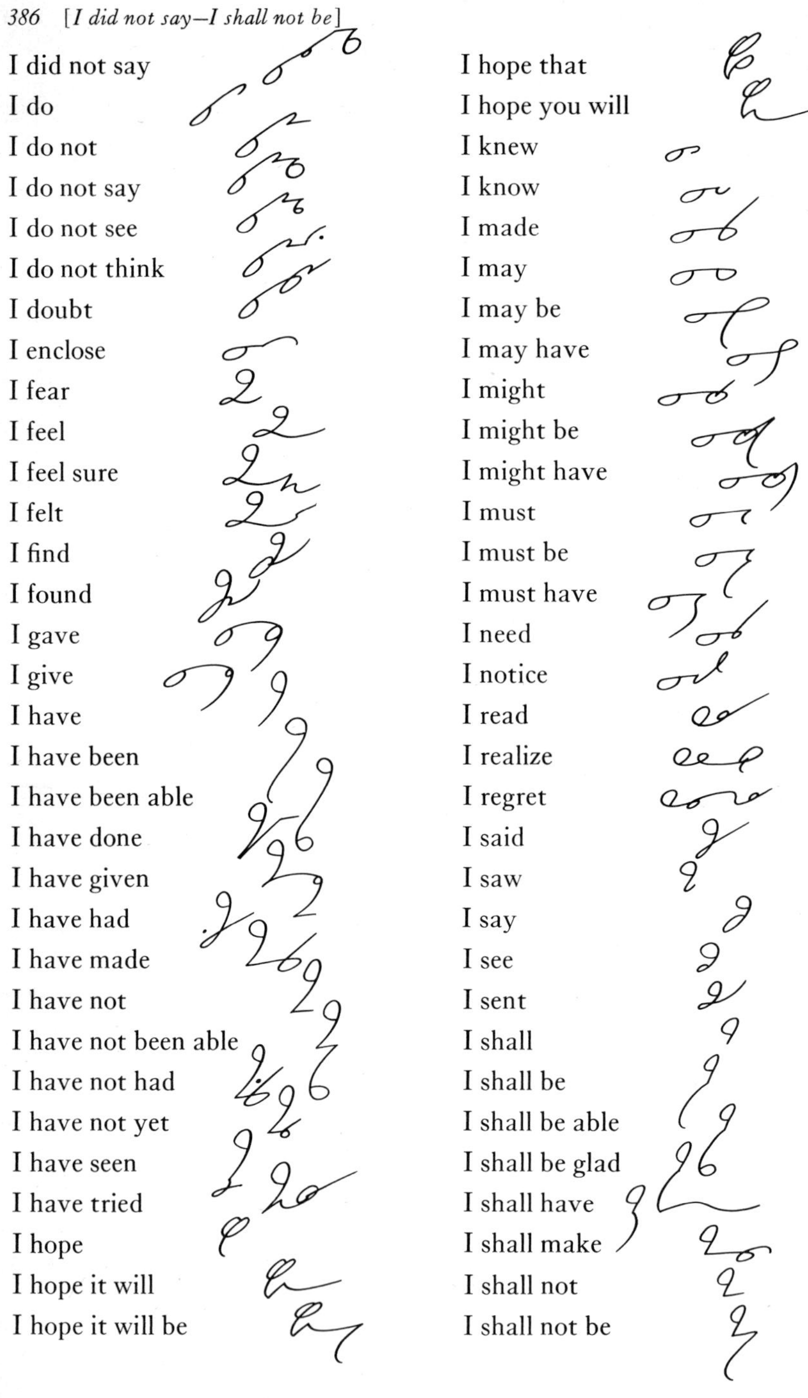

I did not say
I do
I do not
I do not say
I do not see
I do not think
I doubt
I enclose
I fear
I feel
I feel sure
I felt
I find
I found
I gave
I give
I have
I have been
I have been able
I have done
I have given
I have had
I have made
I have not
I have not been able
I have not had
I have not yet
I have seen
I have tried
I hope
I hope it will
I hope it will be
I hope that
I hope you will
I knew
I know
I made
I may
I may be
I may have
I might
I might be
I might have
I must
I must be
I must have
I need
I notice
I read
I realize
I regret
I said
I saw
I say
I see
I sent
I shall
I shall be
I shall be able
I shall be glad
I shall have
I shall make
I shall not
I shall not be

I shall not be able
I should
I should be
I should have
I suggest
I talked
I thank you
I thank you for the
I think
I thought
I told
I took
I want
I want to see
I wanted
I was
I will
I will be
I will be able
I will have
I will not
I will not be
I will not be able
I will see
I wish
I would
I would be
I would have
I would not
I wrote
I wrote you
if it

if it is
if it was
if it will
if it will be
if my
if not
if so
if that
if the
if there are
if there is
if they
if they are
if they are not
if they can
if they cannot
if they may
if they would
if this
if this is
if we
if we are
if we can
if we can be
if we cannot
if we could
if we do
if we have
if you
if you are
if you are sure
if you can

if you can be
if you cannot
if you could
if you did not
if you do
if you do not
if you give
if you have
if you know
if you may
if you must
if you need
if you think
if you want
if you will
if you will be
if you will have
if you wish
if you would
if you would be
if you would have
in a few days
in a few minutes
in a few months
in a position
in addition
in addition to the
in behalf
in case
in fact
in his
in it

in order
in order that
in order to be
in order to be able
in order to obtain
in order to see
in our
in our opinion
in part
in particular
in question
in relation
in spite
in such
in such a manner
in such a way
in that
in the
in the future
in the past
in the world
in them
in these
in this
in this matter
in this way
in time
in which
in which case
in which it is
in which the
in which you

in which you are
into it
into the
into this
is it
is not
is not yet
is that
is the
is there
is this
is to be
it has been
it is
it is the
it isn't
it was
it will
it will be
it will have
it will not
it will not be
left hand
less and less
less than
less than the
let us
let us have
let us know
let us make
let us say
let us see

letting us
line of business
line of goods
long ago
long time
long time ago
make the
many of the
many of them
many of these
many of those
many other
many times
may be
may be able
may be done
may be sure
may have
men and women
might be
might be able
might have
might have been
might not
might not be
might not be able
months ago
must be
must be able
must be done
must have
my time

need not be
next day
next day or two
next month
next time
next year
next year's
no doubt
none of the
none of them
not only
now and then
of course
of course it is
of his
of its
of mine
of my
of our
of such
of that
of that time
of the
of their
of them
of these
of this
of those
of time
of which
on behalf
on his

on it
on our
on our part
on request
on sale
on such
on that
on that day
on the
on the part
on the question
on the subject
on these
on this
on this case
on time
on which
on your
once a month
once or twice
one of our
one of the
one of the best
one of the most
one of them
one of these
one or two
one thing
one time
one way
only one
only one of these

other than
ought to be
ought to be able
ought to be done
ought to have
out of date
out of the
out of the question
out of them
question of time
quite sure
reach us
reach you
realize that
relation to the
Respectfully yours
safe deposit
seem to be
seems to be
send him
send them
send this
send us
send you
several days
several days ago
several months
several months ago
several other
several times
shall be glad
shall have

shall not
shall not be
shall not have
she can
she cannot
she could
she could not
she could not be
she is
she is not
she may be
she must
she would
should be
should be done
should be made
should have
should have been
should not
should not be
should see
since that time
since the
since this
Sincerely yours
so far
so long
so long a time
so many
so many of the
so many of them
so many times

so much
so that
so well
some of our
some of that
some of the
some of them
some of these
some of this
some of those
some time
some time ago
some years
some years ago
suggest that
take the
than the
thank you
thank you for
thank you for your
thank you for your order
that are
that are not
that can
that can be
that do
that do not
that does not
that have
that is
that is not
that is the
that is to say
that it
that it is
that it was
that it will
that it will be
that may
that may be
that must
that our
that this is
that the
that there are
that there is
that these
that they
that they are
that this
that those
that time
that will
that will be
that will not
that would
that would be
that would have
the only thing
there are
there has been
there have
there is
there may

there may be
there might be
there must be
there was
there will
there will be
they are
they are not
they can
they can be
they can have
they cannot
they cannot be
they cannot have
they can't
they come
they could
they could not
they did
they did not
they do
they do not
they have
they may
they may be
they may be able
they might
they might be
they might not
they must
they must be
they must be able

they must have
they think
they want
they will
they will be
they will be able
they will have
they will not
they would
they would be
they would be able
they would be glad
they would have
this can
this can be
this cannot
this cannot be
this case
this did not
this information
this is
this is not
this is the
this matter
this may
this may be
this means
this month
this morning
this must be done
this one
this time

this was
this way
this will
this will be
this would
this would be
through its
through that
through the
through this
throughout the
throughout this
to be
to be able
to be done
to be sure
to become
to begin
to believe
to buy
to call
to change
to charge
to check
to choose
to come
to continue
to convince
to cover
to do
to do it
to do so

to do the
to face
to fall
to feel
to fill
to find
to follow
to form
to forward
to furnish
to get
to give
to give me
to give you
to go
to have
to have been
to have you
to his
to it
to keep
to know
to make
to me
to participate
to pass
to pay
to persuade
to place
to plan
to please
to prepare

to present
to prevent
to print
to proceed
to produce
to prove
to provide
to publish
to purchase
to put
to say
to see
to sell
to serve
to serve you
to ship
to speak
to spend
to surprise
to take
to talk
to tell
to thank you
to thank you for
to that
to the
to their
to them
to these
to think
to this
to those
to time
to try
to turn
to us
to verify
to which
to which the
to whom
to you
too much
twice as much
two months ago
two or three
up to
up to date
up to the
up to the minute
up to this time
upon request
upon such
upon the
upon the subject
upon this
upon which
Very cordially yours
very glad
very glad to hear
very good
very important
very many
very much
Very sincerely yours

very small
very soon
Very truly yours
very well
want to see
was done
was it
was made
was that
was the
was this
we are
we are not
we are not yet
we are of the opinion
we are sending
we are sure
we can
we can be
we can have
we cannot
we cannot be
we cannot say
we can see
we can't
we could
we could be
we could have
we could not
we desire
we did
we did not

we do
we do not
we do not say
we do not see
we do not think
we enclose
we feel
we feel sure
we felt
we find
we found
we give
we have
we have been
we have been able
we have done
we have had
we have made
we have not
we have not been
we have not yet
we have your order
we hope
we hope it will
we hope that
we hope that the
we hope this will
we hope to have
we hope you will
we hope you will not
we knew
we know

we made
we mailed
we make
we may
we may be
we may be able
we may have
we might
we might be
we might be able
we might have
we must
we must be
we must have
we need
we realize that
we shall
we shall be
we shall be able
we shall be glad
we shall have
we shall not
we shall not be able
we should
we should be
we should be glad
we should have
we should not be able
we thank you
we thank you for
we thank you for the
we think

we tried
we try
we want
we will
we will be
we will be able
we will have
we will not
we will not be
we will see
we will send you
we wish
we would
we would be
we would be glad
we would have
we would not
we would not be
we would not be able
we wrote
week or two
week or two ago
weeks ago
were not
were sure
what are
what has been
what is
what our
what was
what will
when that

when the
when they
when this
when those
when you
when you are
which does
which has
which have
which is
which may
which may be
which means
which must
which they have
which was
which way
which we are
which you can
which you cannot
who are
who are not
who can
who can be
who cannot
who could
who could be
who could not
who desire
who do not
who have
who have done
who have had
who have not
who is
who is not
who know
who made
who may
who may be
who might
who might be
who might have
who must
who need
who should
who should be
who should have
who want
who will
who will be
who will be able
who will have
who will not
who will not be
who would
who would be
who would have
who would have been
who would not
why not
will be
will be able
will be done

will be glad
will find
will have
will not be
will not be able
will you
will you please
wish to say
with him
with his
with our
with such
with that
with the
with them
with these
with this
with us
with which
with whom
with you
within the
would be
would be able
would be done
would be glad
would have
would have been
would not
would not be
would not have been
written you

years ago
years of age
you are
you are not
you are sure
you can
you can be
you can be sure
you can get
you can give
you can have
you can make
you cannot
you cannot have
you cannot pay
you cannot see
you could
you could be
you could have
you could have been
you could see
you could not
you could not have
you couldn't
you desire
you did
you did not
you did not say
you did not see
you do
you do not
you don't

you gave
you have
you have been
you have had
you have not
you have not been
you have not been able
you knew
you know
you made
you may
you may be
you may be able
you may be sure
you may have
you might
you might be
you must
you must be
you must be able
you must have
you need
you order
you see
you shall have
you should
you should be
you should be able
you should have
you should not
you think
you want

you wanted
you will
you will be
you will be able
you will be glad
you will be sure
you will find
you will have
you will not
you will not be
you will not be able
you will not have
you will see
you would
you would be
you would be able
you would be glad
you would be sure
you would have
you would have been
you would not
you would not be
you would not be able
you would not have
your inquiry
your name
your order
your orders
Yours cordially
Yours sincerely
Yours very sincerely
Yours very truly

# PART FOUR

Part Four contains abbreviations for 120 expressions. A suggested shorthand outline is given for each expression.

Some expressions are dictated and transcribed almost exclusively in abbreviated form, such as *FOB (free on board)*. Others may be dictated and transcribed either in full or in the form of initials, such as *AC* for *alternating current*.

There are many variations in the use of periods and capitals in abbreviations. For example, the expression *revolutions per minute* may be expressed by *rpm,* or *r.p.m.,* or *RPM.* In the following list of abbreviations, the forms used are those given in Webster's Seventh New Collegiate Dictionary.

# ABBREVIATIONS

| | |
|---|---|
| AA | Alcoholics Anonymous |
| ABC | American Broadcasting Company |
| AC | alternating current |
| ACE | American Council on Education |
| ACTH | adrenocorticotropic hormone |
| AEC | Atomic Energy Commission |
| AFL-CIO | American Federation of Labor and Congress of Industrial Organizations |
| a.m. | ante meridiem |
| AMA | American Medical Association |
| APO | army post office |
| ARC | American Red Cross |
| ASCAP | American Society of Composers, Authors, and Publishers |
| AVA | American Vocational Association |
| AWOL | absent without leave |
| BA | bachelor of arts |

| | |
|---|---|
| BBC | British Broadcasting Corporation |
| B.C. | Before Christ |
| BS | bachelor of science |
| Btu | British thermal unit |
| CAB | Civil Aeronautics Board |
| CBC | Canadian Broadcasting Corporation |
| cc | cubic centimeter |
| CIA | Central Intelligence Agency |
| CIF | cost, insurance, and freight |
| CNO | chief of naval operations |
| COD | cash on delivery |
| CPA | certified public accountant |
| CPO | chief petty officer |
| DA | district attorney |
| DAR | Daughters of the American Revolution |
| DC | District of Columbia |
| DDS | doctor of dental surgery |
| DFC | distinguished flying cross |
| DOA | dead on arrival |
| DT | delirium tremens |

| | |
|---|---|
| EKG | electrocardiogram |
| ESP | extrasensory perception |
| EST | eastern standard time |
| ETA | estimated time of arrival |
| et al | et alii (and others) |
| etc. | et cetera (and so forth) |
| FAA | Federal Aviation Agency |
| FBI | Federal Bureau of Investigation |
| FCC | Federal Communications Commission |
| FDA | Food and Drug Administration |
| FM | frequency modulation |
| FOB | free on board |
| GB | Great Britain |
| GI | general issue |
| GM | general manager |
| GOP | Grand Old Party (Republican) |
| GP | general practitioner |
| HEW | Health, Education, and Welfare |
| HQ | headquarters |
| IBM | International Business Machines |

| | | |
|---|---|---|
| ID | identification | |
| i.e. | id est (that is) | |
| ILA | International Longshoremen's Association | |
| IQ | intelligence quotient | |
| IRS | Internal Revenue Service | |
| JV | junior varsity | |
| kc | kilocycle | |
| KKK | Ku Klux Klan | |
| KP | kitchen police | |
| LI | Long Island | |
| LLB | bachelor of laws | |
| LLM | master of laws | |
| MA | master of arts | |
| MC | master of ceremonies | |
| MD | doctor of medicine | |
| mm | millimeter | |
| MP | member of parliament | |
| mph | miles per hour | |
| MS | manuscript | |
| MSS | manuscripts | |

| | |
|---|---|
| MST | mountain standard time |
| NASA | National Aeronautics and Space Administration |
| NATO | North Atlantic Treaty Organization |
| NLRB | National Labor Relations Board |
| OAS | Organization of American States |
| PAL | Police Athletic League |
| P and L | profit and loss |
| PBX | private branch exchange |
| PGA | Professional Golfers' Association |
| PHA | Public Housing Administration |
| PhD | doctor of philosophy |
| PHS | Public Health Service |
| p.m. | post meridiem |
| PN | promissory note |
| POW | prisoner of war |
| PS | post scriptum (postscript) |
| PST | Pacific standard time |
| PTA | Parent-Teacher Association |
| PX | post exchange |
| q.t. | quiet |

| | |
|---|---|
| RAF | Royal Air Force |
| R and D | research and development |
| RBI | runs batted in |
| REA | Rural Electrification Administration |
| ROTC | Reserve Officers' Training Corps |
| RSVP | répondez s'il vous plait (please reply) |
| SBA | Small Business Administration |
| SEATO | Southeast Asia Treaty Organization |
| SEC | Securities and Exchange Commission |
| SRO | standing room only |
| SSA | Social Security Administration |
| TV | television |
| TVA | Tennessee Valley Authority |
| UK | United Kingdom |
| UNESCO | United Nations Educational, Scientific, and Cultural Organization |
| UP | United Press |
| UPI | United Press International |
| US | United States |
| USA | United States of America |
| USO | United Service Organizations |

| | |
|---|---|
| USSR | Union of Soviet Socialist Republics |
| VI | Virgin Islands |
| VIP | very important person |
| WI | West Indies |
| wpm | words per minute |